ROBIN

Comprehensive Treatment of a Vulnerable Adolescent

Other Books by the Same Author

Personality in Young Children

Vulnerability, Coping, and Growth
(WITH ALICE E. MORIARITY)

The Widening World of Childhood
(WITH COLLABORATORS)

ROBIN

Comprehensive Treatment of a Vulnerable Adolescent

LOIS BARCLAY MURPHY

J. COTTER HIRSCHBERG

Basic Books, Inc., Publishers

NEW YORK

Library of Congress Cataloging in Publication Data

Murphy, Lois Barclay, 1902–
    Robin, comprehensive treatment of a vulnerable
adolescent.

    Bibliography: p. 350
    Includes index.
    1. Child psychotherapy—Case studies.   2.   Brain-
damaged children—Rehabilitation—Case studies.
I.   Hirschberg, J. Cotter, 1915–   .   II.   Title.
[DNLM: 1.   Neurology—Popular works.   2.   Nervous
system diseases—Therapy—Popular works.   3.   Nervous
system diseases—In adolescence—Popular works.   WS 340
M978r]
RJ504.M87   1982   616.8'5884   82–71213
ISBN 0–465–07060–4   AACR2

To Robin and her parents

and to all those

who helped her

to start blossoming

Contents

PART III

ROBIN'S THIRD YEAR IN TREATMENT

Acknowledgments

We deeply appreciate the generous assistance of Dr. Ishak Ramzy who not only helped to design the structure of this book but also offered discriminating editorial clarifications of the narrative. Dr. Gordon Barclay was a helpful consultant on terminology. Ruby Takanishi, Dori Mintzer, Anthony Tripp, and Patricia Allison also read early versions of the manuscript and offered helpful suggestions. At different stages of revision, Drena Owens, Marge McElhenny, and Lucy Whittier each provided excellent typescripts of the manuscript. We are also deeply grateful to the Harris Foundation for its generous support in preparation of this book.

The treatment process we describe owed much to the devotion and resourcefulness of the Children's Hospital team at the Menninger Foundation, and also to the firm commitment of Robin's parents to help their initially despairing daughter. The fact that we can share this story of Robin's progress from potentially severe incapacitation to becoming a useful citizen is due to the wish of Robin and her family to help other neurologically damaged young people with multiple vulnerabilities.

All names of people and places are pseudonyms except those of the authors, the Menninger Foundation, Dr. Karl Menninger, and Topeka, Kansas.

Preface

J. COTTER HIRSCHBERG

In this preface I shall try to answer several questions that may be in the reader's mind. Why would a book need to be written about the many aspects of a comprehensive treatment process which are so crucial in helping a neurologically handicapped and developmentally delayed individual? Partly it is because the medical profession is now able to "save" children with birth difficulties who formerly would have died, children with severe infectious illnesses who formerly would not have survived their high fevers, and children damaged by accidents. Consequently, the actual number of children and adolescents with a variety of neurological difficulties has increased. Owing to the complex, sometimes vague, subtle problems in adjustment and in learning which these children have, there are many gaps in understanding how to help them. Basically, the task of helping centers on the development of an integrated personality that achieves its optimal capacity for growth.

Robin was just entering adolescence at the time of her evaluation and the beginning of treatment; the interactions of primary (organic) and secondary (reactive) problems with which she was struggling had brought about not only maturational gaps and imbalances but difficulties in emotional modulation and control, organic deficits in orientation and perceptual interpretation, continual variation in the interaction of the cognitive-motor-affective functions, as well as secondary problems in reaction to the ridicule, exclusion, and rejection by peers and others. In coming to a total understanding of this adolescent girl, it was necessary to look at all the aspects of her equipment and development. To focus on the central deficit was only a beginning. There may be and often are many additional, though more ordinary, factors in vulnerability—some of them specific and remediable and some of them diffuse and persistent. It is a matter not only of spotting these vulnerabilities and considering their individual and separate impact, but also of watching for their interaction with brain handicaps and their sequential or cumulative impact on the child's functioning. An integration of medical, psychological, and environmental assistance was thus needed in order to reduce the exacerbation of neurological problems as psychological disturbances.

Along with this, there was the need for constant concern with the interaction between all of these organic problems and what otherwise would be normal vicissitudes and stresses in sensitive developmental phases. Neurological and physiological interactions and their internal pressures would inevitably hamper the normal developmental progress, while the combination of internal changes and interactions with the changing external world would add stress to the persistent vulnerabilities.

In such a case, the psychological and medical approaches had to be developmentally oriented, and treatment had to be targeted toward recognizing normal developmental problems in the midst of the basic neurological and physiological difficulties. In this interdisciplinary process, it was necessary to acknowledge the stress of environmental and family demands which understandably overlooked the girl's actual difficulties in orientation, her limitation in problem solving, and other integrative aspects of coping at a difficult developmental stage. With a child at such a critical stage, whose problems included those caused by brain damage and other physical difficulties, neither a medical model nor a metapsychological paradigm would be adequate for evaluation.

This book was written as an outcome of a pluralistic conceptual understanding and technical training; it is an attempt to show theory coming to life in practice. It is also an attempt to help the reader see a developmentally handicapped child empathically: that is, not only from the point of view of developmental standards but from an awareness of what is experienced and what the child wishes and needs. It is hoped that each reader will resonate to what this teen-ager feels. It is hoped that it will become clear that helping such a child is a loving responsibility, a living relationship.

Each reader is well aware of the importance of individual differences in children as they relate to the therapy process—variations in constitutional and biological factors, variations in growth and development, variations in individual experiences, variations in social context, and the interrelated significance of all of these in the child's life. This book illustrates how positive experiences can meet a particular need and improve the total functioning of the individual.

It will be noted that the therapist always reached out for the whole *person*, not just the words, not just the behavior. The therapist was a flexible, caring, concerned individual, reaching out, as a mother does to an inarticulate baby, with a perception that is as individual as the child and as fresh as the shared moment.

Neuropsychological data illuminated the difficulties, and clinical diagnosis contributed information; both provided a basis for the therapist's work but did not distort her immediate perceptions. Time and time again it was evident that the therapist and the girl in this living relationship, this loving responsibility, were guided by a comprehensive theory at its best. The therapist transcended the shackles of rigid therapeutic techniques, recognized the difficulties in Robin's efforts to integrate a response, to react to a stimulus overload, and took into account not only vulnerability but coping efforts.

The therapist and the child responded as a system in which adaptation and change, continuity and discontinuity, sometimes illuminated, sometimes initiated, and sometimes stimulated growth toward an optimal level of functioning. Every person has strengths and weaknesses, limitations, ways of communicating at many different levels. When the therapist accepted Robin's *whole personality,* and both empathically worked toward the integration of that whole self, then the freedom to be a *person* existed for both therapist and adolescent.

I, as Director of the Psychotherapy Service for the Children's Division of the Menninger Clinic, had to select a therapist whose own personality could provide the neurologically handicapped, developmentally delayed child with an individual who was always a humanly confident person, a person who would make use of her skills and experience in the therapy process. This meant selecting a person who was basically flexible, with the freedom to make use of play, drawing, or interpretation; an individual was needed who could always be "tuned in" in relating to Robin, taking her seriously, enjoying the process, and not role-playing or affecting an artificial pose or a detached stance.

The neurologically handicapped child needs a therapist who has worked with normal children, with vulnerable children, and with emotionally disturbed children. Lois Barclay Murphy, Ph.D., was selected as the therapist who had the ability and the qualities to undertake the task of working with this multiple-problem child. Dr. Murphy had had wide experience with children of different ages and social conditions. She was a developmental psychologist experienced in multidisciplinary developmental research and had taught many others, including more than one generation of educators and clinicians. She could support the developmental process and discern its vicissitudes, and serve as an identification figure for the child, who was groping for growth and a place in the adult world. She had the capacity to absorb the anxieties of the child through the relationship, as well as the ability to *feel* herself into the child's needs and attitudes without losing her own identity as a therapist or her comfortable, warm approach. Further, Dr. Murphy could cooperate with the treatment team in work with the child's relationships with her parents, her relatives, and her siblings in the extended family in which she grew up, lived, and belonged.

A treatment was designed that would create between the therapist and the teen-ager a relationship that was continually accepting and yet realistically firm, and that was consistently reliable and directed toward enhancing the girl's ability to mobilize her assets, accept her irreversible limitations, and raise her sense of personal worth. With such a neurologically handicapped girl it was necessary at times for the therapist to serve also as an alter ego for the patient and provide her at other times with guidelines for optimal functioning; these took into account the biological, the cognitive, the emotional, the social handicaps and assets. The girl thus was able to emulate the model of the therapist instead of getting bogged down in disorganization or overwhelmed by a sense of failure. The therapist responded to the girl's signal of the need for such therapeutic involvement; the therapist did only what the girl could not do for herself. The therapist thus extended the teen-ager's ability to cope in an integrated way in the tasks of daily living, as an individual, and as a person interacting with others. The therapist always waited to discern the teen-ager's ability to accept, to make use of sharing, to have companionship, to enjoy, and to be loved safely. Restitution was as necessary for the child as was re-education.

This book tries to illustrate the undemanding, healing quality of being "loved safely." The love of the therapist for the child as a whole person was a love that did not require being loved in return. Perhaps this is best seen in the therapist's constant acceptance of the wide range of Robin's defenses, her needs, her feelings, and the conflicts and adaptations that these, as well as her maturational lags, imposed on her. And above all else, the therapist constantly sought to recognize and stimulate the patient's recognition of her own strengths, of her abilities in the real world. In the treatment relationship the teen-ager and the therapist participated in an effort to live through successfully what were previously stultifying experiences. The goal was always both an educative one and one which at the same time allowed the patient to acquire a new, more rewarding feeling about herself.

Such a therapist-child relationship achieved two things. First, it offered the child an opportunity to react to the relationship with the therapist and to recognize present meanings in the relationship; the teen-ager was encouraged by therapeutic interpretation and comments to express her emotional reactions to the treatment situations. As she became able to express her real feelings in the therapy hours, she was able to carry over into her outside life—the reality of the world itself—her increased ability to react emotionally. Second, this relationship offered Robin an opportunity to express emotional reactions to the therapist that were really those felt about the parents, feelings that with the work of treatment could cease to be disguised repetitions of attitudes felt toward the parents, the family, and others. Thus, once more a goal of an integrated personality remained the purpose of the work.

Large-scale statistical studies can reveal patterns widely characteristic of a group selected according to specific criteria—geographical, ethnic, age level, pathological, and others. However, such general characteristics do vary widely from one individual to another and cannot be considered as the main determinant in dealing with the individual. Dealing with the individual certainly requires, in addition to his place in this statistical range, a careful focus on his own complex of assets and liabilities. An intensive study of one individual can thus serve as a model for understanding other individuals. This method can be enormously fruitful when the selection of the individual is carefully made in order to contribute to the understanding of similar children. This is the justification for presenting the intensive study of one child with a pattern of neurological problems within a broader context of vulnerabilities at the sensitive developmental stage of early adolescence—a study that I believe will be applicable to many others who are in dire need of such a comprehensive approach in the treatment of their difficulties and problems.

Introduction

Robin was a new learning experience for all of us who worked with her at the Menninger Foundation. Not I, or the child-care workers, or the psychiatrists understood at first the subtle, complex effects of her neurological damage in its interaction with multiple vulnerabilities. She was different from a child with aphasia or an obvious learning difficulty; her problems in orientation and processing sensory input and of integrating plans for response to demands and opportunities were profound obstacles to coping, unrecognized at first by anyone. Treatment had to include constant new evaluation and openness to new discoveries of the precise effects of her organic problems of many dimensions.

What could I bring to the task of helping a child with the range and depth of frustrations with which Robin struggled? She was twelve years old; and although I had not treated a brain-damaged child or an adolescent in psychotherapy, I did know something about middle-class twelve-year-olds from our longitudinal study in Topeka.° These children told us this was a scary stage—this transition into a brave new world. Some mothers said, "They are impossible to live with." A California longitudinal study (McFate and Orr 1949) had reported that children were more constricted at that stage than before or afterward, thus indicating how stressed these children were. I had seen them change, move on into adolescence, and grow up.

The stress of this transition was probably an added factor in Robin's misery, and I knew that I could help her with that. I have faith in a child's drive to grow.

Although I was totally inexperienced in treating brain-damaged children, I had given much thought to vulnerabilities within the normal range. I had been concerned with sensory sensitivities that lower a child's thresholds to stress of noise, bright lights, or complex new group situations. I had been deeply impressed by Dr. Roger J. Williams's (1956) documentation of individual differences in the internal anatomic structure as well as commonly recognized external differences. And I had long been

---

° As Director of Developmental Studies in the Department of Research, I headed a series of interdisciplinary teams that studied a group of approximately sixty children from the preschool stage through adolescence. *Vulnerability, Coping, and Growth* by Lois Barclay Murphy and Alice E. Moriarty (Yale University Press, 1976) gives the most comprehensive account of the series to early adolescence.

interested in the variability of the autonomic nervous system from child to child and in the same child in different situations—a variability affecting emotional intensity and control as well as heart rate, control of sphincters, and gastrointestinal functioning. This variability sets a limit to "what a person can stand."

I felt that I could watch for indications of interaction between these and other sources of vulnerability with brain damage and their effects on many different areas of Robin's functioning. Clues to such interaction would be found in nonverbal expressions, conscious and unconscious, and in facial expressions, incidental movements, and unspoken as well as spoken communications, all of which I was accustomed to watch for in working with younger children. In all my work with small children, I had used play materials; miniature life toys and drawing materials would be there on my large table, in case Robin wanted to play with them. I would follow her lead.

I had seen handicapped children of many kinds around the world, in hospitals, convalescent homes, special schools—children severely affected by polio, cerebral palsy; blind and deaf children; children with Down's syndrome and other sources of retardation. I had seen children's energy, hope, joy, and intense satisfaction with any small bit of achievement and progress within their capacities—their drive to cope with the challenges and frustrations they faced. I had also seen miserable, hopeless children in severely depriving settings. Robin was begging for help, so I felt that she must be one of the hoping children. I was not disappointed.

Because Robin was both a challenge and an example of the thousands of children and adolescents who cannot be neatly classified, according to the federal guidelines, as "L.D." (learning disabled) or "E.D." (emotionally disturbed), I kept a detailed record of my experience with her after each therapy hour. And at the end of her three years in treatment, after she had transcended the overwhelming obstacles in her path and learned how to use her zones of strength to cope with her weaknesses, I decided to share that experience with others who might be living with, teaching, or trying to help children and adolescents who were struggling as Robin had. The words of Robin, child-care workers, teachers, and parents, as well as my own words, are taken directly from my detailed records of the treatment of Robin. The interpretive comments and reflections on the process are taken from my records of conferences with Dr. Hirschberg. Often these are his words.

In writing this book, I have tried to distill the nearly two hundred hours of therapy plus other hours of consultation with teachers and shared learning with the professional staff of the children's hospital where she spent the day while living at home, and to offer glimpses of the many different aspects of both therapy and teamwork that released and supported Robin's drive to grow and discovered her previously unrecognized potentialities. These glimpses include evidence of the many dimensions and levels of Robin's difficulties which baffled or frustrated, challenged and rewarded those who worked with her. Many of these difficulties and most of her strengths had not been seen under the limiting conditions and stress of the preliminary diagnostic work.

Sometimes growth came by startling leaps ahead in one area while it lagged in others. Sometimes progress was two steps forward, one step backward. Certain problems recurred over and over again, while others were solved once and for all. Sometimes progress in one area released the possibility of growth in another. The drive to mastery, to understanding, to coping, emerged with incredible force. Her awareness that I was trying as hard as I could to understand and to help was our greatest support.

Naïve as I was in responding to the challenge of Robin, I could not have helped her without the constant deep understanding of Dr. J. Cotter Hirschberg, our supervisor, who is therefore my coauthor now.

Implications for Treatment of Other Young People with Impairments

Every child is unique, in a unique situation with unique needs and unique resources for progress and recovery. Does this mean that our treatment of Robin teaches us nothing that will help the next child? Actually, although details vary from child to child and family to family, certain basic conditions recur and these require similar treatment approaches.

First, since many children suffering from multiple impairments feel woefully inadequate and worthless, *treatment aimed to improve the child's self-image* is fundamental.

With Robin this had to include:

- Medical help with menstrual discomfort and allergies that contributed to her stuffy nose and fuzzy speech.
- Orthodonture to replace congenitally lacking front teeth.
- A social setting in which depressing ridicule would not occur and in which she would have assistance in learning to participate in groups and in using her initiative.
- An educational approach that used her interests in order to maximize motivation and effort, provided opportunities for her to satisfy her curiosities, and also appreciated her creativity, and gave her the quiet and security in protected space that prevented distraction.
- A cognitive reorientation to universal balances of strength and weak-

ness, to the range of individual differences among people, and to
typical stress at her developmental stage at puberty.
- Increased mastery through recognizing options and choices, clarification and use of her strengths, and learning about the cause and nature
of her deficits.
- Recognition of her parents' needs and burdens, siblings' feelings, and
child-care workers' problems in understanding the relation of her subtle neurological problems to her coping problems.

All children with neurological deficits have some pattern of open or
suppressed feelings about the frustrations they experience in learning, in
participating in peer groups, in reaching their own goals, in gaining the
love of those who are most important to them, in the bodily and mental
losses of which they are constantly aware. Consequently treatment aimed
at dealing with feelings is always needed. This will include the recognition of, sorting out of, and clarifying of: (1) overtly expressed feelings of
anxiety, anger, longing for love, and mourning for losses; and (2) unrecognized feelings of conflict and confusion. In addition it will include exploring effects of these feelings on learning, social behavior, interactions with
family and with therapist, and sense of self. Unconscious and preconscious
sexual urges and wishes to be different will gradually emerge and need to
be dealt with.

Along with these experiences of ventilation, clarification, and understanding of feelings others had not understood, all damaged children and
young people need to feel valued, accepted, enjoyed, understood, and
loved—and to feel pride, exhilaration, and hope as a response to the new-
ly adequate learning and coping that emerge during treatment.

As progress is made, treatment aims to clarify possible life roles built on
the strengths of each individual. In Robin's case we supported the role of
being a helper, discussed realistic possibilities, and supported her initiative
as a volunteer in a crippled children's center, as a helper in the school and
residence, and as a baby-sitter.

Pattern of Treatment

With many damaged young ones it would be necessary, as it was with
Robin, to develop a common ground on which the treatment relationship
can grow—to counteract the sense of isolation. Then it is necessary constantly to *stay with* the patient (not "at the end of a ten-foot pole," as
Robin felt with the diagnosticians). This includes sharing interests and
pleasure, appreciating positive gains and work, assisting and supporting
efforts—always participating in a caring one-to-one relationship with a
young person in whose capacity for growth one believes.

As part of this, the therapist follows the child's pace and watches nonverbal communications and bodily clues as well as the implications of

what is said. The therapist also has to be sensitive to the level of awareness—what is conscious but anxiously withheld, what is not quite conscious (preconscious), and what is unconscious.

The therapist relieves the anxiety that inhibits the conscious feelings or ideas that are suppressed; brings the not-quite-conscious feelings and ideas into consciousness, and moves unconscious items (as in dreams) a little closer to emergence—always sensitive to what is the principal struggle or conflict at the moment, and at what pace change can be brought about.

With the neurologically damaged child or young person, the therapist has to assist connections and integrations more directly than with normal people who are working on conflicts and anxieties. Also it is probably generally unsound to attack defenses, which will often disappear spontaneously with increased mastery and progress in self-feeling.

Collaboration with the team cooperating in help for an impaired child or young person will typically involve:

- Conveying the physical, social, and stimulation needs to the social worker, and also the child's feelings about the parents.
- Explaining factors in "inappropriate" behavior to child-care workers (difficulty in responding quickly, in carrying on a sustained conversation, and so forth).
- Suggesting topics of strong motivation to teachers, also modes of optimal functioning (for example, oral versus written).
- Recognizing levels of best potential and importance of providing opportunities to use strengths as well as to work on weaknesses.
- Explaining the child's need for explicit standards and reports on work.

Recognizing the Contribution of the Impaired Child or Young Person

Most children or young people with deficits or damage are sensitive to relationships and stimulated by a warmly accepting, understanding relationship. Most of them gain a feeling of progress and pride in even small achievements. This feeling of progress evokes energy, persistence, a capacity for work, and cooperation with treatment.

All of them have *some* positive resources that can be appreciated and used. With Robin, these included insight, creativity, expressiveness, and a talent for communication, often through metaphor, as well as a deep loyalty, and commitment to becoming a useful person. In the following pages I will document our gradual progress in learning how to help Robin and her surprising progress in using her previously hidden strengths.

PART I

THE FIRST YEAR
IN TREATMENT

1

Robin's Dire Need
for Help

Robin's dire need for help was described to me several weeks before I met her. I was told that she was a brain-damaged girl of twelve who was willful, negativistic, angry, and depressed. She was severely retarded in school, bogged down in second-to-third-grade work, and often went to sleep in the classroom. Other twelve-year-olds were in seventh grade, junior high school. Her violent temper tantrums were upsetting to her whole family.

She moved around with a hangdog expression and retreated to childish play with dolls which her parents considered inappropriate, and her mother reported that Robin wore, hanging below her skirt, a worn-out, torn slip of her sister's which Robin had pulled from the ragbag. Her poor coordination made it impossible for her to play team games or jump rope at the pace of other girls, so that she was rejected and ridiculed by her peers. She was so hungry for affection that her parents were afraid she would get involved sexually.

Robin's misery and pleas for help, the difficulties she caused the family, and their anxieties and sense of inability to help her had led them to take a drastic step: they moved from their Nebraska ranch and came to Topeka to seek help for her at the Menninger Foundation.

The first step was an evaluation by a multidisciplinary team, which included a psychiatrist, a neurologist, a psychologist, a neuropsychologist, and a psychiatric social worker; the members of this team interviewed and tested Robin over a period of several days. I will quote excerpts from their reports.

The psychiatrist's examination was summarized as follows:

> Robin is a tall, homely looking, pale girl who looks her stated age. She wears glasses, has several missing upper teeth, wears corrective shoes for her flat feet, and is generally awkward in her movements. Her self-concept is that of a defective and different child with an ear problem, flat feet, being in a special education class, lack of friends in school. . . .

The psychiatrist also noted Robin's mumbling, unintelligible speech when talking of stressful areas, and her low energy level, constriction, awkwardness, and passivity. She had developed intense feelings of difference, isolation, and loneliness because of her defects and difficulties and had different interests from other children. Emphasis was given, primarily to a "chronic brain syndrome associated with diffuse congenital encephalopathy of unknown cause" and, secondarily, to "adjustment reaction of childhood, habit disturbance, manifested by passive-aggressive behavior, tantrums, excessive doll playing." Psychological impairment and liabilities noted included Robin's "infantile and archaic ways of handling life situations."

The psychologist commented that while Robin had an average I.Q.,

> she displayed an erratic or fluctuating performance, that is, on occasion her abstractions were very good and, in the next moment, her thinking would become concrete and illogical. The abilities she demonstrated were never seen over any extended period. It is impossible to determine to what extent this [variability] was due to her organic limitations or to her emotional conflicts or [to] the interaction of these two deficits.

Robin's neurological examinations reported mild micropthalmia (a small eyeball), asymmetries of face and skull, flat feet, frank chorea (tremors) most severe in her right hand, hypotonia (low muscle tone), difficulties in balance involving unsteadiness in walking tandem, which is conspicuous evidence of autonomic variability. Her wristbone age at twelve was that of a ten-year-old girl. At this time, the electroencephalogram was considered normal, along with skull x-rays.

The summary neurological report was of a "diffuse congenital encephalopathy of unknown cause, manifested by certain areas of deficit in motor skills, abstractions and other abilities, as well as by a definite generalized chorea, relatively mild, but noteworthy in that it has some of its most severe effects in the right hand." The neurologist urged that proper attention to the organic factors should be given in the conference with the parents "as well as the specific and special challenges in preparing a proper educational program."

A neuropsychological study was added to the diagnostic investigation and noted that detailed study of her Wechsler Intelligence Scale for Children showed a wide scatter: with weighted scores of 10 to 12 (average and above) on Information, Picture Arrangement, Picture Completion, and Similarities, in contrast to scores of 5 to 6 (far below average) on Digit Span and Coding. This extreme variability among areas of cognitive functioning was paralleled by the results of neuropsychological tests, where she showed extreme impairment of space perception. *Of her ratings, 83 percent were in the impaired range.*

A few highlights of the neuropsychological report that I found helpful included:

> She has deficits affecting spelling and handwriting; some perceptual disorders; and she lacks adequate fingertip perception on the left hand ... Areas of impairment include abstraction capacity, psycho-motor problem-solving, tactile perceptual skills, visual-motor coordination, receptive and expressive language skills.
>
> On tasks involving combinations of these skills she is likely to be severely impaired. Her adjustment is likely to be considerably less adequate than her I.Q. scores would indicate.

This report was especially helpful to me, since it clarified difficulties that needed to be recognized as organic realities, and that were interfering with Robin's ability to cope with ordinary demands and were causing her overwhelming frustration.

We know from the work of Dr. Roger J. Wiliams (1956) that there are variations in sizes and shapes of all bodily organs; and William J. Sheldon (1940), Herbert R. Stolz and Lois M. Stolz (1971), and others have documented individual differences in body build and growth patterns. Moreover, item analyses of intelligence tests show wide variations from one child to another in patterns of performance on verbal skills. The I.Q. that is the average of the scores on a test is misleading when it is the average of very high and very low scores in different areas. Robin's deficits were redundantly demonstrated, but her assets implied by her high scores on certain items were not adequately recognized in the evaluation. Her handicaps were seen as the irreversible expression of organic damage, and their gravity overshadowed the evidence of her positive resources. The evaluation as a whole was conspicuously lacking in discussion of Robin's potentialities.

In the final conference with her parents, some time was spent on these organic problems. (From subsequent work in therapy, it appeared that Robin's extreme difficulties in orienting and adapting to new situations, to changes in plans or structure, to sudden events, to overstimulation, were only slowly being grasped.)

I believed that she would have to be understood as always requiring a quieter, simpler, and more stable environment than her siblings needed. The interaction of cortical deficits, multiple other vulnerabilities, and cumulative effects of stressful experiences would expose her to certain unmanageable problems. But therapy could try to liberate her assets and help her to compensate for her deficits; this might help to correct her sense of defeat and assist her to accept her limits without despair.

From the social worker's report, we learned that from birth Robin had been in a difficult situation. An unresponsive baby to begin with, she frightened her mother when she "passed out" during x-ray treatment for hemangiomas (localized lesions of the skin), and brought her mother little reward and much worry from the first. The mother's anxiety about baby Robin was naturally increased by the infant's tendency to startle easily, by her slightly asymmetrical skull formation, asymmetrical ear placement, microphthalmus, mildly primitive ear formation as well as by the scars from the treatment and other deviations, such as hypotonia.

As the third, and problem-burdened, daughter of responsible parents who wanted a boy, Robin was left largely to the care of a nanny, Sadie, while her mother devoted her attention to her two preschool-age daughters—Ann, who was five years older than Robin, and Eve, who was two years older. The mother's next pregnancy began when Robin was a little over a year old. Separation anxiety and temper tantrums, which are not at all unusual at this stage even in normal toddlers, began about a month before her little brother Jim was born. The fact that the mother then devoted herself to the much-desired small son, and continued to leave Robin to the care of the nanny, must have added greatly to the little girl's insecurity and to her anger, which continued to burst out in severe tantrums disturbing to the family.

Her mother's feeling that Robin was an "unresponsive baby" deserves special consideration. What traumatic effects might have remained from the early experiences in the hospital? What relation is there between the hypotonia reported later and possible slow development of expressive patterns? What affective atmosphere did this "different" baby meet whenever she was handled by her mother who had been traumatized by her own early separation from an ill mother and was frustrated by the arrival of a third daughter with grave problems?

Robin's vulnerabilities were increased by the effects of severe glomerulonephritis following a contaminated immunization shot at the age of two and a half. It is impossible to know exactly what aspects of her organic problems were due to this shot.

As Robin grew to the stage where most children enjoy and are proud of displaying motor skills, her flat feet, inadequate balance, and poor coordination must have presented confusing problems and daily frustration. Corrective shoes did not ameliorate the problem of balance since it was organic as well and was also aggravated, in all probability, by her angry and anxious feelings and her growing sense of being inadequate and rejected. Evidently, the fact that she tended to trip and fall was not understood as being due to the combination of her visual difficulties and her problems in balance as well as with her feet. The lack of understanding help could only add to Robin's frustration, which was mounting with her inability to master ordinary self-care skills such as buttoning, and tying shoelaces.

As she entered school, her difficulties in small-muscle coordination and the tremor in her right hand must have made attempts at writing very frustrating for her, a frustration magnified by the fact that teachers insisted that she drop the block printing—with which she doubtless felt more secure—and adopt cursive writing, which she was physically unable to master smoothly because of her chorea and sensory-motor difficulties. Brain damage brought spelling problems, reversals, and incomplete sentences; and these problems were undoubtedly aggravated by mounting feelings of confusion, frustration, and anger. In addition to major difficulty with large-muscle sports and games, hobbies and handicrafts requiring good perceptual-motor coordination would have been hard for her.

It was known that therapy at the age of eight had focused on helping the family to be a functioning whole and to include Robin within it. Her mother struggled with helping her to ride a bicycle; and, evidently after three years of heroic efforts by both of them, Robin finally succeeded. But she was not able to jump rope with other girls at their ordinary pace; she could manage it only when the teacher or her mother slowly turned the rope for her. Robin was left out of most of the girls' games requiring speed. Such items give a picture of a child doggedly struggling to master a few of the skills that contribute to the fun, tension discharge, and sense of competence of the average well-endowed child.

Along with everything else, Robin was allergic to certain common environmental factors such as house dust, one of the most uncontrollable allergies for anyone who moves from one place to another. Thus, she had a chronic drippy nose, which would be likely to antagonize other children at this stage when they tend to be critical of little deviations in appearance.

At the elementary school level, many, if not most, children are suspicious of any child who is a handicap to a team or slows down a play activity, as well as looks a little odd because of the tremors of mild chorea, of which some alert children are highly aware. Moreover, at this developmental stage, children are developing peer groups that help them to achieve some emotional autonomy as they begin to extricate themselves from emotional attachments to parents. A child with realistic needs for help from adults, who threatens the level of mastery the group tries to attain, is a "drag." Thus, rejection by other children, including Robin's own siblings nearest in age, was to be expected. This rejection may well have been increased by her explosiveness, which was intensified by the constant and cumulative frustrations in every zone of childhood peer experience, as well as by her parents' ambivalence and efforts to help her develop control by punishing her tantrums.

Up to now, I have dealt with some of the expectable problems in adaptation related to Robin's damage, the cumulative deficits increased by her anger at frustration and anxiety about ambivalent, tense reactions from stressed parents and rejection by peers. Because of her unpredictable temper, her mother left her at home with her nanny occasionally when she took the other children to visit her own mother for several days when Robin was a young child—a vulnerable period for separation problems in many normal children.

But there are still other factors in her emotional development. She was evidently an active, hopeful little girl; in the face of her difficulties in achieving age-adequate developmental mastery she played animal, crawling on her hands and knees. Thus, in all probability, she enjoyed temporary immunity from the falling to which her difficulties in coordination contributed. Certain major supportive influences evidently helped to balance Robin's rejection by her peers and her nearest siblings and the conflicted relationship with her parents. Her oldest sister, Ann, is said to have been sympathetic and supportive, apparently understanding that Robin had objective difficulties. And her Aunt Samantha, the wife of Robin's maternal grandmother's brother, reportedly showered affection upon her. Possibly the love and support from these two did much to salvage and strengthen the "determination" Robin is said to have shown.

It is interesting to reflect on the sharp contrast between Robin's behavior and her fantasies expressed in her play. The explosive, destructive reactions to frustration (and what she experienced as deprivation) had no counterpart in fantasy. On the contrary, her doll play reflected a desire to be loved and admired (a princess) and deep interest in and attachment to family life. Her positive fantasies implied potentially healthy longings and strivings and gave me confidence in the possibilities for progress. It seemed that she did not internalize or identify with destructiveness—she evidently longed at the deepest level to be accepted.

In the course of therapy, all these inferences and speculations would have to be checked, supplemented, and extended as we listened to and got acquainted with Robin. Therapy would have to continue the diagnostic exploration, watching especially for the exact ways in which brain damage and other vulnerabilities affected her efforts to cope with the challenges of her life.

The evaluation emphasized Robin's interpersonal conflicts, problems she created for her family, and her maladaptive defenses. It did not recognize the profound humiliation, the blows to self-esteem, and the daily frustrations contributed by her multiple bodily limitations as these were detailed in the physical and psychological examinations—or the depth of her feelings of rejection, especially by her peers, and the extent of her anxiety about new encounters which might involve more humiliations and rejections. Thus, it did not clarify the relation of her direct and incessant frustrations to her coping and defense patterns, which relied so heavily on ways of warding off these dangers and maximizing available safe gratifications in fantasy play, bike riding, and time with those adults who were apparently most tolerant. With a child who is burdened both by neurological problems and multiple physiological problems, the impact of these on self-image and self-esteem has to be considered independently as well as in relation to social behavior. Moreover, the evaluation did not deal with the basic contributions of developmental disequilibria at puberty to the total pattern of interacting zones of vulnerability.

In the context of the developmental process we needed to clarify the many factors affecting Robin's efforts to deal with new developmental challenges: direct effects of neurological damage, secondary effects and physiological instabilities accompanying puberty, emotional reactions to the physiological discomforts and to the frustrations caused by the damage and by the responses from all of the environment—and the impact of all of the many interacting factors on the child's experience of each new developmental challenge.

Robin's Problems in "Getting To Be a Teen-ager"

The efforts of the school to assist her by placement in a special class had created the difficulty that she was separated from her age group. At the pubertal phase when normal children are aware of the need to leave childhood behind and are also anxious about entering the sometimes frightening world of teen-agers, Robin realistically and healthily did not want to be relegated to the world of little children. She shared the typical puberty anxiety about facing the pressures, seductions, difficulties in impulse control, and adult demands for more assumption of responsibilities which are part of entering the teen-age level.

Moreover, at an age when most children begin to rebel, get sulky or angry, or aggressively resist adults, in an effort toward autonomy and weaning from the childhood mother, Robin's rebellion was confounded both by her own objective limitations, the confusion caused by the mixed pattern of strengths and weaknesses, her ambivalent feelings about her family, her damaged self-image, and diffuse adaptational problems in every zone of functioning.

It seemed natural that she should have turned to fantasy, a resource not entirely seclusive since her Aunt Samantha had promoted and shared her story-telling activities when Robin was younger; and her doll families carried on quite realistic lives. In and of itself, doll play at twelve is not unusual—many normal girls indulge in a last fling at this childish activity, just as some normal pubertal boys enjoy regressing to younger activities with wagons, scooters, and the like.

Her drive to grow up, moreover, might be further blocked by the anticipated loss of the support of her sister Ann, who was going away to college, and also the loss of her other chief supporters, Aunt Samantha and her nanny, when the family moved away from their home to come to Topeka. Robin might then feel that she would be left unprotected, at the mercy of her critical teen-age sister Eve, whom she had to watch daily doing the things at school she herself had so much difficulty in managing—and at the mercy, as well, of her brother, whose own approach to puberty was likely to bring with it the intolerance common to children at that stage.

No wonder that Robin had difficulty in containing her anger and resentment. At this point, Robin was under cumulative strain that contributed to insecurity and frustration in all areas, a sense of inadequacy and damage. Her difficulties in control of impulse and thought, her outbursts of anger, and her shifting thought processes must have been the result of these many interacting factors.

No wonder she was disturbed at this vulnerable transition stage of puberty, when many normal children withdraw out of conflict and ambivalence about growing up and are discouraged or depressed about their futures as well as angry about the unmet needs of childhood. Longitudinal studies, as well as other data, document this withdrawal or constriction in many children. Moreover, it is widely recognized that transitory acute disturbance at this stage can yield to better resolution of conflicts at a subsequent stage. We might, then, consider that there is some chance of Robin's mobilizing determination and active efforts to solve her problems. Her protests against being grouped with younger children, her active wish for help, her anger rather than deep inhibition, were positive indications.

Consideration of Treatment Needs

Would I take Robin in therapy? One of the examiners who saw her during the evaluation told me that she was a "bad therapy risk" because "she was getting so much secondary gratification from her situation."

I thought it was unsound to believe that psychotherapy alone could accomplish enough for a child in such deep trouble at the difficult stage of puberty. I felt that a comprehensive approach would be needed—a school situation with teachers with whom I could consult and who would be flexible and resourceful in working with her learning problems; a setting with other children who would not reject her; medical help, as well as help for her parents.

The director of therapy, Dr. J. Cotter Hirschberg, agreed to my plans and arranged for Robin to be accepted as a day patient in the Children's Hospital of the Menninger Foundation. Here she would attend its school and have a room for use during the day in a small residential unit with seven other boys and girls, some of whom were about her age, some younger. The child-care workers were experienced with children who had acute problems. The psychiatrist/director of the unit, Dr. Moore, was warm, sensitive, and practical, able to challenge as well as support. An experienced social worker would have conferences with Robin's parents to communicate Robin's needs as they emerged in treatment and to share home problems with us.

In addition, the Children's Hospital staff included a group worker who had organized the Assembly Committee with the responsibility to develop evening programs, and the Council to deal with problems, complaints, and needs conveyed by the children in the hospital. Also, Dr. Hirschberg himself would help to integrate the process as supervisor of the treatment.

The resources of the Children's Hospital provided much more help than I asked for, and I was able to begin my discussions with Robin with the good feeling that comprehensive educational, social, medical help would be part of the work with Robin, along with, and integrated with, psychotherapy.

We could not predict or guarantee that Robin would be able to make enough progress to have a good life—at that point the problems seemed discouraging. But Robin had desperately asked for help, and her parents were supporting her.

The Therapeutic Task with a Heavily Stressed Child at Puberty

The complexity of the multiple growing-up task in adolescence is overwhelming to many normal adolescents. The period before and after puberty is normally a plastic phase, sensitive to changing pressures from inside and outside the child. For instance, the two hundred randomly selected subjects of the Guidance Study at the University of California showed increasing constriction on their Rorschachs just before puberty (McFate and Orr 1949). They recovered after a year or two to their previous levels of openness and spontaneity. Morever, Dr. Fritz Redl (1943) wrote long ago of the resistance of the prepuberty child; and some mothers of premenstrual girls in our Topeka longitudinal series complained that for the six months before menstruation the girls were "impossible to live with."

At any point in childhood, the deviations from socially acceptable behavior which are regarded as "disturbed" or "unmanageable" are often simply extremes of expected patterns. Change is needed primarily in terms of modulation and refinement of control. At puberty, the normal physiological imbalances, the disruption of the latency self-image, and disorientation in reaction to changes in the social structure on shifting to junior high school contribute to lability and sometimes defensive rigidity, which make modulated control very difficult.

If neurological difficulties are also present, they must be seen in relation to the adaptational problems which would normally be expected at this developmental stage. If problems are typical of children without special handicaps or unusual internal or external pressures, we can expect more extreme behavior from children whose neurological problems create much greater difficulty in processing and integrating stimulation from changing inner states and variable external conditions.

Longitudinal studies of normal children also show evidence that, for many, puberty is a time of deep narcissistic threat. They don't know how to cope with the uncertainties of body changes and sometimes withdraw into a limbo of vague, uncertain waiting or, in some instances, are depressed for a time. When, to these normal uncertainties and anxieties associated with the ambiguity of a body in transition, are added the certainties of actual damage or incompleteness, the anxiety is inevitably deepened. And so it was with Robin.

With Robin's multiple sources of vulnerability in addition to her neurological problems and a complex of external impacts, the narcissistic threat and anxiety would be still greater. We could not understand the continuing day-to-day variations in Robin's somatic and psycho-social-emotional functioning without constantly looking through double lenses, as it were, at the interaction of more or less autonomous internal (physiological and neurological) pressures and the changing external supports and threats. We had to watch both of these closely, in relation to her feelings about them and to their impact on her feelings about herself.

Typical Problems of Children and Adolescents with Neurological Damage

For all children with acute physical or neurological problems, a major threat is that of humiliation and rejection. Being different or deviant is hard and some children mobilize as many resources as they can to minimize their deviance—by meticulous dress and grooming or by ultra-conforming behavior, which they think will help reduce the risk of ridicule. But this behavior can boomerang. Society expects a child to conform enough, but the over-conformist may be ridiculed as much as the eccentric child.

Other children send pleas for help through messy clothing, garbled speech, frantic behavior, or a retreat into forlorn isolation. Formerly, many apparently retarded, disturbed children were "put away" in institutions where deprivation of affection, of stimulating resources, of encouragement, and of help in coping with their problems resulted in further deterioration. Federal mandates for "mainstreaming" handicapped children stimulated schools to provide teachers trained to deal with their problems. Progress is being made, but it is slowed down by arbitrary classifications such as "learning disabled" and "emotionally disturbed," when in actuality many children are both. And both groups often have other organic or physical problems as well.

Principles of educating the retarded child do not apply to the neurologically damaged child, precisely because the child with neurological difficulties may be gifted in some areas, average in others, yet severely and mysteriously inadequate in others. Moreover, both the inadequacies and the strengths may be variable and inconsistent. Such children may handle some social skills well under certain circumstances, yet go to pieces in strange, new, or complex situations; they are often disturbed by even ordinary stress.

Along with neurological deficits that can be ascribed to damage to the central nervous system, the child may also be subject to a wide variety of other sources of vulnerability. The child may have problems in vision or hearing; he may be flat-footed or have other problems in coordination. He may have skin sensitivities or allergies. He may have unusual autonomic lability and may also have tendencies to upper respiratory problems. The child may have incompatible tendencies to be very active and also easily overstimulated; thus, his own activity drive may expose him to overwhelming and unmanageable encounters. The child typically has poor control of affect, is labile or even explosive and thus experiences angry retaliations from playmates and siblings or punishment from parents. Brain damage thus brings different patterns of cognitive, motor, and affective difficulty with different children, depending on the diffuseness and areas of damage.

If, in addition, the child is in the midst of a critical developmental transition, the insecurities typical of the stage interact with the frustrations and anxieties contributed by the brain damage and the other areas of vulnerability. The cumulative stress threatens the child's equilibrium, clarity about self, and hope for an effective identity. Relationships with family are increasingly disturbed; both security and love are shaken. Understanding, tolerance, and helpfulness of the family may help the child to maintain some degree of control, but if his emotional instability, outbursts, and demands are met with ridicule, punishment, or rejection, severe regression often results.

In early childhood, it is often difficult to tell the difference between the problems growing out of these various interacting vulnerabilities and the normal developmental problems of the young child. But the poor coordination of the child with neurological difficulties does not improve as fast; his temper tantrums may not come under control as soon as those of a normal child; and finally, when school comes, he cannot cope with the complexities, frustrations, and confusions of group life, or the early learning tasks.

The child is bewildered and frustrated and so is his teacher, who might be better able to help a crippled or cerebral palsied child because the sources of the child's difficulties would be more visible and therefore easier to analyze. His family, his teacher, his peers, and the child himself all feel puzzled and disturbed about why he may be successful in one task and "stupid" in another. The successes that he does have may tend to make the hopeful family feel that he is "really normal," so they pressure him, or punish his failures.

As a result, the child struggles in school with confused, embarrassed, self-rejecting feelings, anger, or even rage toward the world, along with constant anxiety about what (often unpredictable) failure will disgrace him next. He is plagued by fear of further rejection and is filled with resentment at the grown-up world which does not understand how hard he is trying and whose irritable responses to his difficulties make him feel unloved and add to his stress and his incoordination. If the family has other emotional problems—illnesses, vocational frustrations, deep personal losses, intense destructive rivalries, or just the ordinary stresses of middle age—the confusion and conflict generated by these add further burdens to the child's struggles and confusions.

Thus, for many a "brain-damaged child," the specific learning difficulties, neurological deficits, or other realistic organic problems are enmeshed in a confused congeries of emotional reactions to the frustrations of his own coping efforts, the residues of his sense of inadequacy in the presence of his family and his peers, and traces of disturbing emotional interactions in the family. The brain-damaged child may, as a matter of fact, sometimes be living in such a disturbing family situation or with so many other interacting vulnerabilities, that he would have severe adaptational difficulties even if he did not have neurological problems.

A developmental approach can focus attention on the interaction of the many sources of difficulty with the problems, challenges, changes, and insecurities of the developmental phase. While the critical phase of puberty can impose the most severe stress on the multiple vulnerabilities of the child, each developmental stage involves its own pressures and risks, as, for example, the teasing and ridicule that elementary school children direct at their peers who cannot keep up in the race or be an asset on the team. Further, a developmental approach can recognize the plasticity of the child and hope for the improvement that is possible with this plasticity.

With Robin we saw how brain damage with its unstable mental and emotional functioning influenced the process of coping with adolescent losses, challenges and social tasks, as well as schoolwork. Her organic vulnerability meant that the therapy process followed a wavering, winding path—with switch backs and regressions—two steps forward, one step backward, then ahead again. Robin could not move ahead in orderly sequential steps toward the achievement of a sense of personal wholeness and a secure identity. It would be untrue to the process to impose on it an artificial structure. Rather, we are trying to share with the reader Robin's experience and our experience as she valiantly struggled with her deficits and as she, along with us, learned to cope with them. At the same time, twice a week therapy sessions over three years and a great many conferences with other team members have to be reduced to manageable space; this makes it impossible to do justice to the recurrent upsurge of certain persistent problems. We are forced to limit our account to major periods of progress and struggle.

Robin's Situation at the Age of Twelve: Ambiguity and Self-Doubt

What was it like to be twelve years old and less than twelve years old in some ways and more than twelve years old in other ways all at once? If Robin had been a small, slow-growing child, her lags in school achievement and play resources and her peer group difficulties would have been less conspicuous. Being a large girl, already menstruating (and in this way somewhat advanced), the lags were more conspicuous.

How could we understand Robin's "hangdog" expression that bothered her parents? A sense of utter defeat? If so, defeated efforts, hopes, wishes, aspirations? And with these, defeat of a vital, eager, hopeful orientation to life which might be evoked with help? Or was her expression one of overwhelming embarrassment? Could she develop a different image of herself as a person with useful positive capacities? Was she overcome with guilty feelings about mistakes, messes, unhappiness she had caused? If so, could she develop a greater capacity to foresee consequences of blunders and outbursts and in turn forestall them?

Such questions could not be answered ahead of time—only gradually, during therapy hours, might we begin to understand Robin's hangdog expression and watch it change to a proud self-respecting stance if we could succeed in helping her.

There were other questions. What was the meaning of her way of wearing torn and discarded underwear of her sister's? Did this convey her feeling that inside she was damaged, too, and rejected, left aside, because of the damage? Was she using this nonverbal communication because her feelings were too complex to put into words, or because she did not trust anyone to respond or understand? Similarly, the worn old scarf she wrapped around her hand incapacitated by frank chorea certainly seemed to say that her hand was useless and unattractive—and perhaps that she felt as unattractive as that scarf.

A *Possible Therapy Approach*

Robin's parents were worried about her hunger for affection, which they felt could lead her to be sexually exploited. Why was she so "hungry for love?" Did this reflect a sense of deprivation? Did it imply a vigor and strength to reach out? What did this mean for therapy? Perhaps being loved, safely—could free her energy for work on her problems. This would be effective only if it were sincere, if Robin were indeed lovable. Since I enjoyed children, and quickly grew fond of them, in family, neighborly, and even research contexts, and did not tend to get too involved with them, this warm approach did not seem to present problems.

On the hunch that Robin did indeed feel damaged, discarded, rejected, useless, defeated, and unattractive, we wanted to help her feel by contrast attractive and capable in our world. My approach was rooted not only in years of research in child development, and in psychoanalytic training with an unusually sensitive and flexible analyst, but also in a little first-hand acquaintance with the empathic, warm approach of Frieda Fromm-Reichmann, and in Marguerite Sechehaye's (1951) remarkable story of the healing power of corrective love and support.

I wondered how we could help Robin feel less different from others. I wanted to help her see that the world is not a place with a high fence between all the people who think they are "normal" or perfect and people who are damaged or incomplete. Most people have some limitations, and it occurred to me that I could illustrate this with examples including some of my own obvious limitations, having arthritis, not being good at sports or swimming, and so on.

Just bringing her into a world of people with a range of strengths and weaknesses would not, however, be enough—could we stimulate a feeling of pride and pleasure in being herself? We know that what we say nonverbally as well as verbally, sometimes covers the opposite. Perhaps her miserable demonstration with torn clothes that she felt so damaged and unattractive covered a deep wish to be a pretty girl instead. How could we bring out the pretty girl? She had a well-formed graceful body except for her flat feet, and she had beautiful, blonde silky hair. The missing front teeth, and stuffy allergic nose distracted both herself and onlookers from her charm. These could be taken care of, if her family could get the appropriate care as soon as possible.

The Need for a Comprehensive Approach to Treatment

When the child has to struggle with all these realistic problems, a therapy oriented to internalized conflicts alone is not sufficient. Moreover, professional training focused on helping the child to cope with his learning deficits or physical problems is not enough either. Good teaching may be frustrated by the child's depression, self-depreciation, lack of confidence that progress can be made, and the chronic cumulative anxiety and anger at previous failures and difficulties.

Distractibility, organic difficulties in handling spatial perception, spelling, handwriting, math, and other problems, may make the child hypersensitive to criticism, with tendencies to sudden collapses of effort. His inability to concentrate, especially when embarrassed, may defeat the teacher. Stress at home or apparently minor physical discomfort may undermine the child's stability and capacity to focus; or noises which would not disturb another child may disrupt his integration.

A model of treatment is needed, then, for these emotionally disturbed, neurologically damaged young ones which will integrate special teaching and therapy for emotional disturbances as well as help with medical problems, social relations, and realistic difficulties in the environment, all of which add to the emotional disturbance and discourage the child.

The therapist for such a child does not work alone but rather as the central member of a team in communication with the teachers and others who are working with the child. The teacher who works with very small groups will be able to adapt the level of work in each area to the wide variation in levels of functioning of each child. But even when these variations in level have been clarified, the teacher may need to search for the particular materials and approach that will evoke the most sustained effort.

The therapist must constantly help the child to relinquish the self-image of one who is hopelessly inadequate and gradually develop the image of himself as having a certain "checkerboard" of strength and weaknesses that many other people have. The therapist can reinforce the teachers and help while also assisting the child to develop more confidence in his capacity to manage or to compensate for his weak areas.

In this book we have tried to keep in mind how it feels to be brain-damaged, at the sensitive developmental transition of early adolescence, and how these feelings interact with the difficulties directly caused by the neurological lesions. These include difficulties in developing an accurate visual map of one's world necessary for appropriate response to the environment, in organizing one's observations and reactions in order to respond to and manage inner and outer changes of all kinds. The brain-damaged child has trouble with transitions and shifts in activities or changes in the day's schedules, with delays or frustrations when someone fails to keep an appointment; changes that are difficult for others are almost unbearable for him—a move from a home town to a new city, or even from one hospital residence unit to another; the absence of a person relied on; or the loss of a beloved relative or friend. And always there are difficulties in keeping up with or participating with one's peers, not only in competitive games in which one could never hope to win or succeed an average share of the time, but also in social situations requiring a quick, flexible response to cues, atmosphere, and interactions among a group of persons. Finally, the normal insecurities and anxieties about becoming a teen-ager are intensified by the interaction of the physiological instability accompanying changes of puberty with the neurological damage.

This study began at the onset of Robin's puberty, and therefore it provides an opportunity to understand more deeply the interactions of developmental pressures with a child's organic and emotional problems at this critical phase. We found points at which the initial careful diagnostic study did not reveal a complete picture of either the child's limitations or positive capacities as these emerged through the interdisciplinary treatment. In the course of therapy, we looked for the ways in which zones of good functioning could be utilized to cope with severe adaptational threats. Each person on the treatment team contributed both to an increased understanding of Robin's weaknesses and her strengths, and to the use of strengths to balance and cope with her weaknesses.

It goes without saying that normal developmental challenges at puberty, including the problem of achieving a sense of identity, clarity about sex-role, and a beginning orientation to future plans, are more acute in a child with multiple organic problems. The identity problem is shadowed by the issue "Am I doomed?" or "Will I be able to manage?" Such heartbreaking questions are complicated by the psychosexual residues from earlier stages and the urgent need to achieve more autonomy from parents despite anxieties about potential competence.

Therapy Involves Extended Evaluation

Therapy would not merely help Robin to cope with problems identified during the initial evaluation. It would give an opportunity for extended evaluation, with continued observation of her responses to experiences over time and the meaning of these experiences to Robin, to provide a sharp picture of the variety of her specific adaptational problems and coping resources. This is also true of the brain-damaged child or adolescent and other children with organic handicaps which create realistic difficulties to which anxiety is a reaction rather than solely a primary cause, although anxiety aggravates the problems. It is risky to diagnose the child's character in these instances, since behavior patterns—withdrawal, resistance, and the like—may be useful temporary steps in orientation and eventual mastery, as we saw in our longitudinal study (Murphy 1962; Murphy and Moriarty 1976; Moriarty 1961).

In our ongoing evaluation in therapy we would need to watch the impact of neurological damage on Robin's developmental situation. We would have to be alert to the relation of the damage to experiences she could not handle, the alignment of acceptance and avoidance of challenges and opportunities, and the possible change in the pattern of responses to varied new experiences and activities which might be created by gradual success in certain areas.

New successes might be expected to reduce the load of frustration and anxiety, evoke new pride and confidence, along with a changing self-image. We hoped the hangdog posture would vanish. And we hoped that Robin's family would begin to see her differently, appreciating her problems more clearly, her efforts, and her feelings.

In this account of Robin's treatment, a concise picture of high points of understanding reached by the team, and progress made by Robin, would not be true to the uncertain, irregular course we had to follow. We have chosen to share with the reader our experience and Robin's experience—in the struggle to master the problems that so nearly defeated her, and threatened to relegate her to the group of those permanently or almost totally incapacitated.

2

We Get Acquainted
with Robin

My first meeting with Robin was a surprise and a contrast to the observations of the examiners during the examination. To be sure, tests and examinations are stressful—they put the child on the spot; and anxiety adds to difficulties in functioning. Difficulties in coping with tests contribute to frustration and undermine self-respect and confidence in the future.

Robin had begged for help, and coming to therapy probably revived her hope. Let us follow her beginning responses in her twice-a-week therapy hours, in order to see her in a quiet situation free of the overstimulation of school and home and the stress of tests.*

Robin's First Hour in Therapy

Robin was brought to my office promptly for her first hour with me. I saw a rather tall, blonde, girlishly rounded, and naïve girl with an extraordinarily sensitive face which quickly mirrored every nuance of her fleeting emotions: at first shy, wistful—as if hoping that we would like

*In the passages that are set off by the symbol ✝ , I share with the reader some of my thoughts and reactions to the observations and the exchanges during the hours of therapy.

and enjoy each other. Later, sometimes humorous, sometimes disparaging, sometimes annoyed feelings were reflected, as she talked to me about some incident that had made her angry or sad. Occasionally her face would be covered by a bland mask. At such times, the appealing and attractive expressiveness vanished, and she seemed unapproachable and unattractive. Mostly, I found myself resonating to her moods, often with a sense of being mutually in tune. She was always quick in her acceptance; and sometimes a subtly appreciative "we understand each other" expression appeared after I had acknowledged some feeling she reflected about events that she had encountered. I couldn't catch everything she said: her words tumbled out soft and mushy as she was missing two front teeth; and the stuffiness of her allergic nose made it harder to understand her.

Occasionally Robin would fall silent. When she did not break the silence, I asked a question related to what we had been talking about, and she always responded instantly, with intense eagerness and effort to communicate. I tried equally hard to understand. She gave precise descriptions of where she lived and compared her present home with her Grand Island home. (The latter was bigger and for a child much more interesting.) She reviewed many losses she had suffered in addition to that of her home—her dog, her cat, her grandmother, and also her therapist of four years ago. She vividly described the horseback riding she preferred (bareback, so she could grab the horse around the neck), her dolls, stuffed animals at home, "hobbies," former pets, and other pleasurable items and memories.

✝   At times her conversation was rather sophisticated: for instance, she mentioned somebody who had teased her by calling her "an Arctic witch," to which she had replied that the other person was an "abominable snowman." Not only her vocabulary—which at moments seemed definitely like a teen-ager's—but also the range of her affective expressions and pick-up also seemed subtle and like that of an older teen-age girl.

At the same time, she had moments of seeming younger than her age—a characteristic that I have found to be not uncommon in children who are between twelve and thirteen, crossing the bridge between childhood and the teens. There was often a fluid alternation between regressing to younger levels of functioning and older teen-age attitudes and behavior.

Robin talked rather freely about what she and the different members of her family did when they got mad: "Father says it is all right to fight back as long as you fight the person who really made you mad and don't take it out on someone else." Her mother wouldn't let anybody else swear or hit. "Things are frustrating when you do the dishes with her because if you drop something yourself and break it, she gets angry and blows up, but if she breaks it herself there is no way she can let out her angry feelings." Robin recounted the ways she fought back at her brother and sisters at times. She loved her older sister, Ann, whom she described as "sweet and gentle." Ann helped Robin with her hair and was generally kind and helpful. Robin was also quite positive in her comments about Eve. Robin did admit that her younger brother teased and tickled her, sometimes very annoyingly.

In school, she imagined that she would like history, which would use her own vivid detailed memory and interest in places. Spelling and sometimes arithmetic were hard, "depending on what kind of arithmetic I have to do."

After exploring her feelings about leaving Grand Island, being here in Topeka, having me instead of Kathleen Kirk, her therapist when she was eight years old, I asked what other kinds of things were hard and which were easy for her. She was reluctant to respond to this question as if she didn't want to get into a discussion of difficulties in this first hour. Later, after giving her a further chance to talk about positive things, I referred to her difficulties in expressing anger with her mother and said, "I am sure you know from the time you had with Kathleen Kirk that there are no rules like that here in therapy; you can talk about how you feel." She smiled a knowing "we understand" smile and then said, "I'm just not in the mood today."

Then she described falling out of bed that morning, apparently in reaction to a dream. She denied that she had hurt herself when she fell on her back. When I asked her whether this happened often, she said it did happen every once in a while.

✛   This kind of motor reactivity in a state between sleeping and waking might be expected in a child of rather fluid responsiveness and some difficulty in central control. I didn't pursue this but noted it as something to check on in getting a fuller picture of the conditions under which good control is maintained. The fact that she claimed to be at ease with horseback riding (and I planned to have the social worker check this) suggests that her large-muscle coordination was under fairly adequate control in a waking state.

In striking contrast to her frequently mature vocabulary, fluent expressiveness, and ease of description of places, people, and so forth was her tendency to lisp—perhaps due to her two missing front teeth—to talk very softly and, at times, to speak so rapidly and in such a low tone that it was hard for me to hear. When I asked her to repeat what she had said—saying that I hadn't heard very well—she slowed down and repeated the sentence with an understanding acceptance of my difficulty in hearing her.

In general, I was impressed more by her lability than by her retardation, and also by the possibility of her having a wide range of responses to different people.

In view of the likelihood that Robin might be imitating her older sisters in certain ways, I wanted to explore how she felt about the girls at school, such as Prudence and Lisa. She talked about both of them rather objectively, describing differences in their interests, saying that she got along with Prudence better; Robin revealed considerable capacity for observation and detached judgment. I asked her if it bothered her to be with girls who got more upset and had more troubles than she did, and she replied humorously that she wasn't sure that was true and then gave some accounts of how she got upset at home.

Later she said she liked the school, and then added that she got away from home as much as she could—that was why she went to camp and why she went to visit relatives when she got the chance, and that was also why she undertook evening activities here at school when she could. I commented that we would need to talk about this more and try to understand it.

✝   While we were able to talk about angry feelings, feelings of loss, difficulties of getting used to new places and new people, I did not confront her with the deeper feelings of unhappiness which I thought she must have had in view of what she said about wanting to be away from home as much as possible.

She touched on several other topics usually rather briefly. Her family was quite susceptible to infections: viruses, colds, and so forth. She said that Ann got the worst colds. She herself had a number of allergies. She demonstrated with her hands how thick the folder was that kept a record of her allergy history. When I asked her specifically about them, she mentioned corn, pork, citrus fruits, and one to two other foods, along with dust, cats, and others.

She seemed to be rather concerned about boys, probably afraid of encounters that might lead to sexual excitement. She mentioned that her parents have made a rule that no one can go on a date until the first year in high school, and this was said with perhaps a little pride that her parents were firm about this rule. She also mentioned her annoyance when her brother tickled her. There were two questions here. Could she be helped to defend herself and cope with it independently? Did she need some support from her family to eliminate this kind of physical stimulation?

After commenting that I would see her next Tuesday and that the hour was up now, we went out into the waiting room, which is also a kitchen where we have a little coke machine. I asked if she would split a coke with me and she agreed, saying, "Dr. Moore said we could have a party together. I don't know why you remind me of Dr. Moore—I keep wanting to call you Dr. Moore." I also asked her to share a cookie, and we finished our treat just as the child-care worker came to get her. As she left, I put my hand lightly on her shoulder, saying, "Good-bye, Robin," and she neither resisted, evaded, nor acknowledged it, but as she stepped out of the door turned back to smile.

✚   It seemed to me that her round, soft, full face and rounded build was quite attractive and could mean that she might well appeal to boys before she was ready to cope with their responses. The fact that she was tall and verbally facile and also rather perceptive and responsive, at times at least, could add to her appeal for somewhat older boys.

Since the evaluation process had produced such a negative impression of Robin, I had wanted to put her at ease and to explore potentialities that might not have been revealed under the stress of the examinations. In this less stressful situation, Robin indeed looked different. She seemed to have a capacity for great rapport and sensitive responsiveness, with honesty and sense of values, a capacity for pleasure and for interests, and a cooperative attitude toward working together—while at the same time she was sometimes stymied and confused by mixed feelings.

She certainly wanted to present a positive impression of herself as growing up, as having skills and resources and wishes of her own, along with both negative and positive feelings and problems in the family which she could only indicate in a general way in this first hour.

I got the distinct impression that this was a child with basically good perception and intelligence with spotty deficiencies—as if a plate of fine metal had been shot full of holes. She seemed to have clusters of seriously disturbing difficulties along with assets. I also had the impression that it would take time to get a clear picture of the range, scope, possible reversibility, and ways of coping with her difficulties, as well as a picture of the specific ways in which brain damage interfered with mastery.

In this first session, I felt that she was making a great effort and accenting the positive to the extent that often she denied difficulties. To be sure, after her initial denial, she would sometimes come around to a concise, quick illustration of this or that difficulty, then run away from it. She was most at ease when talking about situations which she had handled well.

In view of her tendencies toward denial and shutting out, it was possible that some of her school difficulties were increased by suppressed angry feelings. This possibility was reinforced by her report of her mother's difficulties in accepting Robin's angry feelings and by her difficulties in expressing feelings about frustrating experiences within the family. Her voice became particularly bland at these times.

I felt that there was much to work on with Robin, but it might be hard to help her to a realistic, balanced view of herself. Her warm feelings toward Ann and emphasis on Ann's helpfulness implied that the image of being a kind and helpful person might be an important focus for us. Possibly her interest in animals or an interest in children could lead to care-taking roles without handicapping her by requiring much in the areas in which she had most difficulty

Her alternation between, or even at times almost integration of, a subtle combination of maintaining a grown-up teen-ager style while also seeming dependent and younger illustrated the conflict between relinquishing childhood and moving into adolescence which is so common in normal children at the age of twelve to thirteen.

With her sensitivity and perceptiveness there probably were some areas in which she could produce something interesting. It would be important to give her support in every concrete area in which she could develop competence and creativity and to adapt demands to what she could comfortably manage.

Robin Shares Her Interests and Feelings

Robin came in carrying a jacket embroidered with names of her friends and teachers at Grand Island and also a blue nightgown with an embroidered design on it which she had made for her sister Ann. She explained who the boys and girls and teachers were who had written their names on the jacket, and pointed out which names Ann had embroidered for her and which ones she had done herself. The total effect of the soft pastels was very pretty so it was easy to admire it. On the nightgown, "Sweet Dreams, Ann" was embroidered in large letters near the bottom with a large cat above. I asked her how she had made the letters and cat so neat; she used stencils for drawing them on the nightgown, but she had herself drawn in the cat's face. I commented on the yellow and gray eyes and asked whether her cat had had eyes like that, and she said yes. Then she called my attention to the one white whisker which she had enjoyed putting into this work of art.

I commented on her blouse, a print in tones of yellow, rust, brown, and beige, harmonizing nicely with her hair. I said "I wish I had had such lovely hair when I was thirteen." She added that earlier it had been "too fine, like baby hair," and I guessed that she was glad that it had become a little stronger; she agreed, saying that formerly she couldn't do anything with it at all. She explained that she uses lemon oil to keep it light and to bring out the highlights in strands that are more golden than the rest. I inspected her hair carefully, noting where these were, along with her pretty barrette.

She seemed to enjoy this appreciation and told me that she washed her hair every other night because it was apt to get oily and then her forehead broke out. Washing her hair before going to bed kept her up late, and when I commented that she seemed a little sleepy, she said it was because she had overslept, having gone to bed about eleven o'clock.

Since she had mentioned Ann as helpful again, I remarked that she and Ann seemed to be in tune with each other, and she agreed, but made a disparaging face and added, "She's the only one." I asked about Eve who, she had said, was more critical. She said Jim was having a hard time with arithmetic; he didn't like to do his homework. She explained that in Grand Island they had gone to a small school, and it was hard now for Jim to be in a class of twenty-five or thirty children when he was used to being in a class of ten. She said she was in a small class now, which was what she was used to, and Jim would like to come to her school at the Children's Hospital, but the family budget couldn't stand it. Later, she commented that she and Jim had always been a little slower in school than their sisters and needed more time for their homework. They had found some subjects harder.

✝   These remarks about Jim reflected empathy and understanding of his needs, and perhaps considerable rapport with him.

She repeated that the schedule at school "didn't seem very school." If school lasted until four o'clock, she would like to be studying something else.

Rather rapidly then, she said that she had a lot of curiosity, she was nosy, she liked to get into things, liked to find out about things. When I asked what she would like to find out, she said that she had found some books about handicapped children and when she was grown-up she would like to have a place on a farm where she could have animals and help handicapped children. She sounded enthusiastic and confident about this. I agreed that this was a wise ambition and that it was also a big ambition, and she reflected that she would have to learn a lot to be able to do it. She then said, "When I conquer some of my weaknesses, I think I'll be able to do it."

When I responded that deep down inside herself she knew that she could do some good and important things, she smiled a most enchanting, partly shy, partly knowing, and partly confident sort of smile. I said this was very important and I felt sure she would be able to find a useful and satisfying niche in life and that helping handicapped children would be one good possibility. I asked whether she had talked this over with anybody else, and she said that she had mentioned it to Michael, one of the child-care workers.

Soon she went on, telling me things that she said she had never told anybody. She enumerated the people she felt comfortable with, to whom she could talk—her grandmother, whom she had lost last spring and to whom she said she had felt very close, and also her Aunt Harriet in Wisconsin. She discussed the nuances of her feelings toward so many different relatives that it was hard for me to remember them all. I commented that she really loved Ann and she had really loved her grandmother and that it was very important to have people one loved; when one has loved people and been loved, one can give love to others too, and this might have some connection with why she wanted to give something to children who needed it.

She nodded shyly and earnestly and talked a little tensely, softly, and seriously about people by whom she had felt "genuinely loved." She said that at home she gets "plenty of love, all the love I need, but the trouble is it isn't genuine love." I commented that it felt as if they were dishing it out. She said, "Yes, you can take it or leave it." I added that she felt that it wasn't a love that went with understanding, and she nodded again and then added that that was the difference between the love that she felt from her grandmother and Aunt Harriet as compared with others.

I commented that she understood a great deal—more than she let a lot of people know. At this, she flushed and laughed, drooping her head a little and looking at me from under her eyelids, smiled in a knowing way, and said, "Yes, that's it." I added, "And so there are lots of people who don't know how much you really do understand," and she nodded. Then she went on: "I take my time before I decide how much I can let out to a new person. I don't trust everybody." She communicated more on the theme of trusting in a quiet, confiding, and rather tender way.

I asked, "Why do you 'hide your light under a bushel?' " She replied, "Because if I let people know how much I understand, they would expect too much from me." I said, "In this way you keep people from knowing how much you have to give and how much understanding you have, and perhaps you do the same thing with some of your school work." She wanted to know what I meant, and I said, "Maybe your feelings make it hard for you to do as well in some of your schoolwork as you really could."

✝ I was deeply moved by Robin's honest, accurate perception, her communication of her problem, and her way of coping with it to make her survival possible. I felt an inner conviction that with that strength she would make much progress. There was a solid island of insight and expressiveness in her sea of deficits.

Robin had begun the hour with more sharing of positive feelings. In contrast to the evaluation reports of lack of friends, her jacket reflected her pleasure in friendly gestures from peers and teachers, and also her simple creative efforts. As part of my own wish to balance the negative image seen in the evaluation sessions, I genuinely appreciated her beautiful hair. This not only supported healthy narcissism, but gave us a bond.

It was interesting to see how her empathy with her brother's difficulties followed this supportive gesture, then her interest in handicapped children was expressed along with an identification with a helper role and an assertion of confidence in her ability to be a helper. In addition, she became more confiding, sharing feelings about family members she loved and by whom she had felt genuinely loved—in contrast to people she could not trust. Her insightful comment that if she "let people know how much I understand, they would expect too much from me" was realistic. Her understanding was far ahead of her capacity to cope with tasks requiring skills threatened by her neurological damage.

I was startled and touched by this sharp, accurate realization of her contrasting insight and limitations, and the frankness apparently evoked by my sharing a feeling about being thirteen. This was an extremely helpful hour, revealing her hidden confidence in future mastery and usefulness, the healthy narcissism expressed in care of her lovely hair (a narcissism that had been hidden by her discouraged sense of damage so obvious in the evaluation), and the useful defense by which she protected herself from unrealistic demands. I was amazed at the revelation of her potentialities and gained great confidence in the prospects for good development; and I felt that she trusted me and that we could work together well. It was evident to me that a task for the team would be clarification of her strength along with clearer recognition of her organic deficits.

In a talk with her teacher I mentioned Robin's fondness for animals, including horses, and said that I thought if she could be given a book about horses, she would probably want to read it; I felt that building on her maximal motivation would help her progress in school. Her teacher agreed.

At the next therapy hour Robin brought a book "all about horses" along with a paper she had written at home and was going to correct at school. The paper was clearly and neatly written with few errors, considering the number of big words. As I looked through the book, commenting on the interesting information about horse history, she showed me her favorite picture of a mare nuzzling a kitten. Then she talked about her puppies and how her mother had given them their first bath, perfuming each one with a different scent to tell them apart. Robin knows them by a slight difference in color.

Beginning to Probe Angry Feelings and Learning Problems

I commented on her liking to write about horses and remembered she did not like arithmetic; I wondered what parts she didn't like; and she said "the times." When I asked her to recite some multiplication tables, she did not know 10 times 10 but did know 2 times 2 and 5 times 5. (Hardly a second-grade level.) I said it was strange that she could manage such big words about horses and had trouble with such little numbers. She smiled her "knowing" smile, and I recalled her saying that she had trouble with things she disliked or got mad at and wondered whether she got mad at arithmetic. What else did she get mad at? She did not resist this probe but shared some protests: she described how her father helped her brother with his arithmetic and promised to help her, but he merely helped Jim longer. I recognized that she felt her father had let her down, and I asked whether he felt that she was getting a lot of help in therapy while Jim was not. She protested with a slightly disgusted smile, "He has a tutor!" I said she felt that Jim was getting help and that it was not fair for her father not to help her—it was a gyp. She smiled again her "now you understand" smile, then added that Eve helped her sometimes when her own work was finished.

When I asked again what else she got mad at, she said that she sees more of her father now than she used to—in Grand Island he hardly ever came home to dinner, but now he did, and she could get to know him better. Still, now that he had started classes it was not so good. "He's always writing out his lectures, and then he reads them to us," she said with a distasteful smirk. "And I can't play football with him and Jim because he analyzes me if I say I want to!" I suggested that she probably felt one therapist was enough, and she smiled her "exactly" smile. I asked whether she told her father that she wanted him to be her father and not a therapist, and she intimated that she tried but it was hard. She continued that his lectures were "about the id, superego, and ego," and when I asked what these were, she said, "The superego is the watchdog over your inner ego that doesn't always do the right thing, and the id is your temper." I wondered whether she knew the story of Pinocchio, and she smiled, "That's another good example."

When I asked what she did when her temper acted up, she described throwing beanbags and other things on the floor as if that were a safe way of letting out angry feelings. I commented that she had not had a temper tantrum here, but I wondered if she didn't get mad at me too, for instance, for my being away for one of our therapy hours. She denied this firmly, and when I persisted that she might feel I was also letting her down and that I could make it up next week if she wanted to, she declined casually in a tolerant way as if to return some of the acceptance she felt here.

✝ It would take time before she could express anger at me along with her anger at others.

Feelings of Neglect, Frustration, and Loss

In the following therapy hour, the theme of being let down was elaborated after initial denial and resistance. Robin had had many frustrations, with a teacher sick and absent (along with an absent child-care worker) and not enough to do at school; besides that, one of her two pet eels had died. After I noted the relationship between these various ways of feeling neglected—when people go away, get sick, or die—Robin smiled appreciatively, then complained about getting to bed late. When I explored the reasons for this, she commented bitterly that supper might be any time between six and nine o'clock, whenever her mother gets it ready. When I related this to our previous comments about being let down here, adding that "even at home you can't count on your mother to get your supper when you're hungry." Robin smiled even more warmly.

I asked whether she had ways of coping with these many frustrating things that seemed to happen all at once. She replied, "I can get a fish that has real eyelashes and winks at you," and she explained this compensation quite seriously along with describing an aquarium that she might get for it. She added that she might have to get rid of her turtle because a turtle might attack the fish; but this did not lead to a discussion about siblings.

✝ Her pattern appeared to be one of finding compensations to balance frustrations.

Robin volunteered that on November 13 she would be thirteen years old, and that that would mean twenty-six days of good luck. When I asked how it felt to be getting to be thirteen, she said, "I don't know yet, I'm not thirteen yet," and I commented that different people feel different ways about getting to be thirteen, partly excited and happy, partly worried. Robin did not talk about new things that she might do, but said: "There is something I want to tell you. I want to have a doll collection." Here she reviewed the many different dolls—a Barbie doll, four different boy dolls, a Midge doll, and others in that set; then she also told about her bone china set of animals and her set of little plastic horse models. She said she was going to keep these "hobbies."

She went on, "Some people think it is childish to keep dolls after you get to be thirteen." She then described how her mother had given away some of her childhood books that her mother felt were too young for Robin. I said, "You want to decide for yourself when you are ready to give up things. You don't want to give up everything at once."

She then reviewed again all the things that she had lost: friends that she had played with, her grandmother, an uncle, leaving Grand Island; and then added dolefully, "And the horse I've had for twelve years is nearly twenty-four years old." I said, "You are afraid that you will lose him pretty soon." Then I summarized, "You lose people that you care about, and you can't count on the ones that you have; even your mother let you down by not giving you food when you are hungry, and by giving away things without asking you."

The mention of the supper and food reminded Robin of the problem of schedule. She said, "When I was at camp, we got up at seven o'clock, had breakfast at seven-thirty . . . ," and she outlined the camp schedule in the greatest detail from morning until bedtime. She added, "I think a schedule like that would be good for a family, too." (The social worker noted that the mother did find it hard to maintain an organized plan.) I reflected, "It's hard for you when you can't count on people and things, and one way of managing is to plan a schedule so at least you can count on that." Robin again agreed warmly.

✦   I deliberately reinforced her feeling about wanting a schedule since a brain-damaged child has difficulty in meeting changes, dealing with shifts and disappointments, and does realistically need to be able to organize things in a dependable way.

I then said, "I'm sorry that I was away last week when so many disappointments happened." Robin protested, "You wouldn't have wanted to see me on Thursday. I was so upset." I smiled, "I'm such a fragile old grandmother you think I couldn't take it, but what am I here for?" Robin continued that she was upset when her art teacher told her that she would come here weekends for a lapidary class. She had wanted to take lapidary but her family went to the farm every other week, and it would not be practical to be absent half the time.

✦   It was interesting to see her increasingly positive feelings about the hospital school leading to a conflict about trips to the farm.

I reflected again, "You had been disappointed by so many things and just when you thought of something that would be satisfying, the door was slammed." Robin agreed, "I'd be happy on the farm with the horses, but we can't go back for five years." She then detailed all the reasons why they had to stay here for several years. She added that she was not sure they could go back then because she and Jim would be in high school, and it would not be possible to get to this high school from the farm.

✦   It seemed to me that the transition to the teen-age stage was making her more conscious of years ahead.

I said that she seemed doubtful about *anything* ever working out— when she loses so many dear friends and family and so many disappointments happen. She agreed soberly that this was so.

I noted that she had been talking about very important things that day, and we would need to talk more about them on Thursday and try to think what could be done about disappointments and how it might be possible to make good plans that could work. She started out the door rather slowly as if she didn't quite want to go, then turned to smile again one of her warm smiles but with a wistful quality that seemed to be expressing a mixture of hope and doubt.

✚   The long list of losses and frustrations foreshadowed recurrent efforts to cope with problems like these.

Difficulty in Making Shifts and Coping with Disasters

At our next hour, Robin rushed in carrying a huge morning-glory blossom, which she put into my hand; I kept it while we sat down to talk. She was silent at first as she often was, as if it were hard for her to get started, to make a transition, or to shift her orientation from one situation to another. But since she seemed to feel better, I asked whether her teacher was back, and she said yes. So I commented, "It seems to feel good when things are going along on schedule in a normal way, while it is hard when unexpected things happen and people are away or sick," and she nodded.

✚   Her difficulty in getting started is common for people with various kinds of neurological damage. She never seemed to resist my help with this, and I often had to help her get started; I rarely found this necessary with other children.

Then she began a review of disasters: one was a tornado that had hit several places in Grand Island at one time. She felt she had had a narrow escape because when she tried to get in the door at her Aunt Samantha's house it was locked, and she was afraid for a moment that she couldn't get in, until her aunt came to the door to let her in. I summarized that a lot of bad things had happened in her life—that once she had told me about being thrown several times by horses. She belittled this, "I'm used to it, I've never really been hurt." I commented that she could take some things in her stride, and it was easier to do this when there had not been too many other bad things at once. I recalled that on Tuesday she had been upset because supper had been late the night before and she had been late getting to bed. She accepted this and added that last night supper had been on time at six-thirty and she did feel better today.

Wish to Be a Helper

Robin then moved to her great wish to help people. "I want to help old ladies the way I did in Grand Island. My father said I can not do anything until I am fourteen because of hospital rules; and my allergies could lead to colds and be a risk to others." I suggested, "Since other people helped you, you would like to be able to give something too," and she agreed, adding that many people had helped her. I said that there were many people who needed help, not only old ladies (I did not say "like me") but crippled children, retarded children, nursery-school children, and I thought it might be possible to find a situation where she could be of help a couple of hours for an afternoon or two a week. She grew absolutely radiant at this and went on with a triumphant smile, "I do want to help—I've had so much, and I can't give Aunt Samantha anything." Then she continued, "But I get upset with some kinds of children. I can't help children who have something missing like a defective heart or something like that."

I responded, "You feel that something in you is missing, because you have such a very hard time with arithmetic and spelling even though you do have other abilities." She looked thoughtful and said, "That could be." Then she went on, "And I can't help children from broken homes like Missy. I get very upset when I think of what they don't get from their homes." I suggested, "They remind you of some things your family does not give you, and often you try to forget this because you are aware of how much they have done for you." Robin then said, "They give me plenty of love, but they don't see what is really important to me." I just commented, "They don't really understand." Robin had edged her way again to this core feeling of a lack of mutuality.

Then I ruminated aloud, "You say you feel you can't give Aunt Samantha anything; maybe you feel that you would like to give me something too, because you feel that I am trying to understand." She nodded, and I went on: "But you do give me something. I am interested in helping children with different kinds of strengths and weaknesses, and you help me to understand." She accepted this in a calm, thoughtful way, and then said: "Father says I couldn't be a psychiatrist—that I had better go into medicine." I was amazed and said, "Well, you have many helpers, child-care workers, and teachers. They all have different kinds of experience and training. A person doesn't have to be a doctor to help people, does she?" Robin accepted my thought and described two workers who were very gentle with children who needed gentleness. I now encouraged her,

"You understand how much some children do need gentle grownups. You could be understanding and gentle."

Managing Her Temper and Communicating Needs

Robin reflected her doubt, protesting, "But I have a bad temper. Sometimes I can be vicious. I don't want to lose my temper, but sometimes I do." I said, "Well, we're beginning to understand that when you have a bad temper it's like the straw that breaks the camel's back—when too much piles up on you at once. What do you think you can do about it?" Robin thought out loud, "I can go out to some quiet, lonely place by myself, a lonesome place, and after an hour I've cooled off."

I said approvingly, "You do have some ways of managing; giving yourself time to cool off is one way; another way is to understand what makes your temper pile up, then try to prevent letting things pile up too much. On Tuesday, you were angry because so many things had happened at once—supper was late, and you got to bed late, and Diane was away, and I had been away, and it was all too much for you. But couldn't you talk to your mother about needing to have supper at a regular hour?" Robin agreed that perhaps she could tell her mother more.

I asked her whether she had told her mother about some other things she had mentioned—that her eyes and her teeth needed attention, and that she needed another allergy checkup. Robin said she had, and her mother had made a dental appointment and had told her that after she was finished with the dentist she could go to the ophthalmologist again. I emphasized, "So you do feel that if you keep at it and tell your mother, she will take care of things." Robin agreed, then said, "There was a time about five years ago when I could talk to her. I don't know why—out under a tree when no one else was there, we could talk." I commented, "But now it seems hard to find a quiet time like that with her." After a moment or so, I said, "I'll be here Tuesday, and we can talk some more then."

✝   The quiet time in therapy evidently meant much to her, and helped to evoke her hopes as well as to release feelings about deprivation— both in her body and in loving attention at home. The review of external losses had led to a franker admission of internal losses and inadequacies. Balancing these was her identification with a helping role—on the surface a way of sharing what she was given; at a deeper level, an assertion of her own strength.

The next hour, Robin brought a delightful, soft cuddly, bright yellow toy dog which she put into my arms, saying, "I wanted to show you one of my hobbies"; and I shared her pleasure in his cuteness. But then she began a long series of tales of woe. First, Eve had had a party last weekend, and a boy crashed the party and stepped on one of the puppies. The puppy was not badly hurt, but Robin was upset. Then she lost her eel down the drain. I suggested that by now he was happily swimming in the river, and she agreed. She added that she was getting a little mouse, and I recognized the importance of finding a substitute as a way of coping with loss and frustration.

Then she told of how her mother had forgotten something. And her father had not given her her allergy shot. Yesterday, when she went home she hit the wall, and I suggested that perhaps she had been irritated because of these frustrations and accidents over the weekend. She seemed a little doubtful about this, and I added that along with the frustrations or annoyances that she had mentioned, I had not been careful with the morning-glory she had brought me last week. I should have put it in water; without the water it had not survived. Robin then gave an illustration of some error she herself had made and tossed off all the complaints as not amounting to very much.

✛   This use of denial after my admitting carelessness contrasted with her previous elaborations of frustrations.

I did not feel like letting it go and said, "Well, you were cross enough to hit the wall, and if all these other things really didn't amount to very much, there must be something that did." She agreed, then said, "I was awfully upset because I didn't understand what was in the 'Weekly Reader.' We read things, then have to answer questions, and I didn't understand correctly."

I commented, "You want terribly to understand and you do understand many things, and I get the impression that it makes you furious when you can't understand." She laughed and began to relax and loosen up a bit. I added, "I can't understand everything either—there are things that grownups find hard to understand too. Sometimes it does take all of us time to understand things, but it is good to keep on trying." Here, Robin became considerably more relaxed, and I added, "Perhaps some of the difficulties you have in learning make you awfully angry at times," and she agreed.

Anxiety, Withdrawal, and Recovery

This led to a discussion of some of her learning problems, for instance, in arithmetic. She said she knew most of the "fives" now, but in showing me what she knew, she stalled on 10 times 5. When I showed with fingers that multiplying is just like adding up one 5 and another 5 and another 5, she agreed that she knew that. Then she painstakingly counted by 5s up to 45 and stopped before 50, and I wondered why it was hard for her to make that step.

She seemed to withdraw a bit at that, and yawned. I asked her if she was sleepy and what time she went to bed. She said eleven o'clock. I recollected aloud that this was the evening when her father was late for supper and everything was late at home.

✝   This example of a shift away from a topic we were discussing implied some anxiety about not being able to take the next step.

We talked a little more about how things were shaping up at home. I explored whether she had ways to help her mother or any regular responsibilities. She said that she did what she was asked to do when she was asked to do it. I mentioned that she had said earlier that she would like so much to help, and I wondered whether she still had the feeling that she would like to help some younger child. Again, her face became absolutely radiant, her grumpy, sleepy mood vanished completely, and her eyes lighted up with eagerness. I said that I would need to talk to Dr. Osborn, the resident doctor (who worked with the children on plans)—it would take time to work out—she was pretty young, but she would be thirteen soon.

✝   Obviously the eager arousal at the mere suggestion of helping reflects her drive to be active, a giver, not just a recipient, of help. She wanted to use her initiative. Next she illustrated another way of doing so.

Robin said that she wanted to have a birthday party at the hospital. She would not be here for Halloween, but she would like to have a party where the children could wear the costumes from their Halloween party. She would have four groups, and she mapped out in detail her idea of how to run the party, with prizes for the best costume in each of the four groups, then reducing to two groups, then to one. I agreed that it was important to begin to make the plans. She said she would talk to Dr. Osborn, but she did not get to see her very often or have much time to talk to her when she did. I commented that this seemed like a double remark, a little bit pessimistic and a little bit optimistic, and she agreed. I asked, "Why don't you give her a chance?" Robin grumbled, "I don't get a chance to give her a chance." But she said she would try when I urged her to go ahead. As she talked a little more about the party, I referred at one point to "the kids." Robin laughed and said, "They are not billy goats," then laughingly apologized for correcting me and explained that somebody else at the hospital referred to the children as "kids," and she corrected her. I commented, "You don't like to hear children called 'kids,'" and she agreed. The tone of all this was gay and happy in planning ahead toward her party.

I reflected aloud, "You know, it seems quite interesting to me that you are so happy planning about your birthday party, and you were so grumpy the first part of the hour. Maybe you really feel two ways about your birthday—partly, it is going to be good to get to be thirteen, and partly you are not so sure." She agreed, adding, "Well, a good thing about it will be that when I am thirteen, maybe Eve will treat me better." I commented, "You'll both be teen-agers then," and Robin assented comfortably.

✝ I was impressed by her imaginative plans for the birthday party and by her wish to have it at the hospital which implied a feeling of greater security here than at home in the new neighborhood. And I was also delighted by her freedom to criticize my referring to children as "kids."

The ambivalence about getting to be thirteen which was apparent in her contrasting moods in the therapy hour did not interfere with making the most of her birthday.

Spontaneity: The Puppy Episode

Robin had asked whether she could show me her puppies here in my office. I had agreed because I felt that it would give me an opportunity to observe her functioning in a pleasurable situation, which would supplement the evidence of tendencies to disorganize under stress. Her mother rushed in with the puppies about half-way through the hour—evidently by arrangement with Robin who had said that her mother would come and leave the puppies while she went on an errand. Her mother hastily dumped the puppies and said we had better put some newspapers on the floor because she had just taken them to the vet. I had the impression of an attractive, upper middle-class, suburban matron, slender and petite, well-groomed and tastefully dressed. She said that Jim didn't like the puppies but Robin did. I commented that it was hard to please everybody in a large family, but she quickly withdrew.

With the puppies, Robin was extremely relaxed and playful, explaining things to me, commenting about what they liked and what they did not like, and so forth. The puppies were very lively and played by batting at each other; Robin said they did that a lot but never hurt each other. They also nibbled on the toes of my shoes and snuggled into my lap, licking my hand. Robin laughed heartily when they started licking my neck and face, and I objected, pulling them down, telling them they could lick my hands but not my face.

✝   In this situation, Robin was utterly spontaneous and functioned like a normal, well-integrated girl who knew what to expect of the puppies, felt in command of the situation, wanted to clarify for me what they could and could not be expected to do, and was amused at my protests when they went too far. I felt that it had been useful to have them here, for the glimpse I had of Robin in her happiest, most relaxed and spontaneous mood was an even greater contrast with the negative evaluation picture than I had seen so far. It became clear that Robin's difficulties were greatly exacerbated by stress and that this involved not just cortical but autonomic nervous system damage.

It was also important to me to see firsthand the marked contrast between her mother's dainty build and Robin's larger-boned body structure. Quite apart from her neurological damage, I think Robin was physically the kind of child her mother would have difficulty feeling close to—I have known other combinations like this in which a dainty mother found it difficult to relate to a large daughter. But in view of all the things the mother tried to do for Robin, I got the impression that she was trying hard.

"Getting to Be a Teen-ager": Experiments, Dangers, and Doubts

Robin came in this day in a slightly slower tempo than usual, but her cheeks were rosy, from running, she said. She was wearing a becoming pale green blouse with a green and soft red plaid skirt to harmonize, and a green velvet ribbon in her hair, which was done up in a knot on the back of her head. She had a well put-together thirteen-year-old look that seemed natural and charming—neither as harum-scarum as she occasionally looked, with her hair flying and wearing blue jeans with some blouse that didn't go with them, nor as pretentiously, even if experimentally, young-ladyish as she sometimes looked when she was wearing something very grown-up. She said that the blouse and skirt belonged to Eve, and this led to discussion of how she could wear all her teen-age sister's clothes and how they shared things. I commented that she and Eve seemed to be getting along better, and she agreed. I added that sometimes older sisters were critical, and Robin also agreed that Eve was, "sometimes." She criticized the lipstick that Robin had just started wearing—so light that it was hard to tell that she had any on. She said Eve lectured her about not using anything but lipstick—no eye shadow and so forth—"but I wouldn't use that anyway."

I asked whether the dogs had gotten home all right, intending to give her an opening to talk a little bit more about Tuesday afternoon. However, she talked about what was going on with the puppies at home—Charlie had gotten hold of a plastic bottle of alcohol and had dragged it around the house; she got into lots of mischief. Then Robin said she liked horses because she could trust them. "A horse won't go over a bridge if it's dangerous." She gave examples of dangerous things that cars did that horses didn't do, and how nervous she felt when she was in a car and the driver did something dangerous. With a horse, when she rode bareback she could hold it around the neck and hold onto its mane. She hated saddles and talked about how risky she felt they were because they could slip under the horse, and if you went down with the saddle, you could get stepped on. She added that she also felt nervous when trotting or galloping with a horse, but not when walking. It turned out then that she hoped she would get a horse for her birthday. She reviewed horses they had in the country and hoped a couple of them could be brought to Topeka so that she would be able to ride after school.

✝ The recurrent references to dangers implied an undercurrent of anxiety that flowed into any channel available—not an unusual pattern for damaged children who cannot count on control and a capacity to integrate ways of coping with unexpected situations.

After she had finished describing her feelings about horses and hopes for a horse, she looked at me in a challenging way, cocking her head with what seemed a slight defiance. I said, "I wonder how you're feeling; it seems to me that you look as if you expected me to disapprove." Robin agreed instantly and said, "Yes, because a lot of people disapprove of my talking about horses so much." I added, "So you think that I might feel it was wrong to talk about horses or to like them. But I don't feel that way. My family had pets and we had fun with them."

Robin nodded, and I went on, "But it seems to me today that you feel a little restless or uncomfortable." She agreed and said that she had an earache. I explored this and, before long, it turned out that she was also menstruating and that when she menstruated she also got constipated and felt that nothing much helped it. Her periods had come at different times since she started in July; I noted that it was usual for periods to be irregular at the beginning of menstruation. Robin said that she knew that.

She then told me that her school class had seen a movie called "How Wonderful It Is to Be a Woman." She made a face, and I commented that she looked as if she didn't feel that it was wonderful to be a woman. She laughed appreciatively and said, "Well, not right now." I added, "In other words, it can be wonderful to be a woman, but menstruating is a nuisance." She laughed again appreciatively and agreed. Then I said, "Well, what are the things that are wonderful about getting to be a woman?" Robin said emphatically, "Well, you get more privileges, that's for sure." I asked, "What privileges?" and she said, "Well, when you are sixteen you can drive, and when I'm fifteen maybe I can begin dating." I commented that that was quite a while to wait; what did she think would happen when she got to be thirteen, and she repeated that she hoped to get the horse for her birthday and to be able to ride more.

Robin still seemed restless, and I asked why. She said she felt comfortable with some people over at the residence but not with everybody. She felt comfortable with Amy, but not with some of the other child-care workers, nor with Dr. Porter. When I asked why again, she explained that she felt comfortable with people who were gentle but not with people who said, "Don't do this and don't do that." She liked people to be "firm but kind." She was very sensitive to anything that sounded harsh, cold, or autocratic.

✛ Along with her undercurrent of anxiety, her sense of inadequacy tended to make "cold" responses sound critical or rejecting. Unlike many normal children who "close their ears" to harsh comments from cross adults in authority, she was unable to cope with them.

When I asked what people she could remember from earlier in her life who sounded that way, she couldn't remember anyone; and I commented that when we get awfully upset about people who seem authoritarian, it is usually because of earlier experiences. Robin said she knew that, and she reviewed various teachers she had had at school without giving any very definite impressions of them, and then said, "I try to forget it—I can't remember it." I said, "You can't remember the 'what' part of it, but you can't forget the feelings." Robin agreed.

Difficulty in Making Friends

Then she seemed a little sad, and I commented on this. She said, "Well, I have a hard time making friends. I did have a friend in Grand Island, Libby, but I'm not really sure whether I had her." I commented that just recently she had been telling me about friends who were coming to visit and had seemed quite happy about them. She agreed, and I asked, "But still you have doubts too?" and she nodded. She then reviewed the things she had in common with a new friend, Jean—they liked Barbie dolls, they liked to play dress-ups with their hair, and so forth. I said that she felt there were things that she and Jean would probably enjoy doing together, but she still wasn't sure, and Robin agreed. I suggested that perhaps she could plan some things to do that would be fun, and she disagreed, saying they did not do things by plan, they just played.

At one point in the discussion about friends, I said, "We can think about it and try to figure out what are the things that make difficulties with friends. Sometimes you use very big words with me, and if you do that with girls, it might make them feel that you are ahead of them; and when a person is ahead in some ways and behind in other ways it makes the friendship hard." Robin said, "I just don't fit." She talked more about her hopes and doubts in relation to the coming visit with Jean.

I added, "Sometimes angry feelings can interfere with friendships." She said that over at the residence she sometimes kicked a footstool, but she did not hit people. When I asked what made her so angry, she referred to the people she did not get along with very well, whose tone of voice was upsetting to her. I said, "Well, sometimes friendships need to be helped along, like growing plants—they need to be watered and to have some fertilizer."

Shifting the Topic as an Effect of Organic Looseness

Robin did not disagree, but in a moment she began to talk about some bulbs that Amy was helping her with. She had a name for each bulb and each bulb would get a slightly different treatment. This was to be a science project, and she would watch them grow and then see which bulbs thrive on different kinds of treatment.

✛ My comparison of friends with growing plants that need to be helped along led to her associations to the project with bulbs which would receive different treatment—and she left behind the issue of difficulties with friends. This was a shift from an anxious to a comfortable area. Shifts were both directly and indirectly related to her brain damage. I did not yet feel certain about such patterns in the sequences of her thoughts when she free-associates abruptly to an example or metaphor in a way that departs from the main issue. Sometimes this shift is the result of resistance, sometimes it is a direct effect of brain damage, which prevents integration and close thinking because of organically determined discontinuities in her associations. Robin's mood through the latter half of the hour was serious, earnest, confiding, and a little sad as she reflected on dangers and doubts.

Experiments with Teen-age Ways

In early November, Robin increased her experiments with hairdos and clothes and often discussed what getting to be thirteen would mean, both the losses and gains. She said she would, in a few years, reach driving age. Teen-age girls date boys and wear lipstick. But her mother, she said, forbade lipstick until later, and no dating would be allowed until she was fifteen.

✛ She was glad and seemed even proud of these limits, which turned out to be largely her own invention.

She complained that her parents probably would not get her the horse she wanted for her birthday but only clothes. But on the whole, she continued to accent the positive, talking more about her "hobbies"—that is, her dolls, her interest in horses, and her way of riding them without a saddle, holding the horse around the neck. Dogs and cats were important to her too. She described times that were fun and her enjoyment of outdoor activities.

Robin also talked about hurts and angry feelings, being ridiculed by other children and left out; she could accept comments about her ways of avoiding hurts, ways of dealing with anger, possible factors interfering with friendships and with work in school. And she also expressed her frustration with the Topeka house, less ample than the big house in Grand Island.

Other problems recurred, evidently related to her brain damage: her difficulty with changes in schedule, with undependability of meals, with shifts of plans. She needed to be able to count on people and plans as part of her need for structure. It was hard to get along with several people at one time, either at home or in the hospital; this was a result of organic difficulties in integration. I accepted these as real problems which we would need to find ways of managing.

Robin's Changing Relationship with Her Parents

Robin's accounts of feelings and experiences at home and in the hospital were helpfully supplemented by reports from the social worker who was having conferences with Robin's parents twice a week, and by the chief child-care worker who was helping Robin. Robin's mother was trying hard to help Robin—going on outings and shopping together, buying Robin some teen-age clothes. She taught Robin how to iron and also tried a little dancing with her; Robin seemed too awkward and embarrassed to get very far with it. The social worker tried to help Robin's mother evaluate the many demands Robin was now making and realize that these demands contrasted positively with her previous hangdog expression and retreat. Many misunderstandings resulted from Robin's difficulties in differentiating her mother's anger toward the other children in the family from feelings directed toward Robin, and her mother worked at clarifying these and other confusions.

At this time the treatment team had felt that it was not sound for Robin's father, a small-town doctor, to administer allergy shots or to provide other medical care; this would be done by the resident doctor. And the social worker discussed with Robin's father Robin's need for other father-daughter activities. His wish to be more active as a father was reflected in his gratification that Robin had discussed with him her wish to learn to play the piano. He and his wife were trying to work out weekend plans with other families with daughters Robin might enjoy. Attending a movie and a concert and shopping together had worked out well.

Still, he reported, she tended to sit around with the adults and especially to pop in on her parents' conversations with such remarks as "Am I interrupting anything?" And, at night when she was reminded to go to bed, she became quite angry and accused her parents of not wanting her around. Evidently, the feeling of having been left out went so deep that even though both parents were now spending time with her, she continued to project feelings of being rejected onto her parents. In another incident, she burst into tears and said in a very accusing way, "I can never talk to you," crying on her father's shoulder.

✝ It is not uncommon for a teen-ager to feel he cannot talk to his father, or to say his father "doesn't listen," or he "disapproves of everything I say." What was unusual was Robin's ability to try to reach her father—some teen-agers run away from home unable to cope with the feeling of a father's lack of understanding. And it was natural that Robin's deep feelings of past deprivation could change only slowly.

The Birthday Party at the Hospital

The group worker was glad to accept Robin's plan for the birthday party. Robin was disappointed that the staff psychiatrists could not come and pleased that I could. Evidently, attention of parent figures was needed to reassure her that she was cared for. In addition to her earlier plans for the party, Robin obtained her mother's help in preparation of a "Hobo newspaper" and gave me suggestions as to what to wear and bring.

However, at the party she sat on the sidelines insecurely directing me to take her place with the children. She was overwhelmed with embarrassment at her difficulty in cutting the birthday cake because of the tremor in her right hand, and could not participate in games. But she was very satisfied with my performance as her substitute and with the fact that I was given a prize for my knapsack (part of my costume requested by her).

✝ She needed to live through me—at this time my presence was more than evidence of my caring and support; I was an extension of herself when she could not fully participate.

In the next therapy hour Robin also described times that were fun and her need for more out-of-doors activity. Despite the fact that she could talk about ways of dealing with "wild feelings," she became extremely anxious whenever inner thoughts or fantasies seemed in danger of being exposed, or when they threatened to evoke overwhelming emotion she could not modulate.

✝ Her compulsive control seemed to me to be part of her positive efforts to handle impulses and achieve well, along with actively trying to get what she wanted without being crudely aggressive about it.

Therapy up to now had focused on clarifying and differentiating bad feelings from what brought good feelings; what successes she was having; and what solutions were available for the difficulties she faced.

The "Checkerboard"

In my work with Robin, I continued to clarify for myself the ways in which her functioning was influenced by her brain damage: anxious reactions to organically based problems of orientation, shifting, integrating responses to new situations, and her ways of trying to control or deal with both the difficulties and her anxiety. I continued giving attention to her interests and capacities, trying to help her obtain opportunities to use these in her experiences in the school and the residence and also outside the Children's Hospital.

In addition, I tried to begin to help her to accept her limitations as part of a total picture that included many positive potentialities as well—that is, to balance the pessimistic, discouraged feelings and the defeated self-image she reflected in the diagnostic period. "We all have a *checkerboard* of strengths and weaknesses—I have arthritis, which limits what I can do, and I'm not always well organized," I said. "You have a checkerboard of strengths and weaknesses, too, and so do most people." She seemed thoughtfully accepting of this idea.

I also tried to help her clarify her feelings about experiences with different people in order to facilitate acceptance of further help on dealing with negative feelings which obstructed her progress—Robin's blaming her parents and child-care workers was making it hard for them to respond to her, as they reported to me.

Changes in Robin: Expressiveness and Speech

Robin's expressive level had changed dramatically over the first three months of therapy. From uncontrollable, tense tremors and chorea-like movements sometimes of her face as a whole and at other times around her mouth, when I first saw her, her face became unusually expressive in fresh, differentiated, and appropriate ways. She was able to convey nuances of feeling through her facial expressions to such a degree that at times she did not bother with words at all but merely agreed when I verbalized her communications. She always enjoyed my response to this process.

✝   Evidently, the feeling of being understood was precious and gave her deep gratification.

Her speech had decreased in variability, never being as extremely rapid and unintelligible as it often was at first. In general, I attempted to avoid evoking anxiety since she was so quickly disorganized—especially by any reference to possible steps toward dealing with the anxiety itself. The speed of disorganization by anxiety implied that cortical damage interacted with hypothalamus damage.

✝   It still seemed necessary to clarify what she *could do* before dealing with all of her feelings about herself and her limitations as distinct from her feelings about interactions with others and events in the external world. Building confidence might help to reduce the constant vulnerability to anxiety, whereas stimulating anxiety could reinforce it.

She was able to acknowledge frustration, disappointment, and sadness at events that did not work out as she had hoped, and at losses which she deeply mourned, especially the death of her grandmother, and also the departure of workers in the Children's Hospital whom she had liked. She was able to express embarrassment, shame, and feelings of self-consciousness in social situations and got some relief from ventilating these feelings and absorbing my steps toward putting them in a wider context: "Lots of girls and boys feel self-conscious at this stage when one's body is changing and so many readjustments have to be made."

Persistent Organic Problems and Ways of Learning

Robin continued to have acute problems in adjusting to change, shifts in schedules, new situations, or sudden demands, and in responding to a group—problems reflecting her organic difficulties in orientation and integration. She wanted to know what she could count on. She wanted to be informed of everything that was coming far enough in advance so that she could get adjusted to it and plan her own actions.

She was often disorganized by a new stimulus. She was not able to carry on a smooth conversation involving exchanges with others. The child-care workers reported that she tended to shut off or shift the conversation instead of sustaining an exchange. This was a more extreme pattern that was similar to her shifting to non sequiturs, which I had seen. This also seemed to be related to her difficulty in speed of assimilation of a new stimulus, a new idea. The longer sequences of her talk in therapy usually had the quality of something she had thought out ahead. Sometimes she fell silent, and when this occurred she always responded positively to questions or remarks when I broke the silence, as if she needed this help.

Robin craved intake and liked to listen to adults, as when she hung around and listened to her parents talking at the dinner table. She said, "I learn by eavesdropping," and she considered it a major way in which she had picked up vocabulary, information, and ideas.

In connection with her need for intake, as reported by child-care workers, she complained about the emptiness of her second hour in the morning. I worked with the school to add a project that she suggested and wanted intensely—an experiment with mice, which involved her making a cage for several mice, preparing the needed equipment, obtaining their food, and keeping a log of what happened to them under a plan that gave better nutrition to some than others.

She was also very urgent in her wish to participate with the teen-agers in watching movies, such as the twenty-minute Dickens movie which she, as a member of the elementary school group, was not permitted to attend. The problem of getting enough stimulation required very special management with her since she was afraid to go around the hospital environment alone or go anywhere alone in Topeka. In comparison with the life of a typical thirteen-year-old who has one or more weekly events with peers—including going to the movies, going to school games, and so forth over the weekend—her weekend life was often empty.

She wanted to be out-of-doors and to explore, but here she was timid about going out. All this probably intensified her wish to go hunting with her father and brother; this became an issue because her parents did not consider this an appropriate interest for a girl and perhaps because they were afraid of her handling a gun. Robin herself, who liked to dress in a feminine way and had none of the masculine mannerisms of some of the other girls in the Children's Hospital who had not achieved a feminine identity, thought of womanhood in strong terms: "strong women helped to create this country." She resisted any approach to interpretations of sources within herself for her frustrations aside from recognition of her many periodic and chronic physical difficulties such as allergies, recurrent kidney infection, menstrual discomfort, and so forth.

✚   In some ways, Robin's egocentricity was similar to that of other girls at the puberty stage, when many children feel that no one understands them and that grownups obstruct them. Because of her special difficulties in sequential interaction in conversation and cooperative activities, it was important to help her understand that others also have the need for time, need for being told what to expect, need for opportunity to make plans, and that it was important to learn how to work together with others and to help others to help her.

Robin's strength was apparent in her persistent demands for activities which would meet her need for opportunities to carry on her interests in animals, in nature, in crafts, in cooking, and in other productive spheres. While she got angry when she was frustrated and when she felt people were not helping her to reach her goals, her aggression tended to come out more frequently in retaliatory teasing or frustrating others.

Progress in Social Activity, at School and at Home

Robin's great determination and courage were particularly conspicuous in connection with the Christmas social events. While she was intensely worried about the self-consciousness that she would feel at her first evening party, in her first "heels," she was determined to go. She handled the situation quite well despite some "nervousness." She talked to the workers and was apparently not disturbed by the fact that she was the only girl who was not asked to dance by one of her peers.

✛   I had the impression that the achievement of going to the party was in itself satisfying. This was a step ahead from the birthday party, when she needed me to act for her.

She also showed great poise in a controlled and careful style of handling herself at the open house which she had urged me to attend and where she first served refreshments and then escorted me around.

At the Christmas sale, Dr. Porter reported that Robin took the initiative in persuading her to buy something made by one of the boys' groups. When I arrived, Robin was at first shy and detached, then a little later she pulled herself together to approach me and inform me where the things she and her group had made were located. These episodes illustrate the efforts that Robin was making, the pace at which she could respond, and her deep commitment to being a participant.

When things did not go right, however, she was apt to be overwhelmed again as she was at her birthday party. At the children's Christmas party for exchange of gifts, the boy who was to give Robin her gift made the mistake of opening it himself, which brought her to the point of tears. In all these situations, which Robin put herself through with such vigorous effort, her need for adult support was repeatedly in evidence.

She was able to use her therapy hour to deal with her anticipatory anxiety about another evening party. Her deep desire to feel part of a group was also reflected in her devoted work on gifts for her family and many relatives. Many of these she brought to show me and to explain how they were made. She also attempted to use gifts as a way to make contact with other children in the residence, and child-care workers helped her to shift from this to working *with* the group rather than just doing things *for* the group.

Her preoccupations seemed to be influenced greatly by current events in the hospital; while before her birthday she was extremely preoccupied with rehearsal of thirteen-year-old behavior, hairdos, and patterns of dress, this had now almost disappeared. The residues of this were seen chiefly around such new experiences as shoes with "heels" for parties.

My informal discussions with child-care workers and teachers individually included consideration of her continued difficulties in cooperation and interaction. But her reading teacher reported excellent memory for auditory material. Her art teacher commented on her tendency to break up the page into small units, which I suggested was an expression of her need to master small sections at a time.

✞ While I gradually clarified for myself some of her difficulties in functioning related to her brain damage and exacerbated by her anxieties, and tried to support her coping efforts, Robin used therapy to validate her capacity for integrated functioning under "comfortable" conditions; to be at ease in a quiet situation where there was a one-to-one contact with less confusion; to get help on problems of mastery in social situations and on meeting her needs for input and for gratifying activities.

Her active zeal for mastery of craft skills, social events, and acquisition of knowledge through various channels; her need and desire for gratification and fun through activities with animals; her efforts to achieve emotional control, to deal with anger, and to begin to face anxiety, along with her attempts to be attractive, appropriate, and correct in her social behavior and also to be a helping person were consistent and conspicuous. She recognized and tried to deal with many problems, for example, handling her problem of allergy to the Christmas tree at the Children's Hospital by trying to stay away from it as much as she could.

I gradually tried to help Robin recognize the interrelation of her different areas of vulnerability—her "sensitivity," as she referred to it, and the connection of this with her anxiety; the interaction of these vulnerabilities with difficulties quite typical for her developmental level; and the interaction of all these with problems arising from real difficulties at times of stress in the family and residues of earlier angry feelings and resentments at feeling rejected.

I also tried to help her teachers see how these interacting factors interfered at times with her work in school. I emphasized how much the sense of mastery, through school progress, contributed to her confidence and helped to develop increased ego strength for coping with her social and family problems.

In other words, *therapy went hand in hand with educational efforts in a two-way process:* therapy hours revealed aspects of Robin's functioning, sources of her problems, and unexpected potential which could enrich and strengthen the educational process. Similarly, detailed reports from and discussions with teachers contributed to my work in helping Robin to develop a positive view of herself and, at a deeper level, to develop greater ego strength—to cope with her realistic organic difficulties and with the complex feelings related to these.

In addition, when she brought me a spelling paper that contained many errors, I asked her to spell the words orally then and there. She succeeded so much better that I suggested to her teacher that she be given oral tests in order to get a fairer picture of what she knew; her teacher was glad to do this. Robin said, "I know how to spell the words but my [trembling] hand mixes up the letters."

I had also talked over with her teachers our need to build on her strongest motivations. Since Robin had expressed a wish to do an experiment in breeding and nutrition of mice, this was arranged with her. Robin's idea was to compare the offspring of the mice that had had superior nourishment with the somewhat undernourished ones. She kept careful notes of her work with the mice, and the experiment seemed to provide her a sense of satisfaction. The project, however, became a nuisance to both the teacher and the workers, who had to care for the mice on Robin's weekend absences, especially when the workers involved had deep prejudices against mice.

✝ These assignments did reinforce Robin's commitment to learning and to school—and in our many discussions through the next months she almost never complained about the school, in contrast to her many protests about experiences in the residence where life for her was more complex, undependable, and frustrating, despite the real devotion of child-care workers.

Continued Mourning of Losses and Longing for Love

Robin continued to be nostalgic for Grand Island, and her mourning for her grandmother, along with separation stress in regard to the workers, seemed to be associated with a deep existential feeling of the unavoidable disappointments of life. She still had severe problems in achieving independence and entering the unknown; for instance, she refused to try a new group like the Topeka Rainbow group while she had belonged to a Rainbow group in Grand Island; and she still longed to feel accepted and loved and understood.

✟   I felt that Robin would not be able to believe in or to accept the love of others until she accepted and liked herself despite the deeply frustrating actual limitations that made it so hard for her to feel that she was part of her achieving family. Her defenses were helpful to her in progress toward the control and poise she desired and in mastery of certain skills. She needed to use delay and to reduce or break up her goals, and she showed some capacity to be gratified with less success than was achieved by some others. Her uses of repression, projection, and denial, however, at times blocked her capacity to respond and to make optimal use of the help offered her. I expected that therapeutic work dealing with these and with the anxiety which she tried to handle through these defenses would probably be much slower than the work during the first three months, which had been directed toward the transition to teen-age status and optimal use of the opportunities in the hospital and at home.

While Robin and I and her teachers were working on developing her positive resources, the social worker and her parents were also trying to understand Robin's difficulties at home. Her father felt that she often blamed him inappropriately—for instance, when he suggested a special channel while she was looking for a certain program she wanted on television, she protested that he did not want her to watch the program of her choice. Her expectation of being rebuffed or reproached or criticized was so deeply rooted that she sometimes interpreted even helpful efforts in a negative way. She continued to talk at home about how her parents did not love her; she even tried to achieve a feeling of closeness with her mother by crying about a lie, and then saying how glad she was that she could talk with her mother.

✟   This persistent longing for closeness and love from her parents was, of course, very different from the rebelliousness of many thirteen-year-olds who are trying to detach themselves and to achieve autonomy from parental authority. I have seen very normal pubertal girls (who grew up to be very effective cooperative adults) stamp their feet in protest at parental direction. Robin's deep need was for an intimacy, closeness, and love she felt she had not had. It looked as if the sense of being understood and accepted by me evoked a longing for and belief in the possibility of comparable closeness and understanding from her parents.

Meanwhile, Robin's mother was feeling warmer toward Robin, began to enjoy doing things with her, and was interested in Robin's activities in the hospital; and her father also felt that despite the many problems, the family was finding greater closeness. We felt this was essential to Robin's further progress and eventual independence.

3

Increasing Our Understanding of Robin

My frequent contacts with the Children's Hospital professional staff helped me to see Robin's actual difficulties in dealing with new situations and with people, as well as with her learning problems. These contacts included notes from the chief child-care worker, the psychiatrist, and the social worker, conferences with each of them, and occasional phone calls. They welcomed my visits to the residence and the school, where I could get acquainted with the people and the settings in which Robin's current experiences were providing both new problems and growth.

The Teachers' Strategies

My contact with Robin's teachers illustrates one area of integration in Robin's treatment: in my observation of the teachers' methods of working with Robin and in my discussions with them, I saw the ingenious, flexible ways they met her needs—by arranging "a peace-and-quiet spot" free from distraction, in a supply room or even a lavatory; by letting Robin work at her own pace and with materials of her own choice; by helping her to break up a task into manageable units. The flexibility of her teachers in structuring small group and quiet spots to work meant that Robin was presented with challenges she could meet. School quickly became, and remained for the next several years, an area that provided not only avenues for release of energy but also zones of steady, visible, and rewarding progress. Robin regularly shared the tasks, materials, and progress of her schoolwork with me, along with certain practical problems she encountered, and also her need to have explicit recognition of what she had accomplished. I felt that my support of her progress in mastery was important as a foundation for later therapeutic work. While, ultimately, Robin would need to get a clear picture of her organic limitations, I considered it important to build her areas of mastery first, so that she could fully accept her checkerboard of strengths and weaknesses.

Monthly Team Meetings

In addition to the spontaneous exchanges that helped to integrate our collaborative efforts to help Robin, there were monthly team meetings in which I participated with the entire group in discussing problems that puzzled us. Problems of attitude, social interaction, areas of acceptance and of refusal occupied early team discussions. Robin's concern about how she would be regarded, as well as her longing for closeness, probably underlay certain kinds of behavior distasteful to the child-care workers: for example, a tendency to stay very close to people and peer into their faces. And her uncertainty about areas of competence probably underlay some of her demands which were resented by the child-care workers. However, all such behavior was outgoing, and whatever pressure it seemed to exert on people working with her, I felt that it expressed her active efforts to cope with her uncertainties. We could also see how positive was her focus on nonthreatening experiences and activities—dogs and horses would not ridicule her, neither would dolls. These activities provided zones of response where she could actively invest in the world outside herself without danger of being rejected. In addition, the kinds of handling involved did not require high levels of coordination impossible for her.

Child-care workers also reported that Robin was self-protectively distant and hesitant about participating in the residential group meeting—she sat on the edge and contributed little. She "needed to be drawn out, to be asked." Although she had seemed interested when "grounds privileges" were first mentioned, she did not seem to know what to do with them; it was puzzling to everyone why a girl who had enjoyed the outdoors so much before was apparently not interested in exploring. Nor did she care to go out for a walk with the other girls or meet boys on the grounds. Evidently the strange area and strange children evoked her anxiety about newness.

There was mutual distance in the relation between Robin and the girl nearest her age, Alice, perhaps resulting from the difficulties created by their respective awkwardnesses—Robin's rigidity, which is typical of some brain-damaged children, Alice's approach as a schizophrenic girl. Robin's situation in the group was different from that of the others; she was the only day patient and in this sense "odd man out." Her position might have been easier if there had been other day patients.

I commented that Robin did not reflect a sense of inner isolation in therapy hours—on the contrary, her big extended family, which included fond aunts and uncles and also congenial cousins, constituted a warm and comfortable inner world. This inner population made the immediate external relationships somewhat less important to her—and also made her more demanding. It was as if she felt, "If the people around are not as responsive, fun, and comfortable to be with as my relatives are, why should I bother to pay attention to them?" She was, as she herself acknowledged at times, "spoiled" in the sense that she was used to her relatives' acceptance of her and lacked the drive to explore different relationships which is so vigorous in many young teen-agers who are eagerly building their own world. Beyond or beneath these feelings, there was the apparent paradox that while she had many complaints about her immediate family she felt comfortable with them in contrast to her insecurity with new people.

The child-care workers reported that Robin's irritability was reflected in her intolerance for their delays, interruptions, or other incidents that might imply lack of sustained attention. Her intolerance of adults' delays might be another expression of the difficulty in maintaining continuity shown in her shifts in conversation. The professional staff recognized that with her parents' preoccupation with problems of her siblings, she might not be getting much support at home and was sensitive to being pushed aside or overlooked. It was evidently hard for her to accept the fact that with other children to care for there would inevitably be interruptions and delays. This kind of irritation was minimal, of course, with me—here the one-to-one relationship sustained during the therapy hour seemed to be deeply satisfying, and partially balanced the threats she experienced from competition with other children at home, in the residence, and at school, and the interruptions in attention to her which she experienced in groups.

In defense against her anxiety about most new and complex experiences, she mobilized plausible excuses—she could not go to "Fun Night" at the YWCA in town on Fridays because she was "too busy" Friday nights (sometimes going to Grand Island).

She persistently defended herself against the possibility of other people knowing that she went to the Menninger Foundation, a defense that included various cover-ups and dodges. It was as if she wanted just to go to school and go home the way other children did who went to the public school.

She was afraid that if teen-agers outside of the Menninger Foundation knew that she was going to school there she would be regarded as strange. Undoubtedly, this had some element of projection related to her own bewilderment about herself. She found it hard to develop relationships with girls who had serious emotional problems—and this may have been sound since she had so many reality problems of her own. She consciously identified with the strong members of her family and reinforced this with other people who seemed strong to her. (This identification with strength in her family was not challenged in therapy; it seemed to be a constructive defense that would support her efforts toward mastery and protect her from the danger of giving up and identifying with disturbed members of her family and of the school.)

This combination of reinforced anxiety, on the one hand, and defense through identification with strength, on the other hand, had double effects. Robin was able to talk about her anger at people both in the residence and at home; perhaps she intuitively felt that anger was on the side of strength. But she was also able to talk about disappointments, frustrations, and sadness at the loss of her grandmother, her Grand Island home and friends.

Robin's resistance to participation in physical education at the Children's Service and also to exploring activities at the YWCA such as swimming or horseback riding with saddles, to which she was not accustomed, can be understood in relation to her anxiety and the sources of it. In addition to organically rooted problems in coordination and balance, she was unusually susceptible to bruising, a tendency perhaps related to the labile quality of her tissues. These changed visibly in texture during her menstrual periods and also with intense affects and varying physical conditions such as colds and allergic reactions. She had actually had certain injuries in connection with a fall from a horse and also from a bicycle.

Such injuries are rather common among active, growing teen-agers, who often take them in stride without residual anxiety and continue precisely the same activities that led to the injuries. But with Robin, such injuries were complicated by her tendency toward bruising and, probably, by a deep inner sense of having been damaged—although she, of course, could not have consciously known the earliest sources of this at that time.

This anxiety about physical damage was probably also reinforced by her sensitivity to being hurt by the ridicule and rejection of her peers when she could not participate effectively in their games. While she returned rather matter-of-factly a number of times to the physical injuries, it was the hurt feelings that were poured out more often in therapy hours. But ventilation of these feelings was not enough to help her cope with them.

Her areas of outgoing responsiveness reflected strengths. And the fact that, despite her anxious refusals to explore activities which threatened her, she had the capacity to be enthusiastic about her animals testified to the vitality of her inner drives. Her teachers commented on the vigor of her determination to master her "weaknesses" and her consistent hard work at school.

Robin's pattern of strengths, demonstrated by a capacity for persistent effort and enthusiasm where she felt secure, combined with equally persistent avoidance of certain difficult areas presented a complex picture to those who worked with her—with the result that few were able to "see the whole elephant" at any one time. Some persons could see only her tendency to cope with problems by denial, evasion, projection of blame onto others, tense resistance, disdainful rejection of others, and stubborn resistance to help in areas that evoked maximal anxiety. When such devices and moods were uppermost, they prevented workers from seeing the discouragement, feelings of hopelessness, fears, and threats with which she was struggling. Even more, they prevented others from seeing the delight, warmth, humor, and charm that sparkled in situations where she felt secure.

The extreme differences in her functioning at different times, related to her interaction with different people and their different demands, created recurrent difficulties in mutual understanding among people working with Robin in different contexts where they saw different sides of her. It was hard for everybody, including me, to see the whole girl in those early months.

Team Members Share Understanding

The neuropsychologist had commented that when the mildly and moderately damaged areas were interacting in complex situations, the outcome showed the effects of several centers of brain damage. Our major task was to try to understand the varying impact of the neurological problems on Robin's daily functioning.

By the December team meeting, it was possible to differentiate between the respective levels of intake and output. Teachers summarized that Robin had "more difficulty in giving out than in taking in." She herself had commented, "I learn by listening, looking, and touching." "Giving out," either in speech, writing, or action was of course hampered by the neurological damage affecting visual-motor coordination and use of her trembling hand, while sensory intake was very little affected by her type of brain damage. Her need for intake was discussed in terms of her need for more experience, stimulation, outside supply, as well as her need for activities which would bring input. It was noted that she felt depressed when nothing was coming in. We agreed that good movies would contribute to this need.

In therapy, she had talked about her grandmother, her aunt, and her nanny who had given her much attention, along with satisfying activity outlets. It seemed clear that much of her activity was oriented toward bringing something in. Her art teacher told us that her perception of materials in art was sensitive, and she had a fine awareness of color. Her teacher in reading, writing, and arithmetic commented on her good memory for what she was told.

Robin's need for input was discussed with her social worker, especially in connection with Robin's inability to get around town on her own and the distance of her home from resources in town. She needed a once-a-week experience of a movie, trip to a museum, or other experience which a normal thirteen-year-old would be having. Since the family lived so far from the center of town, Robin's ability to reach such experiences was blocked, and she needed her family's help to get this enrichment.

The team also discussed the fact that she needed opportunities to do things that she could realistically accomplish, and that it was important to support her own initiative; for instance, her mouse project was discussed in terms of its value to her. It met several needs simultaneously: providing a learning opportunity that involved looking and touching; caring for the mice met a strong need for little things—babies—to take care of; and observing the process of reproduction met her adolescent need to clarify her understanding of sex, pregnancy, and birth, and the roles of male and female.

We recognized that she needed to take things in slow, separate steps; complexity was hard to grasp. She needed time to master each step of learning; while *insight* often came to her spontaneously, the basic tools of learning, arithmetic, and spelling came hard. Her piano teacher said that she worked on simple American Indian pieces involving minimal work of combining both hands; combining was hard for her. It was obviously necessary to discover her optimum level of learning in each zone, not demanding too much but also not leaving her deprived of stimulation and challenge.

It was also noted that she was floored or paralyzed by sudden demands, changes, and shifts. To such demands, she usually said no at first, but this seemed to be a device for giving herself time to absorb the demand and to organize her resources since she usually responded later.

Child-care workers told us that she participated when she could, as in carol singing; she was helpful at the table, spontaneously getting the flatware, for instance. But she was at the point of tears when a boy pressed her to join him in playing a guitar and singing. At moments like this, it seemed that Robin wanted to very much but was overwhelmed by her doubts about whether she could manage.

Through her active efforts, Robin was sending the message "I need to develop greater mastery," which she had in fact stated clearly in an early therapy hour when she said, "I want to conquer my weaknesses." She was not ready to deal with anxiety about conflicts, or with her resistances, but was preoccupied with questions of how to cope with everyday adaptational tasks. She wanted to be a doer.

Her teachers understood her need for time—time to get oriented, time to get started, time to finish a task. They understood her need to choose, that is, to select what she felt able to master. And they responded to her need for explicit ratings of what she had accomplished. Many of these needs were familiar to them from their work with other brain-damaged children and even with vulnerable children they had encountered in public schools before coming to the hospital school. Robin's initiative and independence, her awareness of how she could learn best were all considered good resources to be encouraged. In the residence, she was not exposed to autocratic pressures, but she was encouraged to cooperate on her terms.

My opinion was that we could not understand Robin's social behavior adequately without seeing it in the context of her total functioning—as a physical organism, a sensitive pubertal girl with multiple sources of vulnerability and strength who had arrived at a difficult developmental stage and who was a member of a highly stressed but valiant family, all of whom were struggling with cumulative personal pressures, conflicts, and worries which colored their daily lives. Beyond this, since there had been no adequate school setting in which Robin could get appropriate academic help and the Children's Hospital school was the only place where this could be provided, she was in a group of children more deeply disturbed or damaged ("schizophrenic," "borderline," "aphasic with partial deafness," and so forth) than she was. An acute problem existed about how Robin could be part of the group without identifying with their illnesses, at this adolescent stage when imitation of peers as part of identification is usual and, among normal children, adaptive. Gradually, she developed a few one-to-one relationships with girls who were somewhat congenial.

The child-care workers felt that Robin expected everyone to understand her completely. She felt that if they did not understand, it must be because they did not care enough about her to try. If a worker commented that she was angry, Robin evidently felt that this was a criticism and that they did not realize that objective frustrations made her angry. If they did not give her what she felt she needed, she seemed to assume that they were angry or did not care enough about her.

The social area was more complex and involved more reflection, more discussion of the nature of her coping problems, more reorientation—and, finally, more work in therapy toward developing a sense of choice as an alternative to all-or-nothing acceptance or refusal of unmanageable challenges. The child-care workers reported that Robin seemed to feel obligated to go to parties, even at the implicit risk of acute embarrassment and of the kind of disorganization she experienced when she was overwhelmed at her birthday party.

The group also shared their first glimpses of Robin's ego-ideal, conveyed through her comments about the strong pioneer women of this country, the women "who helped to create this country." It was felt by some that she was "anti-prissy" and would also reject any feminine image of the "doll" or "cute" type. But there must have been some conflict about "prissiness"—that is, concern with proper behavior and manners—since some girls and staff members felt that she was prissy in the sense of being overcontrolled and critical of any "show-off" behavior of other girls or sloppiness or anything at all off-color. She was so embarrassed or even shocked by one girl's self-display in a song and dance skit that it seemed to reflect considerable conflict about self-exhibiting. The other girls were turned off by her disapproval and felt her to be "uppity." In all this, we could see Robin's need for and use of structure, constriction, and distance in order to manage organic problems of control and integration.

Her major teacher observed that Robin's behavior was more integrated in a very small group—she tended to become disorganized, confused, or upset in a larger group. This was congruent with her effort to keep detached and stay on the sidelines at her birthday party. In line with this, her difficulty in combining and integrating was discussed and her resulting need to take one step at a time and to be allowed time to master a task at her own slow pace. Her art and music teachers, as well as her teacher of reading, spelling, and arithmetic worked with her in this way.

With Robin's difficulties blurred by such a complex group of vulnerabilities, we could see how difficult was the task of clarifying reasonable expectations for her at any given point. Her family had attempted to help her to "act her age." Much of the time, efforts in the residence proceeded on a "try this, and try that" basis, offering opportunities that served as diagnostic sieves to sort out what she could use and what she was not ready to use.

Robin's Basic Strengths

Along with the clarification of Robin's problems and needs, I saw strengths. Discovering the child was the first goal of my time with Robin after my review of the evaluation. I saw her subtle expressiveness, her differentiated perception, the boldness of ideas in her art work and writing, and so forth, which had begun to be apparent very early. It was these observations that led to my inference of innate creativity—related to the subtle perceptiveness, range of affect, and energy potential. These were important resources not glimpsed in the evaluation.

Evidence of drive was reflected in her determination to master "weaknesses," her wish for love, her active cooperation along with her active protest and, when she was doubtful about how much she could do, her assertion, "I can try." Spontaneity was seen in the initiative she took to bring her puppies into therapy, showing me how relaxed and natural she could be when she felt more secure than she was with peers or with adults. This led to the exploration of other areas of good functioning and of strong investment such as eagerness to communicate and to share; eagerness to absorb—as she did by eavesdropping as well as horning in on discussions among adults, as her parents reported.

An underlying hope and confidence was reflected in her shy nodding agreement to my comment, "Deep inside, you really know you can have a good life." This evidence of positive orientation included recurrent anger and protests at what she experienced as external interferences. The fact that she could protest implied that she felt she had rights.

Robin's Way of Using Therapy in the Early Months

After her tremulous beginning and efforts to convey positive aspects of herself, Robin used therapy hours to get acquainted, explore my areas of knowledge, correct my ignorance, and discover common zones of familiarity and points of view. She tested my attitudes, especially about whether I would disapprove or be critical of her interest in dolls, horses, dogs, or her "hobbies."

She repeatedly expressed her sadness at losses, in mood and feelings as well as verbally: the death of her grandmother, the loss of her friends and home in Grand Island when they moved, along with the activities, horses, and so forth, which were part of life there. Doubtless her sense of loss was also deepened by her unexpressed sense of loss of parts of herself, which she could not yet talk about.

She reflected her own *feelings*: as partly a tomboyish, outdoors-loving, horse/dog girl, with "hobbies" including dolls and crafts; a growing girl getting taller and bigger than her mother, stronger in some ways. She had started menstruation; she wondered what it would be like to be a teenager; she tried out new "hairdos" and new ways of dressing. She was also anxious about teen-age activities and impulses and welcomed restrictions and limits from her mother—such as not using lipstick, and delay in dating; I assumed that she felt these limits would protect her from what boys might do.

She was able to talk openly about her anger at her mother's difficulty in getting meals done on time, and her father's tendency to professionalize his relation with her, her disappointment due to her family's not giving her the birthday gifts she would like, and her mounting anger when frustrations accumulated.

She was also able to talk about what she wanted to do and be: to help others (and by implication, to be a worthwhile member of her professional family's clan); to accomplish things; and also by implication, to be attractive, to have friends, to understand others, to be an acceptable teenager, and to grow into a kind, gentle, and understanding adult.

She expressed aspirations and interest in caring for animals or helping children, and assumed that she would go to college—apparently unable to consider the possibility that her academic difficulties would prevent this. (I did not suggest this possibility to her.) Her good vocabulary and conscious use of it tended to support an impression of basic intelligence.

She was not able to talk about or to tolerate reference to deficits or damage except in terms of "things that are hard to do," like arithmetic, or general deficits in skill and control, her "weaknesses."

Her low frustration tolerance, low thresholds for anxiety and anger, and labile affective responses combined with her organically determined fluidity in thought and sudden shifts away from a touchy topic to apparently unrelated topics. This added to difficulties in relationships and to problems in learning directly rooted in her organic deficits. These included problems in abstraction, arithmetic, writing, spelling, adapting to transitions, change, and so forth, as outlined by the neuropsychologist in the evaluation. The anxieties of her parents, their difficulty in understanding her basic problems and needs, many of which were directly involved with her organic limitations, added to her difficulties in solving problems.

Robin's variability was extreme. At times when she was tense, she might talk so rapidly and with so much slurring that it was almost impossible to follow her, while at other times, she was wholly articulate or even eloquent and sophisticated in her conversation. At times she seemed closely responsive, related to me, and empathic, but at other times she seemed distant. She could be spontaneous and relaxed—as with her puppies—but when anxious or attempting any delicate task she had a noticeable tremor and her coordination deteriorated.

She could be angry, sad, gay, humorous, warm and tender, sharp in a sophisticated way, or dreamy and nostalgic. She had days of seeming moody, pessimistic, and not feeling good, and other periods of being positive, hopeful, and enthusiastic. Her variability did not seem to be within much control. It was rather an expression of the inner difficulties in integration and control related to her organic deficits.

She tried to cope with her problems by selective denial of their severity; by projection of some blame onto others; by tense, proud, or even disdainful efforts at control to achieve an acceptable result. She attempted to elicit help to get opportunities to do things that she could succeed in doing and could enjoy (which led to the reactions of adults that she was demanding and unadaptable). Her determination to make something positive out of life gave way at times to discouragement, feelings of hopelessness, and feeling that it was no use to attempt some suggestions for reasons generally projected onto others (sometimes realistically, since it was hard for others to see how intensely important to her were the things she could do).

Robin made her goal very clear: "I want to conquer my weaknesses." By implication, she was telling us that she saw herself as strong enough to accomplish just that with help. Her identification with strong people, especially the strong members of her extended family, became clear as she described her strong, firm aunt and uncle, and strong people in the Children's Hospital. These descriptions also carried the message that she wanted to be strong. But strength did not exclude sweetness; she described Dr. Moore as both sweet and strong.

Robin's goal of conquering her weaknesses told us that she would respond to help in coping and in developing mastery in school subjects and other tasks, and we would have to learn what other weaknesses she would try to conquer. At this point, we did not feel that it made sense to face her with her neurological limits. In fact, we could not really predict how far she could go in compensating for her disabilities. What did make sense was to support her effort, to reinforce her latent ego strength, to help her reap the rewards of effort and develop a sense of competence in as many areas as were realistically possible; and to help her with relationships with adults and children.

Keeping this goal in mind meant that while all of the team could support her through emotional crises as they might come along, I would not—in this stage at any rate—involve her in deep analysis of conflicts which she was not yet ready to deal with; this might conflict with the treatment oriented toward increasing her mastery and competence.

Questions might be raised about this approach. What about her explosive anger? Here, we felt that since almost everyone expressed anger openly in the setting in which she lived, it would be a waste of time to make this a major issue. Rather, we could deal with specific episodes as they came up, to help her get clearer about the various triggers for her anger. Moreover, insofar as cumulative frustration and physical discomfort lowered her thresholds for anger, progress in controlling these areas would come naturally as increasing mastery reduced the amount of frustration and as medical help reduced irritability. As her comfort and confidence increased, and as relationships improved, the time would come when we could help her face the realities of neurological damage, other organic problems, and analysis of her conflicts.

Up to this point we have described how Robin worked in treatment— guided by her own desire to share interests as well as problems. In this way I became her ally, not only in helping her to understand some of the problems and how she might deal with them better, but also by communicating her interests and needs to her teachers and, through the social worker, to her parents.

End of the First Three Months

Our developmental approach had raised a series of questions that were to be kept in mind when thinking about Robin's treatment:

Is she facing the same problems faced by other children at this stage?
Exactly how is Robin's neurological damage affecting her behavior?
To what extent is Robin's neurological functioning at this time made worse by developmental disequilibria?
To what extent do her feelings—anger, anxiety, excitement from any cause—exacerbate her neurological problems and also her developmental problems as she becomes a teen-ager?

To what extent is her emotional disturbance (sense of defect and defeat, and anger) a reaction to realistic frustrations, and to what extent have deeply rooted character problems become established, which would prevent progress in therapy?

Can Robin's anxiety be reduced by help toward greater understanding of the nature and causes of her problems and by help toward better coping methods?

To what extent would support of Robin's overall development and help with typical developmental problems reduce specific handicaps? That is, would specific symptoms be decreased by improved integration resulting from support for development?

What are reasonable goals for treatment? How do these goals differ from those for a child without Robin's neurological problems? What are the priorities, and what sequence in treatment can be foreseen?

What have we learned from the first three months of treatment?

Our gradual learning about Robin and understanding her did not follow the outline of our questions. These had grown out of the evaluation reports; these were so limited that we learned, in treatment, a great deal about Robin's potentialities that was not foreshadowed in the evaluation:

First, Robin was flexible and very responsive to support of a positive self-image, to recognition of and belief in her potential, to being enjoyed, to empathy with the stress of becoming a teen-ager, to cooperation with her educational interests and with her needs for medical and dental care. She responded positively to challenges that were related to her own goals and were perceived by her as within her capacity.

Second, she was not able to deal with anxieties or discussion of her organic difficulties and causes of them as yet.

Third, she could be extremely "stubborn," both in the effort to master difficult problems she was ready to attack and in resistance when she was not ready to deal with a problem. Her stubbornness was an expression of strength, actual and potential, and progress was made by respecting her own times of readiness and unreadiness.

Fourth, she was deeply committed to "conquering" her "weaknesses" and to becoming a useful person like others in her family. This was related to her stubbornness.

Moreover, she had been described as a "poor therapy risk," while by contrast, she was very eager for help. The extent of her insight and the situations in which she could function best had not been revealed in the evaluation. On the negative side, almost everything is harder for the brain-damaged child; difficulty was created by, for example, her variability in mental functioning and her autonomic nervous system instability, especially during menstruation, which undermined emotional control under stress.

In addition, the diagnostic study did not reveal the background of
many of her odd coping methods, which were developed in the context of
her relationships with elderly care-givers; her ideas of being polite and
well mannered did not fit the patterns of contemporary teen-agers. Nor
did the study reveal her hypersensitivity to malicious teasing and ridicule,
and the resulting disorganizing, overwhelming feelings of defeat, resentment, and anxiety.

Reformulating the Problem after the Early Explorations in Therapy

After a few months of therapy, we came to see Robin's problem in a
different way from the initial description of her in the diagnostic process.
The diagnosis had focused on the damage. We now saw this damage in
the context of the normal stress of transition from the twelve-year-old to
the thirteen-year-old developmental stage. Further, we saw the damage in
the context of multiple reality stress in the family, as well as in the context
of multiple physiological vulnerabilities which interacted with the major
problem. Thus, we now saw the problem as how to help Robin cope at
this stage with all these factors in a way that would help her to develop
into an attractive teen-age girl.

I had often been deeply moved and awed by a child's will to live, to
have a good life, and the delight in achievement of the smallest sort
which evidently gives the child confidence that progress can be made. I
had seen this indomitable spirit in blind, deaf, cerebral palsied, and orthopedically damaged children, and children with polio. Here again I saw it
in Robin, with her diffuse difficulties.

I saw her demands and her protests as well as her positive efforts, her
selectivity in regard to what she would and would not attempt, and even
her defenses as evidence of a strong drive to make a good life for herself.
We needed to understand her in the context of both developmental and
organic stress; it was not fair to judge her in terms of age norms that were
not relevant to the multitude of biological problems she faced. She would
need more time than other children.

The Adaptational Problem of a Brain-Damaged Child in a New Situation

Failure to appreciate the adaptational problem presented by strangeness and newness easily leads to misinterpretation of the child's behavior. In the case of many young children, limited experience means that a new person, in a new place with new materials and new demands—as in the testing situation—cannot be perceived and grasped quickly. It takes time to get familiarized, to feel safe, to feel free to respond.

In the case of brain-damaged children, the situation is still more complex. When Robin first entered the school at the Children's Hospital, she could not copy accurately the simplest forms, such as a square. This distortion of space perception and of perceptual motor response would mean that the task of making a cognitive map of new surroundings, of grasping opportunities, of integrating action responses in new settings would be enormous. And the more complex the situation, the more people in a group, the more difficult the task would be.

Some brain-damaged children react to complexity and newness by "hyperactive," scattered behavior. They are easily distracted. When the external situation is simplified, as when the child is settled into a cubicle without distraction he settles down to focus on a school assignment. This change of behavior can be understood in terms of the reduction of the task of perceptual mastery in a simpler setting.

But it is generally not recognized that the same problems of organizing and integrating perceptions of the surroundings must exist for the brain-damaged child everywhere he goes. And if the environment is not simplified for him, he has to do this for himself. He may do so by maintaining distance, by selectively relating to one part of the setting by "clinging" to one or two people, by rejecting demands too confusing to manage. Thus he appears to be resistant. This resistance may evaporate with surprising speed when the situation is clarified for the child by providing more structure, simplified options, and manageable avenues of activity. All this—the distancing, clinging, the rejecting—appeared with Robin, along with responsiveness when mastery seemed to her to be a real possibility.

Related to these ways of coping with difficult problems of orientation was Robin's need to take things slowly, step-by-step and piece-by-piece. Breaking a task into manageable units was a prerequisite to mastering it. She herself recognized her need for time, her slowness, and accepted this with more security than others showed understanding.

Robin's need for clarity and simplicity also underlay her rigid clinging to right/wrong dichotomies and moralistic conforming to what she had been taught was proper; thus the team observed the apparent paradox of her conforming and resisting. Another major clue to Robin's conforming/ resisting variability came from the pattern of her identifications and the relationship of these figures to her ego-ideal. She conformed with demands which fitted her image of what she wanted to be, and she resisted pressures to respond to opportunities felt as alien to her self-image.

The incompleteness she felt was evidently experienced as a deprivation and a loss—as if she had not been given enough; she was much concerned with being given to and with giving. She seemed demanding. Yet, she was never one to hoard what she was given. Rather, it seemed that she wanted to be given to so that she could give. She was concerned about another child to whom she felt the workers did not give enough and, in general, was alert to the issue of who was and was not given enough.

4

Therapy Deepens

During the first winter of therapy Robin's labile reactivity to stimulation made it difficult at times to appraise the overall direction of her progress. In her first therapy hour after Christmas, following her return from her beloved Grand Island vacation to the hated Topeka, I was startled by her expression. Her face was distorted with rage—at moments she looked like a trapped wildcat. There were also sudden explosive outbursts—such as, "Cut it out"—that seemed irrelevant to the topic we were discussing or to anything I had said. While she expressed protests against unbearable pressures outside the therapy hour, it was hard for me to integrate this intense disturbance with the Robin I had seen during the fall. This was a strange girl, and I was puzzled.

Occasionally an obscene word uncharacteristic of Robin leaked through the misspellings in her written work, but she insisted they were due to carelessness. Contributing to the extreme irritability were unhappy shifts in her world of attachments—her beloved aunt and uncle were going away for the winter, and some girl friends were also leaving. At home her parents' attention was increasingly preoccupied by the hospitalization of her sister Eve after an accident. This involved for Eve the loss of her world of active companions and sports for several months; the home atmosphere was dominated by Eve's stormy complaints, self-pity, and angry attacks on the rest of the family. Along with this, Robin's younger brother had school problems and contributed his share to the emotional chaos in the home, which must have been more than any two parents could handle with equanimity. It was only as the overwhelming accumulation of stress was revealed that I could understand Robin's fierce, angry reaction.

Remarkably enough, Robin maintained her efforts at school, persisted in dealing in her own way with questions about sex and reproduction that were made conscious and acute by puberty, tried determinedly to respond to social opportunities and pressures in the residence, and after the first violent regression, cooperated in therapy.

She seemed to cope with various stresses differentially—her sense of deprivation at home while her parents were so preoccupied with her siblings, and while her relatives (formerly dependable sources of support) were away, contributed to increased dependence on child-care workers. Without her favorite child-care worker, she could not go in to the dining room for lunch. Her feelings about loss of peer group friends and longing for a pal were reflected in her tender valentine to me signed, "Your pal."

In contrast to the initial primitive rage, in subsequent hours her feelings of being overwhelmed sometimes led to a frozen immobilization. But the hour also became a haven of peace and quiet where at times she didn't feel like talking; she just seemed to rest.

Her new bodily feelings of puberty development were channeled into narcissistic interest in clothes, hair, and cosmetics—with, for the most part, attractive results; with occasional exhibitionistic accents not atypical of young teen-age girls. Her questions about reproduction were answered partly through her mouse project, partly through exploring resources in her home library, partly in therapy hours.

The autonomy and initiative reflected in various ways of using the residence, the school, and therapy to meet her own pubertal needs were impressive—particularly when compared to the inhibitions of many children who go through this phase covertly. Robin was herself growing up in her own way despite the physical stress inside her body and turmoil at home, and again I was moved by her vigor, courage, and directness.

At the same time that she was struggling, with marked ego-strength in the midst of inner and outer stress, for mastery of typical pubertal problems she was overconscientiously pushing herself to meet certain expectations of her family and the child-care workers. These had to do with progress in "establishing myself in my peer group," by attending dances, overnights, and so forth. Robin's sense that "they will reject me if I don't" was part of the pressure; "I should" was still more.

In view of all the strain—physical, social, and emotional—that Robin was bearing I was astonished to hear that her mother reported that she "enjoyed" Robin more and that the feeling seemed to be mutual. I surmised that Robin's progress in school, personal care, and her social efforts, all contrasted with the difficulties currently presented by her siblings; and that, in effect, Robin had become the good, rewarding one, to some degree a relief or consolation to her mother in contrast to her previous status as the trouble maker and chief focus of anxiety. Certainly Robin was trying—to make progress, to be good, to meet expectations. And her efforts were rewarded by recognition from her teachers as well as from her mother. By now she was channeling her stress into therapy which made possible greater ease at home.

Robin's multiple problems meant that many professional persons were involved in helping her—the doctor, who gave her the allergy shots, the orthodontist, the dermatologist, as well as her therapist, social worker, child-care workers, the psychiatric director of the residence, the psychiatric trainee assigned to the residence as assistant director, the group workers, and her teachers. This variety of helping personnel may in itself at times have been another strain on the integrative capacities of a girl with neurological problems. But Robin, it seems, coped with this pressure by identifying with the helping figures and trying to be a helper herself. Appropriate opportunities for helping arose as she sensed the greater plight of an aphasic girl two years younger than herself.

Robin's many problems and needs required timely communications between the different people involved in helping her, especially between me and the chief child-care worker, the social worker, and the teachers.

The First Two Hours after Christmas Vacation: Regression and Progress

Despite the ups and downs, the two steps forward, one step backward pattern of Robin's development, I was not prepared for her severe regression when she first returned from Grand Island after Christmas vacation. I saw a level of disintegration and disorganized expression of anger which was repeated only once during the next two years—in a situation of intense frustration. I was, however, accustomed to her autonomic lability—which included a tendency to alternate regression and progression, as is often the case with young adolescents. In contrast to the teen-ager posture after her thirteenth birthday, she came in after Christmas looking more like a latency child: she was wearing a plaid wrap-around skirt, which was much shorter than what teen-agers were wearing at that time, and long red knee socks, with a Scottish flavor; her hair was loose and rather uncombed, quite without the teen-ager grooming typical of the fall.

Her face was flushed, but more remarkable was the labile, ambivalent combination of expressive movements and chorea-like activity of her lips through most of the hour. The rest of her face was not involved in the rapid movements; it looked as if she was trying to exert considerable control. But the rapid movements in the oral zone heightened the regressive impression contributed by her childlike dress. Along with anger, disgust, and rejection, much resistance and denial were expressed. At one time she bared her teeth in a way that looked like an animal in a rage. Hostile expressions came chiefly when she was talking about her frustrations with Topeka, how dangerous it was, how she hated to leave Grand Island.

✝ This seemed to be a pattern of discharge of anger which was perhaps related to her preschool temper tantrums—here she tried to control her rage, but it overflowed into these primitive expressions.

Paradoxical moments of happy expressiveness occurred when Robin talked about a trip she took with the family to Washington, but these happy and sometimes impish moments alternated with angry and disgusted expressions. Along with the protests about Topeka, I felt that her new work with a male teacher, combined perhaps with things that had happened during the vacation, was being reflected in transference rejection of me. Overtures from me were greeted with a new tinge of defiance as she answered in a laconic or even mechanical way. I was astonished and puzzled, and I proceeded cautiously, just listening to see what I might be able to understand, trying to make sense of this confusion of feelings.

Finally, I commented that she acted as if she didn't want to come back at all. At that, she smiled rather warmly—the warmest moment of the hour—and I commented empathically on how homesick she must be for her home town. With this she relaxed and opened up to talk about what she had done in Grand Island—going to the movies several times with her sister, her aunt, her family, and twice alone. In contrast to Grand Island, where the movies were only four blocks away from her home and where she felt perfectly safe, she commented that she could not go to the movies alone in Topeka—"It is a dangerous city."

✝ Her surprising shift, after she felt that I understood her, testifies to the depth of her appreciation of understanding of rage; she evidently experienced this understanding as a new and welcome response instead of the punishment for temper tantrums she had received when younger.

This led to a discussion of what made Robin feel the city was dangerous. She first mentioned the destructive teen-agers who had crashed her sister's party, throwing beer bottles around and breaking things. Then she gave examples of plans that she and her family have made to cope with possible threatening intrusions: when her parents went out in the evening, there would always be two of the children together, and, if anybody came to the door, one child was supposed to go to the phone while the other opened the door; in case of any danger, the one at the phone could immediately call the police. There was also a rule that she was not to go out of the house alone at all after dark, not even to cross the yard or cross the street. This description of the dangers of Topeka as compared with the safety and comfort of Grand Island was elaborated and repeated—Grand Island was a good, safe town while Topeka was an unattractive, dangerous city.

✝ It seemed evident that her parents also felt that Topeka was dangerous, although perhaps they were simply trying to help the children cope with their own feelings.

After I acknowledged how hard it was to be feeling that Topeka was so dangerous, her mood shifted even more, and she comfortably reviewed the gifts that she had received for Christmas, including a kilt. This led to a discussion of kilts and Scotland and her wish that she could get a map of Scotland's clans with information about different plaids. I assured her that it would be easy to get this, and she responded with renewed rapport.

An extended discussion of her different family lines followed—some Scottish, some Irish—in which we exchanged information about Scotland. She then described an earlier family trip to New York, then south to Tennessee during which they had had some amusing experiences—for example, arriving at a rather fancy hotel without having changed their very casual dress. In this discussion, as earlier, her facial expressions were very mobile, and she sometimes giggled at the attitude at the hotel, which first had seemed to reject them and then had accepted them after their reservations had been found. In disgust, she emphasized what a snobbish hotel it was and how the family had, as it were, put one over on it by coming in "looking like tramps." In New York her father had made a rule that the girls, who were together at one end of the hall, should not open the door if anyone knocked but should phone their father, who, with their mother, was in another room.

Thus, the theme of danger and the need for protection against danger was recurrent throughout the hour. But, once her angry and anxious feelings were recognized, the initial overflow of hostility and anxiety did not exclude considerable pleasure about Christmas gratifications and fun on the family trip. In an extended discussion of the three dogs that she and her brother now had, Robin commented on differences between dogs and cats and their feelings about travel, about being away from home, and their ability to find the way home if they ran away. I commented that she probably would like to run away and get back to Grand Island, and she agreed.

She then talked about the mouse project. Her teacher had asked her to look up the definitions of three words and make the beginning of a design for a cage. When I commented that her teacher gave her specific jobs to do, Robin said, "Yes," decisively, "And he explains things."

She went on to talk about school and said that she wanted to have grades, and that she could work harder if she knew what her grades were. For instance, if she got a C minus, she might be able to bring it up to a B; she felt sure she could work hard enough to get As and Bs if she knew exactly what her marks were. She also said that her teacher was firm and that she likes firmness. I commented that this feeling was something like her feeling about an aunt whom she might visit. She wanted to know when school was finished. I said that it was probably about the middle of June. To this, she looked disgusted again and remarked, "I thought it would be the end of May, like the schools in Grand Island."

✚ Robin expressed a much wider range of feelings—from wild hostility to warmth—than she had ever shown before, with more affect- and impulse-pressure. The Christmas vacation at home in Grand Island had highlighted the frustrations, emptiness, and dangers of Topeka and had triggered the overflow of deep rage which illustrated the extreme difficulty in managing intense emotion for a neurologically damaged girl. Yet her recovery also illustrated the floating or disjointed quality of her cognitive-affective functioning, as if the lack of integration made it possible to shift into a completely different mood.

On the positive side, she was satisified with work at school, except for her desire to have definite marks, and she was making a real effort. Her teachers reported that she had been reading more and obviously had learned a good deal, since she gave a coherent report on her reading. But when faced with questions formulated by the teacher and written on a piece of paper to answer independently, Robin was not able to mobilize her knowledge. It was as if she did not have the flexibility to restructure what she had absorbed: when given assigned questions she could only give out answers in the form in which she had taken in the material. But when writing on her own initiative, her assimilation and capacity to use information she had absorbed was often impressive.

Following up on her wish to have marks, to know exactly where she stood, I talked to her major teacher who quickly agreed to discuss Robin's work with her.

Our next therapy hour was dramatically different: Robin looked more poised, more mature, neat, and attractive, so that I commented on the contrast in her mood and appearance, adding that it was not necessary to keep angry feelings bottled up until they exploded. I actually offered her a whole series of angry remarks `with which she could verbalize feelings that had been previously expressed both with somatic symptoms and through criticisms and accusations of people and places. She responded warmly but reproachfully, as if verbalizing angry feelings would not be socially acceptable, and later added that she liked to go down to the basement when she didn't feel good and talk things out with herself and try to understand why she felt the way she did. She said that she could "understand better if I talk it out to myself alone, without anybody else in the room."

Following up on her expression of the wish to know exactly where she stood in her schoolwork, I told her about my conversation with her teacher and her teacher's promise to talk to Robin shortly about how she did stand in her work. The teacher had told me that she might be promoted very soon. I asked Robin whether she felt that if she worked hard she might go into sixth-grade work next fall (in order to test her confidence, desires, and possible wish to be challenged still further). With honest doubt and a somewhat depressed sigh, she said, "Maybe," and agreed when I commented that she gave me the feeling that she felt it would be hard going.

I reminded her of the times when she had felt that people underestimated what she could do; she nodded vigorously, so I added, "I know it's important for you to have as much as you can do," and she agreed. I continued, "It's also important not to have more than you can really manage well." She agreed very firmly with this. I summarized, "We have to work together to find what is the right amount so that it is not too much and not too easy," and Robin agreed even more firmly. This whole discussion was cooperative and realistic.

After showing me an electrical gadget that she said resembled something her brother had, she began to discuss things that she and her brother liked to do together, but she added that in games, "He always wins." I suggested that he probably won—in checkers, for instance—"because he could think several moves ahead and plan how to arrange the most jumps," and she nodded. She mentioned other games involving arithmetic and then said that her brother was bad at math, too, and did not like to play those games—and that, as a matter of fact, everybody in the family was bad at math. She also reported that all four children had eye problems requiring glasses, and that all four had some odd troubles with their teeth. When I commented, "Everyone has his own share of problems," she agreed rather solemnly. In addition to identifying herself with the firm, strong members of the family and feeling proud of the Scottish clan she was descended from, she was now seeing herself as one of a family group who shared similar problems.

Interestingly enough, after she told me about her homework, and I commented that homework was sometimes quite a burden, she said it took time to get used to it, but she was "better adjusted to it now." I explained that homework was one way of trying to help her make more progress in school, and that we hoped to bring different areas of her schoolwork closer to the level of her understanding. I said that she thought and understood like a teen-ager, and that if we kept working on it, her reading level could catch up to her thinking level. I said that her teacher had told me how much better she did on oral reports than on written ones in answer to questions written by the teacher.

From this realistic discussion Robin shifted to talk about the possibility that their dogs (a collie and a poodle) might mate and produce a "collie-oodle." Then she gaily chatted about naughty moments when one puppy turned over a bowl of food which made a mess for her mother to clean up. This displacement of naughtiness onto the dogs was paralleled by a denial of any expressions of "real anger" since she came here. When I asked whether she meant that she had not been really angry here in the therapy hour, she insisted, "Not here or at the residence." Without challenging her denial at this point, I commented that therapy hour was a time when she could be free to say anything she wanted to and that she might get on with her schoolwork faster if she didn't bottle up her feelings so much. I added that when she had frustrations at school, it was possible to talk them over with her teachers as we had talked over her wish for the mouse project, her desire to have something to do at nine-forty-five in the morning, and her need to know exactly how she stood in school. I added that if she wanted to talk about anything that she did not wish me to discuss with others, she could tell me and I would keep it to myself. But in line with her denial, perhaps, she replied that there had not been anything that she needed to talk about that couldn't be shared.

✝   In these two hours I saw vivid examples of extreme shifts in both emotional expression and thought, illustrating again the looseness of integration and difficulties in emotional control and sequential thinking. Since this fractured psychic functioning was related to the stress of her conflict about leaving her Grand Island home and settling in "dangerous" Topeka, I felt that therapy must continue to be supportive, to try to avoid stress, and to help her to communicate feelings in order to prevent her being overwhelmed.

Improved Relations with Her Mother

The social worker's contributions to our work with Robin had already been significant. In weekly conferences with Robin's parents, the social worker had reported on Robin's urgent physical needs—and, in turn, had reported to team meetings and to me individually on family interactions involving Robin. During this period, when Robin was discussing school problems in therapy hours, these reports were especially important. At the end of January the social worker phoned to tell me that the family had been extremely upset lately for several reasons. Eve was going into surgery for an operation on her knee. Robin had mentioned the operation in therapy but had either needed to soft-pedal it or did not realize how serious it was. Eve had been so depressed about the consequences of the surgery that she had been intolerant of anyone else's feelings or problems. She had made her friends chiefly in tumbling and other vigorous activities which she would not be able to do for some time, and she was afraid that she would not have any friends. She probably would not be allowed to go back to these activities for a full year.

Recently, when Robin had come in crying about something else, Eve had yelled at her, "I'm the only one who is allowed to cry around here." Both Robin and Eve had then laughed over this. Robin's brother Jim continued to be very depressed about school, and the father formally requested treatment for him. Jim himself had requested treatment. This would be an added expense for the family.

Robin had recently asked her parents how they happened to bring her here, and they were a little troubled as to how to explain her difficulties to her. As a matter of fact, Robin herself had asked to come the year before.

In connection with Robin's interest in the mice, I had previously asked the social worker to check with Robin's mother as to what sex information she had given her. The mother said that she had explained menstruation to her; Robin had not been told about, nor had asked about, intercourse. She now recognized that Robin's interest in the animals—in breeding mice, and so forth—reflected active interest in reproduction. Robin's mother was more than willing for me to explain intercourse to Robin and said that she felt it would facilitate Robin's ability to ask her mother more about it. I felt that since Robin was thirteen and very conscious of "dangers" from boys it would be important to work on this in therapy.

Against the background of Robin's age-appropriate sexual curiosity and her variable protests and interests in activities and parties which might involve encounters with boys—in whom she was evidently interested as well as being frightened of dangers they presented—some shocking events occurred in Grand Island. Several girls became pregnant within a few weeks—girls whom Robin had known when she lived there. In the spring this became a major problem for discussion.

Her social worker also commented that Robin's mother was warmer toward Robin now and actively enjoyed doing things with her. It was the mother's idea to read *Born Free* to Robin, and both of them had been enjoying this. She also enjoyed the chop suey dinner prepared by Robin, although it was rather a nuisance getting all the materials because Robin had spotted some fresh water chestnuts somewhere and wanted very much to go back and find them. I was interested in this as another example of Robin's alertness and curiosity.

Progress in Our Understanding of Robin's Variability

The next team meeting revealed our paradoxical tendency both to understand Robin warmly and to misunderstand her. The principal of the school commented that he had originally overestimated Robin's ability and that she was not working at the level he had thought her capable of. This was not surprising in view of the wide discrepancy, on intelligence tests, between her good Verbal level, both in Comprehension and in Vocabulary, and her multiple difficulties not only in Space Perception, Mathematical Concepts, and the like, but also in written spelling and reports.

One teacher commented that he had tried different devices to communicate with her at times when she could not spell, and he felt that these had been partially successful. He experienced her as a warm person who did not hesitate to "mix it up" with her teachers and who really tried to do adequate work. He was puzzled by the fact that on one occasion she had worked through six sets of multiplication tables and had done them quite well, but on returning to a set which she had previously done adequately, she had been unable to repeat the performance. He commented that she would remark "I can't remember that today," and he admitted that he was beginning to believe that this was really true—that at certain times she could remember and at other times she was incapable of doing so. This could be seen as part of her variability in many other areas.

I pointed out that Robin did not seem to feel beaten by her difficulties or disappointed by slow progress. I also agreed that she actually did function differently on different days. This made it difficult but necessary to sort out what was a genuine neurologically or biochemically-based variation in her capacity to function and what was the result of emotionally defensive operations.

I noted that on her return from Christmas vacation she seemed very depressed and angry and she also functioned at a low level somatically. Everyone on the residence unit had noticed this. One member of the team asked how we could discuss Robin's fluctuations in functioning with her. I said that I preferred to focus on a related question: could we help Robin to understand what she could dependably count on for herself and to recognize where she would be able to succeed? I also pointed out that Robin was terrified of being in any new situation unless she had thought it all out and so was aware of all the aspects of the new problem and prepared for difficulties which might arise. We needed to help her with this. And I shared my feeling that we could help Robin only by continuing to be patient with her and by trying things out with her in different ways in order to clarify our understanding of her areas of competence and areas of difficulty.

The teachers emphasized the fact that Robin, while progressing very slowly, was able to put to use all that she had learned. At that time, she was reading comfortably at a fourth-grade level. The art teacher commented that in art, Robin tended to go into great detail, keeping things small and tight. I suggested that dealing with small pieces and small units was part of Robin's effort to master a task. The music teacher pointed out that Robin's motor coordination was poor but she was enjoying the piano more; she cried less and no longer blamed her inabilities on her mother.

I suggested that Robin needed the sublimations of art and music so badly that it was important for her to have these even though she might not be making much progress. She felt deeply frustrated by the realistic problems she constantly experienced. She needed to feel able to explore things. I thought it was important not to give up but to continue to help her to master as much as possible and to keep the goals within her actual capability.

One of the child-care workers pointed out that Robin tended to set up a situation in the residence in which the group became angry with her and she became a scapegoat. I said that in my experience she responded to humor and that such behavior might be successfully handled by humorous challenging of her behavior.

✝ This was, in fact, a period when Robin was struggling persistently with her difficulty in trying out new situations. This difficulty, of course, was connected with realistic anxiety about possible failure and also about being ridiculed or not accepted. At times, her anxiety mounted to a point where she not only felt miserable but seemed to want others to know how miserable, how frustrated, and how anxious she felt. Also she was angry that she had such severe problems—and she felt that in some way others were to blame for these insurmountable difficulties.

The child-care workers reported that despite her anxiety Robin did try new experiences; for example, she was committed to going to a Valentine party at the Children's Hospital. However, this responsiveness in the Children's Hospital setting contrasted with her tense rejection of the suggestion that she explore the "Fun Night" at the YWCA, a new setting in which all the people would be strangers except for the child-care worker with her. In other words, she was differentiating between situations with greater and lesser degrees of newness, experiences that she could dare to try out in comparison with those she could not trust herself to attempt.

The child-care workers also reported that in preparing for the Valentine party, she wanted to know what kind of dress would be worn, how long the party would be, what kinds of activities would be going on, and what she could do. She said that she knew that she wouldn't dance, but that she would still like to go. At the party she became interested in a conversation about the trampoline. When she was told that there had to be enough people around to provide spotters to watch those who were trampling Robin argued, "Oh no, you don't need spotters," but the child-care workers told her that here spotters were always used as a safety measure because even the most skilled person on the trampoline could sometimes be thrown off balance and spotters around the edge could help them. Instead of gaining security from this protective measure, Robin became extremely anxious, was too blocked to continue the conversation, and even found it difficult to hold her coke and her plate. It was as if the suggestion of danger—even when the plan for protection against the danger was adequate—evoked so much anxiety that she was unable to maintain her poise and integration. The child-care worker with her helped her move away and sit down.

✝   It seemed that when anxiety about any specific situation was evoked, Robin's thresholds were lowered for other anxieties.

Robin Brings a Dream

Robin had left a valentine on Thursday saying I should not open it until February 14. There were hearts on the back of the envelope, and when I did open it on Valentine's Day, I saw that the message on the front of the card—"Because you're special and it's Valentine's Day"—had been underlined by Robin; the type on the inside read, "A special Valentine goes to you, and I'm sure you know the reason, too." The card was signed, "Your pal, Robin," which she had also written on the outside of the envelope.

✝ Robin's valentine seemed poignant—she needed "a pal" of her own age very badly, and it meant a great deal to her to have someone to talk to. I had sent her a valentine of about the same size, also gold and red like hers, which read, "Happy Valentine's Day," and on the inside, there was a sentiment to the effect that I wished her happiness and success; I had signed the card, "Dr. M." I thought that she might have felt let down by the conventionality of this, but since she had so many other realistic physical reasons for feeling in bad shape, it was impossible to determine that. At any rate, she really worked during the hour. I told her at the beginning how much I had appreciated her valentine and how important it was for two people to have good feelings about each other if they were to make good progress in therapy.

On Monday Robin came in looking droopy and flushed, with her head down. It was soon obvious that she had an extremely bad cold. It turned out that she had gone to the party Saturday night even though she had had a fever Friday and was not feeling well. Moreover, she was menstruating and had been having cramps. She was not very open to suggestions of any kind. In view of how miserable she felt, I thought she ought not to come to school, but she insisted that she would. As to the party, she just said that she enjoyed wearing her red dress and other people thought it was pretty. However, she said no boys talked to her at all.

Robin then asked, "Do dreams mean anything?" I said that they often did, but there were many different kinds of meanings, and it was not easy to tell what they meant right away. I wondered what kind of dream she had had.

She then talked about the dream she had had on Friday night, following which she had fallen out of bed. In the dream, there had been a table and something like a pile of tin plates on the floor and some big gray thing. On my questioning, she said it was frightening, and she then remembered it had a long pink tail like a cylinder. I asked what thoughts she had about the table or other things in the dream; instead of bringing up associations to these she told about another part of the dream. This part was out-of-doors; there had been a well with water in it, maybe a "wishing well." And in another part of the dream, a desk—with magazines on top of it—and a staircase. On the desk was a long green thing like a cylinder, and a circle.

When I asked for her thoughts about any of the items in the dream, Robin was not fluent with free associations to the parts of the dream. I commented that her mood was very droopy and that she was feeling bad, but that in the dream she had dreamed of a well—a wishing well—and that sometimes a dream really does have a wish in it. Robin did not object but did not pick up on this. I tried to explain that each part of the dream might be connected with other thoughts that would come out slowly and that it would take some time to get to the thoughts connected with the dream. I asked whether anything in the dream seemed connected with anything that happened or any thoughts she had had before Friday night. She did not think so.

In order to help her associations, I commented that the big gray thing in the first part of the dream sounded scary. She added that it was "growl-y." I suggested that this might be connected with "growl-y" feelings that she had, that perhaps she felt "growl-y" and angry at being sick. She did not object to this suggestion, but it did not really "click" with her. As I tried to give her an opportunity to bring up any further thoughts, she remained very droopy, intensely absorbed in the dream, and I commented that it haunted her and asked whether any special part impressed or haunted her the most.

She said, "No, just the whole thing did." I suggested that the gray part seemed like a worry, and wondered whether she had been worried about something that might happen at the party. She said no, and then defensively protested that she couldn't foretell what happens in the future. I reminded her that she had expressed her worries about boys and what they might do and that she had just told me that they didn't talk to her at the party. She commented again that that happened after the dream, however, and she couldn't have known that that would be the case.

I mentioned that I thought the wishing well was good. The staircase might have the thought in it that she was going to climb up steps—that is, make progress. At this Robin had a kind of "ah ha" expression, and she said very forcefully, "I'm very determined and I am going to move ahead." I said that altogether the dream seemed to me to have two different kinds of feelings—the gray, worried, and "growl-y" feeling in the first part of the dream and the positive, hopeful, wishing, and determined feeling in the second part of the dream. This was something like the checkerboard that we had talked about before, with good things and bad things together.

I asked whether there was anything else in the outdoors part with the wishing well, or the part with the desk and the staircase, and she said, "No, there were no trees, it was sandy." I said that sounded like a desert and like the feelings she had been having about Topeka. I asked what thoughts she had had about Grand Island lately, and she said she still was homesick from time to time. I asked what Valentine's Day might have been like in Grand Island, but she shrugged and said, "No different," and did not want to talk anymore. I commented that the way she was feeling gave me the impression that she was resigned, and I asked whether she knew what that word meant. She seemed doubtful, so I explained it meant the way one feels when there is something good and something bad together—when one has to put up with some bad things in order to get certain good things and maybe both of those were in the dream.

She asked what the magazines on the desk meant, and I asked her what they were like and what magazines they got at home (she answered, "the Post") and what magazines she saw at school. She did not offer much and I said, "Well, you remember I explained to you about all the tricks dreams play—magazines make me think of your friend in Grand Island." I asked whether she had been thinking about her and she said no.

Then she suddenly said, "Miss Trenton [her former teacher] was my friend in Grand Island and I want to write a letter to her about my progress here, but I don't know what to say. I can't tell her I've gone a grade ahead or something like that." I asked what she knew about her work, and she said that she didn't really have marks and that her teacher, Jacqueline, wouldn't give her a clear idea. I told her that I understood that her spelling and reading and arithmetic were all better and that Jacqueline felt that she had been making progress all along. She seemed so concerned with the letter to Miss Trenton that I said, "If nobody at the residence can help you, I will be glad to help you on Thursday if you will bring your letter along." She seemed to want this very much.

She was carrying some books with her, and I asked to look at her social studies book. Apropos of the dream, the book had some material about deserts in it. Papers had been written by Robin in script that was far better than her former handwriting. I commented on this, and she said, "I'm more careful with it." I added, "I believe you must feel better yourself about your schoolwork," and she said somewhat grudgingly, "Um-humm." What seemed to matter most to her was that I might help her with her letter to Miss Trenton. Robin added, "She was a friend, and she helped me."

✝ It was a clear-cut, well-structured, vividly seen dream with clear symbolic elements at an adolescent level. In view of the fact that she had cramps and felt uncomfortable with her menstruation, one could hypothesize that menstruation gave her "growl-y" feelings and made her feel like an animal. And moreover, that sometimes she felt the plate which she was offered was no better than "one would give to a dog."

Of course, the table and the question of plates on the ground, the regressed feelings to an animal state, the feeling of being treated like a dog, and so forth—if these really represented parts of her dream—could have something to do with the way she felt she was treated at home and at Children's Hospital as well. This could be contrasted with her need to be special, be important, her intense interest in *My Fair Lady*. This would fit in with the message in the valentine she sent me: that I was a "special" person. She wanted to feel that she and I were both special.

The second part of the dream—in which there had been a desk with magazines on top of it, a wishing well, a staircase, and a long cylindrical green thing—contained elements of the way in which she coped with the low feelings: the wishing well contained the positive emphasis on desire, the staircase may have had both sexual implications and wishes to advance and make progress through her effort and study, represented by the desk. Her wishes and her desire to make progress include being able to get along with males, to have a boyfriend perhaps, to have positive feelings instead of fear of heterosexual interaction.

As to the way I handled the dream: I had been emphasizing mastery throughout the therapeutic work with her. My approach was based on the assumption that regression is easily triggered in a brain-damaged child, and that she was—aside from the brain damage—in a very labile, transitional state developmentally. Every possible support should be given for the achievement of more stable integration and, as far as possible, disintegrative reactions should be avoided. So I felt that it would not be desirable to push her associations in a direction which would arouse a great deal of anxiety. It seemed to me that at that time it would be better to risk whatever difficulties arose from taking the dream very slowly than it would be to upset her by connecting it with concerns about boys and sex.

The suggestion about the staircase evoked her very intense, determined feeling about making progress, and my question about her friend in Grand Island brought her own association to Miss Trenton, a friend who had helped her. I also tried to explain that what was seen in a dream was connected with other thoughts and one could not tell everything that a dream meant unless one found some of those thoughts. Robin had brought the dream with a demand for "answers"—she wanted me to tell her "what it meant." She used the dream for communication, with trust in my response and a commitment to working together. I attempted to convey that she would have to decide what she wanted to do with the dream; at the same time, I tried to help her by suggesting ideas that might stimulate further associations of her own and evoke a more fluid response instead of her rather static state vis-à-vis the dream. Actually, this response did emerge with my suggestion of a "progress" implication of the staircase. Her demand to work on the dream reflected her own awareness of this as another way of helping herself by thinking about what goes on inside.

At a deeper level, I could infer that she was dealing with concerns both about sex and wishes for it along with wishes to get well and to make progress. It was important to note the static character of her images of cylinder and plates. Evidently, one way of coping with intense sexual threats or anxieties was to be rigid and to "freeze" her images. Her growliness was in the context of menstrual discomfort augmented by her cold, and suggested some anger regarding femininity along with hopes for positive heterosexual participation—that is, both a negative and a positive view of her feminine self.

The fullness and clarity of the dream implied a level of strength which contrasted with the somatic and affective regression reflected in her flushed, droopy, and ill appearance. The clarity of the dream images, in fact, was consistent with Robin's constant expression of a need to be clear about both external situations and her own status, about steps to be followed in her schoolwork—all of which could be seen as expressions of her intense drive to master the confusions and perceptual difficulties related to her neurological problems.

My approach seemed to contribute to her confiding that she wanted to write Miss Trenton and felt the need of my help in doing so. For this reason, as reinforcement to the whole process, I promised to help her in the next therapy hour, supporting her own initiative and ego strength.

Coping with Tension

Robin's continued problems in coping with tension can be illustrated by the impact of a cluster of inner and outer pressures. Combinations of realistic inner and outer stress made it hard to disentangle real difficulties and to separate them from certain distortions and confusing exaggerations or displacements. What follows is a review of the situation over a two-week period as it looked to the child-care workers, the social worker, and to me as I listened to Robin's accounts of how she felt and what was going on.

The last half of February was a time of considerable stress at home because of Robin's sister's and brother's problems and the concerns of her parents about these, which came to a head about the time that Robin herself was feeling unwell. The combination of, and perhaps the interaction of, these factors contributed to Robin's irritability, reflected in confusion and intensified sensitivity to change, to unclear plans, and to special or unusual demands, and other adaptational problems which she experienced even under the best of circumstances.

The ways in which these difficulties were perceived by the child-care workers were described by their leader:

Last week seemed to be quite difficult for Robin. Her mother was late in bringing her each morning and this bothered her a great deal; she seemed more disorganized.

On Tuesday she talked about needing to make arrangements for the concert. When she returned from her first class, I asked what arrangements for the concert I could help her with. She said, 'I don't care if you want me to go I will go; if you don't want me to go I won't go.' My questions seemed to throw her in quite a quandary in terms of "What do I do now?" She got angry with me and went to her room and slammed the door. I went in and asked her what was the trouble, and tried to help her think through arrangements for the concert, but she could not use my help then.

She later asked if she could "go down and see her." I didn't know whether it was her mouse that she wanted to see, and I said, "Who," and she said, "You know, Sue or Dink, whatever you want to call my mouse; I don't know what you call her," and was quite angry again. At this point she told me, "I am not going to the Community Concert; I am just not going."

Robin seems quite angry with Mr. Cook [her science teacher] any time that there is a change in her class. The change seems to throw her off, and she becomes disorganized and very unsure of herself and demands much more attention from workers during these times, and yet what she wants is not clear. Workers are sure at the time that she needs something, but what it is they are not sure—other than to just help her think through what is happening and how she feels.

Robin seems to need exact, concrete explanations. Or, as workers think through something with her, she doesn't seem to be able to tolerate the thinking-through process, and yet after she has been given some time on her own, she can come and talk it through more easily.

Robin has been very difficult to relate with; it is so frustrating at times—the wanting things *now*; and, if you must delay, as when a worker is communicating on the phone and asks her to wait, by the time she has waited a short time, then she cannot accept your help.

This memorandum from the child-care worker impressed me with its detailed observation of Robin's organically determined difficulties in adaptation outside of the therapy hour.

In the next therapy hour she came in with the remark that she had received an A on her reading examination and on her math as well. She also wanted to know more about the dream and still expected me to have the "answer." She asked whether I had "decided what it meant." After explaining again that I couldn't just decide by myself, that we needed to have more of her thoughts to help us to understand it, she said that she really didn't have any more, that she had told everything before.

I repeated that the last part of it—the wishing well, the desk, and the staircase—hung together and seemed to mean that she wanted to make progress and felt that by sticking to work—that is, the desk—she would be able to make progress—that is, go up the staircase. She agreed that this made sense and seemed to be quite satisfied.

On further discussion, she did not find it possible to see any connection between any part of the dream and worries about boys connected with the party that she was going to the day after the dream. I added that her dreams told us what she was thinking about and some of the problems we were working on in therapy, outside as well as inside the hour.

Since she seemed satisfied with linking the dream to her eagerness for making progress, it seemed a good time to raise questions about the child-care workers' problems in helping her. When I reviewed examples from the leader's memorandum, Robin offered a defense for each item—defenses that always seemed logical from her point of view, but which were totally lacking in empathy with the child-care worker who was trying to understand her. In her anxious way, she was consistently concrete in dealing with each situation by itself, not realizing how the accumulation of irritable or defensive reactions baffled the workers.

She did, however, accept my suggestion that when she did not let other people know that she was not feeling well, or that she had a cold, or some other difficulty in coping with a situation, she made it hard for them to help her. At the same time, she protested that the workers "didn't try to understand." She seemed to feel that the workers should intuitively grasp the total situation as she saw it, along with her feelings, and that if they really tried to understand, they would know what the trouble was. She felt that they were rigid and did not grasp her predicaments—just as they felt that she was very resistant to using their help when they attempted to give it.

At the same time, she gave examples of workers who used to understand her very well, as did the residential psychiatrist, Dr. Moore, who "talks the way we talk together here in therapy."

It seemed that the people she considered "understanding" had been able to avoid threats to her shaky self-esteem—that is, they put things in such a way that she did not feel criticized or attacked. Robin was extremely sensitive to how people were approaching her—the manner of the approach was more important to her than what was said, because of her vulnerability to narcissistic wounds. Close to the surface was the threat that the hurt would be deepened.

5

Resistance and Relaxation

Beginning to Understand Difficulties in Communication

The workers were anxious about how to deal with Robin's problems. They were becoming increasingly clear about kinds of situations that were disturbing to her, but they did not feel clear about the difference between a neurologically handicapped and a neurotic, emotionally disturbed girl. Further, they did not feel at ease in dealing with Robin's touchiness or anticipating how she might feel about questions or challenges.

In the next therapy hour, Robin said that no matter what she said or did, it would be interpreted negatively by the workers: "The other girls tease the workers, and they like it, but if I tease them a little bit, they bite my head off; they even do if I come up and put a hand on their shoulder just in a friendly way." She began to feel overwhelmed and started to cry. Offering a tissue, I told her I knew how hard it must be for her to feel that the workers did not understand her and added that we would need to talk about it some more. But she protested that she hoped we wouldn't take this up again in the next hour, which would precede my departure for a conference.

I also commented that when problems came up they could not all be solved at once. To this, Robin continued with reports of the difficulties that her sister and brother were having, as the social worker had communicated to me.

She then shifted to a cheerful report of two litters of four kittens that her friend's cats had just had. Robin mentioned all the names and then discussed the problems in feeding them. One in particular was very difficult to feed. "You could soak a little piece of cloth in milk, and he wouldn't suck on it, or you could soak bread in milk, and he wouldn't be able to bite it off," and altogether it was hard to find a way to manage him.

✚   Perhaps, unconsciously, she felt this kitten was like herself and that she was trying hard to find a way to help it. From time to time during therapy she would describe some other young animal that needed special feeding, a lamb or a calf.

Leaving the topic of the kittens, Robin described a trip to Grand Island the preceding weekend and some new clothes she enjoyed that her Aunt Samantha had sent her. I commented that she must like nice clothes and probably her mother did as well. She added that her aunt also cared about clothes, and then commented that this aunt had spoiled her and, in fact, all of them.

After commenting on the good memories of the weekend, I asked how she was feeling during her menstruation. Robin reported that it was still going on, and it was still irregular—about six weeks apart—so she could never tell exactly when it was going to come. I remarked that it is often true that one is more upset or irritable before or during menstruation, and Robin agreed, saying that she also noticed she tended to get constipated before menstruation, and then added, "And I do get irritable too." It was interesting that, after some gratifying exchanges, she could acknowledge her contribution to communication problems.

By this time, she was relaxed and left comfortably as if the mutual recognition of a source of difficulty had reinstated her inner self-respect; at the same time, there was no evidence that she fully understood the problems created by the barriers her irritability constructed, or the necessity for her to do her share in helping people to understand her.

In the next therapy hour, Robin talked about some of the fun that she and her brother had with their pets and also about her brother's difficulties, commenting that she didn't think their mother "understands any of us very well, but she understands me a little better than she used to." At the same time, Robin was more flexible in understanding aspects of her mother's experience which might have made it hard for her to understand

children, and which probably made it hard for her to extend her understanding to her own children right now, "because she lost her own mother
last spring."

✝ Just at a time of the relatively limited loss associated with my short
   absence, Robin was open to insight about the connection between her
   preoccupation with loss and her failure to understand the problems she
   created with others. Through some progress in understanding herself,
   Robin was also beginning to be more tolerant and understanding of her
   mother.

She had tried to follow up on the previous therapy hour by talking over
with one of the child-care workers a misunderstanding which we had
discussed; she said that the worker "said she understood," but that she,
Robin, didn't really think that she did.

✝ This illustrated Robin's sharp sensitivity to the feeling-quality of an
   interaction, her awareness of what was or was not genuine.

In the context of my imminent departure for a few days, she reviewed
several invitations she had had for the summer and was glad to be able to
fit these into my vacation time. However, she continued to be very labile
and irritable during the next few days—perhaps displacing her anger at
my absence onto the child-care workers. She complained to me that they
weren't giving her mice the proper attention and care; she became very
unreasonable, saying it was awful that her mice "should be kicked around
like an old boot, and they must feel sad because they weren't taken care
of." The worker had commented that mice did not have the same kind of
hurt feelings that people did. Robin stated that when she got older she
was going to make sure that all animals were taken care of. She also felt
angry with Mr. Cook, saying that he was kicking her around like an old
boot too—he did not show up for half of her classes and was late to some
others. She said that he always made it to his math class and that her class
was just as important as the other class. In this context, she also said there
was only one person who could understand her and that was myself. She
was unable to talk with child-care workers because they "twisted things."
   The child-care workers reported that, at that time, she was exceptional-
ly dependent and clinging in the residence, "spending much time at the
office door and wondering why there isn't a worker with her all the
time." However, she was flexible enough to enjoy the circus Friday night
and thanked the workers for letting her join the in-patient group to go to
the circus. She had prepared for this little trip carefully—asking what

kind of clothes the girls would be wearing and how much money they would take so that she could bring whatever money was needed from home.

✚ Here, Robin was again taking the initiative to get oriented and prepared for the new experience. Just at this time, she was beginning orthodontic treatments that involved rubber bands to provide pressure on her teeth in preparation for installation of artificial teeth in the gap where her own teeth were missing. The child-care workers said that she seemed to be handling the process of getting used to the hooks and occasional pricks which they involved; but here again, we have to recognize that this treatment with its recurrent irritations occurred at precisely the time when she was accusing people of not taking good care of her mice.

Through this period of increased irritability during menstruation and the uncomfortable orthodontia, it was important that even when she apparently resisted efforts to help her understand the child-care workers' situation, she spontaneously shifted to positive themes. Perhaps she was gradually developing more understanding and tolerance than was apparent, or than she could admit at the time; this was reflected in her increased tolerance of her mother.

Coping with Frustration through Action

With Robin, March came in like a lion. Multiple pressures and frustrations had been accumulating. It became increasingly clear that the child-care workers did not like to handle her mice over the weekend, and she was angry at them for this, particularly since she felt they did not have to really handle them but only to give them water and food. In addition, her brother and sister had been having trouble together. Eve had inadvertently spilled some glue Jim was using to make a model airplane; he got angry and hit her leg which was still recovering from the accident, causing her further pain. Also, while Jim had seemed to be eager for help on his problems, he had been dawdling so much that it made Robin late getting to school. Robin was angry at her mother for allowing this, feeling that "If she cared enough about my treatment here she would get me here on time."

We reviewed the interaction of these various difficulties, the trouble they were making for her mother as well as for Robin herself, and how the difficulties were greater since she was still trying to bottle up her feelings about these troubles. Actually, her control was shaky—her mouth mobile in the regressed, uncontrollable way which occurred when she was very upset and which gave a paradoxical contrast to the impassive expression of her face when she was controlling her anger. Her inhibition made it hard to evoke a clear picture of the specific things that were then making her most angry, but her stony expression relaxed when I made a sarcastic remark about how "pleasant" all this might have been. In fact, Robin could relax more quickly at such a remark, which implied some empathy and capacity on my part to feel her resentment, than she could with direct verbal interpretations.

After recognizing the actual difficulties and her anger about them, I asked her how she wanted to use the hour. She said that she had wanted to write a letter to her Aunt Samantha in school, but her teacher was away and the substitute would not cooperate. It seemed worthwhile to test Robin's capacity to make good use of an opportunity for an activity that she wanted, despite the accumulated anger and resentment that had nearly immobilized her. I thought it would be useful to demonstrate that there were things that she could do when she was frustrated in one direction, things that would be more satisfying than getting so bottled up with angry feelings. She immediately agreed when I suggested, "Why don't we write the letter—you go ahead and I'll help you right now." She started in quickly, leaving gaps and giving it to me with the expectation of help to fill in the words she could not manage; then she copied it over.

When the hour was up, I commented, "I thought it might be good to see if we could discover something. Some people get angry and just stay mad, and keep a grudge for a very long time; they can't change their feelings. But here, in spite of the fact that you were so angry and so bottled up at the beginning of the hour, when we decided to do the letter and have something satisfying for you to accomplish instead of being frustrated and angry, it made you feel good." Robin smiled with a slight expression of wonder, and I added, "I think this is a good thing to discover. You could find things to do to get into a better mood when you've had a lot of frustrations that make you feel as bad as you did at the beginning of this hour." Robin agreed in a tone that seemed to say, "I get the point," but with a certain ambivalence as if implying that it was easier if someone else helped you do it.

In the next therapy hour she wanted to continue the letters and her mood was entirely cheerful: the mice were getting along fine; her teacher was probably going to make a maze to run them. However, she showed me a cut on her thumb which had obviously had a Band-Aid on it. I suggested that she ought to have another Band-Aid to protect the cut so that it wouldn't get infected, and located one to put on for her—further indicating the possibility of getting help and using it.

As she wrote, she made a great many mistakes, which she again turned over to me to correct. In view of her exhibition of the cut thumb and the many errors, she seemed to be implying a connection between some injury and the difficulties (errors) for which she was wanting, and willing to use, help. The whole orientation of the hour was toward finding solutions to problems and cooperating with help.

In contrast to the angry, regressive, involuntary movements of her lips in the previous hour, at this time her lips were full and again active, but with the impression of sucking, or even the precursor of a full-bodied kiss. The oral quality of her mood was also reflected in her use of three very soft, cuddly mice among the toys on my table, and her juxtaposition of small animals with larger benign protective animals (giraffes). She commented during the course of the hour on keeping the valentine she had received from me a couple of weeks earlier in her pillow to "keep it safe."

✝   Since Robin had shown so much independence and energy in school, I wondered whether she was now resolving a conflict about using help.

Resistance to Interpretation

Some clues to Robin's feelings about interpretation were revealed in the next hour. She was tense and picked her nose in a way that she occasionally did when she had been irritated at experiences she felt to be intrusive. She repeatedly ruffled her feathers at any remark which she apparently felt as a going in.

Much of the hour was spent finishing a letter, drawing pictures, and writing a poem which began "Learning is a maze of math, spelling, reading, history, social studies, art, music." She wrote, "I made an A in math and 96 in a social studies test," then drew a picture of a maze with an alley at the end of which a mouse could go either left or right. If he went one way he would get food, in the other direction he would not. In the middle of the alley was an electric grid.

She continued to write the letter but when I looked at some of my own papers, she immediately demanded help (as the child-care workers had commented). I said, "Of course I'll help," and looked at the letter which contained many mistakes. I commented that the words with mistakes did not seem harder than others, and I wondered why she made mistakes with certain words. Robin, resistantly objected, "Just because I'm not careful," but she was wholly cooperative in accepting the corrections. When the letter was finished she asked me to mail it for her.

Some tiny toy mice and giraffes were on the table where we worked with the letter, and I asked whether they were a family. Again resistantly, Robin said, "I just put them that way." She had seemed restless all through the hour and when I commented on this, she said that she was sleepy and it was hard to get up in the morning. Then she quickly reviewed the many events of the weekend, including a visit to the dentist. She turned back her lips to show the bands on her teeth. I asked whether they hurt, but she said not now. Just then, her bus arrived with several boys in it, and Robin dashed out, commenting disparagingly, "Full of boys!"

✛ In retrospect, her uneasy fingering of her nose, resistance to interpretive remarks, her painful body treatments, the maze with its alternatives of food and pain, and her defensively hostile feelings toward boys—along with concern about receiving requested help—seem connected. I told her I had called the library to get the correct spelling of Lippizan (horses) in order to reinforce the idea that there are different kinds of help.

Problems: Robin's Increased Resistance and Negative Responses in Therapy

Robin came in cheerfully in a yellow blouse and white pleated, summery-looking skirt. She said immediately that her mouse had had seven babies. We discussed how they looked, what the mother did, and how long it would take before they got up on their feet, and so forth. Robin seemed casual and matter-of-fact about all this. She told about a friend's hamster that had given birth; the father had eaten one or more of the babies. I asked what she would do to prevent this happening with her little mice, and she said the main thing would be to give the adult mice plenty of food so they wouldn't be hungry. I agreed that this was a good idea.

She did not seem to want to talk any more about the mice, so I asked how her brother was getting along, and she said, "Fine," again in a casual, matter-of-fact way. I then went back to the previous therapy hour and the way she had been feeling, and her remarks about going to the dentist and having a shot. I asked whether the shots were painful, and she said they were and, in particular, that Dr. Osborn always seemed to hit a little bump or pimple on her arm when giving her the shots and that made it especially painful. I commented, "Then the last thing you wanted was another doctor when you came to therapy." Robin agreed, but made no further remarks.

I was casting about for something she might feel like talking about and remembered her concern about Lent and keeping Lent. I asked how it was coming along, and she mentioned that she was avoiding all sweets and, I think, meat. I asked whether she was also going to church during Lent; this evoked an explosion. She blurted abruptly, "Cut it out!"

✝ This was another bewildering response—I couldn't understand why she would explode at this point.

She went on to say that she would like to go to church but she couldn't go because her mother never got up Sunday morning in time to go to church. I commented that Robin had once said that she herself liked to sleep on Sundays; and a little angrily, she said, "Not during Lent"—she had always gone to church during Lent in Grand Island, and she would like to go now. Her manner was rebuffing and very much unlike her usual manner in therapy. I was puzzled. It seemed as if everything I said was the wrong thing, but I was so baffled that I didn't even remark on her manner.

✝ In retrospect, her rebuff may have reflected her mother's rebuff to Robin's wish to go to church, and her displacement onto me of her anger at her mother.

I finally did remark, "You really don't feel like talking about anything," at which she laughed, and I laughed. We passed the rest of the hour in rather superficial chitchat.

I asked whether she would be able to get out-of-doors now that the weather was so nice, and she said she thought she could take her books and do her homework outside on warm afternoons. However, she couldn't go outdoors around home "because Topeka isn't safe." I wondered how she felt about boys and whether this was what made her feel unsafe in Topeka—I had noticed that she often made a remark about the boys on the bus that came to get her. She said she didn't like those boys, but there were some boys over at their residence that she did like, and then she added that she liked some boys that she knew, including a cousin.

I commented that I had been thinking about this question of boys because of the way she had spelled "class": she had spelled it "galss." I explained that there were some interesting books about how our minds work—that jokes and mistakes, and so on, sometimes reflect things that are in our minds and that, for instance, she might have spelled "class" that way if she wished there were no boys in the class. She thought this was quite ridiculous, and yet she seemed slightly more open to the idea of talking about what mistakes could mean than she had been in regard to other comments.

✝ Robin found interpretations of almost any kind painful when they challenged an attitude, belief, or bit of behavior. That is, she accepted interpretations that felt supportive and friendly to her, but any slight hint of criticism, or suggestion which might involve a change in her views, was painful. Her need to defend herself constantly against any kind of unexpected stimulus, any shift in routine, or the accepted structure of things, meant that new ideas and concepts could be just as threatening as new situations, unexpected demands, events, or changes. Changes in herself were as threatening as external changes.

Moreover, because she had had to maintain a rigid vigilance against being caught off guard in situations that she could not manage, she was much of the time in a defensive position from which she could protect herself either by raising barriers even higher than usual, or by an action that felt like an attack, a rebuff, a rejection, or another gesture which would paralyze the other person.

This kind of experience had been mentioned by the child-care workers, but since I had not been through it before, I had not realized how paralyzing it could be. Despite Robin's warmth and genuine feeling under certain conditions, when she felt on the defensive her empathy was totally inhibited.

An additional factor in her sensitization this week might be found in Robin's confiding her way of putting letters, and my valentine, in her pillow to sleep on at night. Robin may have been hurt because I did not reciprocate her intensity. This was such a delicate area that I hesitated to raise a question about it during this hour when she was so resistant; however, this may have been a mistake, if the resistance reflected anger at my reserved response.

Increasing Response in the Residence

By contrast to her resistance in the therapy hour, the social worker noted:

> The parents report that Robin has been very little problem lately. She has been warmer, more friendly, and more cheerful at home. Mother responded immediately and very happily to Robin's asking to go with her to the Poodle Club. Mother chastized herself that she had not thought to arrange to have Robin go with her in the first place. She really seems to be enjoying Robin a great deal more.

So it appeared that Robin was confining negative feelings to her therapy hours, and giving her mother more positive responses.

The social worker continued:

> Apparently, however, Robin is being a great deal more obvious about her loyalty pull between her experiences here and at home. She wants to come here even on school holidays and had been irritated at our suggestion that she not come on holidays. She had had a couple of very good weekends in which there were activities with other children her age (initiated by the other children), such as the Young People's Concert, movies, and so forth. She even played the piano for a friend her own age who, incidentally, was polite enough not to play after Robin, as she is a much more accomplished pianist.

The social worker also added that the parents continued to be concerned about Robin's brother; he had been here for evaluation and a decision had been made for him to start therapy. It was not clear what this meant to Robin, who had turned off my question about how Jim was getting along by her laconic answer, "Fine."

✚   The deepening of therapy this winter included Robin's use of it to channel disturbed feelings into her hours with me and respond more positively to both home and the residence.

A Relaxation of Resistance—My Visit to Robin's Mice

Recently, Robin had often been ambivalent and therapy was an alternation of resistance and responsiveness. This session was a more friendly hour. Since it was St. Patrick's Day, I wore some small jade earrings, the only green things I possessed, because Robin had warned in the preceding therapy hour that if I didn't wear something green she wouldn't talk to me! She was wearing a two-toned outfit consisting of a robin's-egg blue blouse and a rather tight green skirt over plaid shorts. She sat down and said, "Do you mind if I pull up my skirt? I'm not comfortable at all." She added rather elaborately, "I wouldn't do this if I didn't have Bermuda shorts on." Actually, the shorts were not Bermuda shorts, which go almost to the knee; these stopped half-way down her thigh, suggesting a slight exhibitionistic tendency. I commented only that the outfit was very pretty.

✝ I made a mental note of the relation between this and her outfit at the preceding therapy hour; a skirt which zipped up in the front from the bottom of the hem to the waist, and a blouse with zipper pockets over the breasts. Robin opened the zipper over the right breast to show me there really was a pocket there and, during much of the hour, she sat fooling with the zipper at approximately the genital area. I had made no comment about any of this but noted the preoccupation with bodily concerns, genital sensations, and the like, for reflection and later discussion of sexual feelings.

Robin smiled appreciatively at my earrings and was companionable through the whole hour. Having in mind her difficulties with large groups, I commented that I disliked big cocktail parties because I couldn't take in so many people; I preferred small parties. Robin said, "But I have to go to dances so I can get established with my own age group." I agreed that this was one way.

✝ It seemed to me quite possible that with her organic problems she might never be much at ease in large groups, and I wanted her to feel that there was a choice.

Yesterday I had gone to see her mice. She had been relaxed, and friendly; we had had a happy visit, seeing the tiny baby mice, still rather like little worms. The parents were neat, attractive little creatures, and Robin and I took turns playing with them, watching them on the wheel and the ladder and squeezing through the little hole they had gnawed in the wall between the two cages.

She let me look at her log. We talked about the behavior of the little mice huddling together, and I wondered whether human babies would like to do that—whether they don't get lonely in a separate crib as they usually are. Robin said, "But babies are much further along than these little mice; the baby mice are more like embryo human babies. They can't see and can't hear and aren't developed as much." She went on with a few similar remarks which all sounded clear and mature; I asked where she got her information. She said they had medical books at home, and she had snooped in those. Later, she said that her father had a model of an eye which you could take apart and put together; also, the visible man and the visible woman, a skeleton, a brain, and a good many other models of this sort which she has taken apart and put together at home.

Beginning to Learn about the Nervous System and the Mind

In order to lay foundations for understanding relationships between feeling and learning, I explained to Robin that the brain consists of parts like the cortex that have to do with thinking, and parts like the thalamus that have to do with feelings. The sensations that come in through our eyes and ears send messages not just to the thinking part of the brain but also to the thalamus; in fact, the sensations have to go through the feeling part of the brain on the way to the thinking part of the brain, and this is why sometimes things are not seen quite accurately. This explanation seemed to give Robin a feeling of being respected and taken seriously.

We turned then to some discussion of school, apropos of my earlier questions about her spelling. She said that when her spelling was very bad it was usually because she wasn't being careful with it. She opened her notebook and showed me a play which she was in the process of writing, about a stepmother and stepchildren with typical fairy story characters in it. "Play" was spelled *p-a-l-y*, and almost every other word was misspelled.

Shifting the topic, she began dangling a bracelet on her hand, and I commented that it must be a good luck bracelet with so many charms. She said it was a travel bracelet—she had been given many charms by her sister Ann and by relatives who had traveled—and she told me the different countries various pieces came from.

When I started to comment about the many places Aunt Samantha and her husband, Robin's Uncle Wayne, had traveled, I made a mistake and said "Wade" instead. She corrected me, but I said, "You know, I have been trying to explain how our minds play tricks on us. I said Wade instead of Wayne, and Wade is my father's name. Let's see if we can figure out why I would have thought of him." Then I said we had been talking about traveling, and my father had traveled a great deal, in Europe, India, China, Japan, and many other countries. I said, "Perhaps all the talk about travel reminded me of my father's travels, so I said 'Wade' instead of 'Wayne.' " Then I explained that our minds have different layers—there are the things that we are thinking about and know we are thinking about, but then there are other thoughts connected with those but which we are not aware of. (I had decided to venture on this rather didactic approach since over many efforts she had been so resistant to exploring the meanings of errors in her spelling.)

She was much interested in what I said, so I continued, ruminating aloud, "Let me see how many reasons for mistakes in spelling we can think of: one is just not knowing how to spell a word; one is being upset and worried and getting muddle-headed and confused; one is getting mad and feeling like messing things up, so we mess up the words."

Robin didn't object to any of this. As we continued to go through her play, we noted that she had misspelled skirt, (*s-h-i-t*). I said, "Perhaps skirt reminds you of shit." She laughed, and I said, "Maybe there are times when you would really like to say bad words, but you are just too nice to really say them so it comes out in spelling words to make a bad word." She seemed receptive to this approach. After we had finished with the page and a half of spelling and I had worked on it with her, correcting it and occasionally wondering out loud why this or that mistake might have been made, she came back to her old theme that it was because she had been careless about it. I felt that she had had all she could take of the spelling problems.

I asked her whether she was still intending to be a veterinarian or a veterinarian's assistant. She said yes. I said that it seemed like a sensible thing to plan for since she had such a natural feeling for animals and enjoyed them so much. She said, "I'd have to go to a vet's school." I asked whether that would be after high school, and she said it would be after college. I commented that it would be a long, long row to hoe. She said, "But my father went to school twenty-four years and, if he can I can." (!) I just commented that she wanted very much to do it, and then said it might be important to make progress on the spelling. She said everybody in the family had trouble with spelling, Eve as well as Jim.

✦ It was as if she'd rationalized that if the others made a lot of mistakes in spelling, then it was all right for her to do it also.

She had worn a silk scarf around her head (it was a very windy day), and she had been playing with it in her lap. She now folded it over, rolled it up into a ball and tossed it to me. I commented that the silk was very soft, like Italian silk, and that it was a very beautiful scarf. She said it was her grandmother's. I said, "Well, we seem to have lots of grandmothers today. I am a grandmother, and you have your grandmother's scarf, and you were telling me that over at the Children's Hospital they have been joking with you about being the mice's grandmother." She had mentioned this earlier. She laughed merrily.

✝ As a whole, this hour had a quality of tuning-in, of reciprocity, and an element of identification with helping roles in contrast to the resistance and confusion of some recent hours. It was as if her conflict regarding loyalty to parents and therapist could be resolved by identifying with the common elements between mother and therapist (being feminine) and between father and therapist (being a helper).

Robin's Hope to Be a Helping Person

At our next therapy hour, Robin came in looking dreamy and vague at first, but soon volunteered that she "had had my cake and eaten it too"— she had gone to Grand Island Friday afternoon with her parents, then they drove back Saturday in time for the dance. She did not go to a wedding to which she had been invited "because I found that it was a home wedding, and their house would be rather small, and I decided not to go." I did not challenge or press her as to other "real" reasons. When I asked her how the dance was, she said, "all right," but nothing more. I asked what she wore, and she told me about a pretty bell-shaped white dress. I got nothing much in response to various efforts to find out more about how she felt about the dance.

✝ It was possible that she had decathected it because of a mildly unhappy experience.

She was more interested in telling me that Aunt Samantha and Uncle Wayne had not come home until Sunday evening, so she had not been able to see them. I commented that she must have been very happy to have the news of their return. At this, she beamed and said, "You should have seen me!" She had "jumped nearly to the ceiling" when her mother told her. They hope to go to see her aunt this weekend.

✝ Evidently, their arrival was much more important to her than the dance.

She was fiddling with another charm bracelet and I asked her about it.

She said her mother had loaned it to her. The little charms were hearts with the name of a friend or a relative who had given the heart to her mother. I counted twenty-five and commented that it must feel good to have these symbols of so many dear ones. Robin agreed comfortably, and I mused that her mother was very generous to let her wear a precious treasure like that. Robin agreed.

✟ This sequence seemed to communicate how much more important to her was the circle of relatives and friends, as well as her mother's companionable sharing, than experiences like the dance.

The tempo in these exchanges was leisurely and Robin did not seem to be in a mood to volunteer anything else. I asked how she was feeling; she said that her nose was stuffy from pollen—it always gave her some trouble. I commented that in general she seemed to be having less trouble with a stuffy nose than she did in the fall, and she agreed that the shots had been helpful.

At the same time, she was running her tongue over the orthodontic work on her front teeth. When I asked whether her gums were sore from the wires, she exclaimed decisively that there were three or four quite sore spots. I empathized that this must be a nuisance and uncomfortable.

After each such exchange, Robin sat quietly and passively. She didn't really get involved until I said that I thought she might like to hear how the day care center, for which I was the consultant, was getting along. At this, she became extremely eager, and I told her about the nine children who were there then, the fact that only one out of the nine had a really intact family, and gave detailed illustrations of how very deprived the children were. Robin said she would like very much to help them; she thought that it would be good for them and good for her if she could. She said, "You know, I have been babied and spoiled so much." I said that I thought that she was feeling that she had been given so much, she wanted to give something to children who did not have so much, and she agreed. Later, I added that there was another reason why people wanted to help other people sometimes and that was to be able to give them something that one had wanted oneself but had not actually had. Robin accepted this without commenting.

Instead, she got very interested in what they might like to do and what she could do with them. From this point on, she was quite alert, her tempo quickened, her face melted into a series of exquisitely expressive smiles and communications of interest, empathy, tenderness, humor, and eagerness. She thought of nursery rhymes and little stories, thought they might like stuffed animals to play with, that some of the songs she had been learning might be appropriate for them. She also looked at my toys, and we picked out some brown animals and Indian dolls. She thought they might like a mommy horse and a baby horse. Her suggestions were appropriate and thoughtful.

While this was going on, she ruminated about some good friends she had had in Grand Island—three or four girls in an Indian family who lived on the other side of town. She described the house in some detail, including the fact that they "didn't have adequate facilities"—evidently meaning an indoor bathroom. All through this entire thirty-five minutes or so, Robin was thoughtful, coherent, relevant, beautifully attuned to the problems, relaxed, and functioning in a thoroughly well-integrated and charming way. I was interested in this because previously this level of spontaneity had appeared chiefly when talking about or handling animals. She was very eager to know when she could go, and I explained that the supplies had not come, there were not enough chairs to sit on, there weren't any plates for the children to eat from, there was no sink or water in the kitchen, and so forth. I said that I had urged the staff not to add other children until things had settled down, the equipment had arrived, and the present group had had a chance to settle in.

Robin agreed with this is a mature way, and then a little later commented that it must be hard for children coming from such deprived homes to go back and forth from the day care setting to their homes with such contrasting conditions. (I had described how exhausted and inadequate some of the mothers were and how few resources there were for the children.) I commented that it was a problem, of course, for many children to go from one setting to a very different setting. Then I added that it was even true of some of us when we were much older—it was hard to go from one atmosphere to another. Robin agreed.

There had been an emphasis on her wish to help through all this discussion. When it was the end of the hour, and we went out, she put on her sweater and asked, "Will you help me with my collar?" I agreed, "Of course I will," and she left very comfortably saying, "I'll see you Thursday, Dr. M."

✝   This is the first time I can remember that she referred to me as Dr. M. when saying good-bye—implying her acceptance of me as a professional helper and perhaps a resolution of her conflict about my valentine. It implied also a beginning of resolution of the grandmother transference and perhaps the consolidation of a working alliance, along with autonomy, ego strength, and identity.

I had felt that, for Robin, when so much of her life involved stressful shifts and changes or degrees of complexity of interaction that were hard for her to manage, it was therapeutic for her to experience times like this when rapport was smooth and untroubled and when she could perceive herself as functioning adequately, helpfully, and responsively.

In contrast to the self-image represented at the time of her evaluation before she came into therapy, her behavior in this session seemed to reflect a hopeful and positive self-image and an assumption that she would be able to be of use.

6

Boys, Girls, and Babies

When Robin came in to the next session, she said that she had a problem with being here the following week because a friend of hers was coming up from Grand Island and she very much wanted to join her mother and this friend at three-thirty. I said that she had been very cooperative about adjusting her hours when I needed to leave for trips to conferences, and I felt that taking turns on making such adjustments was a good principle. We decided that since she had a class at two o'clock, the only available time would be nine–forty-five in the morning. Robin laughed and said, "We are as bad as the child-care workers on changing the schedules." I commented, "Well, that's life, we all have to make adjustments to each other and these changing events do come along. We can get used to them."

✝ I was glad to see that she could make light of the changes.

Early that afternoon, Dr. Porter had called and said that she and Robin had had a conversation yesterday evening, initiated by Robin, in regard to her feelings about the forced marriages of several girls in Grand Island. Robin was very upset, and Dr. Porter told her that she should talk it over with her mother and with me and find out why she was so upset about this.

Robin rather abruptly said, "There is something I want to talk to you about." She went on, "There have been four girls in Grand Island this winter who had to get married because they were 'p.g.' [pregnant]." She said that one of them, Brook, was only fifteen, but worse than that, "Megan is 'carrying' and she has to get married, and she is just my age [thirteen]." Robin had known Megan's family; they were quite poor but a nice family, and Robin was shocked and upset that this would happen. She felt very unhappy about Brook, too, and, at a later point in the discussion, said that the corduroy slacks she had been wearing had been given her by Brook along with certain other clothes but now she didn't want to wear Brook's clothes anymore. I remarked, "You don't want to be in Brook's shoes or any of her clothes for that matter," and Robin agreed. She had many questions and said that both these girls and the other girls must have known how these things happen—she did not think it happened out of ignorance. She was puzzled that they could let it happen, particularly Brook.

I explained how feelings can pile up and become overwhelming and sweep people off their feet. I tried to spell out how a little bit of feeling leads to exploring each other's bodies and then feelings mount up and get terribly exciting and uncontrollable. I also explained that this is the reason why some parents do not allow their teen-age children to have parties without a grownup present. Robin said, with some satisfaction, that their kitchen opens right into the living room and that whenever her sisters have boys around, their mother is right there.

She pressed very hard on the question of why the girl's mother couldn't keep the baby. "After all, if the baby was the daughter's child, wasn't it the mother's?" I then explained how the child is apt to be rejected. I asked her whether she knew the word "illegitimate," and explained what it meant. Then, in explaining how children tease other children or how grownups can talk, I asked if she had ever heard the word "bastard," which is used as an expression of intense rejection. Robin did not see why people would reject the child.

She kept pressing the question of whether the girl's mother wouldn't be able to keep the baby and then pushed it to the extreme, saying, "If this happened to a brother and sister, wouldn't their mother keep the baby because it really would be her baby, then, if it was the child of her own two children?" Here I thought she reflected her intense awareness of possible dangers with her brother. I started to explain reasons why brothers and sisters are not legally allowed to marry, and Robin was very understanding about the biological aspect of "weaknesses" being duplicated. Her feelings had mounted to such a point that I felt it was important to explore what she had gone through, so I asked whether she and Jim ever rolled around together, or whether Jim had lain down on the floor with her. She said quite directly, "Yes," he used to do that when they were playing around with the dogs, but it hadn't happened for some time.

She said that she was worried about it now, though, because she had not menstruated for a long time—it had never been as long as this. I asked her whether Jim had "put his penis inside her," and she said flatly, "No." I said that I thought she would menstruate quite soon—that usually I could tell by the way she felt. She said that she had been feeling signs for some time. I asked whether she meant cramps, and she said yes. I suggested that she keep pads with her because it could happen any day now. Robin said that she would be careful, that she had been caught twice without them, and she thought now she would be able to remember.

I then asked her whether she and Jim were left alone in the house at any time. She said twice since they had been in Topeka, when her mother and father went out. I said, "Well, you remember you told me what you would do if a boy started to do something he shouldn't do—you said you'd slap his face hard. That goes for brothers as well as anybody else." Robin objected, "But he could beat me up, and I don't think I could handle him." I suggested then that if she didn't feel secure about being able to protect herself, and if she felt that Jim was apt to get excited and try to get at her, she really should be protected, and she and Jim should not be alone in the house. She agreed softly that she really felt a need of being protected. By this time, she was crying. Actually, she had begun to cry about the bad reputation these girls were giving Grand Island and how hard it is "when you love a town" to have a thing like that happen.

I commented that she was terribly angry at those girls, and she said yes, she was very angry at them for "ruining the reputation of Grand Island." If she could get down there, she would slap every one of them. I thought out loud that maybe they didn't need any more punishment; they must all be having a hard time. She said that she knew that, but still that was the way she felt. I went on that now they didn't have much room to choose what they would do next; they were so young and yet they now had taken on this big responsibility. Robin agreed thoughtfully with this; at the same time her predominant feeling was that her beloved Grand Island's name had been besmirched.

✝   Perhaps she also had some feeling of not wanting to admit that she came from Grand Island, thus trying to disown her sexual urges; there was some hint of this as she said people in Omaha knew about the pregnancies. She then suggested her family might move to Albuquerque for her health!

She said, "Please don't tell Dr. Porter about this. I tried to talk it over with her, and it didn't work out." I said that I did not have to tell Dr. Porter, but I did need to tell her social worker. Robin agreed that that would be all right, and I made it clear that I felt it would also be most important for her to talk it over with her mother.

✝ Her anxiety about her delayed menstruation was intensified by her disturbed feelings about the pregnancies of teen-age girls she knew, her embarrassment about her home town's reputation, her vagueness about how conception could occur, her fear that contact with her brother might cause it, and her need for protection. I felt that in face of her accumulated stress, direct suggestions for evoking her parents' protection were needed. The primitive activity of the two young teen-agers did, I thought, present a possibility of sexual encounter.

Meantime Dr. Moore had suggested to Robin that she give a little talk at the tree planting ceremony in the garden of the residence on Arbor Day.

Comments from the Team about Progress and Problems

A child-care worker's note to me reviewed a series of positive and negative observations of Robin:

> Robin is doing quite well in working through giving a speech for the Arbor Day celebration. She joked with me about being sick on that day or losing her voice and having laryngitis so that she wouldn't have to give the speech. She knows the material quite well and has practiced saying it. She says that the biggest part is saying it in front of an audience. I agreed with her that this was the hardest part because once you had the information that was fine, but it took practice to be able to speak in front of people; she has been reading the material with me and seems to be more comfortable now reading it to me, and makes less errors in the pronunciation of words.
>
> Robin's father came to see her mice and seemed quite pleased.
>
> Robin does a great deal of standing at the office door while medications are prepared and on occasion has overheard communications about the boys' behavior, or communications about the girls, or workers' conversation on the phone, or comments by a doctor or social worker. Many times she will not stand directly in front of the door, but will stand at the side so that she cannot be seen.
>
> She still corrects other children and also wants to help, as when Missy [an aphasic child] is very unhappy with me about eating her breakfast, or when I have told her that she cannot have something she wants right away (as when she was very unhappy about her glasses breaking and she wanted different ones). Robin pulled her close and patted her on

the back and told her that it would be all right to listen. Robin seems to be quite maternal with Missy; she is quite sensitive to Missy's feelings and is quite protective when others are mad with Missy.

Robin has been writing a play, a take-off on Cinderella, only it is "Sourbella." She said that the group worker was going to produce it for her if she got it into shape.

Robin has talked a little more about trouble with her spelling, and about the awkwardness of using a dictionary when she can't even sound out the beginning of a word. I thought this was very good because it has been so hard for her to discuss this limitation with me.

✚   These notes helped me to see in how many ways Robin was now making use of the residence. Her anger and fear of Topeka as a city was not interfering with her freedom to respond to the Children's Hospital in her own way. She was a different girl in action from the girl seen in the evaluation.

Some teachers commented on problems of integration: Robin had trouble with combinations and sequences. They noted that she made good use of familiar, established patterns, but could not grasp new elements easily. Other teachers noted that when taking in new information she could not hold it while looking at another part—she got along better if she could master one thing at a time. They also noted that she had difficulty in getting similarities and differences, and in relation to this, in generalizing or grasping abstractions. She could not identify elements in complex stimuli, could not identify separate fingers or count on her fingers. One teacher felt that her perception was "fuzzy." He also commented on the weakness of her grip, although he did not connect this with her chorea.

✚   In therapy she often could not see connections between related thoughts, and I had to demonstrate the connections.

Her problem in combining extended to visual-motor coordination; she had difficulty in copying. By contrast, her attention could be concentrated; when she focused on something she "grappled with it, put everything into it."

Her concept formation, they said, was variable; she could learn some things better than others. She had special difficulty in immediate, high-level problem solving, especially in meeting any new situation. The teachers also commented that she had such a good capacity to talk to people (using what she knew) that you could expect too much by assuming that her performance could match her understanding.

✛ This, of course, is exactly what Robin had told me she feared, in an early therapy session.

We also discussed the relation between her physiological functioning (as with colds and menstruation) and her cognitive variability. Frustration, physical disease, or anxiety undermined her ego-functioning; her frustration tolerance was low and anxiety about being rejected was always close to the surface.

✛ There was an enormous contrast between her drive to participate and to master both cognitive and social challenges on the one hand, and her capacity to integrate responses to complex situations, as the neuropsychologist predicted. This great gap exposed her to severity of frustration far beyond what other children experience, and her neurological damage interacting with any physiological distress decreased her tolerance for such frustration. We were all growing in our understanding of the effects of Robin's damage on many aspects of her functioning.

Arbor Day: Anxiety about Achievement and Coping with Tension

It was Arbor Day. I had been invited and went over at three o'clock. (Robin's hour with me had been rescheduled for after the ceremony.)

I had heard reports of how earnestly Robin had worked on her speech; she memorized it and also practiced reading it. Her speech was the first item on the program following a brief introduction by the master of ceremonies. As she came to the podium she seemed to be mumbling to herself a little, but then she proceeded in a fairly smooth but constricted fashion, blocking at certain points. On the whole I was impressed by how well she managed and how smoothly she handled many big words in the speech. She was not comfortable enough to look at the audience much or to smile as she ended, or express any of the gracious amenities of which she would otherwise have been capable; and she made a little face as she went back to her place in line of those giving speeches. After the ceremony, refreshments were served, and we all stood around talking. When Robin was out of hearing, I wandered around to see what some of her teachers were thinking. Her reading teacher said that she was sorry that Robin wasn't able to be more spontaneous and that she had done it very much better during the rehearsals, but other observers thought that she had done very well.

After the refreshments, I drove Robin over to the office. On the way I complimented her and told her quite honestly that I had no idea that she was to give such an ambitious talk. I asked where she had found the material, and she told me that a couple of the older girls from Dr. Nester's group had looked up material in the library and helped her put it together. "I couldn't have done it without them." I said that I felt it was a real achievement. Robin nodded and said that she wished her grandfather could have heard it, that he makes "lots of speeches." I suggested that she could write to him and she said, "Yes, I'm going to." When I asked if she could put in the speech, she said yes, she would.

She wanted to know whether she had blushed and I said, "No, not enough to notice"—that her cheeks had been pink, but they were pink now and it was very becoming. She said, "Well, sometimes I blush so much that you couldn't help noticing it."

When we got into the office she seemed relaxed and happy. She didn't seem to want to initiate anything and evidently had difficulty shifting her focus away from the ceremony. I waited a bit, then tried to give her openings with a variety of questions, some general and some concrete. Inching my way along, I asked whether she had talked with her mother about the things we had discussed at our last session. She said no, and later she said defensively that she is in school all day from eight-thirty to five-thirty and there wasn't very much time to talk to her mother.

I asked how her plans for church during Lent worked out, and she said that she would probably be able to go and that her mother would go with her this Sunday and Easter and the Sunday after. She seemed to have a matter-of-fact, taking-it-for-granted attitude about this, as she often did after a desire had been worked out.

Partly because it tied in with the achievement of her speech today, I mentioned that there had been a team meeting yesterday and that her teacher had spoken of how pleased she was with Robin's progress in music. Her teacher had said that she was going to try to get a recording for all of us to hear. Robin somewhat sourly said, "I know," and indicated that she wasn't very happy about the idea of recording. But then she wanted to know what other people had said. I commented that in general the impression was that she has been making progress all around. Jacqueline had talked about her progress in school work. Robin wanted to know what the child-care workers said, and I commented that they had said that she was cooperative and helpful with the younger girls, rather motherly.

Robin became distinctly wistful about this, and when I asked her why, she said it made her think of Annie; I found that Annie was one of the younger girls that Robin had formerly played with in Grand Island. I said, "I think you are missing Annie," and Robin agreed in a slightly depressed tone of voice. I suggested that being helpful to Vera and Missy, girls in her residence, could be something of a substitute, and that this was an important capacity to have—life did bring us frustrations, and being able to find substitutes was an important way of managing frustrations. Robin agreed but in a slightly doleful tone of voice.

I said, "It's strange, but just when we are talking about how much progress you've made and how well you did today, you seem to feel depressed." Robin began to get a little tearful and asked for a tissue, which I found and offered to her; this time she rose from her chair and got up to get it, with more autonomy than at our last session. I said then, "I'm thinking about a remark that you dropped the other day which we didn't talk about at the time. You said something about first year high school— 'If I ever get there'—as if you felt discouraged and uncertain." Robin said, "You mean about dating?" And I agreed that that's what she was talking about.

Robin then shifted the topic abruptly and commented that tomorrow would be April Fool's Day and she would like to play a trick on her art teacher. She decided that if she had some string she could tie up her paint brushes so that when she reached for one, the whole group would come out at once. I said I had some string—there were different kinds, some of it was straight and some of it was all tangled up. She picked a fine, smooth, gray piece of string which was neatly rolled up. I took a very messy, tangled bunch of string and said, "I'll untangle this string." She asked for a pencil and paper so that she could draw her idea about the April Fool's joke. I started unraveling the knotted-up string. When she got through with her drawing she showed it to me, with some apologies, and I agreed that that probably would work and said it was a nice sort of April Fool's trick because it wouldn't hurt anybody.

Robin reverted to talking about the speech and commented that she had bitten her fingernails again; she also mentioned one or two other bits of behavior that she disapproved of. I commented that that was what she did when she was anxious and tense, that those were tension-relieving mechanisms. She said that when her brother Jim was little he had bitten her once—"That was his tension-release mechanism." She said another thing she did was to tear up her tissue; "I always have some with me when I am in a scary spot, like giving the speech." I said, "Well, tearing up a tissue doesn't hurt anybody either." Robin laughed and said, "Wouldn't it be funny if the tissue turned around and bit me?" I laughed with her and said, "Robin, you're wonderful. With a sense of humor like that, you'll get through life all right." She was interested in this idea and picked it up and gave another instance of her own humor and that of other people who got through tight situations.

Robin made some reference to vacation plans, the fact that Eve would be away for six weeks and the family thought they might all take a vacation in June while Eve was away. I commented that she would then have nearly three months' vacation from therapy. I suggested that perhaps while Eve was away she would have more opportunities to talk things over with her mother, but Robin seemed doubtful about this.

In the context of the limitations on talking things over with her mother, I said, "Robin there are some more things that I want you to know that we didn't finish talking about on Tuesday." I then explained to her the problems involved when a boy and girl embrace and get excited—in the summer for instance, if a girl has on a thin little bikini and a boy has on shorts. If he gets an erection and has an ejaculation so the sperm gets out, if it got onto the girl's vagina, she could get pregnant in this way without having had intercourse. Robin seemed to understand this, although she did not tie it up with the possible experiences of the four girls who had gotten pregnant recently in Grand Island.

Robin looked at the clock saying, "My, this hour has gone fast, hasn't it?" I went to the door with her, and when we looked for the car it was not there. While we waited I stayed with her to reinforce the role of support and protection in the context of the things Robin had been concerned with. I said I thought it was important for her mother to know about what we had discussed and to know of the need for her not to be left alone with Jim. Robin said, "I did tell her that." She added a moment later that she did not think Jim would agree with her, but she didn't want to elaborate when I asked what she meant.

✛   Although Robin was relaxed, and not resistant, she could not easily shift her focus from the anxiety-laden experience. She had to talk about it, ask whether other people could see the evidence of it during her speech (her blush). She was anxious about her anxiety and how evidence of it might affect others' opinions of her. The persistence of this anxiety may be another reflection of her organic problem, occurring even when her relationship with me in that hour was excellent. It revealed her persistent insecurity about how she would be seen and whether she would be ridiculed again. This preoccupation affected the pace of the therapeutic effort; it was necessary for me to be guided by her pace. She had to discuss the external aspects of the experience (her blushing, biting her fingernails). At the same time, her previous anxiety about Jim and sex dangers, or excitement, had abated. But she did seem to be anxious about the long vacation ahead when she would have near-ly three months separation from therapy, as if she were putting the anxiety into a future reality-situation.

Learning to Choose Manageable Experiences

I had a note from Robin's social worker that things had been difficult over the weekend. Eve was attending a high school prom with a high school friend and their dates, and Saturday was busy with the preparations. Robin's mother had said that Robin had brought her bureau drawers down to the living room to empty out and put in order and that in general she seemed out of sorts. The impression was that she had messed things up and the family had been unhappy with her.

I thought on reading this note that I might discuss with Robin the problems that arose when she was in the center of the stage herself as compared with those that occurred when somebody else was in the center of the stage, to see whether it would be possible to help her to accept her feelings of rivalry and acknowledge the need for taking turns. However, I did not get very far with this. She was in a casual mood, not really very much interested in the therapy hour.

I asked how she felt about the Arbor Day ceremony. She said she had liked it in a way and in others ways had not liked it. She had not written to her grandfather yet but still intended to. She said rather abruptly, "I'm shy." I commented that she felt two ways about it, on the one hand being shy was hard, and on the other hand it was exciting to have an important role in something like that. She did not disagree. I asked whether she thought she was the only shy person there, and she seemed to admit that some others were shy but still felt that she had a harder time than the others.

She giggled and shifted the conversation to her "cactus hobby," talking about her different kinds of cactus and their needs for special care. She had learned how to take care of them from her Aunt Alice, who was "not a real aunt but an aunt by marriage." While talking about the cacti, her attitude was rather impish and rambunctious, and I commented on this, asking how we had started talking about cacti anyway. Robin said, "Because I wanted to switch the topic."

I said, "I guess you really don't feel like doing therapy today; there have been so many exciting things recently and more exciting things coming this weekend with Libby [her friend] coming up from Grand Island." Robin agreed but then said that she had been naughty over the weekend.

She had been mean to people, and she had been mad at her orthodontist because he had apparently hurt her a good deal in addition to tongue exercises, and so forth. Her feeling was that her "naughtiness" was mostly in reaction to this discomfort.

I gave an example of how I had been irritable and "naughty" in a rather cross encounter with a service station man. She seemed amused but not willing to talk about ways of handling irritable feelings. She said that what she usually tried to do is go off to her room "and get away from it all."

She did not seem to want to talk about that either, but when I asked whether it had been hard to be a thirteen-year-old with older sisters excited about parties she began an important series of remarks: "I don't like big parties anyway; I've tried to go to them; I can't get adjusted to them; I feel strange, like a cactus." I added, "and soft like the mice, intelligent like the poodles, and rambunctious like the horses." She laughed in hearty, amused, and pleased agreement with each of these suggestions; then I said, "Well, what about this feeling strange?" She said that she felt strange with the girls here because none of them shared her interests and she didn't share their interests. She didn't like the dances that were the current rage; she didn't like the records that everybody else liked. She felt out of it.

I commented that being interested in taking care of growing things and enjoying animals and horses did not seem unusual to me, and I wondered what really made her feel so strange. She said that just wanting one or a few friends and not being able to enjoy parties ("I just don't like big groups!") was part of it because the rest of her family was sociable. I agreed that this was hard, then suggested that in many families there were some people in the family who were sociable and liked big groups and others who didn't, and that one could make one's choice as to the kind of social life one would like to have.

There was a distinct note of defiance as Robin reiterated that she "really didn't like big groups, really didn't like big parties," and I explained that some people got stimulated in a happy way by big groups but others of us felt overstimulated and did not like such big groups. Robin's reaction to this was simply to reiterate again almost defiantly that she really couldn't stand big groups. She could not shift to the discussion of choices.

✛   Through all this she was serious and intent, in contrast to the giggly, impish quality of some of her earlier conversation. I tried to suggest again that it was each person's right to try out different kinds of experiences and then choose the most satisfying kind. I felt that with her difficulties in orientation to complex situations it was important to help her feel free to choose. This option was hard for her to accept because of her sense of obligation to participate in peer group social activities.

As we went out at the end of the hour, I paused because her bus to return her to the residence had not come. Just then, my secretary, who had taken the afternoon off to go to a party at the country club, called and said she had had a lovely time. When I asked how many people had been there, she said, "Oh, two or three hundred." I replied, "Well, you can have it, no parties of two or three hundred for me." I turned back to Robin and said that my secretary, Mrs. Jones, was a very social person and really liked parties of two or three hundred. Robin said, "Not for me," and I agreed with her, trying to give her the realization that others felt as she did.

Anticipating Pleasures Away from School

Today Robin described the family's vacation plans. Her parents would take her and Jim on a trip during the last week of June and the first week of July. They would drive through Arizona to see the Grand Canyon, go on through the desert to Los Angeles, then up to the redwoods and back through Colorado. I observed that she liked to be very clear about everything ahead of time, and that the trip was six weeks off—did it seem near? Robin said, "No, it didn't seem too soon." We talked about the fact that Eve would be away for some time in the summer at the French summer session. Ann would be going to summer school.

I asked how her music was going. Robin said, "I want an autoharp—but I don't know how I could get it without taking eighty dollars out of my education fund, and my father wouldn't like that." I asked why she had to take it out of the education fund. Robin said, "Well, everything goes into that—the fifty dollars that father gave me when he 'sold the horses behind my back'—went into the education fund."

I commented, "You are still angry about that," and Robin agreed forcefully, "Yes, I am." I asked what other possibilities there might be and whether Aunt Samantha might like to give her an autoharp. Robin said she was paying for all this (the day hospital and therapy), "and I don't like to ask her for anything else." I commented that her aunt enjoyed giving her other things—clothes, presents, and so forth—why not let her aunt give her an autoharp when it meant so much to her? Robin seemed to agree with this idea and began thinking about ways of communicating her wish: "I might put a note in my Mother's Day gift." I asked what the gift was, and she said a driftwood piece she was making was for Aunt Samantha. I commented that that was "something that you went to a lot of trouble to do yourself—that's the kind of present mothers and grand-mothers like best." Robin said firmly, "I know that." I protested a little, "But why put the note about the autoharp in with that gift? Why not just let her enjoy the gift for a while first?"

Robin seemed to agree again and ruminated about other possibilities: a friend next door to Aunt Samantha had an autoharp; maybe she could borrow it and play it for her aunt. I supported this and said, "I don't know whether your therapist should be in cahoots this way," and we both laughed. Robin said, "I enjoy it." I continued, "I'm doing it because I think an autoharp is a wonderful idea. People need something to do by themselves. You can play things that you learn, and you can also experi-ment and have fun with an autoharp."

Robin continued trying to think up ways of getting the idea across to her aunt; she was very expressive and sometimes communicated with sub-tle teasing, inviting, and hopeful facial expressions. Sometimes I imitated her faces, and we laughed a great deal. There was a little lull, and I pondered aloud after a while, "Twice in the last two weeks you ended the hour with a story about accidents, and I wonder what is going on." Robin said, "Smokescreening again." I replied, "But where there is smoke there is probably fire." Robin replied, "So?" I went on: "What is it all about?" Robin said, "You can figure that out. . . . It's too bad you are not a mind reader." I replied, "Well, I'm not a mind reader, I'm just a poky old lady who doesn't always catch on very fast." Robin replied, "You are not old," and then went on with some teasing remarks. I said, "Sometimes you like to tease and be mean in harmless ways." Robin giggled. She then said, "I see my bus," and I responded, "Right through the venetian blind?"—she said as she left, "I've had lots of practice."

The next therapy hour Robin was in the doldrums, not contributing much, occasionally teasing; she looked more childlike, with a childish hairdo. I commented that she didn't seem to feel like working today, and she agreed. But then she began to talk about the things on her mind that had to be taken care of in connection with vacation: she thought her poodle, Charlie, was pregnant. If the pregnancy came from a brown neighborhood dog who is "too big for her," her babies would be too big for her to deliver. Her mother promised that they would get the vet to help. We spent a little time discussing what "help" meant. She had trou-ble with the word "abortion," slowly struggling to get it out and finally saying that she did not like the idea but her mother had said that Charlie might have to have one. I wondered whether she had ever heard of abor-tions in people. She said she had not. I wondered whether Charlie knew she was going to have a baby and would be upset by an abortion. Robin thought she would be upset and firmly believed that Charlie knew that she was going to have a baby. Robin suggested that they might let the baby grow and the vet would help her then. I asked if she knew how the vet would help her with the delivery, and she did not know, so I suggested that there were two ways: the vet might give her a little anesthetic, as a doctor sometimes does with a woman who is having a baby, and then reach in for the baby with forceps so the mother doesn't have to struggle with it so much; or the doctor could do a Caesarian, make an incision and take the baby out that way. Robin nodded, agreeing that that was probably what would be done. All of this seemed to be an extension of her concerns all winter about reproduction.

Robin was also worried about what she would do about her mice while she was away. I said that it sounded as if the dogs and the mice were just like children—she enjoyed them very much and had a great deal of fun and satisfaction from them, but they were also a great responsibility. Robin agreed soberly and said that was one reason why she wanted them—so that she would get used to taking responsibility.

I commented that she seemed to have vacation very much on her mind, and she said, a bit sarcastically, "Obviously." I commented, "How sarcastic can you be?" She protested that she wasn't really being sarcastic. She said that when she got back from the trip she ought to "go to summer school." I commented that it sounded as if she didn't want to and, again, she said, "That's obvious." She clarified that she liked to sleep late in the summer, and she couldn't do that if she went to summer school. I said it was quite a conflict—she wanted to have fun during vacation and sleep and at the same time felt that she ought to go to summer school. She agreed with this. I wondered how much she would be able to accomplish if she went to summer school feeling the way she did—would it really be worthwhile? I added that if she could unravel the things that made her mess up words and spelling so much she might be able to make much more rapid progress in her schoolwork.

Anger Affecting Spelling

She was listening with interest now, and I added, "Sometimes you mess up words as if you are making mud pies." Robin picked this up and recounted a time when Ann was making mud pies, and Eve broke them up. I said, "That was even better, the way you mess up words is like breaking up mud pies." I went on to say, "I wonder why you got so angry at them." Robin said defensively, "Well, the mistakes I make are consistent." I said, "Some of them made a lot of sense"; for instance, the time she spelled "class" g-a-l-s-s during a time when she was feeling negative toward boys. It could be that her mind unconsciously did other things like that. But sometimes the mistakes she made did not make that much sense. She turned the words inside out and upside down, put the end letters at the beginning and the beginning letters at the end, and so on. Robin laughed and said, "Well, one word I have trouble with is 'first.'"

I said that was very interesting indeed. What was there about "first" that bothered her? Would she have liked to be first in the family? Robin thought about this and then decided that she didn't really want to be first in the family like Ann. "What I'd like would be to be who I am, but get rid of the troubles." I agreed that that was good and natural and that was what most of us wanted.

+ I felt restless and dissatisfied with the use that we were making of the hour; Robin was ambivalent and uninvolved for the first part of the hour. I felt unsure about how deeply committed she was to working on learning problems. This was apparently so obvious to her that she was concerned about my discomfort to the point where she wanted to get to work on therapy in order to help her therapist! And her comment on the question as to whether she wanted to be first reflected her self-esteem and insight.

Interactions of Fear and Anger

At the next therapy hour, she commented that there would be a break of two days around Memorial Day before the new part of the school session started, and she did not know exactly what would happen after that. I recalled that recently she had said that she had started school too early and had had a bad time. I wondered why it had been hard. Robin said that her birthday was in the middle of November so she had been younger than most children starting kindergarten; all the other children had been ahead of her. A pair of twin boys she had liked very much could do everything and had not wanted to play with her.

I agreed that this must have been terribly disappointing and frustrating. I wondered whether it could have something to do with her feeling so mixed up about the word "first," which she had trouble spelling. She made a face with her "here we go again," ambivalent smile, but then said that she thought it was quite possible. I wondered what else had gone on in first grade, and she said she couldn't remember much until she was in Miss Trenton's room. I thought I remembered that Miss Trenton was a teacher that she liked. Robin said, "Well, all the teachers were friends of the family and that made it harder." I acknowledged that it must have been difficult if she didn't like a teacher to feel that the family expected her to like them all.

She then remembered a big storm: "The wind blew out the window, and the glass broke and fell all around." I commented that she must have been terrified. I wondered whether she could have been working on spelling at the time that happened, so that somehow the broken glass and the fright and broken words got jumbled together. Robin was interested in this and agreed that it might be possible. She said that she had been terribly afraid of storms ever since then, and of thunder and lightning. Whenever a storm came up, she went to Eve's room; she used to go to her parents' room and sleep on a cot. I asked what else she did, and she said she would squeeze her pillow very hard. I agreed that it was a good idea to get hold of some good feelings to chase away frightening feelings.

She reminisced some more about broken glass and cuts and related accidents. Once a boy had run into her with his bike, and the fender was sticking out and had cut her on the thigh so that she had bled badly. She had been about a block and a half away from home, and a friend of hers, Kenneth, had taken her home. It hurt for some time. I commented that this incident might have something to do with her mixed feelings about boys: it must have felt good to have Kenneth stay with her and help her to get home and to have the feeling that you could count on boys; at the same time, this happened in a setting of pain, and it was a boy who ran into her and caused it. She agreed, saying she had thought of that too. Then she ruminated aloud about how she did feel close to boys—how much she would miss Kevin because he was going away in a couple of weeks—and how she felt she really couldn't get along without boys. I commented that, at the same time, she felt that they were dangerous, perhaps even more at this stage, and Robin agreed.

She also commented, "I've never broken any bones," and mentioned Eve who was now out of the cast. We talked about Eve's hurt knee and the fact that Eve would not be able to do sports for some time, if ever, because "her knee goes out." I commented that accidents seemed to be "par for the course" these days. We talked about how quickly bones healed up, and Robin remarked that if a person's head got hurt it healed more slowly. Robin said she thought she had had more than her share of accidents, and I reminded her that she had already told me about being thrown by a horse.

I commented on all these memories of accidents and storms and broken glass and cuts of different kinds from glass and from metal, coming in connection with her thoughts about what had made school hard for her in the beginning and her difficulties with spelling. I said it looked as if the troubles with spelling were all mixed up with frightened feelings and not just angry feelings. Robin agreed. I added that maybe the angry feelings came because she was angry at being frightened.

By now, it was about the end of the hour and, although she had not seemed to see the bus, she got up to go. As she went out the door, I said, "You've remembered some very important things," and Robin demurred, "I'm not quite sure they are all just right." Then I protested, "Well, they had to come from somewhere." She nodded.

✝   Although Robin had reported significant relevant memories, it seemed that she did not want to pursue the implications of her interacting fear and anger. She was not openly resistant, she just did not get very involved. With vacation coming, and the changes it would involve, it might have been that she wanted to avoid stirring up too many feelings at once.

Feelings of Loss and Unfinished Mourning

At about twenty minutes before three on the day of our next therapy hour there had been a tornado warning—a tornado had been sighted northwest of Topeka. A secretary phoned that Robin would not be able to come until the tornado alert was over. She arrived around twenty minutes after three. I asked her whether she had been bothered by the tornado, and she denied it at first. I commented that it was an odd coincidence that we had had this tornado warning today when just last week we had been talking about storms and frightening things that happened in connection with storms. She looked rather limp.

Robin put some books and a big folded sheet of paper down on the table, and I commented that she seemed to be depressed. After a little more denying, she said that she was discouraged. She had done badly in multiplication today. We discussed the fact that she could do addition pretty well but multiplication and division were very hard. I then said that it might be that feelings get in the way of multiplication and division too. Last week she had talked about feelings that get in the way of spelling and perhaps feelings were getting in the way of multiplication. Robin said, "That could be."

She began to talk rapidly about the weekend and soon she was crying and sobbing so hard it was difficult for her to get the words out. Her family had gone up to Ames where her grandmother had lived, but Robin couldn't bear going. I asked whether it was just this time last year that her grandmother had died, and Robin said yes. She talked about how close she had felt to her grandmother and how her mother had not been the same since her grandmother had died.

I commented that it could have been especially hard for her mother because the grandmother had become sick when Robin's mother was about six years old and had been hospitalized, so that Robin's mother had had to live with her Aunt Samantha. I suggested that Robin's mother must have had many feelings about this; she might have been frightened and angry that her mother had left her when she was such a little girl. Then when the grandmother had gotten out of the hospital after Robin's mother had grown up, Robin's mother may have needed to be closer to her because she had not had enough mothering when she was little—usually if a girl had had enough mothering when she was little, she grew up and had children of her own and was able to bear it when her own mother died, but if she had not had enough mothering from her own mother it was harder when her mother died because of all these feelings. Robin nodded through her tears and said, "I think I understand."

I commented that it was natural for her to be sad and to mourn for her grandmother, but I thought that perhaps she was extra sad because of her mother's sadness. At one point, Robin made a slip, saying "mother," and then corrected herself, saying, "I mean *I*." I commented that sometimes she felt as if she and her mother were one, and that was just what I meant about feeling even more overwhelmed because she was feeling her mother's grief as well as her own. Robin nodded.

I asked whether there were things she wished she had done for her grandmother. Robin said that she could have done more for her grandmother, still crying. I said, "Well, last year you were twelve, and twelve is a hard year." Robin asked, "What do you mean?" I said, "At twelve, girls are growing fast, their bodies are changing; they don't know just where they are at, or how to manage, and often they are pretty preoccupied with themselves. That's natural too." Robin nodded.

She said, "When I think about Grandmother dying last year, it makes me think that maybe Aunt Samantha will die and mother will die." I agreed that when one person dies it does make us fearful that other people who are close to us will die. Then I said that all of these things were probably harder because she had recently lost one child-care worker, Michael, and now another, Kevin, was going next week. I commented also that when she feels so overwhelmed by a loss the multiplication of losses becomes even more overwhelming, and she nodded.

Robin said that nobody would ever be like Michael. I agreed that it was probably hard to believe that anybody would ever be as enjoyable as Michael, but there could be another child-care worker who would be satisfying to know. Robin was still crying and said that now that Kevin was going there was nothing worth staying in school for. I asked whether things were really as bad as that, and she said that she did not get along with the other child-care workers—they would say one thing and then do the opposite. I kept pressing gently, step-by-step, and finally she said, "Last Friday one of the workers had said they would try to stay in the living room more when I was there, after I said something about being lonely, and then two of them went into Lisa's room and stayed for about half an hour. When I went to the door to see if they would be coming out soon, they gave me a black look, as if to say, 'You don't belong here.'" Robin said that she felt left out.

I commented that she felt left in many ways—Michael had left her, Kevin was about to leave her, last year her grandmother had left her. She felt left out at camp last summer. Gradually, Robin's tears began to ebb. She kept wiping her eyes and nose, which were now very red, but gradually stopped crying.

I said that when she felt so overwhelmed with her feelings of loss and being left, it was hard for her to remember any of the good times. What would she be doing this weekend? She said she would be going to Grand Island. I asked whether she would be seeing Libby or any of the other girls. She said she didn't know. I commented that she seemed to be feeling so terribly lonely.

I asked what she did when she felt like that. She said that all she wants to do is go to Grand Island, go to her mother and father's room, and close the door. I asked her what she did; she said, "Talk to someone," and I asked, "Who?" She said, "Who do you think?" She was speaking very, very softly and with her head hanging. I said, "Do you talk to God?" She nodded, and I asked, "Do you feel better then?" She said, "A little." The hour was more than up, and I suggested that we would need to talk about this some more. Robin wiped her eyes some more and went out.

✝   Robin seemed so overwhelmed by the realistic losses she was feeling that I did not think it was appropriate to do more than empathize with her feelings at this time. I did not think she was ready to connect external losses with her bodily losses.

Coping with Feelings of Loss

At the next therapy hour Robin came in wearing a turquoise and sage green checked dress that I had not seen before. She said that it was not new, and I commented on its Tyrolean design with lacings up the front. From time to time during the hour she fiddled with these, sometimes tightening them and tying them up. Perhaps this hinted at an effort to control feelings that had overwhelmed her the previous hour.

I asked whether she had been able to talk to her mother since our last session on Tuesday and, in a rather off-hand and slightly defensive way, she said, "Well, sort of—she knows how I feel." A bit later, she said that she had talked to her mother last night "a little bit sharply." I asked why she had spoken sharply, and Robin said that she didn't want to go on the overnight this coming Saturday and her mother wanted her to go. The family was planning to go to Ames to settle some business problems. Her step-grandfather wanted to auction the house that had belonged jointly to the grandmother and to him, and to other members of the family, and then buy it back. Other relatives who owned part of the house felt that if it were auctioned it would be sold for very little and the step-grandfather would end up owning it all and the rest of the family would get gypped. I commented that the rest of the family must be rather angry at him, and Robin agreed. I added that these angry feelings must make all the other feelings more difficult for her. She agreed.

At one point, she said rather forcefully, "I won't go up to the attic." I asked what scared her about the attic, and gradually she explained that her grandmother had fallen from the attic window. I asked how she had happened to fall, and Robin said it had been an accident. I commented that we had been talking about accidents for some time. She agreed in a somewhat withdrawn way.

I asked whether she had felt overwhelmed after our hour on Tuesday. She said, "Well, I was irritated." I suggested that she might feel angry that therapy opened up so many feelings, but I explained that it was important to get at feelings and try to understand them so they wouldn't make things worse for her. Robin agreed again, grudgingly. I said that I had the impression that today her feelings were different from those of Tuesday—today she had the sense that all her own feelings about Michael and Kevin and her grandmother were enough for her to handle without trying to handle her mother's feelings about losing her own mother. Robin agreed.

Robin also remarked that she had been stubborn. I said that being stubborn could be very good at certain times and not so good at other times.

This time, her "stubbornness" came up in order to fight her feelings of being helpless. Robin was a little skeptical about this (although she had commented that when she lost one person it made her think about all the other possible losses, and that thought made her wonder how she would be able to manage or get along if she lost all the people who mattered to her). She switched to other topics of conversation, avoiding further discussion of loss.

She was supposed to put something in the student newspaper. What should it be? What news was there? I asked her if she had seen "Peanuts" today and described Snoopy, the dog. Robin was a little amused. From that, her thoughts turned to the Topeka zoo and the new giraffe. We talked about the giraffe, how it had behaved, the fact that it wasn't really grown up yet, and so on. Robin commented that she didn't like the way they were developing the zoo, the cages were too small and cramped. In Tulsa, they. had large areas where the animals could walk around. It was more spacious. Also, for the polar bear, they arranged to have snow to make him feel at home. We agreed that it seemed too bad to build a new zoo in such an old-fashioned, crampy way. Robin spelled out how the small space would mean that the animals wouldn't live as long; they wouldn't be able to reproduce and they wouldn't be as healthy.

I asked whether she couldn't say something about this in the newspaper—get children involved and see if she couldn't start a crusade to provide better quarters for the animals. Robin was intrigued by this idea and said, "It'll be my turn to do an editorial soon, and I could do that for an editorial." I agreed that that would be a good idea.

✚   While Robin had not completely come to terms with her feelings about her grandmother's death and all it involved, her coping effort was constructive—directed toward helping animals to live longer—as if to turn her passive feelings of being overwhelmed into worthwhile action.

Letting Go of Feelings of Loss

The next week Robin came in with a new hairdo and a white bow on her head, which she said her mother had arranged. She was carrying some books and a package; she very carefully unwrapped the packing from around a little Japanese lacquered coffee cup and saucer, black with a gold edge and a subtle design of muted green something like the color of her skirt. I said the cup and saucer were beautiful and asked her to tell me about them. She explained that her mother had told her step-grandfather that she would very much like to have these, and he was willing to let her have them. It was the only thing he was willing to part with.

I commented that it was nice to have something to remember her grandmother by; it looked as if the trip had gone all right. Robin agreed with some reservation and said, "It was all right except for lunch." They had gone to lunch at a special restaurant where her grandmother had taken her in the past, and they had met the lawyer there who was going to help them with the arrangements. Robin said that her eyes had begun to water, and she had had to excuse herself and leave. I suggested that it was quite natural for feelings to well up at a time like that, and Robin said yes, but that it had been hard to understand because she had been able to go to Ames and to the house—and even go to the cemetery— without crying. I said perhaps it had been the combination of several things at the restaurant, including her memories of being there with her grandmother, which brought the tears, and even if the tears had been embarrassing it seemed that she had been courageous about the weekend. I felt it was important for her to have been able to go to Ames. I explained that when we avoided something like this, it could hang over us, and we could have a bad time with it afterward, but now she must feel good to have been able to do it. Robin said she really had needed to go through with it, and she obviously felt relaxed and satisfied on the whole.

Since she had some books with her, I asked how her schoolwork had gone during this period with so many stormy feelings. Robin said, "Fine," then contradicted herself and said, "I'll show you how I have been goofing up my math." She opened up her math book to the page where she was working on subtraction and division. She worked through the first example: 24 minus 8 is 16; 16 minus 8 is 8; 8 minus 8 is 0. Then she was supposed to divide 24 by 8, and she had a hard time with this. After she struggled with it for a little while, I commented that she had taken away 8 three times, and I reviewed it for her: 24 minus 8 was once, then 16 minus 8 was removing the second 8, and 8 minus 8 was removing the third 8, so that taking away 8 three times from 24 would mean that 24 divided by 8 was 3. At first, she said she "didn't catch," but when I went over it again she said, "Oh," with an expression of insight, and she seemed to get the idea. But then when she tried to go on with the next example, she again found it difficult.

Shifting to an Area of Success and Plans for Vacation

She shut her book, and I picked up the other one she had brought, which was a story about one hundred Dalmatians. She said she had seen a TV show based on the book and explained the story to me. I asked whether she found it comfortable to read a book at this level, and she said yes, started to read the first page, and then pointed out differences between the way the story was told in the book and the way she saw it on television. The ideas were complex, and I was impressed by her clear grasp of them.

Soon she returned to the vacation and the plans for after vacation. Robin said that her cousin Sara might come from San Francisco and stay a month. Robin didn't know whether she really wanted to go to summer school. "I know I should try to catch up, but I just don't want to go to summer school." She emphasized again the fact that she liked to sleep late and the rest of the year never had a chance to sleep as late as she wanted to. She would like to sleep until noon. She was really a "night owl."

I asked whether she had talked this over with people at school, suggesting that some compromise might be reached that would give her a chance to sleep late and do what she wanted to do on certain days while coming to school other days. She said she had not talked it over with anyone yet, then said that it might be all right if she came to school three mornings a week and had the other mornings to do as she liked. Somehow, she seemed a little belligerent about this, and I said, "Well I'm not here to fight with you." Then I added as she raised her eyebrows, "Or maybe you really would like to have a fight. Well, that isn't quite in the books but then we don't always stick to the books do we?" Robin said, "Oh no, I don't like to stick to book rules."

I objected, saying that it seemed that she had a rather good balance of liking to be well-organized and well-bred but also liking to be independent. As she listened to this she was a little arch, in a smiling way, as if she were enjoying a mild controversy. It was about the end of the hour, and I heard her bus.

✝ I had the feeling that she was both comfortable about having "made it" by getting to Ames over the weekend and at the same time a little worn down by the burden of conflicts around her step-grandfather's behavior—even while she felt a contented gratification in having the exquisite little cup and saucer as a memento, as if the gift were some compensation for the loss.

The complexity of all her feelings about her grandmother's death, her step-grandfather's behavior, and her own participation in the visit to the scene suggests that some anticipation of all of this lay behind her mild withdrawal and noninvolvement in recent hours.

7

Therapy Continues

More on Feelings and Learning

Robin came into my office carrying a large music case and some books. She opened the case and showed me her autoharp—labeled "guitaro." She had a book with directions for chords for various songs and showed me how she played "Blue Tail Fly." I exclaimed that it would be fun to try it, and she put the autoharp in my lap; I played the chords and sang a verse of "Blue Tail Fly." I asked how she had managed to get it, and she said it was second-hand and cost fifty dollars—much less than she expected to pay for an autoharp. I commented, "So you did manage to get it."

She then wanted to work on schoolwork, and asked whether she could sort out her papers in my office. I agreed, adding that some other things (feelings) could be sorted out too. We sorted all her papers for the year, dividing them into piles—math, spelling, social studies, reading, and so forth—and we organized each pile according to dates. I commented that in some subjects, the papers showed great improvement from the beginning of the year to the end. Then I went through the spelling papers carefully and talked about some words that were misspelled. For instance, she had spelled "storm" *s-t-o-m-o-n-d*. I commented that she must have had stormy feelings about "storm," and she agreed. I asked whether she remembered how she had spelled "girls" and reminded her that at one time she had spelled "girls" *g-a-l-s-s*-; I suggested that perhaps she really felt that girls were as delicate as glass. She agreed again and said, "I guess I do." She had spelled "sister" *s-i-e-t-e-r*, or something like that, and when I picked this up she said, "I guess I was mad at her that day." Often she seemed all too accepting of possible connections between feelings and spelling. But at times she had excuses. For instance, she had written a sort of poem about spring, and I wondered why that would be done in a messy way since it seemed to be expressing such nice feelings. She said that she had written it out-of-doors on a walk.

From this, I asked whether she had recently been riding her bicycle since this was a word that appeared in the poem, and she said that she did ride it from the residence to school and back. I asked whether she got along all right with it, because she had told me before about some bicycle accidents. She said she had not had any accidents lately, but "I don't trust it." When I tried to explore this, she did not want to pursue the matter.

She also had *One Hundred Dalmatians* with her. She had read perhaps one-third of it. I asked at what level Jacqueline, her teacher, placed this book. She said it was a sixth-grade book. (This reflected two years' progress in eight months.)

Robin said that Jerry, a teacher for the summer session, had talked to her this morning about going to a half-hour reading class in the summer. Robin said, "I know I should." I commented, "But you still have some conflict about it—you do and you don't want to do it." She agreed and then said, "Well, I should do it." I agreed and said that reading was important in other subjects, like history and social studies, and if she could bring her reading level up she would be able to do other subjects at that same grade level. Robin said, "I like history and social studies"; then she added, "We had history in Grand Island but we never got past the Civil War." She repeated, "We never got past the Civil War." I said, "Well, there are different kinds of 'civil wars'—in the house, for instance." Robin looked at me with an "Oh, there you go" laugh; she was not rejecting, however. I added that I thought she had made a good deal of progress in getting past the "civil war" this year.

Robin said, "Well, I *am* going to the reading class, so that's that." I said, "You are resigned to doing it because it will help you to do some other things." I added "Lots of us have to do certain things because they are important to other things we want very much to accomplish." Robin agreed to this too.

While she was sorting out her papers, she complained that she had trouble organizing things. I said "Well, that's funny, you like to look attractive and well-dressed, and you like to have nice manners; keeping things organized is something of the same kind of thing." Robin disagreed and said, "It is completely different," and then added "I come from a long line of family who are not organized." I laughed and said "Here, you have the bad luck to have a therapist who isn't too well organized." Robin laughed hard, and I asked, "But do you have to imitate the things in your family that make trouble for you?" Robin ignored this and went on tidying her papers. She commented, as she was almost finished, "This is a funny way to spend a therapy hour," although she had not been unaware that I was using this process for therapy purposes. I said, "Well, we have been sorting out more than just papers—sorting feelings is important too."

When the piles were sorted out, she wanted to have a table of contents for her folder. She wrote "Table of Contents" correctly. She also wrote "Math" and "Reading" correctly, but on "Social Studies" she put an "l" directly after the "i" and made the same mistake in three more attempts. Finally she was able to stick in the "a" between the "i" and "l" and then continue. She made no more mistakes.

I commented that we needed to understand how she could do things so accurately at times and be so inaccurate at other times. She said, "I can do it when I feel like it."

I paused, then said, "You know, several times you have said things about feeling that you are spoiled. I wonder whether this isn't one of those things." She was interested and asked "What do you mean?" I said, "Well, you say that if you feel like doing it correctly, you do it, and if you don't feel like doing it correctly, you don't do it. Meanwhile, messing things up interferes with things that are very important for you to do." Robin agreed. It was the end of the hour.

Working on Anger in Therapy

Robin came in looking rather ambivalent; she was disheveled and had a few scratches on her hands. First, she talked about the weekend and how she had played with and fed a calf. Soon she said grumpily that she didn't like her schedule for the summer; she was going to be tied up the whole day; and she wouldn't be able to do a single thing that she wanted to do. As she talked she got angrier. When I commented on how angry she felt, she got angrier still. I asked whether she had discussed this with anyone, and she said no—except for Jerry. I said he had told me his plans for trying to give her special help with writing and reading in summer school.

I commented that she was so angry because she had had her own ideas about what she wanted to do for the summer and then this plan had been dropped like a bombshell. I suggested that it was quite possible that if the plan were discussed with Dr. Moore some changes could be made. Robin insisted that this was not true. "They have their clutches on me, and they won't let go." I replied that she felt that they were absolutely rigid and hopeless and there was no chance they would be the least flexible. Robin said that was exactly the way she felt. She continued to be extremely angry, but I noticed that her facial expression loosened up and became freer, and she became extremely attractive.

I commented that she looked very pretty when she got angry, and that she had once said that Eve did also. She said, "It runs in the family. Almost everybody in our family is like that." I suggested that apparently letting the angry feelings out freed her up and that a good deal of the time she must be working hard to keep feelings in. She didn't say anything, and I harked back to the schedule and suggested she talk to Dr. Moore about it. She said that wouldn't do any good, and I protested that she had told me that she could talk to Dr. Moore as easily as she could talk to me. Robin said, "The only reason I am talking to you now is that. . . ." I interrupted and said, "If you didn't, you would explode." Robin laughed and agreed. From here on, there was an exchange of banter and, at times, Robin laughed freely, alternating with angry expressions, but she did not give an inch on the questions of talking to Dr. Moore.

Instead, Robin shifted, saying she had written a book report that her family had liked. I asked whether it was on the book she was reading recently. I complained, "Sometimes my mind lets me down; I can't think of the name of that book." Robin enjoyed this and, step-by-step, helped me out by giving me hints until finally I remembered it. I said that if she could write her reports at the level of her conversation, they would usually be good. Robin said that they are good "when I am careful."

I wondered why it was that she didn't feel like being careful sometimes. Perhaps she wasn't in the mood, but why was it that sometimes she was in the mood and sometimes she wasn't? Robin said that she could write better reports when she was angry or tired. I said this was very interesting and important, and it would be wonderful if we could find out how to get to that point without having to get angry to do it. Robin didn't pay much attention to this remark.

Turning to the schedule, she said that right now she had an appointment at three o'clock on Tuesdays and Thursdays. I said, "Then really you are angry at me." She denied this but actually became much more relaxed. I asked, "Would you like to stop therapy now for the rest of the time before you go on vacation?" She said firmly, "No." It turned out that her mother had gone to Lawrence and left Robin on the way and would be picking her up on the way back. I commented that if she had told me that she didn't have school today and that it was inconvenient to come, I would have been glad to work it out with her.

I then said I would get in touch with Dr. Moore, and I hoped that she and Dr. Moore could talk things over. Robin still was grumpy and said she wasn't sure that she would talk to her. However, she had softened up somewhat.

She was often vivid and humorous in between bouts of angry feelings and resistance to the talk with Dr. Moore. When she was most angry about the summer schedule, she insisted rather obsessively, "I'm going to do it; I know that I should; I only have two more years to get caught up with my group." I commented that she felt she had to and that it was not just that she was being made to. But she still insisted that the program had been imposed. When I commented that it was a shock to have it dumped on her so suddenly, she said she felt like tearing up the whole place. I commented again that it had dropped like a bombshell and that she probably felt like bombing in retaliation.

✝   She accepted these remarks as reflecting the way she really did feel. At no time during the hour did she verbally express any change in her appraisal of the matter, although she did increasingly have warm and humorous moments.

Preparing for the End of the Year of Therapy

At our next therapy hour Robin did not seem to be ready to offer anything, so I commented that I had been thinking about the difficulty I had had in remembering the word "Dalmatian." It occurred to me that this word sounded something like "damnation," and that when she was angry in the last therapy hour, perhaps I was feeling angry with her and felt like saying "damnation," but I knew she would not like me to say it so I was shutting it out and, along with it, I shut out "Dalmatian." Robin was intrigued with this and agreed with the tentative tone of approach—that it was interesting to see how our minds work. She was reminded of a time recently when she had bumped or scratched herself going through a door at home and felt like saying "damn." She was shyly hesitant as she admitted this and stumbled a little; I said something like "I guess we all have feelings like that whether we say the word or not."

Robin agreed but said nothing more. I commented that she would be leaving on vacation in two weeks, so two weeks from today would be our last day in therapy for a while. She acknowledged this, somewhat hesitantly, as if she were ready to fend off something she didn't want to hear. I continued, "This is one reason why I was hoping you would talk to Dr.

Moore—there will be two months without therapy, so it will be extra important to be able to communicate with her." Robin agreed a little doubtfully, and I asked whether she had talked to her. Robin nodded yes but made a face, retracting the right side of her lip in a slightly disparaging way. I commented that she didn't seem to feel very satisfied with the discussion, and she said, "Dr. Moore really didn't know anything about it all—she thought that I would be through about noon." I suggested that perhaps Dr. Moore would be finding out more about it, and Robin grudgingly expressed some doubt. I said I thought she seemed to be feeling disappointed. She didn't respond at first, then said that she felt sleepy. She yawned and talked about how she had not been able to get to sleep until about two o'clock last night because it was always hard to get to sleep as early in the summer as in the winter. Finally, she said, "Kevin left yesterday." I said, "Finally, you tell me—after twenty minutes. No wonder you are feeling sad."

Another Feeling about Boys

We talked for some time about what Kevin meant to her. She said he was like a combination of Joe and John, boys she had known in Grand Island. John was rambunctious, and Joe was shy and liked animals—Kevin was all of these. She sounded so tender in talking about them and in saying that she would like to meet somebody who was a combination of all three of them that I said, "I think perhaps you love Kevin." Hiding her head in the back of the chair, she protested, "Don't be silly." I said, "I don't know what the exact word is, but it seems to me you're fond of him—you're attached to him." She said, "Yes, I am attached." I replied, "Well, I didn't say you were *in love* with him, just that it seemed to me that you have a deep feeling about him and feel close to him and are fond of him." She did not disagree.

A few moments later, she began to brighten up. She wanted to know about the book I was writing. I told her it was a longitudinal study in which children were studied as babies and then at different ages after that. I was working on vulnerabilities, the different kinds of difficulties that different children had; and on stress, the different hard things that have happened to them; and on resilience, the strengths they developed in conquering their difficulties. I said it was interesting to see how personalities of people were shaped by the way in which they mastered their difficulties. For example, Teddy Roosevelt who had not been strong as a

child but who worked hard at getting enough exercise to become a very
rugged person. Then I gave examples of other famous people with
difficulties.

Robin was very alert and interested in this and, after I had given several examples, she said, "I have an uncle who was one of the Rough Riders
and Uncle Wayne has a book about them. He lets me read it in his house
but he won't let anybody take it out of the house." From this, she shifted
to talking about relatives in the Spanish War and the Civil War. Then,
from relatives, she began to talk about Sadie, the nanny who took care of
her when she was little. Robin added that Aunt Samantha had told her
that when she (Robin) was five months old, she wouldn't have a bottle but
insisted on having her milk in a cup.

I commented that babies have much stronger feelings than people
know about, and they can do more than people realize they can do. This
reminded her of a child she knew, a two-year-old who wanted to be
played with much more than the grownups realized. I asked whether she
remembered how she had played, and she talked about the toys that she
had kept, particularly a tiger that she still kept in her bed. "Then, if
anybody comes to the door, I throw it at them." I laughed, saying that
would not hurt anybody, and she said, "No, but it could scare them. And
if I don't have one of these animals, I have a pillow." She would throw
the pillow if she were surprised by anybody coming into the room.

✝   Robin's associations to my comments about coping with vulnerabilities ran to different examples of strength, Rough Riders, for one, and
her own insistence as an infant on drinking from a cup. This evidence
of early vigor had not been mentioned in the evaluation, but it seemed
to fit with the picture of an active girl with a mind of her own.

Sharing Appreciation and Anxieties about Nature

On the evening before my next hour with Robin, a big tornado had hit
Topeka and caused widespread devastation. It had passed within a few
blocks of the area where Robin lived so I had phoned to find out whether
the family was safe and their home intact. Robin had been casual and
cheerful on the phone. She said, "Oh yes," they were fine, their house had
not been touched. They had watched the tornado out the window of the
basement, and it was fun to watch. She had seen a rainbow after the
tornado.

Now in the therapy hour she said that a friend of Eve's, Jean, was missing; nobody knew where she was. Her faintly defensive smirk, followed by a grimace, seemed to convey her feeling that it served the girl right. I said Jean's family must be worried, and Robin relaxed into a more natural expression and agreed. Robin then said that her own family had offered their house to shelter four or five people, but no one had come. She asked whether I knew which people here had been left homeless, and I said one of the teachers at a day care center had lost her home. A little later in the hour, Robin said she had heard that some of the workers at the Children's Division had lost their homes and then added, "Wouldn't it be funny if they were assigned to our house?" I commented that that would be a coincidence.

Then I recalled that we had had a difficult hour recently, and I thought perhaps part of the trouble was that, in addition to the absence of her teachers during the vacation, it had been hard for her to feel that after next week I would also be gone for the whole summer. This made it especially hard to sort out her feelings about the child-care workers being away. Robin said, "Well, my period started on Tuesday, and I wasn't feeling good." She elaborated by saying that before her period started, she sometimes didn't feel like eating, and she hadn't eaten much breakfast or lunch. I said that lots of girls felt more "irritable" when they menstruated, and that it was harder to cope with frustrations and difficult feelings then. I asked just how she felt before menstruation, and she said, "Well, I had cramps a little later, and I have cramps now, but not just at that time." I commented that maybe her body was beginning to have a different feel, and perhaps it was a little uncomfortable, even though it was not like real cramps, and she agreed.

I asked whether she had called Dr. Moore yesterday, and she said yes. I said I was glad, and thought it was important for her to be able to talk to Dr. Moore when confusions came up at the residence. She still seemed hesitant to do this spontaneously, so I emphasized that it would be an important step ahead to be able to do it. I asked her then whether she had met Dr. Edmunds, and reminded her that once or twice she had come in while Dr. Edmunds was in the waiting room. She checked: "She's a little bit heavy and friendly and smiley?" I agreed that she was, and Robin said she felt that she would be able to talk to Dr. Edmunds and was glad that she was going to be taking Dr. Osborn's place.

✛ Although Robin did not say that this made her feel better about the months ahead, I think it supported the more relaxed mood of the rest of the hour.

I asked what she would be doing at home, and with some eagerness she said she hoped she would be able to help pack "the camper" for their trip. I asked what else she would see besides Disneyland and Grand Canyon. She said she wasn't sure, then protested about the dreadful things that were going to be done to Grand Canyon, filling it up and spoiling it.

By chance I had some photographs of Grand Canyon which I had taken years earlier and showed them to her. She pointed to ledges and some of the fine rock structure and said, "Just think how many thousands of years it took nature to carve out these beautiful things, and now some men want to destroy them." Then very wistfully she said, "What will there be for our grandchildren—what will we be able to give our grandchildren?" I agreed that it was dreadful to think of this great and wonderful place being spoiled, but I felt that the public protests had a good chance of changing the plan for using Grand Canyon for industrial purposes. Robin said that if she knew where to write she would like to write a letter herself. I suggested *Nature* magazine.

As we looked at some of the mountains and trails, I talked about the fact that my husband and I used to be able to do a lot of climbing, but we didn't have the strength to do so much any more. I said that we were finding solutions to these problems—I called them "geriatric tricks." Robin smiled at this, and I explained that now that I could no longer climb Mount Washington in a day, I found that I could go half way up in a bus and then climb the rest of the way. Robin made a somewhat disparaging face, and I said, "Yes, but it did mean that we could have the fun of getting up on top and seeing the view," and Robin accepted this.

✚   I offered examples of finding substitutes for activities that were beyond me in order to build a concept of ways of coping with frustration.

Then she began to talk about other aspects of nature. She said "conditions are changing; the ice cap is melting, and there will be too much water in the ocean, and it will cover the lowlands on the shores of some countries. Our climate is being changed because of the fumes from so many automobiles. Besides, every year we are getting a little bit closer to the sun." She thought that perhaps in three years the earth and the sun might fuse; God was going to make something happen again. Then she continued, saying that in the Bible God had made the promise that He would never again cover the earth with water but that He might destroy it with fire.

I said I remembered the promise of the rainbow, but I didn't remember the fire part, and I asked her where it was. Then she began to talk about volcanoes and lava and how lava is very good fertilizer. I commented that was something like the way that feelings fertilize relationships between people.

Robin was interested and began to think about the tornado again. She wondered where the tornado came from. I suggested that it was from the conflict between winds from different directions. She said she thought it was from the conflict between the hot winds from the south and the cold winds from the north, which met and then started to push each other and whirl, and this made the tornado. I added, "Perhaps this is something like the way feelings between people can clash and make something like a tornado." Robin laughed, "Oh, oh!" I commented, "You were surprised that I would say that," and she agreed. I added, "There are many things in the universe that are something like the way things work inside us, and it is interesting to think of possible connections."

On this congenial and intimate note we terminated the hour. She went out to the waiting room and saw a box of cookies. Without asking permission, she helped herself to a number of the cookies. I commented that somehow now she felt much more like eating than she had earlier today, and she agreed.

✝ This was a friendly, sharing hour, probably influenced by her good feeling about Dr. Edmunds, which reflected an awareness that a new relationship could fill the gap left by the loss of an old relationship.

Coming to Terms with Our Separation over the Summer

On the day of our next therapy hour Robin's family was to leave at four o'clock on a trip to Kansas City, so she was restless, her mind very much on the trip. I used this to review her health during the past year, and noted how uncomfortable she had been during the fall with frequent extreme stuffiness and restlessness. We also talked about the work on her teeth and the fact that she was gradually getting a lighter schedule of visits to the dentist as well as fewer visits to the allergy doctor. She agreed that she felt better and was in better health now than in the fall, although there were some allergies that still bothered her and the bindings on her teeth were a nuisance—they caught slivers of food and prevented her enjoyment of caramels, which she liked very much.

I asked about the weekend, and she reported that she'd had a good time in Grand Island. She was astonished that Jim had treated her so well, and gave examples of his courtesy in opening doors for her, along with a great decrease in teasing. She enjoyed Jim more than before. I asked whether she thought that he was growing up or that this was a result of his thera-py, and she said that she didn't know, but it was awfully nice.

She then volunteered that she didn't know whether they would ever go back to Grand Island to live. Her father would have to stay in Topeka longer than he had planned originally. I asked what thoughts she had about where they might go, and she said she didn't know whether they would stay in Kansas. I commented that if they were in Kansas or within a hundred miles in any direction, she would still be able to get back to Grand Island to visit. I asked how she had gotten this impression—wheth-er by eavesdropping or by putting two and two together or by a "sixth sense"—and she said, "Mostly, the last." I asked what else her sixth sense was telling her, and she said, "Well, nothing more yet."

I said I thought she had been dodging getting to the point in talking about my being away for two months. She had talked about how she felt about losing Kevin and Michael and other losses. We had been seeing each other a couple of times a week for a long time now, and it would be natural to find it hard to have this interruption. Robin looked at me with agreement in her soft and tender expression and she gave a little smile as if she were pleased to have me understand this but didn't feel that there was much more to say about it. I asked if she had reached the point now where she could talk to Dr. Moore and Dr. Edmunds if trouble came up. After a little thinking, she said she would be able to do so. I commented firmly, "Good, I'm glad for that." At a later point, she remarked, without connecting it with this discussion, that she found it very hard to read people's handwriting, and I said this was hard for many of us. I added that if she wrote to me, I would answer it with a typewritten letter that would not be hard to read. She seemed to think this over and accept it.

She talked about school and how much she enjoyed having more time to herself last week. She said that she and Dr. Moore had not made any definite plans about how much time she would spend at school after her trip, but she hoped that she would have a good deal of free time. She also hoped that when her cousin Wendy came to Grand Island, Wendy would be able to visit her in Topeka, and Robin wanted a week off to visit with her—that would leave only a couple of weeks in July for school, and that wasn't much. She knew she needed to catch up and do some schoolwork this summer, but she did love to have free time and to be able to sleep late.

I commented, "Well, you have a real conflict there." She wanted to know what I meant, and I said, "Well, you want two things—you do want to catch up in your work, and you do want to have free time so you can sleep late and have fun." She agreed and seemed to grasp what "conflict" meant.

We then talked a little more about the school problem. She said, "I know that if I'm going to be able to get a job and finance myself, I've got to learn spelling and arithmetic and get more education." I repeated that reading was extremely important in order to be able to study other subjects too. She said that she could read some adult books around home. I agreed that this was good, and added, "I expect you think I'm a stubborn old therapist to hang onto this point so much." Robin again gave me her warm and tender smile and said that she herself wanted to make more progress on schoolwork. She still thought that she would most like to be a veterinarian or a veterinarian's helper. It was about four o'clock and, as we went out, she spied her mother's car through the venetian blinds and dashed out to join her.

✝   As Robin's preoccupation with losses faded and she could look forward to new relationships, her willingness to work during the summer increased, even though she still wanted free time. After the ambivalence of earlier weeks, it was impressive to see her commitment to make progress in her education.

Problems and Compensations

At the last therapy hour for the year with Robin, she herself set the tone by bringing two major things she wanted to share with me. First, there was a beach coat she was making of terry cloth—white with a blue collar and large navy blue buttons to match her navy blue bathing suit. She showed me the material and the preliminary stitching which had been done. After this, she brought out the script for the play which she and the other children were putting on that summer. I looked at the beach coat carefully, impressed by the work that was done on it, and asked whether she would be using it in California. She said she didn't know; she might use it there or might just use it here when going to the pool.

She spent some time telling me about vicissitudes with their car. The clutch had broken down, and the motor company was so swamped with problems arising from the tornado that they couldn't promise when it would be done. Their trip might be delayed two days and, if this happened, they would have to cut out their visits to the Carlsbad Caverns and the Painted Desert. They might also have to cut out their visit to the Grand Canyon. I empathized with her feeling of disappointment at the possibility that they might not be able to see those beautiful places, adding that I knew it must be frustrating and must have something to do with the restlessness she was feeling right now.

She was fingering the bands on her teeth, and I asked whether her mouth was hurting. She said that just a few hours earlier the dentist had put the wires on her braces, and she wasn't used to them yet; they were uncomfortable. I commented that this was one more discomfort, and we had talked about how hard it was to have a number of uncomfortable things happen all at once.

After this recognition of her discomfort, she brought out the script for her play, wanting me to read it, and she showed me her part. The script was about a witch who wanted to turn into a good fairy and did not want to be a witch anymore. It was humorous and light and childlike. I commented on the nice theme of turning bad things into good things. I also said it looked as if she did have some things to look forward to. She said that Wendy would be coming to stay with her in Topeka, and she would be able to have the time with her that she wanted.

I noticed that she had an area of scraped skin on her right ankle on the side facing me and that it looked a little inflamed and had a rather large area of black and blue bruise above it. I commented on this and said that the exposed area might be a little infected. I also commented on the bruise. She said, "I bruise easily," and I agreed that she bruised easily both on the outside and on the inside. She insisted that she knew what to do; she would put on some salve, and that would heal it. I commented that she felt she could take care of herself, and she agreed quietly but not enthusiastically.

It was the end of the hour; I suggested that her mother might be waiting, and we went out to have a look. Her Aunt Samantha was there, and Robin commented on this eagerly. Since her bundle containing the beach coat was awkward and the paper bag had torn, I brought a piece of string to tie it up. Robin at first demurred, saying that she could manage all right, then comfortably accepted my tying it up for her.

As she went out, however, she had trouble opening the door; it does stick, with a rather stubborn latch. I was at the door and said, "I'll open it for you and let you out." Robin said, "I do want to go," and I did not challenge her. She ran off quickly to the car to greet her aunt.

✛   The tone of the hour was low key. There was the theme of disappointment about the delay of the trip and losses that this would involve, but there were also very positive feelings—I thought almost eager feelings—about the play they were working on. Her involvement in the play seemed to be great enough to create some conflict about going away. That is, there was a shift in balance of investment: the interference with some of the interesting experiences she was expecting to have on the trip decreased the commitment to that, while her apparently unexpected interest in the play increased the satisfaction of staying here and thus left her more ambivalent about leaving than she had been before. She evidently took for granted that we would see each other in the fall and did not express anxiety about separation from therapy for the summer.

8

Reflections on Robin's First Year of Treatment

Robin and Her Family

At the time of the initial evaluation we did not know much about Robin's world before she came to Topeka, nor did we know how she felt about the move. During her treatment, Robin shed some light on these areas, and the social worker provided additional information.

Robin's family had two houses, one in Topeka and one in Grand Island near their ranch. Robin cherished the Grand Island home and farm and mourned her separation from them with endless criticisms of Topeka, especially by describing it as a dangerous city. Her family was accustomed to upper middle-class standards of achievement. In Robin's case, their demand for behavior appropriate to her age seemed to overlook her realistic problems. Robin identified with her family's expectation of good marks in school and proper behavior, and she soon began to use the Children's Hospital and therapy experiences to try to meet the family's standards.

All members of the family were active, and reactive; according to Robin's reports, most of them blew up at times. This energetic family was characterized by both great anger potential and also warmth, along with strong loyalty and a shared sense of rightness about ordinary aspects of living.

Many of Robin's references to her mother seemed to imply that for long periods she was exhausted and had little to give beyond carrying out the most essential chores for a family with four children. At the same time, both parents and Robin had a capacity to keep trying, to clarify goals, and to mobilize energy to try to realize their ideals of family life. Like the family, Robin's outstanding patterns included, on the positive side, a capacity to sustain diligent effort and, on the negative side (although there are important adaptive aspects here), outbursts of angry protest or retreat to sleep.

Robin felt that she never had the rapport with or tuning-in from her mother which she craved. The intensity of her feeling implies not only that her siblings received this but that she herself received it from someone, probably her grandmother.

She had a vivid sense of heritage from strong forebears, and seemed to use this to provide a balancing sense of inner strength deeper than the surface deficits. The unassailable assurance of strong family origins seemed to support her determination to be recognized in positive terms as, first, a girl and, second, a person with positive abilities, rights, clear views to be respected, and valuable ideas about how the school and therapist could help her.

As background for the parents' difficulty in coping with Robin's deficits from infancy, there was a three-generation history of troubles as well as of individuals of marked strength. Robin's mother's mother was hospitalized when Robin's mother was six, and her father died before she was in her teens. After the hospitalization of her mother, Robin's mother had been cared for in her aunt's home; in effect, she was an only child and, like Robin, she had temper tantrums. Her uncle was seldom home, so she accepted her own husband's preoccupation with work and absence from home as typical of men. Robin's father had suffered traumas in World War II and was both hyperalert to danger and threatened by aggressive impulses which he handled by rigid control. He had also had periods of insomnia. Robin empathized with her father's wartime suffering so much that she seemed to be frightened by the fact that a new doctor was a German refugee.

I knew from our Topeka longitudinal study, on children's ways of coping with everyday problems (see page xvii), that family life in the Middle West often has a richer texture and broader reach than the family life typical of larger cities. Instead of the isolation documented in studies of metropolitan families, the nuclear family in Topeka was typically part of and one with what in India is called the "big joint family"—a network of grandparents, uncles, aunts, and cousins. Some children said that family reunions and visits were the happiest times of the year. Robin's family was like many middle-western families in their devotion to, and satisfaction in, a wide circle of relatives. With many of them, Robin felt comfortably secure.

The range of Robin's experience was characteristic of middle-western culture: vacations spent together by the whole family, visiting relatives, or exploring the scenic pleasures of the Western mountains, canyons, and caves or of California, and excursions for hunting or fishing. Many families had strong feelings of attachment to the land through life on, or visits to, a family farm. All this was part of Robin's life and contributed to her strength.

Typical also in Kansas was corporal punishment—spanking with the hand, paddle, switch, or belt. Such punishment was used in schools and widely accepted by children, some of whom remarked, "They want to bring us up right." The pattern of punishment in Robin's family was similar, but Robin was not abused. In most of our longitudinal research group, chores such as taking out trash, mowing the lawn, helping with dishwashing and drying, and household cleaning, as well as care of one's own room were handled by the children. Robin enjoyed helping to cook meals. The majority of our study group families were church members, attending church on Sundays and other functions during the week. In this respect, Robin's family was different—church attendance was irregular, partly because of weekend visits to their ranch.

On the whole, Robin's family was typical of families in this subculture, and she did not feel that her family was different. Small town and farm life in Nebraska had provided many satisfying experiences, freedom of movement, and opportunities for exploration and discovery. These had been enriching and to some extent balanced the emotional and social deprivations and the frustrations related to her damage.

As I Saw Robin after Nine Months of Therapy

Along with Robin's cognitive and motor control problems due to neurological damage, a psychosomatic direction of influence interacted with an earlier somatopsychic direction and with stresses of puberty. By the age of twelve to thirteen, Robin was experiencing cumulative physical discomfort from orthodontia, upper respiratory infections, allergic congestions, and ease of bruising—along with great autonomic variability, depression, and a negative view of the world and herself. As a child, Robin's explosions probably had occurred whenever a combination of stresses from frustration, fatigue, and overstimulation led to overwhelming tension, a combination likely to occur on trips and visits. Understandably, her mother had left her at home with the nanny and her busy father so that family visits with relatives would not be ruined for everybody. The child, also understandably, had resented being left by her mother.

As she grew older, Robin retreated—to the basement, to her room, or to sleep. She tried to manage her feelings without disturbing the family, but she could not communicate with them in a way that contributed to mutual understanding. Sleeping late may well have made it possible for her to keep going. When she felt misunderstood or felt that she was being seen in terms of her handicap or problems alone while her positive human qualities and interests were ignored, she could be as stubborn as she was cooperative when she felt accepted as a whole person, a girl growing up.

Despite the depths of her recurrent misery, at times Robin could be gay, tender, and loving; and she was staunchly loyal to her family. The sense of membership in her large extended family, with its wide range of strengths and weaknesses, gave her support and hope deeper than the discouragement that darkened her heart at times. Probably both Robin and her family were confused by her swings between good, conforming, and ladylike behavior at one extreme to the angry explosions at the other.

Robin's Coping Problems

In addition to her own organic problems, Robin had to cope with the reactions of others—family and relatives, peers, visitors, strangers, and the hospital psychiatric, caretaking, educational, and housekeeping staff— with all their varying degrees of perceptiveness, congeniality, and appreciation of human differences, handicaps, resources. We saw the pressure to conform, to act "normal," to be like other girls her age although she did not have the adaptive resources other girls had. She felt the ridicule of peers who thought she was strange and the irritation and frustration felt by others who could not understand her slowness, apparent rigidity, "stubbornness." She also sensed the appreciation of a few relatives who had watched her struggle from early childhood.

We saw too the variety of coping strategies and defense mechanisms, which helped her to tolerate the inescapable pressures—retreat, covering up, balking, fighting, along with maximizing the noncompetitive activities she enjoyed. And when all defense failed, we saw her physical, emotional, mental shakiness—the tremors, fluid inscrutable facial expressions, confusions of thought communication. Despite damage affecting 83 percent of the psychoneurological functions tested, Robin was very much alive and never gave up. She astonished her teachers by her amazing determination to master discouraging learning tasks, and, when they appreciated her efforts, she could be "a delightful girl."

Pressures: The Stress of Change

It was only slowly that we came to see what the move from Grand Island to Topeka meant to Robin. For the family as a whole, it was a shift to a community with more resources for everyone as well as a chance to better meet Robin's needs. But she loved the country—its beauty, the freedom it offered her, her relatives there, and the farm animals, especially her big horse. In Grand Island she felt that "everyone knows me" and "it's safe," while Topeka—the "big city"—was "dangerous." Probably no one realized what a strain the move continued to be. Leaving home and the world of home for a new city is stressful to many children. And so it was for Robin.

Before coming to Topeka, Robin had been at ease in certain one-to-one relationships—for example, with her friend Molly, her cousin Kitty and other relatives, and one teacher, Miss Trenton, who had helped her. From earliest childhood, she had found groups stressful—partly, in peer groups, because she could not process the complex combinations of motor, cognitive, and social patterns involved in children's games rapidly enough to keep up; partly because, in any complex social situation, she could not orient to its complexities or integrate and organize levels and sequences of response rapidly enough to feel comfortable and to act. Only in structured situations where the need for such new organization was limited, and where she could learn to follow predictable patterns, was she at ease.

Her adjustment was made more difficult because equivalents of former supports were lacking. In Grand Island, the family lived on a street not far from shopping, movies, and other town resources; Robin was fairly independent on her visits there. In Topeka, the family lived on the far outskirts of town so that Robin was totally dependent on being taken to the shopping center, to church or to the movies. In Grand Island, the pace of living was relaxed, and Robin did not feel so embarrassed by her slowness in counting out change as in Topeka where she felt impatient eyes of the clerk upon her. In Grand Island there were the supportive and loving Aunt Samantha and Uncle Wayne and devoted nanny, along with familiar acquaintances of all ages—younger children with whom Robin had played, old ladies with whom she had talked. In Topeka, there was hardly anyone nearby for companionship. Robin felt lonely, lost, fearful—and so she hated Topeka.

It is not unusual for children to find the loss of roots stressful. Much has been written about "separation anxiety" when the infant loses the mother, but the loss of the child's own world can also be threatening. Nor does it help when people in the new setting are turned off by the child's talk of the beloved past.

Self-Image, Narcissism, and Spontaneity

In the evaluation of Robin at twelve, the psychiatrist reported that Robin "presented herself as damaged and handicapped"; she was considered a "poor therapeutic risk." But in therapy she very early betrayed her insight, and she worked energetically in school. This contrast reflects one of her struggles. In her absolute either-or way, she was trapped in the dilemma: "Am I hopelessly inadequate, unattractive, and unmendable?" or "Am I potentially competent and successful?" This concern was seen at both extremes—in her "hangdog expression" reflecting a sense of defeat and hopelessness, and in her demand for perfection, for As, for success in school which would prove her capacity for ultimate success.

Her persistent and intense effort invested in school work was noticed by all her teachers. But she seldom expressed any sense of triumph at school achievement; she was depressed by failures without experiencing comparable exhilaration at success.

Robin's record included reports of angry screams when she was frustrated, but her crying in therapy was never like that. Although tears were near the surface, she only sobbed at those times when she touched bottom. Perhaps to balance her despair, she dissociated herself from the girls who had severe emotional and mental disturbances that she did not have ("psychotic," "schizophrenic," and so forth). It was as if she had to establish a firm structure within which she could maintain her own integrity as impaired but different from the emotionally sick ones. Her feelings were generally *reactions* to realistic stress; Robin's face could be transiently rigid or subtly expressive of a wide range of delicately shaded affects.

In the evaluation Robin's "hangdog" expression and apparent self-image as a damaged girl actually masked a healthy and basically hopeful wish to be attractive, just as the anxiety about appearance of many pubertal girls reflects the wish to be a pretty teen-ager along with the doubts about whether they can make it. The merest hint of my appreciation of

her pretty, soft blonde hair released a typical early adolescent preoccupation with hairdos and clothes. Along with such typical experiments, Robin
used her appearance as a communication from time to time: she could
dress like a "little girl" or, wearing her older sister's clothes easily, seem
older than she was. Such variations paralleled her widely discrepant levels
of functioning—she worked in math at the level of the "little children"
while in certain scientific areas and in vocabulary she was ahead of her
age level.

Robin's narcissism, then, was both a source of strength in motivating
self-care and self-management, and a weakness in masking or hiding a
balanced picture of her positive resources and her areas of organic
difficulty.

In contrast to her tenseness when she felt threatened, Robin was relaxed
when she was happy. With her pets, Robin was both responsible and utterly spontaneous. She washed not only her own pets but the other dogs
the family owned. She described their habits with pleasure and, when, in
the early weeks of therapy, she brought a couple of puppies to my office,
her skillful, gay, and spontaneous handling of them was a communication:
here I am completely happy and at ease. Thus, she was actually saying,
"Recognize the kind of person I really am—the joyous, relaxed lover of
animals—and I will be able to grow up." Other children in therapy had
said to me in effect, "If you will give me what I need, I can grow up" and
"If you understand that I am not really a brat inside, I can work hard in
therapy." This narcissistic demand to accept her positive self-image included the tacit demand to accept all that she had incorporated into it—
her extended family and her love of country—in short, her beloved world
with her own "constellation of dear ones" and dear things and places.
With a therapist who found strength and comfort in nature and valued
such roots, there was no pressure to wean Robin away from her attachment to "country." The hope was not to break important old ties, but to
enlarge her world, her range of ease and spontaneity. This proved
difficult.

It seemed that for Robin a prerequisite for spontaneity was a setting of
familiarity, populated by the things, people, and ways of relating that
carried a sense of "this is my world," or at a minimum, "this is my kind
of world." She could be her spontaneous self with people like Aunt Samantha, but strangers were threatening and might involve pain. Thus,
familiarity spelled safety and released spontaneity, while newness was im-
mobilizing to Robin.

Adolescent Struggles with Adults

Initially in the hospital Robin had an oddly clinging approach, sticking close to the workers. During the middle of her first year of therapy, she was frequently argumentative, for example, complaining that a busy child-care worker was unwilling to help her. She also had a tendency to push the workers or her therapist at times, as if to test whether they would hold firm or could be strong enough to cope with her and to help her. The child-care leader who was the chief object of this baiting at first was loved by Robin in time and sorely missed when she resigned to have a baby.

While Robin was able to have some clearly positive, warm relationships, she seemed to need a few people for ambivalent relationships. On the whole, she needed to keep me among the positive group and generally disavowed anger when it was suggested that unexpressed anger was blocking her thoughts during the therapy hour. Other spontaneous open relationships, quite free from ambivalence, were sustained with persons who were outgoing, warm, and had a ready sense of humor. But the adult had to reach out to her warmly or the game was lost.

In other words, within secure relationships based on the premise that "If you give me the respect I need, I can give back to you," she was capable of a wide range of expressiveness—subtle, shy, open, earnest, poignant, self-righteous, balky, wistful, generous, concerned, hopeful, confident, disappointed, loving, witty, and gay at different moments. When the warm approach was not provided by an adult she was as unresponsive as a statue, and nothing would move her.

Robin felt two ways about being pushed. She remarked on occasion, "I need a push," especially when she had a hard time getting started in a therapy hour. What she seemed to mean was, "I need a push to do what I am ready to do and want to do"; for she was adamant in her resistance to pressure to do something others thought would be good for her but which she felt unready to tackle.

Robin's awareness of her need for structure was expressed in her respect for "firm," "strong" adults whose clarity undoubtedly simplified her own adjustment and satisfied her need to know where she stood—what the demands were and how adequately she had met them. For a child whose experience in the environment had been confused by organically distorted space perception and complicated by visual-motor difficulties due to her neurological problems, the drive to achieve clarity could become paramount, and she needed the structure adults in authority could provide. She could not afford to rebel as other adolescents did.

The Stress of Menstruation

Menstruation may begin in widely different physiological and emotional contexts which, in turn, influence the way the onset of menstruation is experienced. Some girls announce to their mothers, "Mom, I've made it!" with a feeling of achievement, of delight that a landmark on the path of growing up has been reached. To others, the beginning of menstruation is a shock, a threat, a "curse"—or an embarrassment because of lack of equipment to manage it or lack of emotional or intellectual preparation.

To Robin, her early periods were "a drag" and an embarrassment because they were so irregular that she could not predict when they would occur and, from time to time, she was caught unequipped. While she was not inhibited in discussing it, it seems probable that—occurring as it did when she had not yet left a latency level of functioning in school and out of school—she was not emotionally ready. She had too many doubts about her ability to manage the many aspects of being a teen-ager—and even more doubts, as became clear later, about becoming a woman who could produce a healthy child.

All these uncertainties and tensions may have intensified the cramps she had throughout her period—pain which added to her other chronic discomforts. This pain increased the irritability accompanying lowered thresholds for autonomic reactivity and the related tissue lability (which was obvious enough to make it possible for me to suggest to Robin that a current emotional crisis was being intensified by her period when she had not mentioned it). While Robin was always ready to acknowledge her period and seemed to understand its relation to heightened emotionality, she was not able to sort out this factor for herself in the face of overwhelming feelings.

From the point of view of the work in therapy, the intensification or eruption during a menstrual period of ordinarily guarded feelings had certain productive results: it made possible the opening up of the walls which protected some of her deepest anxieties and facilitated our discussion of her feelings and their sources.

The strain of other body discomforts related to her allergies, orthodontia, occasional bruises, kidney and upper respiratory infections burdened Robin with additional tension which probably interfered with progress in relating to others. She could admit to feeling "droopy" along with feeling bad physically and could recognize difficulties and sources of stress one at a time, but often resisted admitting to more complex problems than her siblings had. She needed to support efforts toward mastery by aligning herself with the strong ones. To admit to very complex problems might imply the possibility of failure, of giving up, as the sickest ones did.

Variability

Over this year of therapy, we accumulated many observations of Robin's variability, which had been noted in the initial report by the psychologist in discussing her response to the intelligence tests and by the neurologist, who mentioned her autonomic nervous system variability. Different members of the team observed her variability from day to day in what she could remember and what she could do, even within short periods of time. This variability was primarily due to instability related to her neurological damage and the fact that physiological changes of puberty interacting with her neurological damage increased the instability. This was also increased by fatigue, illness, frustration, overstimulation in complex situations, anxiety, and the hormonal variations during her menstrual period.

When Robin was in good physical condition, felt confident about what she was doing, was gratified and happy, her level of coordination was better than her own average. Thus, teachers and child-care workers were confused by the fact that at times she could perform a certain cognitive or motor act and at other times she could not. This variability meant, of course, that Robin herself did not have the sustained confidence in what she could expect of herself that most other children have. While the variability was often caused by anxiety, it also intensified her anxiety and this disturbed her reality testing.

The team tried to help her with this by making realistic plans, keeping stress within manageable limits, and accepting her need to protect herself from overstimulation and demands she could not meet. Robin herself became aware of times when she was more vulnerable to external stimuli. Although her behavior might look like nonadaptive "withdrawal" to an outsider, she was adaptively managing her state by modifying her relation to the environment—by reducing outside stimuli and erecting a greater stimulus barrier. In doing this she was learning to handle the multiple vulnerabilities which interacted with brain damage.

With incomplete teeth and poor coordination along with incapacities in school subjects and the self-rejection related to this, it was not surprising that Robin had little or no tolerance for inadequate performance. She persistently wanted to do what she could do adequately—helping a worker get the flatware for a party, joining the group in singing carols, or monitoring a table at the Christmas fair.

Robin's problems of perceptual-motor functioning were problems of integration at a basic level, but the integrative task was much more difficult for her when any degree of anxiety, suspicion, or irritation at frustration was added to the task of integration of perception, memory, and motor expression. These affects were invariably present in test and examination situations, especially where use of her chorea hand was involved. Although severely disintegrative reactions were seen in speech and facial expression when Robin experienced acute threat (as in sudden, unexpected demands like that in the guitar episode) or anger (as she felt at returning to Topeka from Grand Island after Christmas), she could manage oral spelling tests under neutral conditions confidently and smoothly with remarkably few errors.

It is a commonplace in longitudinal studies of children that many normal children do not develop in all zones at the same time—an eighteen-month-old child may be so preoccupied with motor achievements that he is not much interested in speech, and eighth graders are often so preoccupied with new bodily energies and experiences that they are "the hardest to teach." It was not surprising, then, that a child like Robin with neurological and physiological problems would not be able to respond to opportunities and pressures to advance in every area at once. And it was not surprising that Robin gave priority to one zone—schoolwork.

Further Effects of Neurological Damage on Robin's Adaptation

The impact of neurological damage was seen in the parallel of the abruptness of Robin's emotional shifts with the abrupt shifts and discontinuities in her thinking. It was as if the currents of her cognitive and affective processes jumped at times instead of flowing smoothly—and sometimes as if the rockiest moments of her experience plunged her into rough "white waters" of unmanageable feelings.

At times, intense feelings of anger and anxiety were close together, but either feeling could disorganize her control by contributing to deterioration of her motor coordination and her capacity to grasp and evaluate a situation, to find a solution to a problem it presented, and to reach an acceptable response. This disturbance of affective-cognitive-motor functioning was not understood by most adults, who called it "resistance" and blamed her for it. Spontaneity was literally impossible in new complex situations. When she had no time or no help to prepare for a change or new experience, she resisted because of her great difficulty in coping with it. This was sensible, since the more experiences of disorganization she had the greater the likelihood of getting disorganized. If she could protect her need to orient herself and to process her observations at her own pace, she could prevent disorganization.

Her difficulties were chiefly on the adapting, output, integrating, or—as Piaget puts it—the accommodation side. Her teachers recognized her greater ease of intake, and Robin made as many opportunities for taking in as she could. The neurological damage had left an island of creativity, insight, and intuition, which contrasted with her difficulty with mathematics, and motor adjustments—including speech—in new or complex situations.

Along with the interference Robin experienced in making shifts smoothly, she also had difficulty in integration of facts and concepts—that is, in bringing together and seeing connections between thoughts, as in her efforts to understand her dreams. It was easier for her to see differences than to see similarities or connections. Life and ideas were disjointed, disconnected for her.

There were also problems normal for her developmental stage—anxieties about boys, sexual dangers, difficulties in coping with irregular and stressful menstruation, autonomic nervous instability related to the disequilibrium of puberty and reflected in shaky emotional control. Sibling rivalry and mother-hunger, exacerbated by feelings of deprivation, persisted. She needed more help with her relationships within her family. Any departure of child-care workers, teachers, or therapist evoked feelings of loss, and the anniversary of her grandmother's death brought overwhelming mourning, intensified by concurrent experiences of loss.

When she tried to manage social problems in her own way, she was considered "controlling," inflexible, or difficult. Inevitably, frustration brought irritable or angry reactions from Robin when she found criticism of her well-intentioned efforts unbearable.

While all of Robin's pressing adaptational difficulties were often hard for child-care workers and others of the staff to understand, even harder were her jumpy cognitive shifts—her difficulty in carrying on a sustained conversation or maintaining a set over even a short period of time. This was seen in her inability to accept a worker's promise to respond as soon as she was finished with a current task; she could not wait a few minutes as other children could. The abrupt jumps occurred when there was some affective interference, as in therapy when we got too close to a sensitive area.

Another expression of her neurological problem was seen in her difficulty in getting started—it was often hard for her to begin talking in therapy or to start again after a silence; I had to help with questions or suggestions. This difficulty in starting, whether in speech or action, is seen in other neurological conditions—more extremely in parkinsonism.

Thus Robin had a constant, inescapable adaptational risk—the risk of failure in any new cognitive, physical, or social task, the risk of being overwhelmed by confusion, of finding her accustomed patterns of communication, expression, or signaling to others useless. It was realistically difficult to count on herself or the world. Any new step was taken as a calculated risk. Robin lived and grew with the daily question of whether to take the risk this time. Sometimes she voted "yes," sometimes "no." But voting "no" involved a further risk: that she would be regarded as resistant, "stubborn," or as someone with a "character disorder."

Beginning to Help Robin

We have seen that a child with neurological deficits and multiple physiological vulnerabilities combined with disequilibria of a transitional developmental stage has formidable problems; these present interminable frustrations and failures that are magnified when parents and teachers do not understand the causes of her failures and the related irritability. Robin's anger and disappointment about her frustrations escalated in reaction to both the pressures applied by the adults who did not understand and the ridicule and rejection by her peers.

One of my aims in therapy was to evoke a commitment to an active effort by helping her to realize that she had strengths and choices, that she could find substitutes, could set limits to excessive demands and overstimulation, could plan ways of managing new situations, could use and get help when she needed it, could master basic educational problems and get ready for a vocation, and so forth; and that she was not alone in having a "checkerboard" of strengths and areas of difficulty. In other words, I wanted to help her see that like other people she could find ways of coping with her problems.

The child who has been ridiculed by peers, left out by adults, and defeated in school needs a positive relation with the therapist, teachers, and other members of the treatment team at all times. Any negative, distant, cold, punitive, or critical tone stirs overwhelming feelings about past rejection. Not until the child has achieved some mastery of difficulties in the outside world, a secure sense of acceptance, and a capacity to cope with everyday problems can negative responses from others be tolerated.

The first strategy with Robin, therefore, was to provide the ease of feeling understood, of being accepted without pressure to do the impossible. Along with this went support for doing what was possible in order to reach a better balance of success and failure and thus experience a realistic increase in a sense of competence, of being more like other people.

In order to get clear about what was impossible and possible, a related strategy was to follow Robin's initiative, to let her demonstrate what she could do, whether that was playing with puppies, attempting an experiment with the effects of nutrition on mice, or helping others. Equally important was watching what she could not do, whether it was a matter of difficulty in handwriting, in copying simple forms, in arithmetic, or in participating in a group of twenty children (as in the dining room or at a party), or responding quickly to new situations. Thus, maximizing what she could do and letting progress come as gradually as necessary in mastering the difficult areas could help to build her confidence.

Along with her neurological problems, Robin's multiple physical problems—including the congenitally missing teeth and the stuffy nose which interfered with clear speech and made her unattractive—added to her anxiety and the negative self-image developed out of her failures. Anxiety increased the tremor and also her difficulty in motor coordination which made her appear awkward. All this contributed to the sense of defeat, rejection, and impairment.

Another strategy, then, was to work toward an improvement in her physical condition—that is, to correct the real physical problems as quickly as possible. We assumed that if anxiety about her appearance and speech could be reduced, her awkwardness and perhaps even the tremor would be reduced. Medical help might also reduce her menstrual distress.

A third strategy was to understand the relationship of her organic problems to her social behavior in order to help her work toward better social relationships and to cope with new situations. Robin needed order and dependable schedules to minimize sudden adjustments, which she could not manage. Her constriction, distance, and appreciation of structure were part of her own efforts to cope by controlling impulses that would create predicaments she could not handle; these rigidities had led to others regarding her as "prissy." In addition, Robin had tried to counteract her own feeling of inadequacy by snobbish poses and by reminding everyone of her areas of superiority—at times she tried to play a game of one-upmanship.

Understanding was not enough. Robin, as an active girl, needed action to counteract defeat. Therefore, as a fourth strategy, we recommended that when she was sad, frustrated, or defeated, she needed to be given something to do that she *could* do.

As a fifth strategy, we tried to reduce Robin's great anxiety about going to a party. It was as if she felt it was too great a risk. Here, we tried to help her develop a more relaxed and flexible attitude toward the little school parties, to help her see that none of us can be perfect in our social skills—the sky won't fall if we can't do everything. Preparing and rehearsing before a party helped her to manage better. Child-care workers gave the practical, on-the-spot assistance that helped her internalize these orientations. Therapy alone could not have brought the growth that was supported by the collaboration of the team.

Still another strategy was related to her early sense of not having received "real love" from her family. With her temper, irritability, awkwardness, and failures, it was easy to see how hard it may have been for them to "love" her. I genuinely enjoyed this sensitive, protesting, struggling, defending, compensating, defeated but brave and appealing girl, and let her see my warm feelings for her. Her teachers also enjoyed her. I thought that if she felt loved by me she would gradually become more enjoyable at home; this did occur.

These simple beginning strategies did not include direct challenges to her defenses or frank discussion of the nature of her neurological damage or its partial cause in the contaminated immunization shot. All of that had to wait until Robin felt better about herself, had more confidence in her ability to cope with basic academic challenges and social problems at school, in the residence, and at home.

It seemed clear that we could not blame Robin, her previous teachers, or her parents for their lack of understanding or for the pressures they put on Robin, since most of the experienced hospital staff did not immediately understand the subtlety and complexity of Robin's difficulties.

Specific Steps in Treatment through the First Year

At the beginning of therapy it was not entirely clear how Robin viewed her physical and mental equipment, her situation at the age of twelve, her transition to teen-age status, or her potentialities. Hence therapy needed to provide further diagnostic data—to understand Robin's view of herself as well as to help her cope with her difficulties.

Since Robin's reaction to the evaluation focus on her problems was a discouraged, helpless emphasis on her deficits, I focused the initial treatment on her strengths, the normal aspects of her puberty problems, and an effort to help her revise her image of herself as isolated by difference. It seemed important to bring the picture into balance.

In therapy hours she described herself as stubborn and determined, a tomboy who had grown up with boys and felt at ease with them; she also said she hoped to go to college like her sister and then become a vet. She began to refer to a time "when I've conquered my weaknesses." She had a vivid image of the useful effective person she wanted to become.

In early months of therapy there was no shred of the difficult behavior which plagued the child-care workers, nor did Robin discuss the residence enough for me to get a detailed picture from her of what caused this behavior. In the residence, frustration, feeling left out, not being noticed, not having her needs met quickly triggered her anger.

It also seemed clear that she highly valued a situation or a relationship in which rapport and understanding were available. "I've been given everything except real love." Her expression "real love," as she explained it, meant understanding and "respect for me as I really am"—that is, an inner self that was more important than the defects. Later she remarked of her spelling, "I know what it should be, but my hand [the chorea] mixes it up." Here she explicitly distinguished between the inner Robin of accurate perceptions and the outer Robin with defects that interfered with performing at the level of her inner perception.

At that time, in the midst of the complexities of her behavior, of her large family, of the many problems at home and at school, I did not grasp the full significance of what she was telling me. She was in fact saying that the true inner Robin was far superior to the handicapped, retarded-in-school, awkward girl so full of problems; and that she wanted to envision her future life in terms of this inner superior Robin. Fortunately, at this point I avoided confrontations or challenges that would have undermined her positive hopes, and left the reality-testing to the future.

The "Checkerboard"

Several steps were taken to bring Robin out of her sense of isolation and into the feeling of being one person among others. One step was to convey real appreciation felt for her as a person, a maturing girl who was attractive, interesting, and lovable. She responded to shared humor and a relationship in which her richly varied emotional expressions were evoked, echoed, and responded to.

Another step was to dissolve the rigid dichotomy of damaged versus normal and help her to see that she, like others, had a pattern of strengths and weaknesses—like a checkerboard. I hoped that using my own deficits freely could help bring her back into the role of a person who was not totally different from other people, one who had problems that she could learn to manage. This process, together with my acceptance of her strengths and interests, began to release a charming, attractive girl who was concerned with the normal steps in becoming a teen-ager.

Gradually the therapy process itself came to be used consciously by both Robin and me to continue sorting out the ways in which her organic problems contributed, through interactions with stress, to her emotional and adaptive difficulties. We also attempted to understand what other factors in addition to her neurological problems contributed to her emotional difficulties and to be aware of the way that all of these factors interacted with each other.

The team saw that her rigidity in her demands on others and on herself was a way of protecting herself from the stress of unexpected changes and the threatening demands the environment was placing on her. Because of her great need for protection her defensive operations were never challenged at this stage. I assumed that in the midst of the complex multiple changes from her country home to the city, from latency to puberty, from life in a familiar neighborhood to life in a day hospital, defensive maneuvers could be regarded as inevitable parts of her positive coping efforts.

Along with her defensive efforts, Robin showed great capacity for active problem solving, and she continued to "accent the positive." With gradual success in mastery she began to be able to accept comments about what hurt her feelings or aroused her anger, the ways she handled anger that might interfere with friendships she wanted, and possible substitute solutions; and she also began to admit feelings of "not fitting" and "wild feelings" that needed an outlet.

I tried to help Robin cope with concrete life experiences, as did the child-care workers and teachers. I used various specific devices to assist effective use of the hour—for instance, Robin's difficulty in making shifts and her slow pace in moving into an hour were handled by offering connecting links, bridges, and transitions, which could support her engagement in the process. Her inhibition, affective instability, and fluid expressiveness were treated as communications to be understood, thus leading to integration instead of the destructive exchanges that often occurred in other situations. Disruption of thought was also lessened in this way.

In the transference, I also used concrete experience to help her cope with certain persistent problems such as separation anxiety and anger. For instance, her deep feelings about the many separations in her life from infancy on and the recent loss of her grandmother became available for therapy especially at times of my absence from town.

Thus, Robin's defensiveness and rigidity began to soften as her increasing mastery and security diminished her need for them, and as I tried to help her strengthen her coping efforts. The improvement in her use of undamaged areas of insight and verbal communication contributed to better integration. As she grew in her ability to recognize anxiety about new reality demands such as parties, I tried to help her reduce that anxiety by reflecting on alternative solutions: to realize that it was all right to accept the fact that very complex situations in large groups were actually hard for her and, therefore, she might choose the kinds of social situations in which she could participate; to accept the fact that planning ahead and rehearsing with herself what the demands in a new situation might be could help her feel more secure when the time came; to accept the fact that she did not have to try everything now but could try one thing at a time. These suggestions helped her to participate in social experiences and this, in turn, gradually helped her to feel more comfortable with her peers at school. This support for autonomy helped her to develop a more positive problem-solving approach, which further relieved her of the need to utilize projection (blame and criticism) and other self-defeating defensive operations. Instead, she identified with my problem-solving orientation instead of pressuring herself by rigid demands.

Because of Robin's great need for support of improved cognitive integration, I did not encourage free association and fantasy at first. Only after integration had improved was the expression of fantasy and dreams used as part of therapy work. Her ego development was constantly scrutinized in relation to the needs created by her neurological deficits. And I helped Robin to substitute ego-strengthening activities for ego-disrupting activities.

Accepting the goals of Robin's parents while at the same time helping Robin to modulate her pressure on herself to meet these goals was also important. An effort was made to help both the parents and Robin to prepare for a more mature relationship by helping one to begin to accept the other—that is, not only helping Robin to clarify her feelings about her deprivation but to grow more tolerant of and insightful about her parents' needs and stresses in relation to all of the pressures on them. This led to a period of increased mutuality and appreciation between Robin and her mother—a step in progress which was accompanied by further improvement in Robin's ego functioning.

Transference and Real Person Relationship with the Therapist

Partly because of the problems created by Robin's multiple vulnerabilities, partly because of the complexity of her family relationships, it was important to emphasize the "real person" aspect of my relationship with

Robin; she needed more than the average child needs. The "real person of
the therapist" was an anchor to reality, and the fact that I presented
myself as a person who also had a "checkerboard of weaknesses and
strengths" and who did not deny these weaknesses but shared ways of
coping with them helped Robin to deal realistically with her reality problems, instead of escaping into excessive fantasy as she had been doing in
the preceding years. This sharing process lent Robin ego strength which,
in turn, evoked her own ego strength. Sharing her school problems and
progress, and getting her cooperation in working out solutions with her
teachers which would use her strengths, was another approach. Among
other aspects of this sharing, I discussed with Robin certain interventions
with the school when she was not yet able to communicate needs and
problems directly. Occasionally, when it seemed necessary, a phone call to
teacher or child-care worker was made during the hour. My relationship
with Robin was often directed toward present here-and-now reality; I said
to her, in effect, "I will take a stand and try to help you use reality
resources more than you're now doing" (a more direct approach than I
would have used with a child who had a simpler psychogenic illness). I
also worked directly with her on certain learning problems in arithmetic
and spelling.

I also suggested explicit connections between past relationships with
parents and transference ideas and feelings; I did this more than I would
have with an average neurotic child because of the variable deficiency in
Robin's capacity to make such connections for herself.

Along with being a "real person," I referred at times to the nature, the
opportunities, and the responsibilities of therapy. This delineation of the
path helped her not to get trapped in the excessive dependence that is
often great for an impaired child—dependence on the process and the
therapist. In order to keep dependency within bounds, I emphasized the
importance of using therapy "not just to communicate better with the
therapist but with other people, too."

The treatment process was also used to foster healthy independence and
autonomy in various ways:

1. by fully appreciating experiences of success—progress in therapy,
   steps mastered, achievement in school and in social relations in her
   family;
2. by distinguishing between fantasied achievements and these real socially valuable achievements;
3. by directly assisting and recognizing cognitive growth through contributing increased understanding of her physiological functioning,
   so that the educative aspect of the treatment process became an important tool to support ways in which she could flexibly learn. This

> included acknowledging harder days when tension, physical distress, or distractions lowered her learning capacity;
> 4. by recognizing the importance of Robin's social adaptation—the gratification, increased self-esteem, and response from family and peers that could be gained by progress in adaptation to social groups;
> 5. by encouraging identification from Robin in order to wean her from excessive embeddedness in the family and to help her achieve a more realistic comfort in being herself. I used identification to help her realize that we all have to struggle with weaknesses. This was done especially when she was anxious about difficult new tasks, unfamiliar situations, or potentially disapproving attitudes from others. At such moments Robin made more use of the identification.

This identification seemed to be a major factor in Robin's being able to confront being different and to feel that this was not overwhelming or disastrous. Recognizing her variability in the context of that of others allowed Robin to experience herself in the therapeutic relationship as being lovable, loved, and adequate within her own resources.

At her early adolescence phase, with emerging sexual anxieties along with the rest of her problems, it was necessary to achieve a reduction of anxiety about formerly unmanageable deficits in order to free her energy for progress in other ways. Her rigid defenses, which served the purpose of dealing with internal conflicts, had interfered with growth. As the defenses and coping maneuvers that protected her against disorganizing stress became more adequate, she was better able to deal with internal conflict and anxiety about deficits.

Clarifying the need for modulating or relinquishing certain kinds of internal control (for example, excessive, rigid prissiness) while helping her parents to realize the need for various kinds of outside structure was a constant part of our therapeutic strategy. This clarification helped Robin to develop a more balanced view of her parents and helped her parents to become clearer about Robin's reality problems as well as her emotional needs. The double process was more necessary with a biologically impaired child whose problems were complex and sometimes obscure and who was so overwhelmed by her own difficulties that it was hard for her to realize the problems faced by the adults around her.

It is not unusual for families to be confused by the uneven performance and the unique problems of neurologically impaired children who are not cerebral palsied and do not have other visible problems. A major goal is to help the parents understand the realistic difficulties of the child so they can help instead of scolding and punishing.

Helping Robin and her parents to understand each other's needs enabled them to value each other and appreciate the patterns of strengths and weaknesses they all had. This, in turn, reduced their struggles with each other. All this included helping Robin to realize that I also had needs and limitations along with strengths and that these limitations did not diminish either Robin's or my adequacy and lovability.

Flexibility of the Process

My therapeutic work with Robin was flexible both in my own range of direct exchanges with her and in the extent of my contacts with teachers, child-care workers, group worker, and psychiatrists as well as the social worker.

During therapy hours I supported Robin's activities that were directed toward becoming an attractive teen-ager, and also encouraged her to share her frustrations and difficulties and her feelings about these. As part of my attempt to help her accept herself as one person among others who have varying portions of strengths and weaknesses, I was frank about some of my own limitations. And in order to diminish her sense of difference, I shared her interests, pleasures, and concerns when these actually overlapped with my own. This provided an experience of mutuality which I hoped would remove her sense of isolation and also facilitate more experiences of closeness and friendship outside her extended family. These responses to Robin as a person were in addition to my interpretations of emotional reactions, especially of memories of loss as these were reflected and intensified in the transference, and also to my efforts to help her to recognize the relation between physiological states and emotional ups and downs.

My role as liaison between her and various members of the team was used sometimes to supplement Robin's inadequate communications to them, sometimes to receive their illustrations of Robin's difficulties in using their help. At other times it was used to suggest procedures teachers or child-care workers might use to help Robin.

In other words, I was therapist, a member of a team helping Robin, and a friend—shifting from role to role as the need arose. I felt no conflict between using an educational, expressive, analytic, supportive, and gratifying approach at different moments, while also trying to clarify the realistic needs and limits required by a therapy situation.

Another reason for the need for flexibility was that Robin's progress varied in pace with different problem areas. Her bedraggled appearance and hangdog expression of defeat and hopelessness disappeared rapidly; with therapy, and a comfortable group, there was hope. Understanding help in school and response to her own interests evoked intense effort with resulting improvement in schoolwork; she never gave up or retreated to sleep in school as she had been doing before treatment began. Consequently she steadily made up for lost time on academic work. But the tremor, coordination problems, and difficulties in orientation and processing sensory input were not reduced. In addition to the primary neurological problems, emotional instability continued to be conspicuously greater during her menstrual periods. Equally persistent were her deep rooted needs for attention and reassurance that adults cared for her, her longing to be loved, and her recurrent sadness at loss.

During this first year of therapy, it had not been possible to make much progress on helping Robin understand the way in which anxiety exacerbated the organic problems that in themselves contributed to anxiety. We just began to look at feelings which disturbed her spelling and arithmetic. The last half of the year did bring some acknowledgment of negative feelings, in contrast to the early months when Robin was showing me what she needed, what she could do, what she wanted, what she hoped to become, and her determination to "conquer her weaknesses."

Progress through Comprehensive Treatment

At the end of eight months of comprehensive help, including individual therapy, special education, psychiatric social work with parents, support in group experiences, medical and orthodontic care, what changes did we find in Robin?

Instead of going to sleep in class, bogged down in second-grade to fourth-grade work in school she was reading sixth-grade books, actively struggling to master spelling and arithmetic, and writing more legibly. Instead of a defeated, discouraged outlook, she was hopeful. Instead of a hangdog expression and wearing torn clothes, she was carrying herself well and dressing attractively. Instead of being a chronically worrisome burden about whom her parents were extremely anxious, she was at times enjoyable, and generally helpful at home. In school she was cooperative and had initiative in exploring her interests. In short, she was now actively coping where formerly she seemed to have given up.

Her defenses loosened considerably over the year. A major coping approach and defense during the first half of the year was what Dr. Moore called her "hard-nosed approach" to the child-care workers and to Dr. Moore herself. For months, she was very rigid in her demands on other people, in effect, "You stick to exactly what you said or exactly what the routine is or exactly what you promised, and so forth, and, if you don't, then I will be angry with you, and I won't cooperate." This rigidity had now softened visibly.

Evaluation versus Behavior in Therapy

The contrast between Robin in the evaluation tests and Robin in the therapy sessions illustrates some of the weaknesses of evaluation. Diagnosis in terms of an illness model is not valid for children who must be seen in terms of the developmental challenges with which they struggle. And the adaptational challenges are far greater for a child with neurological problems. Each developmental step brings new demands, threats, and opportunities, along with new emerging capacities; but there is also the loss of old security from known solutions to previous problems. Examinations and tests evoke anxiety in most children, and even more in a girl like Robin. Evaluation of a brain-damaged child should be based on a developmental model that includes attention to the relation of the changing tasks to the vulnerabilities and strengths, as well as a recognition of the meaning of the situation to the young person who is also changing.

Robin's developmental concerns were familiar to me. The problem was to discover the impact of neurological limitations on the normal twelve-to-thirteen-year-old developmental situation. And we needed to discover latent strengths and potentialities not reported in the medical evaluation.

As we approached the second year of work with Robin, what could we anticipate? What gains from the first year would she be able to consolidate? What new problems of early adolescence, as she passed her fourteenth birthday, would she confront? What new types of stress would she experience? What progress would she make in coping with stress? What troublesome behavior patterns and defense techniques would she be able to outgrow? What physical problems—menstrual tension, allergies, skin sensitivity—would decrease in intensity? Would her drive to master school tasks continue at the high level of her first year?

What further steps in understanding herself would she take? Would she be able to face limits related to her neurological damage? What anxieties might be aroused by awareness of these limits? In what way might both objective difficulties related to her neurological status and anxieties about these interact with new external pressures and developmental challenges? What new understandings of Robin would the team gain?

These were some of the questions in the back of my mind as we ended the first year with Robin. We had no way of foretelling the sequence of external events, especially in Robin's large family, which might create new problems for her.

PART II

ROBIN'S SECOND YEAR IN TREATMENT

9

Progress Through Stress

Robin's Summer Experiences and Growth

Robin's summer had included a satisfying trip to Disneyland with her parents and brother, seeing natural wonders en route; a visit from her favorite cousin; participation in a school play; and a month's vacation at home. Robin returned to school and therapy a glowing teen-ager with happy memories of her vacation.

Her inspired and eloquent descriptions of Yellowstone National Park, complete with accurate factual details and considerable maturity in her style of communication and level of insight, foreshadowed possible jumps in the level of her schoolwork. More than once Robin gave fluent, detailed, vivid descriptions of various aspects of the trip—the Grand Canyon, Carlsbad Caverns, cacti in the desert. When I commented on her real talent for description, we compared the difference between her verbal level in writing and that with talking, and we decided to find out whether it would be possible for her to handle still more work orally. During much of the discussion of her vacation and travels, her attitude was one of friendly interchange, wanting to feel that our relationship was not just that of therapist and patient but that of friends. At one moment she seemed to reflect some feeling that any reminder of the therapeutic relationship was a little disappointing or felt cold to her. I explained that our time together was not just to make progress within an hour but to help her share her real gifts with other people and in more groups.

Some inner somatic integration seemed implied by the lessened discomfort of, and somewhat greater regularity of, menstruation; decreased evidence of extreme autonomic lability; and increased control of her hand, reflected in improvement in her handwriting.

September reports indicated that she was functioning better with peers and with child-care workers. She seemed more stable and relaxed. It was as if a consolidation had occurred over the summer which had lifted her to a new level of functioning. She herself was aware of this and reported that on a visit with some relatives, including two psychiatrists, they had commented on her improvement. She said, "They saw me last year, and I'm better now."

And she felt quite optimistic: "I know that I could catch up a year and a half in this year if I could only get interested," and she gave the example that she had learned the lines for her summer play in one day because she was interested. At other times during this month she talked about factors affecting the way she functioned—for example, "After an allergy shot, I talk more" and "If somebody helps me and pumps me, I can talk." She also commented that when she was angry and tired, she buried herself and did not want anyone to bother her. But along with a positive attitude toward awareness of herself, feeling optimistic about progress, she still expressed embarrassment in regard to being at the Children's Hospital school. She wanted to be normal.

New child-care workers and new arrangements with the other girls were discussed. She was now sharing a room with a girl named Lisa and felt that she got along better now with the girls than she did last year; she and Lisa got along well when "Prudence isn't around." Robin liked to mother Lisa and other children. She also discussed rather shyly, but with pleasure, her feelings when boys whistled at her or showed some other attention.

When a social worker friend of the family from Grand Island had been stranded in Topeka, Robin had offered the woman her own room and had moved to a room in the basement. This friend stayed with the family during September and October.

A major problem arose when it was decided by the team and the other children that Robin should be the representative at the Council where patient needs and complaints were discussed. She was intensely anxious about it: "I am not ready for this"; "I can't stand noise and confusion";

and "I know I'm disorganized but I can't stand it if everything else is disorganized." I agreed with her that it was important to her to be in situations that were under control, that helped her to feel controlled herself. Robin and I discussed how her anxiety about the Council was increased by her feeling both upset about recent conflicts with her father and disturbed by Eve's return; added to this was the discomfort of sleeping down in the basement while the guest was using her room.

She also expressed guilty feelings about letting the girls down if she did not join the Council, and her conflict about rejecting it because she herself did want to accept the challenge and to master the difficulties involved. Actually, she did go to the Council meeting with a push from a child-care worker, and she functioned adequately there. Later in the month, she spontaneously discussed the relationship between anxiety and anger: "When I am scared about something, I have to get angry first—I have to get angry and ask for it and then get a push, and I can get over it." Social functioning was stimulated to another jump in the Council, where she rapidly became an active, forceful member. Her increased experience there with boys may have contributed to her greater ease at parties, where she now began to dance and where she helped to balance the group by bringing neighborhood girls to add to the group.

Doubtless in connection with more relaxed relationships, she became interested in different people's first names; and, she discussed the feelings around different names that she had been called. Grownups should be called by their proper names, but she liked to be called "Little Robin" and perhaps still better she liked it when her Aunt Claire called her "Cookie," "Sweetie," or "Honeychild." I commented that she had different systems of names: one was the polite and proper system; one was the mischievous, teasing system; and one was the friendly, loving system. I wondered when she herself used these different systems to name other people. Ruminating in a relaxed way, she was able to describe different circumstances under which she used different names. There also seemed to be hints that she felt some conflict between, on the one hand, wanting love from me and, on the other hand, wanting "a harder push." She clarified that she "had all the discipline that she could take" but, at the same time, some sharp stimulus helped her to pull herself together.

Her teachers made use of new insight into her learning potentialities by introducing more oral work, so that she did excellent work in spelling words two or three grade levels ahead of where she had been in the spring and by increasing the use of projects—for example, a project on molds—to focus reading, spelling, and science in meaningful study. Her work was now at an "advanced elementary school level" compared to the second-to–fourth-grade level where she had functioned a year earlier. But her math remained her hardest subject. At a team meeting the staff emphasized the change in Robin, her better level of functioning in general, getting along better with girls, as well as being helpful in school.

She also seemed to be working very hard on understanding herself and helping me to understand her. She was able to be frank in regard to difficulties with her hand—how her hand got shaky and her writing got bad when she was too tired. In commenting on her various kinds of progress, I communicated the team's wish to have another round of tests in order to get more clear about her strengths and difficulties and the ways in which she could be helped with these. Eager to get clear, she accepted the idea of the tests at this point.

We can now look at the contrast between Robin's blossoming and progress of the early fall and her later "sullen" behavior, along with outbursts she had at home and in the residence.

The summer—with Eve away, more time with her parents, and the multiple gratifications of the trip, her cousin's visit, and the school play— was a time of reduced stress and increased release and satisfaction, permitting integration of gains made during the preceding year. By contrast, the fall brought many traumas and strains—the death of her mother's sister, Robin's accompanying concern about her mother's grief, her sister Eve's withdrawal and disturbance, her brother Jim's ongoing problems, the strains her parents were under, and finally Ann's marriage and, for Robin, the loss of Ann's presence when she and her husband planned to move to Florida. All of this brought an overload of stress and decreased self-control. The depression and anxiety about these events could be only partly reduced by therapeutic work on their meanings to Robin.

✝   Brain damage can provide a magnifying glass that permits us to see more sharply the relation between situations as experienced—that is, the specific adaptational problem in each instance—and the child's reactive behavior, primary and secondary feelings, and coping efforts. Robin's behavior varied between unusual extremes—in somatic, autonomic, affective, motor, cognitive, and social zones. It seemed obvious that if we were to understand Robin we would have to see the range of her behavior in relation both to variations in organic conditions within herself and in relation to these varied external impacts as they were intensified, fractionated, or blurred by the complex perceptual and autonomic effects of brain damage.

Comparing the experience of the treatment team early this fall with their experience of the previous fall, we saw an increase in Robin's openness—she no longer had to concentrate on her positive resources while inhibiting feelings of anger, anxiety, resentment, doubt. She could let herself cry, laugh, protest, resist, defend, despair, and hope. We saw a richly, deeply emotional adolescent girl who expressed both forceful and subtle feelings over an unusually broad range.

While her determination and her identification with strong members of her family were persistent, there were also times when Robin felt like its vulnerable members and was tempted to see herself as weak despite her impressive school progress. Rocky, white water stretches in the river of her experience were seen when internal and external stress interacted— for example, when her parents' fatigue and difficulty in dealing with stress caused by multiple problems with all the children in the family prevented them from providing support to Robin. Still Robin was able to face these situations even when she was close to being overwhelmed. She did not regress as she did in the previous January.

In the following chapters, I shall review some of the treatment process with Robin's varying ways of using therapy hours and help from the treatment team.

Robin Begins the Second Year of Treatment

On the first day of therapy after the summer separation Robin was in the physiological phase in which she looked quite round, with full lips and an open, warm smile. There were few pauses during the hour, and many topics were touched on. She had brought home several new kinds of cacti. I commented that she had told me about cacti and that sometimes she felt like a cactus, and I added that cacti could be prickly. She agreed that some cacti were prickly, but some cacti were not prickly, and she had been particularly interested in a kind that was not prickly.

Talking about a visit to a relative, Edith Fay, Robin said that she had a way of making work feel like fun. They had taken bricks from a greenhouse and transported them across the road. The important thing for her was that she had done this with some other girls, Edith Fay's three daughters and two visitors. They had made her feel like "one of the family," and it had been fun to do things all together. This was a rare and satisfying experience with peers—she needed more.

She also had seen Uncle Mark, a brother-in-law of Uncle Wayne and Aunt Samantha; he was a retired psychiatrist, and his son Tony was also a psychiatrist. She said, "They pick up my signals; they know how I'm feeling. They can tell my improvement." Then she commented, "If I got into a jam and needed someone to talk to, I could talk to them; but," and she made a wry face, "Tony said, 'You know, I think she is doing pretty well.'" Robin gave the impression that she felt let down by this remark even though she also understood it as meaning that she had progressed.

We talked briefly about some books she brought. One was *Cheaper by the Dozen*, by Lillian Gilbraith, about the experiences of raising a large family of children. Robin said that she found this interesting, and she considered it at "a junior high school level." She had a "modern arithmetic" book and found this was difficult; she said she "hates times and division" and did not like the endless little problems in the book.

She said, "I really want to know my grades and if I could figure out how they mark the papers, I could know my grades. The math book is fourth-grade work, and a book called *Science and Life* is fifth-grade work." I commented that she was making a good start, wanting to get ahead in her schoolwork, and I asked whether she could talk to her teachers about the problem of doing work that interested her. She seemed to think that was a little difficult.

We went from this to the set-up in school—her schedule, new teachers, the boys and girls. She had three new teachers. She was the only girl in her two morning classes, and both the boys were younger. She said she had gotten along well this summer with older boys—Bryce, for example, who did the make-up for the play.

As she often did, Robin then shifted to a negative issue. "Sometimes when mother is talking about us she says, 'My son is in the sixth grade and my daughter is in sort of the eighth.'" I suggested that she felt embarrassed about this, and she nodded. I wondered what she said when somebody asked her where she went to school, and she replied, "I say the hospital school, and leave it at that. I don't really tell them any more than I have to." I commented that she evidently felt uncomfortable about this, and she agreed.

She came back to the point that she could learn spelling faster if she were interested and then made the comment, "After a shot, I talk more." Pointing to her right hip, she said, "If I fall on this hip and get a bump, it wavers me a little and I get dizzy and I can't talk at first. If somebody helps me and pumps me, I can talk." I commented that we would need to think more about the times when she could talk and the times when she couldn't. I pointed out that just then, for instance, she was talking, and there had been some bumps this summer.

Robin agreed, "Yes, trouble seems to run in our family. My mother's sister, Harriet, was in a sanitorium. You might be surprised that I would be exposed to this. She was an alcoholic." I commented that she hadn't told me that last year even though she had talked about Harriet. Robin added, "I haven't told anybody; I'm not supposed to." She then said that

Harriet had died of "heart failure" last week. I commented that it must have been hard on her mother. Robin said, "Yes, and on me, too." I asked whether she had been fond of her Aunt Harriet and she said yes. She added that she had seen her just a week before; she had been very frail and weighed only about eighty-six pounds, but "none of us knew that she was that sick."

She added, "It seems surprising that we have so many psychiatrists running around." I took it that she meant family members who needed help with problems, and she agreed. I commented, "But you've also told me about very many vigorous healthy people." Robin agreed and said, "There is lots of good Irish and Scotch blood in the family, a lot of us are strong," implying that she would identify with strong members in the family.

Coming back to the question of bumps and jolts, she commented on the many jolts this summer. Then she added, "I'm proud of myself; I walked over here from school. That might have something to do with my talking now." It was interesting that this permission to be independent made her feel proud but the Arbor Day speech had not evoked that feeling. I commented that she seemed to be saying that she could talk when she felt good and proud, and also when she had had a jolt and needed to talk about it. Robin agreed and then added, "Sometimes when I'm really angry and tired, I bury myself. I don't want anyone to bother me. It's similar to dope—wanting to talk after a jolt. It creates an illusion. I see things and then I can talk about them." Then she added, "You should talk to Dr. Edmunds. She talked to me right after a shot."

She then said, "I've got a habit of talking to people I'm not supposed to. I talk to the residents instead of Dr. Moore." I commented that she had told me that when she was angry she couldn't talk, and I wondered if she was angry at Dr. Moore. Robin didn't say anything about this. Then I suggested, "Maybe you were angry at Dr. Moore because you were really angry at me. You know, sometimes people put their angry feelings toward one person on somebody else." Robin nodded and then said, "That makes me clam up," with a knowing and sharing smile. I smiled back and said, "I have a brilliant idea," and grinning at her, said, "Both names begin with *M*." When I commented that she might have felt angry at me for being away so long, she nodded and smiled sheepishly.

Robin grinned and then went on, "I can't sleep if I switch beds." I commented that many kinds of switching had often bothered her. From this, Robin said, "I'll give you one guess as to who Dr. Edmunds reminds me of." I said, "Well, let me see, she is plump." Robin agreed and asked who else I knew who was plump, and I said, "Oh, Kathleen Kirk." She nodded and said, "I told Dr. Edmunds that but she didn't like it." I said I knew that she had been very fond of Kathleen Kirk. Robin nodded and said, "I meant it as a compliment, but she didn't understand."

Then she shifted to another problem: "Sometimes in class I talk to myself out loud. I get so absorbed that I forget what I am doing." I asked whether there were ever times when she got so blocked that she couldn't talk to herself at all. She gave me a questioning look, and I explained that when people can't talk to themselves, it was really bad. I commented, "What you are telling me is that you talk to yourself when you have something on your mind." She nodded, and I said, "You feel embarrassed about doing it." She agreed, saying, "Some people think it is psychological."

I commented that there were lots of things to talk about, and we had more time. This was the end of the hour, but there would be another hour and another day and another week and another month and a year ahead of us. Robin protested, "I just have a year and a half" (to accomplish all she felt she needed to accomplish). I took her to the door, saying that I would see her on Tuesday.

✝   In this hour Robin swung between feelings of pride (with even a little of the old superiority posture that was shown at times last year) and feelings of embarrassment, sheepishness, and other feelings of slight shame. This conflict seemed very important in relation to her motivation for progress—she wanted to be able to be proud of herself.

The second hour was very full, with Robin often talking so fast that I was not sure I could keep track of it all. She said that her teachers were not completely new to her, and that she got along with them all right. But there were some child-care workers that she liked and some that she didn't care for. She liked the new French girl, Lucy, who was very understanding, had a good sense of humor, and was quick on the pick-up. Robin said that she also got along well with Gretchen, but she did not get along with Claudia, although she couldn't seem to explain why; Jo was "Okay."

She talked a little longer about the boys in school: she said Todd and Garth didn't get along very well with each other, but she felt that she got along with both of them except that their manners bothered her. When I asked what she meant, she said that they sometimes whistled at her. I commented that boys that age did like to whistle at pretty girls, and Robin flushed a little, with a smile that was slightly disparaging but still expressed pleasure, and then gave examples of how other boys had whistled at her. She got increasingly warm and pleased as she talked about this, and I grinned and said, "It really is fun, isn't it?" She giggled in response, agreeing that it was.

When I commented that she seemed to be doing very well, she started talking about the social worker friend of the family who was staying in Robin's room. "She talks to dad a lot—they know the same people. Some things she brings up I don't like—she sounds cold, like a social worker shouldn't be, and so I leave."

Robin then said something about a couch, and that her social worker at the hospital scared her, but she didn't want me to tell her—the social worker scared her just the way a psychiatrist with a couch scared her. More associations to this seemed to take two directions. The first was that a couch was like a treatment table, and once when she had fallen off a horse she had had a painful experience on a treatment table—she still had a scar on her leg from this accident. The second was in response to my question of why we were talking about a couch here. She said, "Well, psychiatrists sometimes have couches in their offices, and one time last year you talked about getting a couch." I laughed and said, "Well, I'm not about to clear things out of this office to get a couch now." Robin said, "I'm not afraid of this office, but last year once you. . . ." I interrupted, "Yes, I remember once when you were feeling very miserable and unwell, I suggested that perhaps you should just rest until the bus came for you and that you could lie down on the couch in the other room. But I wonder what made you think of this now." We clarified that she was at the end of menstruation and also felt very tired. It had been a mistake for me to suggest that she lie down last year, and she didn't want me to repeat it.

I said, "I guess you really don't want me to ask questions now; you don't feel like working hard in therapy today." She said that she had had cramps for three days, had taken Midol for this, and had felt like sleeping most of the time. She also said she felt sleepy today. I said, "Okay, I won't ask any more painful questions. Why don't you tell me more about your trip instead of leading me off after a red herring the way you did, talking about this couch business."

✝ The cagey and mischievous way she had talked about all this made me think that it was a way of getting out of talking about other things.

Robin began talking about the trip eloquently, very expressively describing in accurate and fascinating detail different aspects of it. She was rather disappointed in the Painted Desert, but she did dig up a few plants to bring home. She described the dimensions, the lighting, and the stalactites and stalagmites of Carlsbad Caverns in tones of awe and delight. She described experiences in Arizona in the same detailed way, mentioning temperatures of water, dimensions of areas of space, colors, lights, and other characteristics of the settings. She had not only been open to new visual impressions, but she had also listened with great absorption to the comments of guides and other adults, and she remembered many details. (In the next therapy hour she said that she got most out of travel—facts from books, when she could not see or hear things, did not mean much to her.)

I commented that it seemed like a wonderful trip and asked her how the family all got along in the small quarters of the camper. She said, "Oh, well, Ann and Eve weren't with us, so with Daddy and Jim, and mother and me, we were well balanced." I agreed that it must have seemed nice to her and Jim to have their parents all to themselves, and she agreed. I remarked that it sounded like a fine summer and that now that she was getting along with her family so well, getting along with the other teen-agers at the hospital school and with the child-care workers, it looked as if things were so much better than last year. She agreed.

Remembering last fall I said, "You know, last year you helped me to see how much you could take in and that you could understand more than most people thought you could." Robin interrupted, "Yes, but that's just for you, I don't want everybody to know how much I understand because they will expect too much of me." I protested, saying, "Well really, does that make sense? Lots of us have points that we are good at and points where we are not so good, and it's important to be clear about them ourselves and help other people to get clear about them. We want your parents to understand." Robin said, "They do." I said, "I think we can help others to understand, too, that you take in a great deal, but still there are points where you have difficulties."

Talking about school, Robin said that she had trouble with her math and hadn't felt like working during this menstrual period. She hadn't discussed this with the teachers. She said, "Well, the main point is to be able to find a way to get really interested. I know I could make up a year in half a year if I could get interested enough." After the eloquent account of her trip I could only agree with her, and so I said, "Well, this is something that we will have to work on. Is it all right for me to talk with your teachers?" Robin agreed that this was okay.

✢   There was a chummy, intimate, and social tone in the last part of the hour when we were talking about the trip. I think Robin wanted to feel that our rapport was entirely a matter of friendly interchange. The idea of regarding it in professional terms seemed cold to her—although this did not inhibit her very long since she flowed into such a spontaneous and happy account of the trip.

It isn't necessary to read between the lines to realize that at the beginning of her second year Robin and I had different aims in the first couple of hours. I was so eager to know what kind of summer she had had, and what shape she was in, that I did not take time to get the feel of what she wanted. In her comment on the "cold" social worker, she was probably implying that she wanted to renew the experience of warm rapport that she had felt at the beginning of the first year—while I had taken this rapport for granted.

Overview of October

Physically, Robin continued to seem more stable than she had been last year. Last fall, her irregular menstrual periods had usually been preceded and accompanied by considerable emotional instability as well as marked changes in her appearance—sometimes there had been an almost edematous appearance of her face as well as conspicuous autonomic lability reflected in blushing and paling, and occasional periods of nonvolitional rhythmic lip movement. Much of this had disappeared this fall and, although she might be "under the weather" during menstruation, the changes were like those one sees in other girls. She still needed plenty of sleep and was tired when she had not had enough. It was reasonable that a girl of multiple vulnerabilities, exposed to so much personal and family stress, would need plenty of sleep to restore her equilibrium. In addition, her allergies were under better control than they had been last fall, when she was miserable with a stuffy, drippy nose until she had her allergy shots. However, she still reacted to the allergy shots with pain in her arm, and sometimes she was pale after a shot.

We discussed the improvement in her handwriting, now much smoother than at any time last year. When I asked about her hand tremor, she remarked that it got worse when she was tired; "I was born with it, and I have to take it in stride." She was still conscious of the tremor at times, and she still brought something to hold in her hand to play with or wrapped a scarf around her hand. She complained that she could not manage badminton very well. There were problems in getting enough exercise for an energetic girl.

In order to have a better basis for planning her education and thinking about her potentialities, Dr. Moore and I felt that a new psychological evaluation would be desirable. But Robin objected, feeling that to be tested by Dr. Grant would be hard for Missy, whom Dr. Grant had in therapy. She said that Dr. Grant "represents a mother image" to Missy, and Robin felt that she would be taking something away from Missy. Robin finally agreed that she would do the tests if Dr. Grant discussed this with Missy and Robin was reassured that it would not be a strain on Missy in any way.

Robin brought up her feeling about the traditional school flag; some children wanted to stop the use of the special flag, which had been created by a previous group of children. Robin, however, felt that the flag was an important tradition and that "we should let tradition alone." She was very forthright in expressing her views in Council and intense in expressing them in the therapy hour.

During this whole month, her sister Eve was not able to go to school; she spent most of the time in bed, part of the time not being able to eat much. Robin talked about this rather blandly, apparently not much worried although it was apparent that Eve must have been a concern to her parents. Robin thoughtfully agreed that it might have been hard for Eve to come back and adjust to the demands of the family after a summer of being with a teen-age group traveling abroad.

She reflected considerable strain in connection with my absence early in the month; she said she had no one to talk to because when they went down to Grand Island Aunt Samantha was busy with a guest. Robin was also worried that she might lose Sadie, her childhood nanny, who was in poor health, and also Mattie, (the housekeeper), who wasn't well. We related these anxieties about loss to her feelings about my absence and the strain of not being able to talk over these anxieties with me. She emphasized that she felt that I "treat her as an individual" and that everybody else "tries to program her." In connection with this, we discussed again her feeling about being special and touched on the fact that although she talked a great deal about how much she had been given, she was also sad about things that she would never have and the difficulty of accepting her limitations. She again expressed an intense desire to help, talking about children who needed help and "Negroes who are just like the immigrants who came into this country at the beginning and made this country, except that they [Negroes] didn't have a fair chance."

She also discussed the roles, opportunities, and responsibilities of girls; the kind of strength she felt as a girl; her upsurging sex feelings, particularly around the time of her menstrual periods; her fantasies about boys, and her resentment of the temptations involved when she was expected to entertain her sister's boy friends. She looked forward to being able to handle boys. She described her attempts to distinguish which boys were "safe" and which ones were not "nice." She was also quite explicit about her feeling able to physically defend herself if necessary.

Toward the end of the month, a problem came up in connection with riding a horse. She "showed her fear" while on a certain horse at the West Campus of the Menninger Foundation, and she wanted very much to have a chance to ride him again under circumstances in which she would be able to conquer her fear—that is, to have no one present except Mr. Keith (a riding instructor at the foundation). He had helped her. She wanted to have the horse "in the pasture" nowhere near any barbed wire fence, which frightened her. She cared a great deal about riding and, at the same time, was quite open about her fear of certain horses under certain circumstances.

In discussing what it meant to her to be able to "talk to somebody" in therapy, she repeated that she did not feel at this time that she could have any meaningful communication with her mother. I tried to help her see that her mother must be very burdened and distracted with the presence of a guest, Eve's difficulties, and the problems of chauffeuring Jim and Robin, along with routine household tasks. (I doubt that she had any "life of her own" during this time.) But it was hard for Robin to accept a total view of her mother's situation.

✝ During this month, Robin consolidated the progress she had made over the summer and continued to exert much effort to integrate new feelings related to her sexual development and to respond to new challenges.

Sorting Out Feelings about Being Different

At the beginning of the therapy hour, Robin showed me her spelling book, explaining that her teachers were now letting her spell orally. She wanted to demonstrate to me how well she did, and I tried her out on the current spelling lists. She spelled all of the words correctly and easily, except for one—she spelled "spoke" *s-p-e-o-k*. The book contained a wide range of vocabulary, discussion of the history of words, games for sorting out mixed up words, and multiple choice games for choosing the correct spelling of a word; it was obviously an upper elementary grade book.

She then said that Jessie, one of her new teachers, was going to let her dictate a book review to a tape recorder. Robin was very pleased about this. Her speech seemed quite clear, and I commented on how well she was getting along and on the usefulness of doing more of the work orally. I also commented that the contrast between the way she could express herself here in the therapy hour and the difficulties she had in writing helped us to understand that she could talk things out better than she could write. Robin nodded and agreed, but did not add anything.

I said I had been thinking about the question of the psychological tests, and I wondered if she had any more thoughts about it. Robin shook her head and said that she did not want to have them with Dr. Grant, because she did not want to take anything away from Missy. I commented that sometimes when we thought we were doing something for one reason there could be some other reasons as well. She kept resisting every suggestion and question that I offered, but she did blurt out at one point that she was afraid of Dr. Grant. When I tried to explore that I did not get very far. All she could say was that she had always been able to get along better with elderly people, like Sadie and her grandmother. At this point, I said, "So it's because I'm an old grandmother that you felt comfortable with me?" I said this in a slightly kidding tone, and we laughed. She added, "Well, not just that."

I then explained that a major reason why we had been able to get along so well was that right from the beginning last year she had worked hard and had been so giving; I would not have had any way of helping her if she had not given me so much. She looked at me in an understanding way, but then when I came back to Dr. Grant and suggested that she might find that things could work out well, she began to look very bored. I laughed and said, "You're telling me to stop talking about that?" She smiled shyly and relaxed.

She then discussed the problem of being special. Sharon, a secretary in the Children's Division, had grown up in Grand Island, and with her Robin had a special relationship which she did not want other children to know. Robin said, "I don't want to be different and high and mighty anymore. I've always had everything I've wanted, and I've had lots of love from Aunt Samantha and Uncle Wayne and Sadie, but there's something I want that I don't get."

This led to thoughts about the deaths of her grandmother and Aunt Harriet, how much she missed them, and how she felt that she didn't have any other relative like them. I said it was natural to be grieving about them and to feel that the relationships she had with them might not be duplicated, but that she was growing up and was able to know more people and develop new relationships. Robin cried and repeated, "There's something I want, and I don't know what it is." Then, she began to elaborate again on how she had had all the material things she wanted. I wondered aloud why this came up after I had been away a short time, when it had not come up during the summer when we were apart for a long time. She said, "I was very busy during the summer, and now sometimes I don't have anybody to talk to." When she said again that there was something that she still wanted, although she had always had everything, I commented that she might feel deprived because I could not be constantly available to her as Sadie had been when she was a little girl.

Robin began to cry about Jim, about how he needed what she had; that she was able to make progress, but he was having a very hard time in school, and he should be in the Children's Hospital School too. In addition to her sadness over Jim's situation, she said that if it weren't for Uncle Wayne and Aunt Samantha, she couldn't be here either. She felt that they were giving her everything. She knew another girl in Grand Island who needed the same kind of help that Robin was getting, but that girl's family couldn't give it to her. I said, "I guess you feel that if Uncle Wayne and Aunt Samantha weren't paying for your help here, they would be able to help somebody else," and she nodded.

I empathized with her feeling guilty that she was privileged and had so much help when others she knew could not have as much. I said it was natural to feel guilty about this, but as she grew up it would be possible for her to have her turn at giving to others. For instance, she would be able to help other children in the way she has been helped. Robin brightened up at this suggestion, but then she still worried about her brother.

Thinking hard, I said slowly, "You know, it might be that you felt gypped because you didn't have everything that Jim had when you were little, and you can't stand to have things turned around now and feel that you are getting things that Jim doesn't get." Robin then said that Sadie "always kept things even between us," and now they were not even anymore. I commented that as we grow up we cannot have exactly the same kind of pattern we had when we were little, that each one develops his own pattern of strengths and weaknesses, of things he gets out of life and things he lacks, and so on. Robin said, "Yes, that's what Sadie said once."

I then suggested that maybe she did not really feel that she had had too much, had had everything, but that she was sad about things she would never have. She would never be a boy; with all the progress that she would be able to make, she might still feel different from other people. Robin nodded and said, "Yes, I think that's it." I reflected, "Well, isn't it strange that just when you're making so much progress—you're getting along with the girls, you're catching up in work, and you aren't as different as you used to be—that you would be so overwhelmed now by the little bit of difference?"

Robin then talked about how Aunt Harriet, Uncle Mark, and her grandmother had always accepted her as a girl—they had never made her feel conscious of the things she could not do. But in school at Grand Island—in the special class and also in other situations—sometimes she had felt that people did not want to get near her, that they thought she was peculiar.

I said that now that she was feeling so much closer to being a regular person she could let herself show me how much she had suffered in the past—in a way she couldn't let me see last year. Robin said that was part of it. And I added, "But you still feel sad because you'll never be able to be completely what you would like to be," and Robin nodded.

I said, "Well, all of us have to accept some of these things. When I was your age, I had to say, 'Oh, swimming isn't my dish— I can't swim because I get terrible sinuses from swimming.' You could say, 'Oh, math isn't my dish; there are lots of things I can do and understand, but not math.'" Robin brightened up more, and the tears stopped flowing so hard. She asked what the cause was of a red spot on my finger. I looked at it carefully and said I wasn't really sure. She said she thought it might have been a cut and that a good thing for cuts is to put the finger in hot water for awhile, then in cold water. I gave her a big smile and said, "When you have received some help, you feel like giving some help to someone else," and Robin smiled understandingly.

After she went out, my secretary commented that she did look as if she had been crying hard, and yet she did not look unhappy at all.

✝ It was interesting to see the sequence in the hour from pleasurable progress in school to anxiety about the retests; projected deprivation for Missy, then fear of Dr. Grant; not wanting to be special anymore, feeling that so much had been given to her, grieving for the loss of people who cared for her; anxiety about her brother not getting as much help as she was getting, accepting my interpretation that her present feeling of not getting everything she wanted was related to early feelings of not getting what he got; and feeling bad that she was not a boy, she would always be different, and could not be all that she wanted to be. Then, despite her prolonged crying about these personal losses, after my empathy and interpretation, she shifted to offering me help, evidently identifying with my helping role.

Robin's Urge to Be a Helping Person

Robin looked rather serious when she came into my office, but did not seem overwhelmed at any time during the hour. She talked quite frankly, in a chummy way, about many thoughts and feelings, without any evidence of real disturbance, except possibly a slightly tremulous quality when talking about hurts that she had suffered in the family situation. She said that she knew that Anna Freud was studying blind children who were very young, and there were older blind children who needed just as much help, as well as many kinds of other children who needed help—why didn't the government provide ways of helping all of these children? I asked how she happened to know this and she said, "Well, I know what's going on; I'm not as stupid as you think." I asked her what made her think I had ever thought she was stupid, and she just laughed it off. Then she said that in the past and also recently she sometimes had dreamed that she was helping children. She would wake up with a feeling that she had been in a helping situation and was able to work with children who needed help. Her comments on children reminded me of Helen Keller, and I asked if she knew about her, and she said she did and was very much interested in her. She wished there could be a way of helping an individual child. When they were in Grand Island, their church sometimes would collect clothes, toys, and games to send to children who needed them; she had not even been able to do this lately.

She also talked about the needs of Negro children—"I don't see why they aren't just like other immigrants; they ought to have a chance to progress just as much as other immigrants have done." She continued, "Besides, it isn't fair; at our school here they have colored teachers, so why don't they have colored children?" I suggested that perhaps it was a financial problem, because the colored children's families might not be able to afford it. She felt this was not fair.

She came back to the question of helping and I said, "You are helping when you help all of us understand the needs of children like you with their checkerboards, as we have been calling it, of strengths and difficulties." She was very much interested, and I explained that it was hard for everybody to understand these complicated patterns, and she had been very helpful in sharing her experiences with me.

She said again that she had needed very, very much to talk to somebody, and she felt that I had always accepted her as a girl; that I had never thought it was strange to come from the country, to like animals, or to do tomboyish things; that I had treated her as a girl from the beginning. She felt this was different from the way some other people treated her—thinking that her interests and tastes were strange and thinking that she was peculiar.

I said that I knew she had felt that some people thought she was strange, and I asked whether part of her feeling about this might be because she herself was afraid to get close to other people and so she thought they were thinking that she was strange. Robin agreed calmly and casually, "Yes, I think maybe that's the main part of it."

Variability in Quality of Work

Robin came in a little late; she was carrying her books and said that she was working hard on her homework. She showed me her assignments, with papers she had filled out, which her teacher had marked "100," "99," "97," and so forth. She said she wasn't quite sure what these meant, and I explained that "100 percent" was perfect and all the rest of the marks were almost perfect. This meant that she was doing very well. I wondered whether she would like to be moving faster on her schoolwork (remembering other children who found it rather boring to be doing something that could be mastered too easily). Robin agreed and said she wished the assignment could be flexible.

She spontaneously offered to show me some writing she had done which was actually very poor, and I contrasted it with the good piece of writing she had previously done about birds. I commented that there were wide swings between her rather poor work at certain times and very good work at other times, and I thought it was important to try to understand this. What were the things that helped her to do so very well at certain times, while at other times she did badly?

She said that this rather messy page had been done on Sunday; she had been writing in her lap and hadn't felt much like doing it (words were mixed up and misspelled, and the whole thing looked more like the writing she had sometimes done last year). So I said, "That's a matter of mood, is it?" and she nodded. I went on, "Well, what do you suppose makes the mood so different?" She explained that sometimes it was a matter of being tired, sometimes it was a matter of not liking the work.

Since she was still working ahead on her homework, I said, "I wonder why it is that you don't seem to want to do therapy today? Could it be that last Thursday was so rough?" She denied this and said that she had just been busy doing her homework.

I said, "Well, I do have some things on my mind." With curiosity, she looked up, twinkled, and asked, "What?" I looked at her seriously and said, "It seems to me sometimes you put roadblocks in your way—all this talk about how hard it was to talk to Dr. Moore a few weeks ago, and saying that you were afraid of Dr. Grant, and so forth. These feelings really get in your way." I then explained that Dr. Grant was one of the most experienced persons in the country in helping to clarify exactly the things that we had been working on—to see whether tests could make clear for us what is connected with the high spots and the low spots, her best and her worst in working.

Robin protested, "Well, I didn't want to have her test me because it might hurt Missy." I asked if she really thought that Missy would feel that way, or was she, Robin, just thinking that if she were in Missy's place she would be feeling that way. Robin looked at me very solemnly and in her most earnest tone of voice said, "Well, Dr. Grant represents a mother figure to Missy, and Missy has hardly anyone at home."

I said, "I understand what you mean, and this is a beautiful example of one of the things we've been talking about. Here, you expressed yourself in a very mature, practically professional way, with very good insight. This is an example of what I mean by your mature level of functioning." Robin looked thoughtful, and I said, "It's almost like a flower blooming over here and then over there, there aren't any flowers." She looked sad and said, "Perhaps the candle goes out." Robin then said, very seriously, "The flower is one way of saying it, but the candle is another. It's like our flag at school," and then she described the flag at school. She explained that the lion's head on the flag stands for courage, and the candle stands for hope.

I said, "Robin, are you saying that when I talk about your best level it makes you feel discouraged about having to plug along on routine assignments and that when you get discouraged your work isn't so good?" Robin nodded a little. Then, she volunteered, "Well, I will take the test with Dr. Grant if Missy won't mind." I asked, "Is it all right then for me to talk it over with Dr. Grant and ask what she thinks about it?" Robin nodded.

We now talked a little more about her schoolwork, and I said it sounded as if "you feel you would like to have more flexibility on your assignments." Robin agreed, and I told her I thought her teachers were interested and flexible, and I wondered whether Robin herself had told them she wanted more freedom on her reading assignments. Robin said she had hinted at it. I explained that I would be glad to talk to them again—they had been so responsive to the idea of working orally, dictating, and my other suggestions—but it would be better if *she* could talk to them about the best ways of getting ahead in her work. Robin said, "I did talk to them about doing more orally, and they are flexible."

I asked then how Eve was getting along and Robin said she had trouble with keeping her food down. I said she had told me before that Eve did not want to go to school, and I asked whether she thought that Eve might be having a hard time getting adjusted after being in Europe this summer. Robin thought this was quite probable and then said, "We all feel like breaking over the traces sometimes." I commented that it was fine to want to be independent if one could take it step by step. One had to get ready for it. I wondered if she had thought about what she needed to master before she got to be independent herself. Robin said, "Yes, I've thought about it." I asked, "Doesn't it have some connection with arithmetic, among other things?" Robin demurred at this and said, "Oh, I get along all right." I said. "How about learning to handle a bank account, change, and things like that?" Robin again said, "Oh, I'll be able to manage."

It was the end of the hour and I said, "Well, we can talk about this some more another time. It's all right for me to talk to Dr. Grant then?" Robin said yes. I added, "I'll see you Monday," and she said, "Yes," very firmly.

✛   It seemed to me that she was reflecting considerable satisfaction in growing up—being able to manage to communicate with other people on her own, being able to shove me aside a little, being able to be more flexible herself—while at the same time being courageous and honest about facing some of the problems involved in her wide range of functioning, and also her need for more flexibility in assignments so that she could do as much as she wanted to when she was functioning well.

Ways of Coping with Boys

With the leopard coat and her new hairdo with bangs, Robin looked more like a fifteen-year-old or seventeen-year-old girl today and seemed to have developed a more mature self-image. She said that a couple of cousins had come up from Austin.

She did not volunteer anything else, so I commented that I'd been thinking about a remark she had thrown out last week, when she had said something like, "I guess perhaps all of us like to jump over the traces sometimes." Robin responded with her very knowing expression, eyebrows slightly raised as if she were interested to see what might come next and were impressed that I had picked this up. I smiled back and asked, "Have you been feeling like kicking over the traces yourself?" Robin said, "Perhaps." I commented that she had made this remark, if I remembered correctly, during an hour when she had been late to therapy for the first time. Robin acknowledged this, and I asked whether there had been other ways of kicking over the traces. Robin said, "Well, maybe in talking." I asked what she meant, and gradually it became clear that when she talked with her older sister Ann she had been asking questions "that Ann thought I was too young to be asking." I wondered what these might be and suggested that usually when girls in their teens got together they talked about boys; Robin again responded with her knowing and somewhat pleased expression, and said she and Ann had been talking about such things as "Who am I, what do I want to do, where am I going, and what is the responsibility of a female?" I said I thought these were quite natural things for teen-age girls to talk about.

I added that I thought she had a pretty solid sense of direction, that she had often talked about wanting to do something to help either animals or children. Robin agreed, and then two main points became clear: she thought that maybe being a vet wasn't a feminine occupation since it would be hard for a female to handle a horse or cow physically as a vet would need to do. The second was that science and math requirements for a vet would be difficult. I emphasized the fact that there were different kinds of helping and that taking care of either animals or children was not only a perfectly good feminine interest, but something that also would fit in with having one's own family. Robin protested that she didn't even have an opportunity for dates. "I know I'll be out of here by the time I'm sixteen, but as long as I'm in here I probably can't have dates." I wondered if some of the older girls didn't have an opportunity to have dates, and Robin said they did if they could go to public school. I commented that we didn't know yet at what point she might have more privileges.

From this point Robin moved into very active discussion of encounters with boys, feelings about boys, hazards in relationships with boys, and specific experiences that she had had. Sometimes she was very direct and open, sometimes she handled points indirectly, in subtly expressive ways, with meaningful glances, and she always seemed to feel relaxed when I picked up the implications of her expressive pattern.

A bit shyly, with her head slightly drooping and a hint of a smile, she commented at one point that she had had an encounter with one of Ann's boy friends when Ann had gone upstairs to dress and the boy had been waiting downstairs with Robin present. I asked if he had kissed her, and Robin said "yes," again with her delicate smile and her head partly hanging, and I replied that it must have felt good. Robin nodded, then raised her head and said, "and Ann gave it to me when she got back after her date." I commented that she had made Ann angry, and Robin agreed, but I said, "Well, you're an attractive girl, when you are feeling good." Robin said, "Boys are a magnet to me." I said, "And you're a magnet to them at times." Robin then gave other illustrations; for example, when she had been waiting in the dentist's office, a boy who had been going out the door had said, "Hi Babe," in passing. She did not think that this was a nice remark. I said that even if she did not think he came from a "cultivated" family, the remark might have been made in a friendly way, but Robin did not think so.

She went on giving other examples, including one about when she had been at Ann's dormitory, and a boy who had been "stood up" by a girl he had expected to date had asked Robin if she would go out with him. Robin said that she had just told him that she was pretty busy that night and could not go. I said that was a good way to handle it—evidently she felt that she could handle boys. I asked whether she was acquainted with the phrase "getting fresh" and whether she had ideas about what she would do if a boy "started to get fresh with her." She gave examples of boys whom Eve had refused to go out with because she could not trust them in the car, and I agreed that necking while driving could be very dangerous and added that some boys wanted to go down a side road and go further than that. Robin said that one of the boys Eve refused to go out with would not do anything like that, but still he was dangerous to drive with. I then asked whether she and Ann had talked about such things as the fact that the sexual reactions of boys were different from those of girls. Robin seemed quite at ease about my approaching this question so directly and said, "Well, not really."

I reminded her that at times when she got very angry, she could explode suddenly and did not always have good control over her feelings. I explained that sometimes sexual feelings could flare up, just as angry feelings do, and could be hard to manage. Robin seemed very accepting and understanding, and I went on to say that one important thing to know was that boys got stimulated faster than girls did and that, for this reason, it was not a good idea to "lead a boy on"—things could go faster than one intended.

Robin nodded in an understanding way and referred to the Grand Island girls who got pregnant last winter, and I agreed that she had had some good education on this. I added that I didn't think any of them really wanted to get into trouble.

Robin said, "Well, Brook's family walked out on her and went off and left her alone. I think one reason why she got too involved was that she wanted somebody to be close to." She explained that Brook's family had gone to California and left her with neighbors. Then Robin added, "I think something like that can often be the reason why girls get into trouble."

I agreed that that was sometimes the case and said that I thought she was perhaps telling me that she had a family who stood by her and that she wouldn't need to get too involved with a boy. Robin seemed to accept this, and she added that if a boy started to get fresh with her, she would slap him or kick him—"I know this isn't very feminine."

After some further discussion of various aspects of boy-girl relationships, and the fact that Robin did not trust the boys in the Children's Hospital, it was about the end of the hour and I summarized, "It seems to me that you feel that you have several different kinds of protection. One, you can tell the difference between boys who are safe and boys who are not safe; two, you feel that you could defend yourself physically if you had to; three, you feel that you are too young to get too involved and would try not to." Robin nodded and I said, "But the other side of the picture is that you are very responsive emotionally, and feelings could surge up quickly, so it would be important not to get into situations that might lead to trouble." It was the end of the hour, and I said that we could talk some more about these things another time.

✛   It was interesting to see how open and direct Robin was in discussing these new encounters with boys and the feelings aroused by them. This was in contrast to her difficulty in clarifying her feelings about Dr. Grant, whom she saw as a mother figure to Missy. Her own mother-need was a deep and tense problem, whereas she could be relaxed about boys, with a realistic grasp of dangers, ways to avoid them, and a capacity to use her understanding.

A Scary Dream

The next time I saw Robin she seemed to be rather limp and dreamy, and I asked whether she was having her period. She nodded, saying that she was, and I remarked that she didn't seem as upset as she used to be last year at the time of her period. She then said that she had been rather "tempery" on Tuesday, and she gave illustrations of arguments at the Council meeting. Some of the boys had wanted to take down the flag with the lion's head and the candle of hope, and Robin had argued about it, saying, "We should let tradition alone!" She said she felt this was part of the school and should not be changed. I asked what reasons the boys had for wanting to take these down. They had said that the people who originated the idea for this flag were now gone. Robin did not think that was a good reason. Evidently, she got rather peppery at such times.

She then talked about certain boys she liked at school. Next she mentioned that in a Council meeting, she brought up the question of whether girls could take Shop. She felt that girls should "know how to do things," and "they ought to have a chance to take Shop." I commented that many men pride themselves on their gourmet cooking, and Robin said, "Well, it's not so hard to break through on that as it is on something like letting girls have Shop." We agreed that it would be useful if girls knew how to do more repairs around the house, and Robin came back to her old theme song: "The women who founded this country were strong women, and the country still needs strong women."

Robin then began to make distinctions between "having a strong will" and being "physically strong." She said that she felt physically strong. I asked whether she could carry a couple of pails of water or milk, and she said that she had milked cows and she could do things like that. I agreed that she did have strength. She made a little face and looked doubtful, and I said, "It seems that you're not sure whether you're strong or not."

Robin gave one of her knowing smiles, expressing a subtle rapport, and the conversation then came back to boys. At one point she said, "I like to be with boys. . . . I want boys." I commented that I thought she was telling me that she liked boys as friends, but that at times she had other longings too. I added that sometimes girls have feelings that surge up before or during menstruation. Robin said, "I think I'm in the middle of it."

We talked for some time about how appropriate it was for her to have friendships with boys, and I suggested that the more friendships she had in the next years, the better basis she would have later on for understanding boys and choosing a boy with whom she wanted a deeper relationship.

Robin got dreamy again and groped, trying to remember a dream. She said it was a dream that she had had sometimes before menstruation. It seemed that she and another girl were in a drugstore or at a show at night, and they came out near a dark alley, and a couple of boys came along. There was so much blocking that I said, "And I guess it was scary." Robin nodded and said that she didn't like to go downtown at night. I commented that this was connected to many of the things that she had been saying about liking boys and wanting them, on the one hand, and yet being unsure of herself and unsure whether she would be strong enough to keep a relationship at a friendly level, especially when strong feelings were surging up around menstruation time.

I said that it was good that she was strong enough to be able to face her feelings and that since she was able to do this she would know that at certain times these feelings got very strong. She would be able to say, "Well, I'm feeling sexy and that's that; I'd better watch out." Robin nodded with a feeling of relief.

It was the end of the hour, but she still seemed to need and want to talk a little more. She said, "Last year, Kenneth and I were alone with the mice and nobody worried about us, and it was all right because we were so young." I said, "But now you're afraid that it wouldn't be safe to be with a boy." She said, "Well, the boys at the hospital would be safe."

I suggested that perhaps one part of the problem was her own expressiveness and the signals that she sent out herself. She wanted to know what I meant, and I explained that she had many subtle ways of communicating her feelings and it could easily be possible that when she is feeling warm and friendly, a boy would misunderstand it and think that she was ready for more than she really did intend to give. I suggested that she would need to be careful not to lead boys on to the point where things would get unsafe. She nodded understandingly, and I suggested that we could talk about it again.

✛   I may have gone more slowly than necessary with this dream but I felt sure it would come up again. I wanted to clarify her own wishful contribution to her concern about what boys might do.

Distrust and Challenge

At the beginning of the next hour, Robin said that she had been thinking that in the summer she would like to have either a day care center job or a job with a vet; the trouble was that there wouldn't be any transportation, and the vet was a couple of miles from home. She began to get tense as she said that she could walk it, and I wondered how comfortable that would be in the summer heat. Then she said that maybe Grady could give her a ride on his motorbike. I was astonished to hear of "Grady" since I had not heard of him before, and I asked about him. He lived across the street, and Jim talked to him, but apparently there had not been any actual contact between Grady and Robin.

I asked gently then, whether this was "a fantasy." At this, Robin blew up, and out came a flood of complaints and almost tearful expressions of frustration. First, "nobody at school believed anything" she said, and Jessie, today, told her she shouldn't make statements like one that she made because it wasn't true. I commented that she seemed to be feeling that people didn't trust her, but I thought many people did respect her. Robin quickly said that she knew it was her own feeling—she felt as if people didn't trust her. I wondered then what could make her feel this way.

As we worked on this, it came out that she felt that her family didn't trust her. She would never be able to have a ride on Grady's motorbike because Eve had messed things up by injuring her leg on a motorbike. I commented that she felt that Eve had made a lot of trouble for her in this way.

Robin then exploded that Ann and Eve both expected her to entertain their boy friends when they arrived, while the girls got dressed. "It is just too tempting," and "it isn't fair to be expected to sit down there and entertain their boy friends and not get involved."

I commented that it was almost like being Cinderella with two older sisters who had the boy friends, and Ann could drive a car, and Robin wasn't allowed anything yet. Robin reiterated that she wouldn't be allowed to date and she wouldn't be allowed to go on a motorbike. I empathized with her frustration about these things and asked whether she felt as badly as this all the time. She said it was worse at some times than others.

Then she talked about what a bad week it had been. On Tuesday, she had had a hard time with the horse "Dancer" because she had shown him that she was afraid of him and that was the worst thing you could do with a horse. She talked rapidly, sarcastically, about how humiliating it was. I gradually spelled out that she felt that she wanted to prove that she could ride him; she wanted to prove it to the horse and she wanted to prove it to Patrick, who had taken her out with the horse, and it had been particularly humiliating to have this happen in front of a man. Robin agreed forcefully.

During all this, she said that she would like to be able to go out just with Mr. Keith (whom she trusts and she feels he trusts her) and "show that darn horse that I can ride him." She was afraid that she wouldn't be allowed to go out just with Mr. Keith. I asked whether she had discussed this with Dr. Moore and she said no, she could never get hold of her to talk it over. I said, "You can keep trying," and asked her whether it was all right for me to talk to Dr. Moore about this. She said yes, and I said I would do the best I could to get in touch with her.

Robin left a little reluctantly.

✝ This was another interesting example of Robin's determination to master a challenge and to solve the problem in a way that she could manage.

10

More Progress Despite
Increasing Difficulties

November was a very difficult month for the family and more difficult
for Robin than she was able to communicate at the time except in moods
of depressed "fatigue." But in the midst of family turmoil, Robin continued to make progress in her schoolwork. Her social science teacher recognized her insights and her contributions to class. Her work in science and
English was considered good. Despite this progress, Robin felt discouraged about the possibility of getting to public school, as she had hoped to
do.

By comparison with last year, her birthday came and went without
fanfare. Robin wanted a baby kitten but knew that her mother wouldn't
let her have one. She acquired an uncomfortable and bizarre looking
brace as part of the current orthodontia, which she deliberately and perhaps a little proudly or exhibitionistically "took in her stride."

She said she couldn't talk to her mother and that when they tried to
talk both got irritated. Her need for a baby animal seemed to be intensified by her struggle to cope with her feeling of the inadequacy of her
relationship with her mother. Some of her irritation was probably due to
my absence early in the month because of illness, although at the time
Robin had seemed to accept this realistically.

Robin also reacted to the family embroilment in troubles by repeated expression of her wish to "be an individual," to have a style of her own. She was critical of her parents "not being strict enough" and felt that Aunt Samantha and Uncle Wayne had "helped" her by making definite demands.

On the whole, she seemed to maintain herself through all the family stress until my absence toward the end of the month. At this time, she had her turn at an outburst, like one her father had had the week before. Robin's outburst occurred in the residence, and her protest was focused on my unavailability, which we had discussed the hour before I left for Thanksgiving; her upset also coincided with her menstrual period. The immediate stimulus for her anger was an episode in which four girls in her residence protested separately against taking responsibility for flag raising, and Robin evidently felt attacked.

I will review in detail her frustration at difficulties in communicating with her mother and will discuss her hand tremor.

Mother-Deprivation and Longing

Remembering her birthday I remarked, "Let me see, your birthday is Wednesday," and she nodded casually. I said, "This time last year there were some things you wanted very much for your birthday. Do you have things this year that you would like?" At first, Robin seemed to deny this, then soon began to say that she wanted a kitten, and the rest of the hour was occupied with a discussion of her feelings about kittens and other animals and her desire to take care of them.

She said that, of course, she would really like one of the babies in a new litter a friend had, but it would be hard to take care of the baby when she was going to school. However, she thought it might work because Charlie, one of her dogs, was also expecting early in December and might accept the kitten. This led to a discussion of previous experiences Robin had had with a mother animal that accepted other animals and experiences that Robin herself had had taking care of baby animals. She told about a cow they had in Grand Island, which rejected one calf that was then given to a different cow that took good care of it. The first cow then had another calf and rejected that one as well. Robin herself had taken care of the second calf.

I said that this was very interesting. I wondered what was the matter with the cow that rejected first one calf and then the other. Was the cow upset about something? Robin said she didn't know.

✚   I did not suggest the connection between her own feeling of being rejected and her interest in the rejected calf.

I asked her whether she had talked to her mother about how much she wanted the kitten to take care of, and Robin said she could talk to everyone except her mother. I said I was surprised about this, because I had thought that Robin and her mother had been getting along better recently. Robin said that her mother got irritated too quickly. Then she said, "I get irritated and she gets irritated and I get more irritated, so it's no use to talk to her."

I asked whether she ever said to her mother something like, "I *need*," and Robin said she didn't, repeating that her mother wouldn't listen and would just get irritated. I wondered why her mother might be getting irritated now; probably she felt pressed with four children and all the animals, and the troubles of Eve and Jim. Robin said rather coldly that another mother she knew in Grand Island had five children, the youngest only six months old, and with another preschooler. By contrast, all four in her family were able to do most things for themselves.

I then asked what ideas Robin had about how we might help her mother to understand that Robin needed a baby kitten to take care of. I also commented that what she really wanted was a baby and that she must be feeling that it would be a very long time to wait. Robin nodded with her appreciative smile. I commented that this was a deep longing, and she agreed. I asked whether she thought it would be useful for me to talk to her social worker—and whether she herself had talked to her. Robin said that wouldn't do any good; it would just make her mother more irritated.

I said I understood how much she wanted to have a baby kitten or a baby animal of some kind to take care of, and I thought we would need to find a way to solve the problem. Robin seemed quite pessimistic about that.

✚   In reviewing the hour, what struck me was the deep longing for a baby kitten—together with conflict with and distance from her mother—as if taking a mother role herself would make up for not getting the mothering she wanted. She did say that Eve was back in school now; it was hard for me to judge to what extent her mother might be disturbed by the problems that Eve and Jim were bringing her or whether something else was creating tension between her and Robin. My unavailability early in the month undoubtedly added to the sense of mother-deprivation.

Physical Progress and Individualizing

On the day after Robin's fourteenth birthday, she came in wearing a handsome, rather sophisticated blouse in tones of cream and brown with a sunburst design on the front in a deep gold yellow which matched the gold wool of her skirt. She was wearing a new brace on her teeth (a "bow") that she had to wear fourteen hours a day. This was a conspicuous and startling arrangement, since the heavy wire protruded entirely around the front of her face and head. When she came in, I asked how long she had had it, how it felt, and whether it bothered her. Robin matter-of-factly explained that she had had it for a week—since her previous hour with me. She had to wear it through the afternoon and night. It interfered with eating and, she added humorously, "biting my fingernails!" She also said that it was hard to kiss her parents goodnight, but she managed to do so by protruding her lips above and below the wire and she demonstrated this.

When I commented that she seemed to be coping with it very well, she said she had "to take it in her stride"; the only time it really bothered her was last week at Council, because she was the only girl there and she was a little embarrassed with the entire group of boys.

I commented appreciatively on her gay costume, and we talked about her taste compared with that of Eve, Ann, and her mother. She said, "I'm trying to decide on my own taste now." Ann and her mother had the most neutral tastes of all. This seemed to be another step toward becoming an individual.

In general, her mood had been cheerful. I said that along with the fact that she was doing well at school, and getting along with the others at the Children's Hospital, she seemed to be getting along better at home. Robin's mood seemed to droop slightly at this point, and I reminded her that I would be seeing her this Thursday and again next Monday, but that I would miss the week after Thanksgiving for a conference in Washington, as well as Thanksgiving Day when she also would be away. If there were things that she needed to talk about, it would be important for us to use the time well.

Robin asked, "Did you talk to Dr. Moore about my hand? I said I couldn't remember doing so, and asked Robin why she asked. Robin said, "Because she said something the other day about my hand getting better." This led to a discussion about her hand. I remarked that I had noticed a week ago that she had been carrying a scarf, and I thought she did this when her hand worried her; but I also had the impression that her hand was better, because her writing was so much smoother. Robin said that she always did carry something or other in her hand to distract attention from the difficulty that she had with it. She described a girl in Grand Island who had lost two fingers and who held a scarf so that her fingers came around it and the loss of the two was not noticeable. I commented that she, Robin, must still be bothered by her hand, but Robin again remarked, "It's something I was born with that I had to learn to take in stride."

Her mood became a little droopy, and I said that I thought it was wonderful that she could be the kind of person who would not be stopped by a problem like that—that she developed ways of coping with it and was determined to enjoy the many things that life offered. I asked her if she knew what I meant, and she nodded; I added that I had known other children who became too inhibited because of some such difficulty, but she was different, she had the courage to keep right on going. Robin nodded thoughtfully and wondered why her hand was better.

I tried to offer an explanation—that her "nervous hand," as she called it, was sensitive to other things going on with her. I asked whether it bothered her more when she was scared, angry, or not feeling well. She felt that it did get worse when she was scared. I suggested that one reason why her hand was getting better had something to do with the fact that she was getting more stable—that she was coming out of a period of change that many children went through between the ages of eleven and fourteen, when their bodies were growing and changing. I tried to explain in a simple way about glands and hormones and the fact that there are many internal chemical changes, as well as the changes in size and muscles. All these changes inside could have something to do with her hand getting more nervous, but now that her body was becoming stable her hand was getting a little better.

Robin listened to all of this without a comment. I asked how it happened that she wrote with her right hand when it was her right hand that bothered her especially. She explained that she had developed a good many skills with her left hand, but that she had been made to write with her right hand. I asked whether her hand bothered her in specific kinds of activities. She said that it did, especially if she were carrying something or holding something and unable to manage without dropping or spilling.

✟ Robin's candor in discussing her "nervous" hand (chorea) contrasted sharply with her pattern last year of hiding defects, avoiding discussion of problems. At the same time she was not as confiding or warm as she often was—perhaps reflecting the distance she felt from her mother, as well as defending against my absence.

Stress and Growth: A Dream

The first hour in December was absorbed with repercussions of my absence during a stressful time at Robin's home; her father had had a blow-up that had been frightening to Robin. She seemed rather feeble and pale and slumped into a chair. When I asked how she felt, she at first resisted talking about it, denying, "Okay, I feel all right," and so forth. I looked her over deliberately and said, "Well, I get the feeling that you really don't feel very well." She then said, "Well, you get the signs better than I do—the last time I saw you, you asked whether I was having my period, and it did come right after that." I continued, "But you're not feeling well right now," and she admitted that she had a sore throat and a cold, that she couldn't stand up "more than two minutes," and that she was feeling lousy. I said that she seemed to have the grippe and that usually in that state one stayed home in order to get over it and not get a further infection. Robin said, "But I'm stubborn—I have a project to finish up, and I'm going to do it." I commented that my mother would have said she was cutting off her nose to spite her face, and Robin laughed and said, "I know it, but I'm stubborn and I want to finish my project."

I wondered what other feelings she had; I said it was hard sometimes to tell the difference between physical and emotional feelings. I wondered how she had felt about my being away, whether she had been angry about it. She said, "Well, maybe," and started on a dream, hesitantly at first. "Somebody had been hurt—maybe me, maybe somebody else—and somebody was there with a tray, and I don't remember exactly what was going on." She knew that she had screamed (her mother had told her she had screamed) and had said, "Why don't you wear it for an earring?" There had also been a gun, "but nothing happened with it." After we had worked on the dream, "Somebody was shot four times; there was a doctor, but they couldn't get him, or something like that."

I said I thought it was a very interesting dream. I wondered whether the scream had been an angry or a frightened scream. Robin said she did not know; I suggested that it might have been both. I asked when she had had the dream; it was last Thursday. I commented that the last time I had seen her, two weeks before, she had told me that her mother was hurt and that she herself was hurt in a blow-up at home. I thought this might have had something to do with the dream, but Robin objected that that had happened some time before. I explained that dreams pick up feelings and thoughts that are hanging around from recent days, or some time back, or even very, very far back. I asked how she had been feeling during the two weeks I was gone, how she felt after her father's blow-up. She was not very articulate about this but said it was the first time she had ever seen him blow up that way. I suggested that she liked to think of him as the strong one in the family who didn't go to pieces and that perhaps it was frightening to her to have him blow up, perhaps she felt she couldn't count on him anymore. She agreed that this might be so. I said it must have been very hard for her to have me away just when she was feeling let down by her father, and I asked what other strain there might have been. What was the visit over Thanksgiving like in Grand Island? Only when I asked whether Aunt Samantha's guest, Maude, had been there did she blurt out, "Yes, she was and I hate her and I can't stand her." I said, "You were angry about her getting in your way with Aunt Samantha then, and I wonder whether you were angry at me because the conference people took me away from you?"

Robin's mood changed dramatically; the denying and resistant mood at the beginning of the hour completely vanished. She talked in her confiding, friendly, warm tone until the end of the hour. She said, "I know you had to go, but I guess I was angry that you went." I repeated that it must have been hard for her to have me away just when she felt so upset about the tense situation at home, about her mother being hurt, feeling hurt herself, and feeling she couldn't tell when her father might blow up again.

Robin then said, "Partly I was upset because I didn't know that I was that dependent on you." She clearly implied that she didn't want to be. I said, "Even when I'm away I think about you." Robin said gently, but clearly, "I know that." I said, "I guess what was hard was not having me here to talk things over with." Robin agreed. I asked whether she had talked things over with anybody. Robin said, "Since you weren't here, I did talk to Mother some." I could not get a clear picture of how much she had talked to her mother. I asked about Dr. Edmunds and Dr. Moore. She said she could talk to Dr. Edmunds, but she still couldn't talk to Dr. Moore very well.

Still thinking about the dream, I said, "You know, there's something funny about that dream; that remark about 'why don't you wear it for an earring' sounds like a joke to me. It sounds as if you felt that even when you got hurt and things were very difficult, you could count on your sense of humor to handle the situation." Robin agreed, saying that was how it seemed in the dream. Then, she told how Dr. Edmunds had kidded her and commented on how good it was that she could take teasing. Robin sounded ambivalent in quoting this, and I commented that she seemed to feel two ways about it; that she realized it was a compliment and meant that it was an indication of maturity to be able to take teasing, but still she didn't feel that good about it. Robin smiled again.

But she said, "Well, I'm not grown-up yet, and I won't be grown-up until I'm twenty-one." I said, "You sound as if you think when you are grown-up, you won't be dependent on anybody. Does that make sense?" Robin said she guessed not. I said I felt the good thing was that one could be independent in many ways, and at the same time one needs people, and Robin agreed. I added, "We've talked before about the fact that therapy is not just to have one good relationship, but to help pave the way for other good relationships. You wouldn't have a good relationship with me in therapy if you hadn't had a good relationship before with Aunt Samantha and with Sadie." Robin added, "And Kathleen helped too." I agreed, "She helped very, very much."

Robin then said, "Mother told me the other day that when I finished with Kathleen, they had said I might need to have some help again when I was twelve years old." I explained that the twelve-year-old stage is a hard time for lots of people.

I then commented, "There were many things in that dream from recent and far away times. I'm wondering about that tray; a tray could be like one of those trays they carry babies on these days." I added that the way she treated me at the beginning of the hour, not wanting to talk, was the way a one-year-old baby treats its mother when its mother has been away for two or three weeks. Robin was interested in this, and I added that lots of us have angry feelings when we've been left at a difficult time by somebody we need to be able to count on.

I said then we hadn't talked about the gun, and I wondered about that. Had her father and brother been hunting; did she want to go hunting? She said she didn't want to go hunting, but she did wish she could have been outdoors the way they were when they went hunting. Then she remembered more of the dream. "Somebody was shot four times." I wondered what the four could be about. Robin said, "There are four flags at school, and the girls are supposed to do their share." I asked whether the boys did their share, and she said they did, but there had been trouble about the girls doing it. Robin herself wanted to assume that responsibility. I asked what other thoughts she had about boys, and she said that last Friday Jim had kicked her when she had asked him to button her dress—he had buttoned it, then had kicked her so that the brown from his shoe left a mark on her black skirt. I reminded her that she had told me how gracious and gallant Jim had been during the summer, and she said, "Mostly, he had been that way all fall." This event happened after the dream.

Robin had told me in the middle of this discussion that several times she had had dreams that seemed to foretell the future—for instance, she had dreamed that when riding her bike down a hill she would fall and get hurt badly. That had happened, although she had not been seriously hurt. Another time, she had dreamed that her mother had been burned on the back. She herself had been at Aunt Samantha's and this occurred at home when her mother's loose cotton blouse caught on fire as she turned away from the stove. The other children had put out the fire, but her mother still had scars from it.

I repeated that the dream had many, many things in it and that I thought she had been very angry and very frightened by what happened in the family and very upset by my being away just then, and that all these feelings had piled up together in the dream.

Robin seemed contented and close through all this and, because it was the end of the hour, I said, "I'll see you Thursday."

✝ Robin's dream was her way of saying with ego strength, "I want to explore some of my feelings about my parents." All through her childhood, she had thought of her father as a strong figure. Here was an episode which she saw as an indication that he was human—he also had his limits. She saw him in a more realistic light. The dream implied that she was psychologically ready to accept herself as an adolescent. She was achieving in therapy a self-concept other girls gradually evolve for themselves. In the dream, she was not a grade-school child to her parents.

Still there was a question as to whether she was consciously aware that she was changing her view of her father. She realized that he and her mother were anxious about whether he could finish his professional training. Like many other adolescent girls, Robin needed to maintain an identification with her mother while also clarifying her own identity as a separate person. The solution for her, as for others, was to individualize her identification by selectively retaining her freedom to be like her mother in some ways, as in her cooking, her caring. At the same time, she wanted to achieve the freedom to develop her own taste, to master skills that would be useful in earning her own living, to be independent. Many of her uncles and cousins were in helping professions and she wanted to identify with the helping tribe.

The problem of identity was involved in connection with the conflict about flag raising. While some of the girls resisted, asserting that it was the boys' responsibility, Robin did not feel it was unfeminine. It was part of the range of roles appropriate to "a strong woman."

Robin's desire and ability to work on her dream implied that she understood that dreams could be taken seriously—that they could "mean something"—and that there was more than was apparent on the surface. She had great trouble with arithmetic, but she could work with metaphors. Working on the dream was evidence of her progress in understanding and of her awareness that working on the dream could foster growth. My support of her work on the dream implied that Robin did not have to continue a childish dependency relationship, that she and her therapist could cooperate and share understanding. I tried to keep the dream discussion at a level I felt she could use—in dream discussions, as elsewhere, I maintained a psychosocial orientation, always keeping in mind that potentially threatening interpretations would lead to disintegrative, rather than integrative, reactions.

Strength and Defenses

✚ This was an interesting hour, illustrating both Robin's zones of insight and mastery and her major defenses.

I had received the Council notes before Robin came in and asked how the flag-raising problem had been settled. She said, "Well, since the girls didn't like the idea, I'll have to take it up at Council next time." The younger girls did not want to take the flag down in the evening. I wondered about their feelings, whether they might feel this was a boy's rather than a girl's job; and also whether it was hard for them to do. Robin said the child-care workers helped them; as to sex role ideas, Robin got a little huffy and said that sawing wood is just as much a woman's responsibility as a man's (along the line of her previous discussions of pioneer women). I said I knew that she had a very strong conception of a woman's role, but not all girls did. Sarcastically she said, "Yes, that's the pale, limp, weak type that can't do anything at all." I commented that she had strong feelings about this, and wondered what would happen if she had one kind of strong feeling and other girls had a different kind of strong feeling. What does one do with disagreements in a democracy? Robin tended to dismiss the whole business, saying again she'd just take it back to Council.
I asked about other things that had been bothering her on Monday, such as her father's blow-up. She said defensively, "Well, he's only done it once or twice." I commented, "In other words, you feel as if in general you can count on him to be self-controlled." She nodded. I asked about other people in the family, including Aunt Samantha. She said that her aunt didn't blow up very much. Then I asked who she felt she was like, and she replied that it was hard to tell because she was close to so many

people in their big family. I said, "You mean that you take a little from each one," and Robin nodded but didn't seem interested in talking about this.

Instead, she commented on how much fun Dr. Edmunds was in teasing her, and how much she had enjoyed Dr. Edmunds's kidding her "when I overreact when she's giving me a shot." I asked whether she had had any thoughts about the connection between her feelings and health. She said she knew that feelings were connected with health—for instance, when she had been angry last week she had gotten that sore throat. And before she came to Topeka, when she had to take a test, it would "upset her kidneys" so that she would urinate a great deal. I explained how this works. I said that she seemed to be interested in medical things and that her teachers had commented that she was interested in scientific things. I wondered what she had in her folder. She immediately showed it to me, and I read what she had written on molds, fungi, bacteria, and so forth, on the basis of material in the encyclopedia. It was interesting and concise. When I asked some questions to see how well she understood it, she reeled off definitions, usually getting them quite straight. We talked a bit about some problems in writing, but she seemed to grasp the big words very well. I said that some things were hard for her and went slowly, but other things she picked up quickly. She wanted to know what, and I said, "Well, you have used words like malignant, overreact, and once you told me that Dr. Grant represents a mother figure to Missy."

✝ Instead of responding to the general point I was making, Robin seemed anxious about the possibility of too much being expected of her because of my comment on the area where she picks up quickly. At this point, her flight into the concrete was very obvious. Without acknowledging what I was saying about her ability to use adult words appropriately, she gave illustrations of how she thought Missy felt that she was an older sister.

Moreover, she came back again to some humorous episodes—for instance, how she had spilled her slice of pie at the supper table just after Ann and her mother had both spilled something and the whole family had giggled with hysterics. It seemed that she was using humor as a red herring to get away from the issue of how much learning she could expect of herself, and perhaps also to tell me that the family troubles were not so acute or so constant as they might have seemed on Monday.

Her flight into the concrete and shifting the discussion to a humorous episode were defenses against her anxiety that too much might be expected of her.

Christmas Stress and Robin's Creative Coping

About the middle of the month, Robin's mother had her turn at blowing up. Robin felt "all used up," but commented, "I have to concentrate hard on my work to get away from all the confusion." We discussed the price she paid for not admitting to herself how hard the struggles in the family were for her to bear.

In this context, she began to express a dread of Christmas, which reminded her of her grandmother's death and her aunt's recent death. Robin's feelings about loss were accentuated by her confused feelings about these relatives and also by her sense of the loss of Aunt Samantha, who had been "taken over" by Maude. All these feelings became connected with thoughts of losing me. We discussed the way in which we take into ourselves everything we have received from others and how these things remain part of us after loved ones are gone. We also discussed changes from childhood to being grown-up and the different realities that have to be accepted.

✝ My short absences were in reality helpful to the process of coming to terms with loss.

Along with these stressful feelings, Robin was frustrated because her mother had refused to let her have a horse, and because of her continued difficulties in talking to her parents. She used school as a support against all the family stress, but she still felt anxious about the quantity of work she could manage and about the possibility of ultimate success. She had done a careful, successful project on molds which her teacher had evaluated at a seventh- or eighth-grade level. Considerable writing on this had been managed with a sort of "speed writing" Robin had invented, leaving out vowels to shorten the work. Along with this positive use of school, Robin continued to sort out the ways in which she was like and different from her disturbed relatives; she expressed her appreciation of Dr. Edmunds's humor again; and from time to time voiced thoughts of working as a veterinarian.

The third week of December brought a dream centering on a staircase and a big tomato—which I restated as "to-mate-oh?" not yet knowing about plans for Ann's marriage, which was to take place in January. Robin was expressing more interest in boys and in the dance to come and in sex feelings, which seemed to become intense around the time of her period. She did dance with three boys and actively helped to make the party a success. Therapy use of the dream focused on wishes and conflicts about growing up and about relations with boys.

She was also more ambitious in her schoolwork, choosing an adult book on Pasteur instead of the younger books offered by the teacher. She ended the pre-Christmas week by making a reindeer and sleigh cake, and by expressing pride in me and in the family strengths on both sides of her family. She also reviewed how much she had been given by many people. In contrast to earlier defensive coping, she was now resiliently mobilizing her capacities for creativity and mastery.

Stress, Sensitivity, and Conflict

One Monday morning Robin's social worker called to tell me what had been going on in the family: on the previous Monday, in the late after-noon, there had been another very tense situation in the family which apparently overwhelmed Robin's mother so that she walked out of the house and stayed away an hour or so, coming back later. The result of the mother's blow-up and departure was that Eve and Ann both settled in to be more helpful and cooperative; it looked as if things might possibly have turned a corner.

Robin came in looking slightly flushed, and with a very strained, some-what depressed look around her eyes, and she talked more softly than usual and in a higher voice, without her typical strength or resonance. It did not seem atypical for a young girl, yet it somehow was weaker than Robin's usual voice. She veered back and forth between problem areas and positive things that helped her to maintain her "strength" and keep herself somewhat independent of the family conflicts.

I commented that she didn't look very well; she said she was very tired, and I suggested that one would be tired after struggling with the stress of the last few weeks. Robin didn't argue with this, and I explained that her social worker had told me what had gone on after Robin's hour with me last Monday and this helped me to understand why she had seemed to have difficulty talking on Thursday. Robin accepted this too, understand-ingly, and her mood through the entire hour today was one of sharing how weak she felt—she felt as if she had lost all her strength and couldn't manage very well any more.

I asked what had gone on recently, and she said that Eve had gotten angry and had gone off to a motel, saying that she couldn't study in the room with Ann and she had to have a place to herself. The father and mother had decided to give Eve their room and to use the family room in the basement as their bedroom. I commented that it sounded like a difficult Sunday and, coming on top of other difficult things recently, Robin must have been feeling a little overwhelmed. She said she was sensitive and always had been, and implied that she could not stand much more because all her strength was used up.

I commented that she had had a lot of strength and that she had shown me that despite the ups and downs in the family she was able to keep up her work at school. Robin said, "I have to concentrate hard on my work to get away from all the confusion." I said this was a good thing to do in one way, but I thought perhaps her feeling weak and tired and all used up might have some connection with how hard she tried to accent the positive. That was a good thing to do in general, but when it meant that she wasn't admitting to herself how hard some of the difficult things really were for her, it used up too much energy.

Robin shifted; Christmas was coming, but she couldn't care less—Christmas still reminded her of the death of her grandmother "who wasn't with them anymore, and this year Aunt Harriet died." She hung her head and said perhaps she shouldn't talk about it, that it was hard for her to believe that Aunt Harriet was alcoholic, even though she really did know it.

I commented that Aunt Harriet had died only a couple of months ago and said that a wise friend of mine had once said "grieving takes four seasons." Robin said, "All right, but it's been more than that since my grandmother died." I suggested that perhaps one reason why it was hard to feel clear about it all was that her feelings about her grandmother and Aunt Harriet were mixed up.

In talking about the stress and disappointments, Robin finally brought out that her mother would not let her have a horse until summer, if then. "Mother doesn't trust me" since Eve had been thrown on the barbed wire and had torn her leg. Robin continued that she had been thrown too and had hurt her leg and it still sometimes bothered her, and that, in fact, she was a little afraid of the horse, but she wanted to learn to manage it. I summarized these many different strains—Aunt Harriet's death, Eve's difficulties, the long period when a guest had Robin's room, the disappointment about not getting a horse, her father's flare-up when I was away.

Robin admitted that she was mad, and I commented that she was mad at me as well as at life in general with all these confusions and difficulties. I asked whether she had talked with her mother about her feelings about Christmas and she said that she had tried to, but her mother had been looking at television and said, "I'll talk to you later." Robin had then gone to her father and told him how she felt. She also said that she had talked to him about the fact that she felt she was too sensitive and too easily upset to be a doctor or psychiatrist or something like that, but she might be able to work with children. I commented that there were a number of things one could do with children and that one could get training after finishing high school. Robin objected that she wanted to go to college, and I said that there were things you could get training for after finishing high school and other things you could have training for after finishing college.

Robin then shifted to talking about the dogs. She brightened up and talked in a more cheerful tone of voice about how when things got too upsetting at home, she could always play with her dogs and talk to them. I commented that they gave her a peace and comfort area and they must mean a great deal to her.

I asked how she felt about school, and she said, "Well, I'm trying to do more and I try to keep the quality good, but I'm still not as good on the quantity as I should be." I empathized that it must be hard to do much at home when there was so much confusion. I also wondered whether she was getting enough sleep; perhaps she needed extra sleep in periods of stress like this, and she agreed. I said, "When your energy gets all used up by anxious, angry feelings, it seems as if the only way to build it up again is with sleep."

Her tone continued soft and thin, as if what she wanted during this hour was mostly comfort. It seemed unwise at this time to press too hard. At one point she said, "I'm sensitive and I always was sensitive and I always will be sensitive," and seemed to imply that she felt as if she never would be able to stand anything. I agreed that she was sensitive and added, "But another thing that is very important is that you are at a very sensitive age. I know what it's like to be thirteen and fourteen, and as one grows older one finds ways of managing and getting along with one's sensitivity." Robin said reflectively but a little doubtfully, "I know I'll probably outgrow some of it." I said, "You sound as if you felt pessimistic about ever being able to really manage things successfully in life." Robin smiled warmly at this, the way she did when she got a lift or relief, from feeling understood.

✝ This happened several times during the hour, yet she did not have the complete relief, followed by strong positive feelings, which had emerged in certain other hours. There seemed to be a possibility that she was struggling against identifying with fragile members of her family, or at least with a feeling that she would never get over the sensitivity that made her so vulnerable to stress.

Trying to Help the Sick and the Old

Robin commented that she still couldn't look forward to Christmas. She talked a long time about Aunt Harriet, saying things that she "didn't know whether she ought to say," and I reminded her that in therapy one can say everything.

She had overheard Aunt Harriet's husband telling how bottles of pills had been found in her suitcase, pills that should not be taken with alcohol. I asked Robin whether she was telling me that Aunt Harriet knew that she was taking a risk. Robin said, "Yes, she needed some help so much and used the pills." The discussion had the tone of ventilating things that Robin had not felt free to discuss with her family; I asked whether she could talk about Aunt Harriet with her mother; Robin said, "I can't," that her mother was too upset about it.

She said, "I don't understand why Aunt Harriet had such a hard time, because she had two lovely daughters who would do anything for her and so would her husband." I commented that it was hard not to be able to understand, but that neither she nor I knew enough to understand.

Robin thought Aunt Harriet might have been helped by Alcoholics Anonymous, and I agreed that sometimes Alcoholics Anonymous did help people. Then, Robin said that Aunt Harriet really wouldn't accept any help and that she, Robin, would have liked very much to help her.

✛   Robin's mature grasp of Aunt Harriet's alcoholism problem, the resources of Alcoholics Anonymous, and her aunt's inability to accept help is an example of strength which helped to balance her deficits.

When Robin commented that Aunt Harriet wouldn't let anybody help her, I said that it was true that nobody could be helped who did not wish to be helped. For instance, neither Kathleen Kirk nor I would have been able to help Robin herself if she had not wanted to make progress. Robin nodded seriously and said, "That's what Aunt Harriet wasn't able to do."

I commented that Robin seemed very concerned about Aunt Harriet, and Robin said, "In a way we're the same." I said, "You're the same in the sense that she needed help and you feel that you need help, but in many other ways you're very different." I asked Robin what Aunt Harriet looked like, and Robin described her as very thin and frail—with transparent skin so that you could see her bones. "She wasn't eating anything toward the last." I said, "Just living on alcohol," and Robin nodded seriously. She then commented that Aunt Harriet's husband drank a little too, just a social drink. But one time at Aunt Samantha's when she asked him whether he'd like some ginger ale or other soft drink, he said he'd like bourbon. Aunt Samantha had exclaimed, "What, at this time of day!" Robin said, laughing, that Aunt Samantha seemed to think that wasn't a proper time for a drink, but it was five-thirty or so—as if Robin thought that it was an appropriate time.

I said she seemed to think that Aunt Harriet's husband was able to drink in a healthy way, and I also commented on her laughter and said, "Here again, when you've been talking about something sad and very worrisome, you're able to remember something that seemed funny to you and that helps you keep your head above water." Robin nodded and said, "Life is a sea, and you have to learn how to swim." I added that sometimes the waves and the breakers were very rough, and it was hard to swim. I went on to say that I thought the fact that she felt close to Aunt Harriet helped us to understand why it was so hard for her to accept her loss.

Robin then shifted to Christmas and the fact that it would be very hard not to have her grandmother on Christmas day. This led to more conversation about her grandmother and the fact that her grandmother had helped her make things, like baking a cake. From this, Robin remembered other old people whom she herself had helped, giving an example of one elderly friend who had lived to the age of one hundred and then died after her hundredth birthday celebration. Robin commented, "We wouldn't have wanted her to live any longer." I said that part of growing up was growing to accept the fact that when a person has had a long and complete life, we cannot ask that they keep on living for us. We have to be willing to let them die when the time comes.

Robin nodded seriously and gave some other examples of old people whom she had known and helped—one old lady whom she had read to had also died. I commented that it seemed to me that she was telling me two kinds of things—first that it was hard to accept the loss of her grandmother because her grandmother had helped her to learn how to do things and, second, that there were other people whose loss she felt because she had been able to help them. She was feeling the loss not just of the people, but of the relationship of helping and being helped.

Robin agreed and said that it was hard to imagine having another relationship like that. I said that part of growing up was to accept losing the relationships that we had as children. It was hard to let these go when we did not feel sure about new relationships that might develop.

Robin got a tissue and said, "My nose starts to run when I feel like this, just the way you said it does." Then when she sat down, she looked at the clock and asked what time it was. I didn't suggest that perhaps she was wondering how much longer our relationship would last.

✝   It was important to clarify that while Robin was vulnerable like Aunt Harriet, she had the strength to get help as her aunt did not—along with other strengths.

Anxiety, Loss, and Identification

As soon as Robin came in for her next therapy hour, she said, "I had another stupid dream." She said that it might "symbolize" something, but she didn't know what. First, there had been a great big huge tomato; about all the rest of it she was quite vague, but she gradually brought out that there seemed to have been some other big things, and she thought they had probably been big people. She then said there had been something little, maybe it had been like a fork, but it had had a round end; then as she groped along trying to remember, she said there had been stairs and, finally, something at the top of the stairs—like an attic, and she thought there was a lot of apparatus in the attic. These things came out slowly after help from me, as I asked, "What do you suppose those big things were, what did the little thing look like?" and so forth.

She said the dream was a nightmare, and it came before she got sick at about four o'clock A.M. Friday night after the dance at the Children's Hospital. I asked about the dance and whether she had been with some boys. She said she had talked to Kelly and Charles, and had had a pleasant time with them. Much later she said she did not dance and, pointing to the external brace around her mouth, said that it would be hard to dance with that on.

She kept coming back to "that silly tomato," and I restated it, as with the earlier dream, "to-mate-oh?" Robin responded to this with only a smile.

I suggested that she might have wanted to dance, or to mate, but a year before she heard about the girls in Grand Island who had become pregnant, and I asked if she remembered how shocked and upset she was then. She said that another girl had just had an illegitimate baby and had not gotten married. I suggested that this could have made her even more frightened and upset about what can happen with boys. She agreed and then said she would be afraid to be in a car with two boys, particularly at night, but she would not be afraid to be in a car with one boy in the daytime. She had had some conversation with a boy named Floyd, who went to public school, and I suggested that maybe she would like to go to public school where she would see Floyd; she agreed but said it would be a long time before she would be able to do so. I suggested that this long time before she would be able to go to public school or would be able to dance, or date or mate, was a long flight of stairs that she would have to go up. Robin agreed. She said, "I can't date until I'm sixteen or get to public school, and that will be a long time."

I suggested that both Floyd and fork begin with *f*. It was a little fork, as if she would like to have a little taste of what it would be like to go out with a boy, to date or mate, but it was frightening.

Robin in a quiet, thoughtful, dreamy sort of mood seemed to agree with each step in an understanding way, but without any real relief. I commented that at the top of the stairs there had been all that apparatus in the attic, but the apparatus on her face would be gone by the time she grew up. Robin then said, "If you could connect this dream with the dream before, I think we'd have something."

We went back to the previous dream in which she was so angry and frightened—another nightmare, and she remembered there had been a gun in that dream. I reminded her that that dream had come the day after she had been so angry at the girls for refusing to help with the flag raising, and angry with me because I had not been there to help her. I wondered whether part of her fright in the nightmare was because to blow up in anger as she did at the girls felt something like having a gun or being masculine like her father who had blown up when he was so exasperated. I suggested that that dream might be about the fear of acting like a male and that this dream seemed to be about the fear of having a male. Robin seemed to agree with this too, but still wondered about the little fork with the round end. I suggested that that was a piece of masculine apparatus that was little, but important, something one could want but be afraid of.

I asked Robin whether she had had her period. She said no, and I suggested that she might have it soon and that the dream might be influenced by sexy feelings that are likely to come before a period starts. Robin agreed again, but still did not seem to be relieved. I commented that she seemed very droopy, and she said, "I'm tired." I suggested that she was tired from struggling with all these feelings and that I thought she was struggling with some other feelings too, because for the last few hours we had been talking about her feelings about Christmas when her grandmother and aunt would not be there.

The attic made me wonder what she knew about her grandmother's death, because the attic in the dream might be like the attic in her grandmother's house. Robin described how her grandmother had gone up to clean the attic, which she was not supposed to do because she had a bad heart; that she had opened the window to get some air and had fallen out and her neck was broken. I said that would certainly make an attic seem very scary, and I wondered whether an attic at the top of a stairs could mean something like this: there are things one longs for very much, on the stairs of growing up—like the things that one does with boys and getting married—but so many people she has known have had a bad time, like Aunt Harriet and her grandmother, and it is frightening to think about growing up when she thinks about the people who have had such a bad time.

Robin began to cry and said she did think part of the dream was connected with her feelings about her grandmother. I said I knew how sad she was about losing her grandmother; if she had been thinking that she would never see me again, just the way she would never see her grandmother again, this could make things worse.

Robin said, "I never did see Kathleen Kirk again." I said, "And so you feel that because you lost one therapist and never saw her again that it would happen this way with the next therapist." Robin nodded. I asked whether her father had patients that he still saw. She said yes. I said, "Does stopping one relationship necessarily mean that you never see the person again?" Robin said no. I said that one thing that dreams do is to give us a chance to sort out the difference between all those inside thoughts and imaginings and the way things actually were. Robin was silent, and it was the end of the hour, but I let her stay over for another ten minutes. Finally, after she had been very quiet with her eyes closed for a few minutes, I asked, when she opened them, "Where are all the other people, like Aunt Samantha—people who have had a good life?" I added, "You feel you are a little bit like Aunt Harriet who had such a hard time, but you feel you are like a good many other strong people too."

Robin nodded. She said, "But I don't have Grandmother." I said, "But you have the things she gave you, and some day you might be a grandmother and give the good things which your grandmother gave to you to some other children." Robin added, "And I could give them to my own children or to other children." I agreed and said, "One of the good things about what we receive from others is that we can give those same good things to other people who need them." Robin seemed to be gaining vigor during this part of the conversation and stood up. She had brought me a package at the beginning of the hour and told me to open it. It was a little decorated tray of cookies. Now at the end of the hour, I said, "Wouldn't you like a cookie?" She said, "But should we open it?" I said I thought it would be easy and found a way to take the lid off without disturbing the gift and offered her a cookie, which she took. I said I would see her Thursday.

Team Meeting: Family Stress, Robin's School Progress, and Anxiety

At the next team meeting, the social worker decribed the episode she had told me about earlier, when Robin's mother had become very angry with Jim, Eve, and the father all at once and had left home for an hour, after which she had returned and decided not to lift a finger. She had gone on strike, as it were. She had threatened to send Eve and Jim to boarding school. Ann then pitched in to help the mother, while the mother sewed something for Robin. Robin was the only one who did not fight her, the only one who got up in the morning after being called once. The mother had made an outfit that was supposed to be for Eve but "accidentally" didn't fit, so Robin had gotten it.

The father seemed to be worn out. He had always tried to see himself as the strongest in the family, but now he was sick and tired. He dreaded coming back from work, with all the problems he had there, to more problems at home and would have liked to avoid them. When the social worker had tried to show the parents Robin's recent school reports, they had not wanted to see them, and they could not deal with the question of retesting Robin.

When somebody commented that things were going more smoothly with Robin than with anyone else, I commented that she had, however, had two nightmares lately; I reviewed them and suggested that one of them seemed to be concerned with being afraid that her own blow-up would mean that she might be like a male, like her father who had blown up a few days before.

The discussion continued with other aspects of Robin's good functioning. At the dance, the child-care workers reported that she actually did dance with several boys (which she did not tell me—she told me that she had "talked to" several boys). Robin helped get the boys together, and asked Melvin to dance with Elaine, a friend Robin had brought. (Robin might have been sexually stimulated by dancing with boys and embarrassed to tell me that.) The child-care workers also commented that she was speaking much more clearly and it was much easier to understand her than last year.

Dr. Moore and the social worker discussed Robin's closer relation with her mother. It seemed that Robin identified with what her mother worried about. The mother had panicked about Eve's dating, and there had been much talk about it. Ann had decided not to go to London on the International Living experiment as had been planned, because of her boy friend. The mother was upset about this too.

The social worker reviewed a fight that Robin and Jim had had about a chair where Robin had been working. She had left the chair, leaving her things at the table. Jim had come up and shoved her things away and sat down. He had then left, and Robin had come back, pushing his things aside, and got her own again. Then Jim had come up and pulled out another chair. Eve, coming along at this time, had commented, "Well, Robin will win." The group laughed and said that somehow everybody had this feeling. Robin did get involved in hassles and did win. The flag situation was an example.

The social worker added that there was a new theme of sacrifice, that Robin felt that Eve should be considered first now, that a great deal had been given to her, Robin. She had made such remarks as "They [her parents] don't have time for me right now because Eve is most important." She had also referred to feelings that she ought to be earning her own way because her uncle and aunt have to pay so much for her treatment. I felt this concern was important background for Robin's fear of losing me.

In school she had made a unique and original owl mural using different textures and shapes; she helped to clean up and was less attention-getting than last year. Her math teacher commented that her math had improved and she was now able to do fifth-grade work. Robin was frequently tired and had said it was hard to get enough sleep. She made self-depreciating remarks at times but, on the whole, seemed much less frustrated than formerly.

Jessie described Robin's study of fungi for science. Robin had four "culture slabs." She cooked her agar solution, kept notes on the fungi, bacteria, and so forth, did research on these and on mildew, and made slides. Jessie said that she has seen eighth-grade students tackle "lesser projects and do less well in them." As to spelling, if Robin sounded a word out slowly she could spell, but at times she got frustrated and did poorly then. Robin brought four adult books from the library and was slowly reading a book about Pasteur. Jessie also said that Robin was so expressive in class that she was a threat to Garth. For instance, when Jessie asked for a description of winter or a tree, Robin would bring out a vivid and expressive statement, but Garth was not able to do this.

It was suggested that Robin wanted very much to be an adult and thus tended to overreach herself. I suggested that she wanted to get away from being a child; she probably wanted to demonstrate that she could do more advanced work. Her teacher said that she would understand part of the book on Pasteur. It was suggested that Robin's molds might be displayed; this would be good for her and stimulating to others, too. Robin used to take homework home last year in order to get her father's help; she did not do this now, although she always seemed to have homework at home.

The child-care workers told of Robin's hesitations and apologies—"I shouldn't be saying this"—her tendency to be overcontrolled regarding saying the right thing at the right time. She also tended to drop clues instead of telling the whole story about something that was bothering her or making her angry.

The team also discussed Robin's relation with her mother. Dr. Moore believed that Robin and her mother must have talked a good deal about Aunt Harriet's death. There was some thought that even if Robin had worked through her angry feelings toward her mother last year, the mother had not worked through her own feelings, and also might be encouraging Robin's identification with her. Moreover, it was valuable to Robin to be "the one who was not picking on mother."

I suggested that all the attention that Robin was getting in therapy and in her special education might create a problem for the other children, which Robin, feeling guilty perhaps, wanted to terminate or resolve. This might be related to the anxieties about loss which seemed to have been reintensified currently.

Growing Up, Sources of Strength and Sweetness, Fears of More Losses

In contrast to all of her sad anticipations, in the last therapy hour three days before Christmas Robin was gay, sometimes giggly, though there were thoughtful, earnest, direct moments. Her tone seemed to be in harmony with her gay costume—a pants and jacket outfit in warm bright tones of gold, green, lighter yellow, and some blue. After I noted that she was much freer and more open now, more in contact with her unconscious, and able to deal with dreams and feelings much more spontaneously than she had been last year, and that this was progress, she took off the jacket, showed me the inside and in particular showed me a tag which said "do not clean."

✝ The hour was "dancy" and seemed to weave back and forth between gay, sometimes teasing moments and at other times serious thoughtful themes. The pace was rather fast, and Robin was often quick to make a warm, laughing remark that had the quality of a tit-for-tat type of repartee.

After we had talked about her pretty outfit, I gave her the small Christmas gift I had brought for her (which she had glanced at without making any comment), saying, "See if you can guess what it is." She smiled and guessed that it might be something ceramic. I said that she was right, It was something handmade. "It's a little dangling thing, but it's very feminine." She opened it and found the little silver poodle bracelet charm. She exclaimed, "Oh, that's cute," and looked carefully at the arts and crafts label on the box. Then, she told me about a school in Tennessee where handcrafts were taught.

Then, I said apropos of design, "We didn't talk about this interesting card you gave me with the cookies, on Monday. Here are these four hearts, and the four is interesting because in your dream you dreamed about a fork and four seems to be important in your life. Your grandmother and Aunt Harriet and mother and you make four; and your mother and father and Aunt Samantha and Uncle Wayne make four; and your grandmother and Kathleen Kirk and I and you make four (I'm grandmother too, for that matter); and there are four children in your family," and so forth. Robin was interested and said, "I like fours." I said, "There are lots of fours." Robin seemed to object then and said, "I was thirteen last year and thirteen brings good luck." I asked, "How about fourteen?" She seemed a little dubious and said it was good to be fourteen in some ways. I said she seemed to have mixed feelings about it and asked what the mixed feelings were about, since she seemed to be doing so well in school and had had a good time at the dance.

She mentioned talking to Kelly and Charles at school; Kelly teased her and, with a little blush, she admitted that she liked it. She also said that when he had come in to the dance, he had said, "After I get warmed up, will you dance with me?" And Robin had said, "You'll get warmed up faster if you get out into the middle of the room."

After talking about Kelly and Charles a little bit, she said, "But I changed the subject, didn't I?" I commented, "You're weaving back and forth." She seemed to want to get back to the Christmas card, and I commented that it was also interesting that it was pointed at one end and that it had a round opening at the other end. Robin laughed and protested gaily in a "Oh, there you go" tone of voice.

Then she got serious and said, "What about that dream. I had it again last night." I commented that if she had had it again, it certainly must mean that her dream mind wanted to tell us to get to work on it. I asked her just how it had been this time. She said that there had been big people and stairs and between them had been the tomato. She wanted to know what all that was about.

Just as I started to ask a question, she asked, "Did you talk to anybody about this?" I said, "Yes, you know that even a therapist my age talks over a patient with a supervisor and Dr. Hirschberg is our supervisor." Robin agreed quite comfortably. "What did you and he think about it?" I said, "Well, we went over the things that you and I had talked about, and he agreed that you were very much concerned with problems of growing up." I asked whether she knew what the word "heterosexual" meant and she looked interested. I explained that it means being able to respond to the other sex—if you are a girl or woman, being able to respond to a boy or man, and if you are a boy or man, being able to respond to a girl or woman, and that growing up means to be able to have heterosexual responses.

Robin seemed to feel pleased or possibly a little flattered that I would use this big word to describe what she was going through, and she nodded, again a little flushed, but in complete agreement. I said, "You remember how we were talking about how you want to grow up, and this means relations with boys, and at the same time you're frightened of what happens when girls like those in Grand Island go too far too fast in their relations with boys." Robin agreed.

Even so, she switched again and began to talk about Aunt Samantha and Uncle Wayne. I said, "Let me see, Uncle Wayne is what relation to you?" Robin said, "He's grandmother's brother, and Aunt Samantha is related to me just by marriage." I said, "Well, that's interesting. In other words, you're telling me that Uncle Wayne represents strength on your mother's side." Robin nodded, interested.

I said, "I'm interested in this, because mostly you told me about the sweetness on your mother's side—of your grandmother and others." And Robin nodded. "But you had always given me the impression that you felt the strength was on your father's side." Robin now said, "But there is strength on my mother's side too." I agreed and said, "Yes, that's what you're saying now, that Uncle Wayne represents strength on your mother's side too. In other words, you get sweetness and strength, and you get strength from both sides." Robin agreed thoughtfully.

Then she said, "And Sadie did a lot for me too; she always had lunch for me when mother wasn't up to it yet." I agreed that she had many people who gave her a great deal. Then, she went on giggling, "When Jim and I used to have fights, Sadie would say, 'If you two don't stop that, I'll go home'—and she lived way across town so we always did stop it." I commented very seriously, "You mean that she controlled you by threats?" Robin said, "Just that one threat." I said, "I think that's very interesting—it might have something to do with why it's so hard for you to say anything that you think isn't the right thing to say in therapy. You're afraid that if you did, I might go away and leave you." Robin nodded soberly and said, "That might be so." Robin laughingly said to me, "I'll be in Grand Island all next week." So I laughed back at her and said, "And now who is leaving whom?" Robin giggled some more.

Here I was impressed with Robin's flexibility and capacity to respond to positive aspects of Christmas along with her ability to think about the ramifications of her experiences of loss and fears of more losses. She was stubborn in her determination to master challenges but not rigid in an anal-character way. She was energetically trying to grow up.

Progress in the Fall of Robin's Second Year of Treatment

The first four months of her second year in therapy, with some work at the junior high school level, adult reading, progress in social participation, response to boys, ability to deal with sexual pressures, and clearer speech, looked like a giant step ahead—a dramatic contrast to the previous September's depression, hangdog expression, tremors, anxieties about participating in groups, tendencies to become unintelligible and to lose control, and second- to fourth-grade schoolwork at the time of her evaluation. Many of her concerns were healthy adolescent preoccupations, which she worked on actively while still struggling with problems directly and secondarily related to her neurological deficits.

The progress was partly due to developmental changes and maturation; some stabilization of menstrual periods; some reduction of autonomic nervous system variability, which had been exacerbated by normal physiological instability of puberty. Improved control of her allergies and the prospect of improved appearance with restitution of the missing teeth supported her increasing confidence with boys and courage to participate in teen-age social events. Progress in school was fostered by the flexibility of her teachers, who used her maximal motivation; child-care workers helped her to prepare for social occasions; and her group worker appreciated her participation in Council. Therapy supported Robin's integration of the many aspects of her progress.

Her capacity to focus on schoolwork in the face of the extreme stress at home and the anxiety caused by my absences was impressive. Robin had given us many surprises, but still I was amazed at the continuing progress in her internal development, individuating and clarifying her identity with a balanced view of her similarity to and difference from relatives, and of the sources of "sweetness and strength," reaching a more realistic view of her father, while developing typical teen-age heterosexual interests.

As part of Robin's growing up, she felt a loss of childhood, as many children do in the transition to adolescence. The losses of her grandmother and aunt who she felt had helped her absorbed some of her feeling of the loss of part of herself in the process of growing up. Included was the loss of her daydream of becoming a veterinarian, which was more unrealistic than she realized in view of the difficulties with technical problems her disability in mathematics would cause.

For a girl whose neurological problems made all changes and transitions uniquely difficult, the recognition of losses and changes in the process of growing up were inevitably painful. Added stress came as a result of the conflicts between different girls' and workers' concepts of what were appropriate jobs and behavior for girls. There was tension beneath Robin's persistent forceful assertions that pioneer women who "made this country" were strong, "not pale and weak." She continued to identify with the image of the strong pioneer woman in order to defend herself against temptations to give up when she felt weak.

Along with these various sources of strain in the process of growing up, was her awareness of being a "slow learner" and of the necessity to struggle with this limitation to the pace, and perhaps the possibility, of reaching her goals. Her identification with strength supported her "stubborn" determination to conquer her weaknesses. She still had not completely faced the implications of neurological damage.

11

A Checkerboard and
a Mosaic of Self

More Sex Education

The winter of Robin's second year of treatment continued to bring stressful experiences. By January 1, Robin knew about two pregnancies in girls in Topeka—"a blot on Topeka." Robin and her family spent the week from Christmas to New Year's in Grand Island and returned to Topeka for Ann's wedding.

Ann's marriage, and then Robin's knowledge of Ann's pregnancy, again mobilized feelings of loss ("Ann was the only one I could talk to"), resentment against the coming baby ("I'm not ready to be an aunt"), feeling left out of the Ann/Jonathan relationship, feelings of anger ("I don't want to talk to her"), feelings of rejection when she tried to talk to Aunt Samantha, helplessness, some despair, and shakiness in reaction to the cumulative tensions of the fall when her parents seemed unable to manage the stress they were under. She again felt anxious about losing other supports, such as Sadie, and, by implication, me, and therapy. Robin reproached her parents for not talking to her and expressed her feeling that she could talk only to Ann, a reproach that made it hard for them to respond. Later, she had blown up angrily at Eve and the family after a relatively slight incident on the day she had worked on preparing dinner for her parents' anniversary.

Still, she tried to maintain her equilibrium and succeeded much of the time; she continued to work well at school, although she was morose in the residence. In therapy, after release of feelings about the loss of Ann, she turned to thoughts of future plans—whether she would be able to go to public school or to France as Ann and Eve had done. She could manage the trip to France if her cousin Leslie could be with her because "Leslie takes me for what I am, with the weak points and the strong points." Concern and anger about being taunted as a "nut" because of being in the Children's Hospital was balanced by pride in her science project.

We talked about plans for the psychological tests, to check on development in order to clarify plans for the future. Discussion of her anxiety was followed by acceptance of the test plan, but she was depressed and withdrawn in the therapy hour on the day the testing began, unable to continue to work at understanding her feelings. The idea of the tests mobilized feelings of despair that she would never be completely like other girls. At other times, feelings of loss were handled by denial, and narcissistic blows by compensatory haughtiness at moments.

We discussed her defensive patterns and also the checkerboard of weaknesses and strengths, and Robin creatively developed a richer concept as she worked on a bold and original mosaic combining a multitude of textures, smooth and rough, and of colors, dark and light.

She also used the sexual concerns intensified by Ann's marriage to press for more "sex education" in the Children's Hospital, as well as a science project on the body, and especially the nervous system. She was extremely interested in some elementary facts about interactions contributing to emotional upheavals of the central and autonomic nervous system. This helped her understand the way in which her mind could exaggerate the meaning of a disturbing event.

The multiple stresses of this period had a double consequence; they threatened Robin's integration and also stimulated growth through efforts to understand and creative coping. It is worthwhile to review a few therapy hours in some detail.

Robin's placid mood after Christmas vacation gave me the feeling that she must have had a satisfactory talk with her mother. Robin said she had. Her mother had talked with her about sexual intercourse and had said it was not right to have sexual intercourse unless you loved the person and were married. Robin mentioned the pregnancy of one Grand Island girl, Marcia, and the fact that she had lost the baby. Robin felt that it was a blot on Marcia, and she also talked about another girl in Grand Island who had gotten pregnant this fall and could not get married; Robin did not know what would happen to the baby.

Rather abruptly, Robin said, "Did I tell you that Jim hugged me yesterday?" I asked her how it had happened. She had thrown a pillow at him and they were roughhousing, then suddenly he had hugged her while she was sitting on the bed. She "wasn't lying down, so he couldn't do anything to me." She added that she didn't think he could anyway, he wasn't old enough. I took this rather seriously and suggested that perhaps they were both old enough to be outgrowing that kind of roughhousing and that one kind of excitement could lead to other feelings. Robin said he couldn't do anything to her because she could kick and bite.

I thought there might be some connection between these thoughts and feelings and the dream about the "tomato." She mentioned that she used to have a dream over and over again which she had not had since she "had been here." "It's a little box, and there are matches in the box, and if one match gets lighted, they all get on fire and I couldn't stop them." I reminded her that for many years she had had trouble in controlling her temper and that perhaps she had felt that she had a temper that was as hard to control as fire. She added that in the middle of the box of matches was a little sign saying "Don't strike me." I suggested that she was asking not to get touched off or frustrated, that she didn't want the kinds of experiences that touched off her uncontrollable temper. She agreed, and I said that perhaps she thought of it now because other feelings could be hard to control, and in this experience with Jim, perhaps she was thinking that feelings that started with teasing or play or a little aggression could turn into different feelings, and Robin agreed knowingly.

Then she added that this might be how "accidents" happened. I asked what she meant by an accident, and she said "like Marcia." I said that if a girl got pregnant because she has had intercourse when she should not have it, it was not really "an accident"; I agreed that Marcia could have been carried away by feelings. Robin began to stumble and get embarrassed—her nostrils had been dilating and closing increasingly, although her manner was still quiet and somehow strangely contented and mature. She said, "There are still some things that I don't understand—perhaps I shouldn't say this." I reassured her that there were not any rules here about what she should or should not say. Finally, she was able to bring out that she really didn't understand how the female body worked. They had had movies in school, and she knew some things about reproduction, but she felt she still did not understand all about it. I suggested that this could be one reason for going ahead with a project on the body—there would be things that would help her to understand how the female body worked, but also there were things to understand about feelings and how they worked.

Robin said she thought that there ought to be more sex education in high school—that when so many girls got pregnant, they needed to know more than they do. I asked how much she had learned from being around her animals. She told how one of the girl dogs "in heat" jumped on a boy dog, and this excited him and started them off. I said, "Yes, it is true that girls can start the excitement and the boy isn't entirely to blame." I went on to say that girls and boys often do not understand how some feelings can lead to other feelings and how they can get carried away by them. Robin seemed relaxed as she nodded.

Abruptly she shifted to say that over the weekend she had done some baby-sitting. She had stayed with a seven-month-old baby and a three-year-old baby for the entire afternoon from one to six o'clock, with her mother staying with her the first hour or two to give her a start and Eve being with her for the last couple of hours. She described how rambunctious the seven-month-old baby was when she tried to change him and how often he needed to be changed. She also described feeding him and putting him to sleep, and so forth, as well as comforting him when he cried. The three-year-old mostly wanted to be read to. I said it sounded like a satisfying experience and wondered whether she would be able to baby-sit by herself another time, and she thought that with this experience she would be able to. She was obviously gratified by her mother's support in the baby-sitting experience.

She continued with another example of progress: she had learned to ice-skate yesterday. A child-care worker had helped her, first supporting her until she got the feeling of skating and keeping her balance, and then moving away a little distance and saying, "Now skate over to me"; and she had succeeded. I agreed that this must have been a wonderful feeling.

✛   It was interesting that my recognition of her comfort in, communication with, and help from her mother—in contrast to her recent anger— triggered the abrupt shift to an open discussion of several anxieties, then a good experience with a baby. Robin's concerns about sex and pregnancy were typical for young teen-age girls; and like many normal teen-age girls, she experienced baby-sitting as a preparation for having children of her own later.

In the next hour Robin said that after her mother had told her about Ann's pregnancy, she, Robin, had been so upset she couldn't talk about it; she had cried all night, hugging her big stuffed elephant. I commented that when she was terribly upset, the stuffed animal was a comfort to her. Evidently she felt that the baby would take Ann away from her even more than Ann's marriage to Jonathan would do.

She brought me a drawing, a complex abstraction, unfinished, with a checkerboard area in the middle with carefully drawn blue and red squares in it. I ruminated aloud, saying I thought it was interesting that there was a checkerboard in it, and we had talked so often of checkerboards. This one seemed to be a checkerboard about feelings, with half the squares blue and half red; blue might have something to do with sad feelings, and red with warm feelings. Robin said that Lucy, a child-care worker with whom she could talk, had also asked her what it meant. I commented that it was interesting to see how feelings and minds worked together: she comforted herself with a stuffed animal, then she did something creative. Robin was fascinated with this and half-believed that the design could have something to do with her feelings. I said that I thought she really had two kinds of feelings—that along with feeling sad and upset, she had good feelings.

She was now more relaxed and positive, and the angry, depressed mood lifted. For the rest of the hour Robin was occupied with a variety of factual questions, sharing information and also a "funny" episode. Lisa was starting to menstruate but did not have her sanitary belt and pads with her; Robin was menstruating herself and could not lend her a sanitary belt. Then, Missy ran out into the hall, dangling her sanitary belt to offer it to Lisa, just as "one of the male workers walked down the hall." Robin thought this was hilariously funny, as apparently all the girls did.

✝ The sequence of ventilating feelings, having them accepted, achieving further cognitive mastery, lifting of depressed mood and resurgence of humor was a concise example of her coping process.

She asked questions about how babies got started, and I commented that sometimes it was easier than people thought; for instance, if sperms got on the opening to the vagina, they might go right up into the uterus. Robin reflected, "They must be active little things. I've heard they look like tadpoles." I said that there must be a book called *Growing Up* by de Schweintz in their school library or, if not, she could probably see pictures in an encyclopedia to get a clear idea about these anatomical matters.

By now, she seemed very cheerful, and I commented that I felt that, although it was natural to feel upset about losing Ann, it seemed that she really didn't feel as furious at Ann as she had earlier; she might even feel like going to visit Ann. Robin asked, "You mean on vacation?" and I said yes.

She seemed relaxed, and seemed to have worked through most of her intense, upset feelings. I mentioned that Dr. Grant had said she would have some time next week to start testing, and Robin agreed comfortably, "That's fine."

✝ In this hour it was interesting to get a glimpse of the multitude of ideas and questions in her mind related to sex and how babies got started, and also her openness in clarifying what she needed to know.

Stress Involved in Sharing Her Thoughts with Her Parents

In the next hour Robin had several things on her mind: first, the stress involved in discussing with her parents her feelings about Ann's marriage; second, her worries about Jim's explosiveness and fear that he could hurt her; third, her concerns in school—her fear that if her math teacher was changed as she expected, she would not be able to make much progress; and finally, that she would like to take a speech class because she felt this would help her in other things in addition to speech itself—she could use help in speaking more clearly, not cutting off her words so much, not talking so fast. She talked now in a rather quiet, open, confiding way. She said she had hurt Ann and she had hurt her parents. She had told Ann that she "loved her so much that she was angry at her." Ann couldn't really talk with her. I suggested that in time they would be able to talk comfortably.

She then said that on Sunday night when she and her parents were driving back from Grand Island she had tried to tell them how she felt and said that she had been closer to Ann than she had been to them because she always felt that she could tell Ann how she felt. As she described this, she said that she thought her parents had been hurt—they had clammed up and had not said anything. However, later she remarked that her father had said, "That's a feeling, it's not reality." Robin said that it was a feeling *and* it was reality.

I was so overidentified with Robin's struggle to try to communicate with her parents that I laughed when she quoted her father's remark. Then, I said, "Well, I guess I laughed because I was feeling with you so much in your trying to talk to your parents, and I know just how you felt when your father made a remark like that. You want him to be your father and you want to be his daughter, not be treated like a patient." I added that there might be another problem for him right now. She was not a little girl any longer, she was an attractive young lady; and it could be that her father felt that it was important to keep the balance and not to get too close. Robin said, "Yes, but now that I'm losing Ann, I need to be dependent on my parents." I said, "Yes, you need to be able to talk to them, but you also have said you want to be an individual, to take responsibility, and to be independent." I reminded her of how upset she had been when she thought that she was too dependent on me.

This led to a discussion of differences in her feelings at different times—how comfortable she was when she left in the middle of June, and we were separated for nearly three months, and, by contrast, how upset she was when I went away in the fall. I suggested that it was much easier for her to get along when she left me than when I left her. Robin said there was an important difference: during the summer, she had the trip, and the play at school, and Wendy was visiting, but in the fall she had to settle down to schoolwork that was difficult and not so satisfying.

I agreed that this was a real difference. Then, coming back to the question of her communication with her parents, I thought that this could work itself out gradually and that it would be important to keep in mind the need for a balance between closeness and independence, because if she got too close and too dependent she might find herself getting upset about that. Robin agreed with this.

She was playing with a sketch and I looked at it. There was a tight checkerboard in the center and vital dynamic lines reaching out in all directions toward the corners. Soft colors in many shades and tones made it very charming. Although it was somewhat geometrical and controlled, it was also vivid and spontaneous. I commented that it seemed tight in the center but reaching out in all directions, and Robin agreed. Later she commented that she had been trying to tell her father that she felt that life was a checkerboard but that he had not seemed interested. She said that she also felt that life was something like a lake where the water gets very rough at times, and I agreed.

✝   Here she was internalizing, integrating, and extending the concept of a pattern of positive and negative capacities and experiences as part of a process of coming to terms with the frustrations and satisfactions of her life.

After that hour I called our social worker to tell her about the hour before she talked with Robin's parents. Since Robin had also expressed concern about changing her math teacher, I called the new teacher and mentioned this to him.

The social worker told me that Robin's mother had also talked about the ride home from Grand Island and had said that Robin had been very angry, saying that she had never been able to talk to them the way she could talk to Ann, and had accused them of various kinds of neglect in the past. They felt very upset about this and could not realize that it was Robin's way of trying to reach out and get a closer relationship with them, which she needed at this time because of the feeling of the loss of Ann.

When Robin came in for the next therapy hour I asked how things were going at home, and she said laconically, "They're going better." I explored with general questions, but she did not respond and seemed rather inhibited. She had brought another sketch and wanted my reactions to it. I thought it seemed to reach out in all directions, or maybe to be exploding in all directions, but one could also see it as showing pressure coming from every direction. Robin asked why it was so gay and said it reminded her of a carousel. I commented that she had gay feelings in herself too, along with feelings of discomfort and anger.

Soon she began talking about an intense argument between her mother and Aunt Samantha, who had been angrier than Robin had ever seen her. I commented that it must have been very hard for Robin's mother to have her aunt so angry and that it looked as if they had been so upset that neither one had been able to see the feelings of the other. Robin agreed with this but in a somewhat pouting way, as if adults should not behave that way.

She opened her notebook and made a design for a "mobile." Part of it was in the shape of a coiled rope, and part of it looked to me like an embryo. There was another little item in it, just a thin acute-angled triangle. I commented that the coiled rope looked rather like a snail and that another figure looked like an embryo, and Robin said she had not thought of that. She turned over the page to another design she had drawn; what attracted me was the grade at the top with As for science, reading, oral spelling, but a lower grade for written spelling. Robin was very pleased to have these good marks.

She then returned to her discussions with her mother and said that she wished that she had a tape recorder to show me what she had said. I responded that she had been very angry. She agreed and said, "I couldn't talk that way unless I was angry—I couldn't repeat it now." I commented that she did two things: one was to clam up as she did at times so that nobody knew what to say. I was stymied and did not know how to help her when she shut me off, and probably this happened with other people. The second thing that she did was to get so angry that it made it hard for people to respond.

Robin did not disagree but shifted to talking about school, and about her embarrassment—how hard it was to talk about school with anyone except me and Dr. Edmunds. She reminisced about how she had felt in

Grand Island as if she were being treated like a half-breed, not like the others, and how now she felt embarrassed about talking about school. She also reminisced about an episode at her birthday gathering, when the cake was very hard to cut; she was very embarrassed when Dr. Edmunds helped her, although she was glad that Dr. Edmunds did. Then soberly, and somewhat wistfully, she said that she felt her hand was getting better and that she could do more with it now. While she said this, she let her left hand lie on her knee in such a position as to make her new fingernails visible. I noted her wonderful progress with her nails, and said that it must also be satisfying to have her hand get better.

I said I was still thinking about the connection between all these things and the difficulty she was having in talking with her parents. "Robin, you have a hard time, but so have your parents. And you make it hard for your parents to understand and respond just as you did for me." She made a face at this, but I laughed, "Isn't that true?" Robin smiled delightfully and agreed.

I suggested that we might think about how to help. "You have trouble talking to people because you're embarrassed." Robin said, "I'm sensitive." I agreed, and continued, "Probably your parents suffer too; parents can worry very much over their child's difficulties. Maybe you and your mother need to have a good cry together, and you could explain about the checkerboard, how embarrassed and overwhelmed you've been at times about hard things but also how you're glad you are making progress."

She listened carefully and said, "I was starting to try last night." She had been talking about something which made her eyes water and her mother had responded, "Your waterworks are showing." Robin thought this was amusing, and I asked whether she let her parents see the charming Robin that she let me see. I said, "You have a good sense of humor, and you are delightful when you let it come out." She said, "I try to let it out at home," and then added that it used to come out more with Aunt Samantha and it always did with Wendy—"she always understands all of my six sides."

I paused, then said, "Hmm-m-m, that's an odd pun, isn't it? It sounded as if you were saying your sick sides, and I wonder whether that isn't what you're feeling when you are depressed and discouraged and forget about the good progress you've been making in your schoolwork and in relationships with the boys and girls." Then I said, "It's the end of the hour, but we need to talk about this some more. Meantime, could you maybe give your parents a chance?" Robin agreed warmly.

✝   It is interesting to note how her design reflected her increasing capacity to contain in metaphors her perception of others' and her own explosive feelings—her way of integrating her awareness of her varying impulses and affects.

Rough Waters of Life

In a late January hour I could hardly remember a time when Robin looked so lost, discouraged, hopeless, and limp. I reminded her that she had told me that she was going to cook a meal for Ann and Jonathan, and she said she had, but she had not felt "at ease." I said this was natural when any member of the family got married; we had to get used to the fact that this person "belongs to somebody else," and we find it very hard to know where we stand. In time we do feel included.

While explaining how left out she felt, how she did not know whether Jonathan really wanted her there or even whether Ann wanted her there, she said in a forlorn tone of voice, "It doesn't matter; they'll be going away in the summer." I challenged her, saying "What a whopper!" She smiled warmly, but without any real change of mood, and asked what I meant. I explained that she was trying awfully hard to throw it all away and pretend to herself that it did not matter. Also, because sometimes she had warmed up to an intellectual explanation, I asked whether she knew what the word "defense" meant. She was curious, and I explained that when we have sad or angry or other unhappy feelings about something, sometimes instead of trying to find a solution to the problem, we just try to get rid of it by throwing it away as she was doing now.

Robin responded with a laconic "m-h'm" to this, without any real change of mood. I commented that it seemed to me that she really felt very lost, and so many sad feelings were mixed in together—her feeling of losing Ann and not knowing where she stood, her feelings of anger that Ann had let her down, her feelings of being rebuffed by Aunt Samantha, the difficulties in communicating comfortably with her parents—all these things had piled up. She said that after supper with Ann and Jonathan she didn't know whether to go or stay, didn't know whether she was wanted or not. I empathized with her about how disappointing this was along with all the other feelings that she had.

Soon she mentioned, "My tests started today, as you know," in a discouraged, depressed tone of voice. I asked why the tests made her feel so discouraged. She said in a limp way, "I always have had limits, and I always will have." I wondered whether she felt that she had to accept the fact that no matter how hard she and I worked together or how hard she worked, she would never be able to get to be what she wanted to be. She said if she could have a kennel to take care of animals or could help a veterinarian, she would be able to do what she wanted to do (neglecting the main point, and I did not bring her back to it).

I commented that she seemed so lost and sad that I wondered whether she was angry at me, and again she denied this. She said, "I'm tired; I was up late Saturday night and last night; if I could sleep till noon, I'd be all right." I did not think that just plain fatigue could make her feel as badly as this. Was she having another period? She said, "Not yet," and I commented that it was only about three weeks since her last one. She demurred, "But I'm irregular." Then, she said that she had been having cramps; she particularly gets cramps when she eats sweets, but "as long as she could stand up" she was not going to do anything about it. She also commented that her mouth hurt so much that she couldn't eat fruit. Her braces had been tightened—her teeth obviously were moving, they were tender and sore—and she had trouble even with bread.

I commented that she had physical pain as well as painful feelings about everything that had been going on, and probably each kind of pain made the other worse; Robin agreed. We talked about how very painful feelings could be intensified by physical pain and vice versa, and I commented that recently she had said that life was like a lake and sometimes the water was rough. She remembered this, and I said, "And sometimes one can keep on struggling and swimming hard, and sometimes one has to tread water and wait." Robin accepted these remarks rather firmly, and her face relaxed.

Toward the end of the hour I commented that it seemed to me that she was at a point where she felt there were a good many things that she couldn't do anything about and that she was being stoical. I asked her whether she knew what that meant and she said, "Sort of." I suggested that we would need to think some more about these things.

✝ After the previous hours, when Robin had been able to mobilize positive feelings to balance frustrations and to integrate a concept of the complex pattern of pluses and minuses in her life, this was an hour when she had lost her grip on the positives and needed direct help in coping.

A Mosaic of Feelings

In the next session Robin came in loaded with books and carrying the art work she was working on: a piece of wood, roughly in the shape of a fish, filled in with a very complicated mosaic, using pieces of many different textures, shapes, and colors. Very carefully she opened an envelope containing more tiny bits of stone, to fill in some of the gaps with certain colors and textures. It looked like a daring and complex undertaking—I could not imagine trying to combine such an extraordinary variety, and I told her so. I commented, "This is the creative Robin today. Last Monday you seemed so far away." She looked at me wonderingly, and we talked about the mosaic; she left it in my office.

✝ I had a feeling that between her gay costume, the mosaic, and her manner, she was trying hard to mobilize quite a fancy statement of herself, almost as if to cancel out the gloomy mood of Monday.

In an equally deliberate and absorbed way, I looked at the books she had brought. The first one was on preparation of meals, with many colorful illustrations and basic information presented in an interesting way. I asked Robin what grade level it belonged to, and she said "eighth grade." I noted lists of calories, quantities of vitamins, and so forth, and exclaimed over the fact that one would have to get on with arithmetic to understand all of this, and Robin agreed.

✝ Since she enjoyed cooking, this was an assignment that must have been gratifying and could motivate effort on the arithmetic.

She also had brought a new book organized around topics, one of which had to do with "keeping safe" and accidents. (Dr. Edmunds had told me that yesterday Robin's sister Eve had torn another ligament in gym, this time in her right leg. Robin had been very angry and open about this with Dr. Edmunds and had said she did not see how she, Robin, could stand it.)

Now, as I looked at the section on accidents, Robin told me about Eve's accident. She described it almost casually, but I exclaimed irritably, "My God, one more thing." I asked how it happened—Eve had been tumbling in the gym—and then I asked how she, Robin, and her mother felt about it. With only mild irritation in her voice, she said it was a nuisance because Eve might be laid up for a month or more, she might have to have an operation as she did last winter, and "I remember how cross she was last winter and how awful it was those weeks that she stayed home with her bad knee."

I empathized with her, feeling that this would be one more difficulty. Wondering how it had happened, I picked up some sentences from the book dealing with the relation of feelings to accidents. Robin did not resist but said, "I can think of examples with me. Sometimes I've had accidents because I'm stubborn."

I leafed on through the book and came to a section on nerves. I said I thought nerves were interesting, and we found diagrams giving a simple view of connections between the brain and the sense organs.

Robin also had her notebook with her, and I noticed that the writing was conspicuously smoother at certain times than other times. I said, "You know, one thing that's interesting about nerves is the way they send feeling messages that get mixed up with signals to move or to act, so that when we are anxious our coordination is not so good." I asked if she remembered telling me about how upset she had been when trying to cut the cake and suggested that the anxiety had probably made it harder for her to do it. She was interested, and I said, "There are lots of interesting connections like that. For instance, when I had my Ph.D. examination, my hands were dripping wet afterward. I was very anxious naturally and the nerves carried messages that made me perspire too much."

Robin was fascinated and said, "You know, one time last summer when I was in Nashville, we were playing a game called Spoons"; at one point when the competition got high, "I laughed so hard that I relieved myself." She said she had excused herself, and when she had come back her aunt had asked, "Are you all right?" She had said, "Oh yes, it's just a little wet," adding that she had been terribly embarrassed. I agreed that this was another example—when we got to laughing so hard we could not control it, the "tree of nerves" sent out messages too widely and the excitement overflowed, as it were, so that we lost control of the bladder too. I said there were lots of ways in which feelings were spread by our nerves, so they get beyond our control.

It was getting on toward the end of the hour, and Robin said, "Something just happened today; I got awfully upset at noon. I wanted to get this mosaic to show you and told Lisa that I was going back to the art room to get it and asked if she would tell Jo. She forgot to tell Jo, and Eloise asked me if I had called Jo. I said I had, meaning that I had sent a message, and then Jo said I told a lie because I didn't call her." Then Robin giggled and said that Dr. Edmunds teased her because she was "kicking herself" and feeling so guilty about it and had said, "If you don't stop kicking yourself so much, I'll pick you up and turn you upside down." I laughed and asked Robin if she thought Dr. Edmunds could, and she laughingly agreed that she probably couldn't.

When I asked Robin if she were feeling better now about the tests with Dr. Grant, she said yes. She said she had been doing some puzzles too. I commented that on Monday she had been so overwhelmed she could hardly talk. She agreed and said she had felt ashamed of herself. I asked why she would feel ashamed—that to have so many feelings that one couldn't talk about them wasn't anything to be ashamed about. Was she ashamed because she couldn't do as well as she wanted to on some of Dr. Grant's tests? She said, "Maybe," but she didn't seem to want to discuss that further just then and went back again to her mosaic.

✝ In this hour there was a quality of "peace offering" as if she were bringing me as much as she possibly could in order to bring things back to a level of comfortable communication, as if she wanted to make up for letting me see her at her lowest on Monday by showing me the creative, active, competent Robin.

Reflections on the Mosaic

In the first year, we had been trying to help Robin get a reasonable perspective on her strengths and weaknesses. She wanted to "conquer" her weaknesses but, in view of their nature and the fact that there were unknown organic limits to the extent to which she could do this, it seemed important to help her accept varying levels of functioning. Consequently, we referred time and again to the checkerboard of areas that were easy to manage and areas that were hard to manage; for some people the difference between the easy and hard areas was greater than it was for other people. We did not attempt to find a more flexible and complicated image than the checkerboard.

However, Robin herself implicitly dealt with this. Her interesting mosaic included bright and dark bits of glass and stone of many different tones and shades of color, juxtaposed in an interesting pattern. It was as if she were suggesting, "I am more complicated than a checkerboard. To be sure, there are bright and dark areas, and there are many different degrees of difficulty. At the same time, the whole me is vivid and strong"; as indeed she was. Certainly her strength was shown in her ability to make use of the opportunity to control and limit stimulation when she was in a sufficiently flexible setting, as she was at school.

This nonverbal communication was the climax of the series that included her colorful drawings and was important to me as evidence of her capacity to integrate the wide range of her feelings. Nonverbal expressions are important at any age, not just at the stage when children are unable to verbalize feelings.

Beginning to Understand the Nervous System

At the next therapy hour, Robin came in with a magazine that her teacher had given her as part of a project and opened to pages where suggestions for baby-sitters were reported by teen-agers. Robin said that she got nervous when she was baby-sitting if a baby cried and she could not soothe it. She added that when babies got to the stage when they knew the difference between the mother and other people, sometimes it was hard to comfort them. I agreed and also said that there were differences between babies, and what would comfort one baby was not satisfying to the next; we have to try different things until we find what is most satisfying to a particular baby.

Robin said this was one of two projects she had; the other one was on the nervous system. I thought it might be worthwhile for us to think about some more facts about the nervous system that could help us understand what happened with her. I drew a simple diagram of the cortex and the thalamus, with connections to muscles, to stomach, and to adrenal glands. I used this to explain how messages from the outside world come to the brain, where they stir up connections to other thoughts, then send messages down to the thalamus, which stirs up feelings, and these send messages back to the cortex so that more messages start scooting around.

Robin said, "I know what you mean. Last night when I was very tired, I curled up in my electric blanket and pushed my kitten off the bed so I could go to sleep, but she got back on it and bit me. While I was sleeping or dreaming, I thought it was a sword." I asked about the sword, and Robin said it was not very big, perhaps a yard or a foot, but then she measured with her hands not much more than about seven inches. I said, "Yes, this would be an example—because a kitten's bite isn't going to do much to you, but a sword could hurt you." I asked if she had ever seen a sword like that, and she said the only sword she had seen was her grandfather Mason's sword.

Robin thought of another illustration: on Saturday night she had been cooking dinner, and when Eve had been standing near she had accidentally dropped some hot mashed potatoes on Robin's hand, not hot enough to really burn it but hot enough to frighten her, and Robin had exploded, raging at everybody for ten or fifteen minutes. "I know I overreacted." She explained that she had been very tired, had not had anything to eat since breakfast, and had been working hard on the dinner for her parents' anniversary. I explained that thresholds can get lowered at times so that a small stimulus can be much more disturbing than it would be ordinarily.

She then added that she and Eve had not stayed mad very long, and she had helped Eve with her crutches and getting dressed.

We came back to the diagram, and I asked whether she could remember any of her thoughts when she felt so overwhelmed last Monday; I had never seen her so discouraged and hopeless. Robin said, "Well, I really wasn't all here. I've been like that a good deal of this week, and part of last weekend I wasn't all here either." I tried to get her to explain more about it, but she said that she just could not think of any thoughts that she had had. I commented that when she got that overwhelmed it seemed that she went blank, but then she recovered, the way she had on Thursday, bringing in the interesting mosaic to show me the creative things that she could do.

Robin jumped and said, "I thought of another example. Before I came here, one night when I needed an allergy shot, I was sleepy and didn't want to stay up till daddy got home; I went to bed and told mother to tell him to give me the shot after he got home. I was lying on my right side, and he came over and said, 'Don't move, this won't hurt,' but I dreamed it was a porcupine that said, 'Don't move, this won't hurt.' " I said, "Yes, that's another kind of exaggeration, the way the sword was an exaggeration. A shot is made with something that pricks—just one thing—but a porcupine has a thousand needles that prick." Robin was vastly amused and also seemed to be gratified by swinging along and thinking about illustrations of ways in which associations elaborated or distorted or exaggerated a specific experience. I explained that when we were awake we tried to control our thoughts in a logical way, but when we went to sleep it was the logic that went to sleep and our brain worked more like a baby's brain.

I reminded her that once she had said to me, "I need somebody to talk to so I'll know I'm alive." I said, "This is the way a baby must feel—because a baby doesn't have much memory, it doesn't have much imagination about the future, so it needs to have the reassurance of the familiar person right there. When you felt so overwhelmed at losing Ann, it was these baby feelings that were coming up, that you had always been able to communicate better with Ann than anyone else and Ann understood you better than anyone else." I added, "But the fact that Ann was a good big sister to you and could understand and communicate with you probably had something to do with your ability to communicate with Kathleen Kirk and then with me. What Ann gave you was inside of you, and it will make it possible for you to communicate with other people. For instance, you have good communication with your teachers."

Robin said, "Well, Jessie accepts me. She treats me as if she feels that I can do any project that I want to do. She doesn't treat me as if she thought I was just somebody who needs help." I commented, "Well, one reason why she is able to recognize what you have to give is because you're able to communicate what you want to do. There will always be people you'll be able to communicate with, and you will be able to find ways to do what you want to do. Right now, there is Dr. Edmunds, as well as Jessie. The important thing is that you are able to communicate with people and work with them and help them understand what you are interested in doing and how you feel."

Robin glanced up at the clock—it was about six or seven minutes to the hour, and she seemed ready to go back to school.

✝ This was an hour of gratifying cognitive mastery which paved the way for later discussion of the damage to her nervous system. While Robin was struggling with her feelings about losses of intimate relationships and frustrations in communication with her parents, and also progressing in school and in self-understanding, she was integrating a picture of the positive and negative aspects of her life. I was fascinated with her ability and drive to achieve integration at this time of overwhelming feelings. Her neurological damage contributed to her disintegrative responses while her island of insight and creativity provided resources to absorb them.

12

Understanding Robin's Neurological Damage

Overview of Therapy in February and March

At the beginning of February, Robin talked about Eve's accident to her knee, the operation this again required, the fact that Eve would miss additional school beyond what she had already missed and perhaps lose credit for the year, and Robin's feeling that Eve needed therapy but would not accept it and also the family would not be able to afford to pay for it. Robin felt "privileged"—and perhaps a little guilty because Aunt Samantha was paying for her therapy. This reflected only one of many aspects of competition and struggle between Eve and Robin. Eve often attacked Robin verbally, and sometimes physically, along with her many verbal attacks on the rest of the family. Robin's physical vulnerability— getting bruised easily—and psychological vulnerability—not having the speed or integration to defend herself well verbally—left her often angry and hurting.

These and other stresses interacted with the recurrent physiological instabilities accompanying menstruation—Robin's cramps, intensified autonomic reactivity, affective and sometimes cognitive lability—to produce acute disturbance. She had some hours of resistance in therapy beyond what I had ever seen before, as well as more projection and more anxiety. Especially when her parents were preoccupied with Eve, more intense feelings of being left out erupted; resentment and anger put her into a double bind; she was pulled between conscience (wishing not to be an added burden) and wanting to demand her share, and her desire for autonomy and maturity conflicted with her intense craving for attention and concern. A milder form of this conflict is experienced by many adolescents who want to be secure within parental care while also wanting to become independent. The interaction of Robin's vulnerability, experiences of deprivation, and current stress made the conflict unmanageable.

During this period, she was going through retests with Dr. Grant. The testing had begun after considerable delay because of multiple family stresses, but instead of going on under improved conditions, as was intended, the tests were being given under even greater stress.

Robin reported that during the tests the tremor of her hand was worse, her speech became mushy, as it had two years before, and she could not do her best. In the context of anxiety about the testing, she had a dream about threatening storms, lightning, and tornadoes, with associations to a frightening time in the first grade when a storm broke windows and scattered pieces of glass around. Therapy connected her thoughts and dreams about external storms with her internal storms at this time of external and internal stress.

Along with the testing, new work in math involving estimation and abstract work, coupled with difficulties in writing down recipes for home economics, probably intensified her stress. She talked about these school difficulties and accepted my assistance in helping teachers to understand them. Her math teacher decided to give up the "new math" approach and go back to drill on multiplication and basic combinations.

While Robin had periods of being desperately discouraged, she mobilized various positive resources to support feelings of competence: for instance, models of the body assisted her study of the nervous system. Her desire for mastery was satisfied by my participation in discussion of the nervous system and application to her own problems. She was extremely gratified at being given the facts and "finding out why" she had so many difficulties, and she seemed to gain strength from the realistic informative process. ("I have had tests and tests and tests, and no one ever explained to me why I have these problems.")

However, later she misinterpreted the information about neurological difficulties, jumping to the conclusion that this would affect her capacity to have a baby, and sobbed in despair. I explained that her kind of neurological difficulties would have no connection with the functioning of her reproductive system. This was confirmed by a pelvic examination with the doctor's report that that area was normal.

She also despaired about mastery of math, feeling that she could not bear "to still be doing fourth-grade math." At such times, this discouragement became overwhelming so that the therapy task was to separate the realistic difficulties from the areas in which she was distinctly competent, such as art, social studies, and Council. After total ventilation of intense affect, she responded positively, with a shift to hopeful, constructive feelings and receptivity to the reality testing I provided.

Through all this, adolescent interest in boys was developing, complicated by the progress of Ann's pregnancy. Robin wanted to know exactly when babies can and cannot get started, and so forth. She discussed the problems that certain girls had had in not being able to wait, how this was a blot on their marriages, and how she intended to wait until sex could be part of love in marriage.

When a friend, Megan, planned to run away, Robin told a worker; then for a couple of weeks she was upset because of fear of losing Megan's friendship. This was another source of despair aggravated by the instabilities accompanying her menstrual periods, and it led to further discussion of the way feelings get exaggerated during the unstable period of menstruation. Robin expressed her feeling that she was glad she had a woman therapist; she did not think she could talk to a man about these things. Increased difficulties in functioning were also exaggerated when Eve ran away from home. In connection with the variability in her hand tremor, Robin commented that coffee seemed to help stabilize her hand, and we related this to individual differences in the effect of drugs on nerves.

Robin pressed not only for the results of current tests and examinations but for possible early factors in her difficulties. She mentioned an accident at the age of four when her forehead was badly cut, which she thought might have contributed some damage. While her great pressure to find the answers may have been overdetermined by sex curiosity, it was also part of Robin's desperate effort toward mastery and her determination not to be like the girls who "gave up." She wanted to get enough education to be able to support herself.

Her mother's preoccupation with Eve, including a trip to Grand Island alone with Eve, contributed to Robin's increased irritability and protest, and also to a transitory attempt to compensate for the lack of attention from her mother by getting attention from her father. While this was loaded in part with oedipal implications, it was important to see it in relation to the continuing and intensified feeling of privation in relation to her mother and her various efforts to get attention. Robin could say that she "wanted her share." Later, Robin shifted her emphasis to "I need to feel needed" and "I need you." During this period, she seemed to alternate between regression and a progressive wanting to take responsibility and to give. She completed a plaque in art class—an owl with the legend, "Be Smart"; Robin commented that he had a smirk and agreed that he looked smug.

During this period when her mother was preoccupied with or away with Eve and both her residence doctor and I were away at professional meetings, her sensitivity to being teased by others seemed to increase as well.

Despite the intensity of Robin's craving for attention from her mother, it was apparent that when her friend Libby and an older friend who had been her teacher were visiting in Topeka, Robin had less need for her mother. I interpreted that she craved intimacy and companionship and that as she could develop more friendships outside the hospital, her desperate need for her mother would not be so overwhelming.

Robin's interest in boys was expressed in excited reactions to mild physical contact when boys in the hospital touched her hand or held her hand at a party or in a Council meeting. While this was thrilling and she wanted to talk about the meaning of it, her anxiety was reflected in dreams of sexual attack and more discussions of girls who had gotten into trouble.

We can now look at some of the therapy hours.

Giant Steps in Learning

The first hour in February, Robin had brought along a notebook and a book from school and was fingering them. She said that she got her grades that day; they were actually A for everything except math—A in oral spelling, English, social studies, and science. In math, she had gotten a C. She was concerned about the C; she just didn't understand math. They were supposed to be working on "estimating," and she didn't know how to do it and had a hard time with it. I agreed that it must be very frustrating when she was making progress in everything else. I added that it was good that she had been able to progress at school all fall when things had been hard at home, but it had been at a price—and the price was that her reaction to the stress was to have more severe outbursts this year than she had had last year, and we still needed to work on them. Robin looked very thoughtful and nodded.

I told her I thought she had taken some giant steps, and then I said, "Last year you were reading books about horses, and I never would have been able to predict that you would be reading about Pasteur in a grown-up book a year later. Last year you were making that sweet little decoration with the tiny shells, and I never would have been able to predict that you could do something so complicated and with such imagination as your mosaic." Robin's eyes were shining. I said, "People can't take giant steps all the time. You take some giant steps, and then you keep on working and consolidate things and get things integrated."

Then she talked about fun in the speech class—in order to "get them started," her teacher had suggested that they "break all the rules," and they evidently had a quite hilarious time doing this.

She said that they were going to have a dance soon, and she was going to bring two girls. The boys had suggested that she bring them, "And that's about the first time Melvin has talked to me." Then, she added, "I don't know whether I should bring this up here or not, but when I was talking to Eve about the boys, she asked whether I couldn't bring them home to supper." I asked how her mother would feel about it, and Robin replied that her mother had heard the question and had said she thought it would be a good idea.

Robin then said that she and some other girls had talked with the group worker about wanting a course in "sex education." She said, "There are a lot of people who don't know what they should know. This place is supposed to help people with their problems, and sex is one problem." I asked whether she could tell me the kinds of things that she might want to know more about, and she seemed at first rather blocked, so I tried to give her some possibilities: "You might want to understand better the feelings that you get at a party or when you're dancing with boys, or you might want to understand more about the feelings that may come before menstruation or during it or after, which are sometimes very intense for some girls. Or, you might want to know more about just how babies get started and so on."

Robin said, "Well, I think girls ought to know about whether babies can get started during menstruation or before or afterward, because sometimes they think they can't." I said, "Yes, usually the ovum comes out of the ovary"—and Robin nodded her head—"into the uterus in the middle of the month between menstruations, so that is the time when most babies are conceived. But it can also happen that a baby could get started before or during or after menstruation—it differs with different girls."

Robin said, "I think girls need to know things like that." I said, "You mean that if they're going to try intercourse, they should have that kind of information because of fear? Is that the only reason?" Robin hastily replied, "No, of course not, but still that's important."

I agreed, and asked whether it wasn't also important to know more about what sex is all about, whether sex is just for excitement, or just for relief, or whether sex is an important part of love. Robin then made the contrast between a girl who had intercourse at age thirteen in Grand Island, and Ann who really loved Jonathan, and I said that was part of what I meant; it was important not just to learn what not to do, but to understand more about what it means for sex to be part of love—Robin was the kind of person who would be able to love in a deep way when the time came, and I hoped that she would be able to wait for sex until it could be a part of real love. She said, "I will be able to."

✝   While I do not think prohibitions are of much use with adolescents, I
    do think that learning about commitment to somebody who cares and
    with whom one is identified can be helpful. I talked very quietly and
    meaningfully with Robin and she responded in the same tone.

The next week a relaxed Robin came in with a large pile of books and a tape recorder. I asked how she was feeling, and she said "fine," so I asked how the math was working out. She explained the system that her teacher had suggested of recording multiplication tables on the tape recorder so that she could listen to it and use her hearing memory. I thought this a very good idea, since the oral spelling had helped so much. I also said I wondered how much she had done visually. I took out a dollar bill, some quarters, dimes, nickels, and pennies and asked her how many quarters there were in a dollar, how many nickels there were in a quarter, how many pennies there were in a nickel, how many dimes there would be in a quarter and what would be left over, and so on. She had to think very hard, but actually got most of the answers right—apparently having made real progress since the last time I had done this some months ago. I exclaimed, "Once you really remember all of these facts you have most of what you need in order to make change and not get gypped when you're buying things." She agreed and seemed to feel comfortable about focusing on this.

I asked how things were worked out in class, and she said that the two boys were doing something that was "ahead of" her, but she liked to eavesdrop. She said, "You know, I get along better when I'm in a class with some people ahead of me, because then I can listen to what I'll have later on and it's a challenge to look forward to. If I'm in a class with children younger than I am, it gives me an inferiority feeling." I commented that this was a healthy way to feel—there were people who felt inferior if they were in a group with people who knew more, and they only felt comfortable when they were with others who did not know as much as they did because they had to feel on top.

✝   Actually this was an amazing commitment to and perception of ways of learning for a neurologically impaired girl.

She now wanted to show me an exercise book for handwriting. Recently she had been having trouble doing the writing that she was supposed to do in her speech class, and her teacher had given her this handwriting exercise book to work at and told her that when she had difficulty writing out words that she needed, she could practice some of the exercises instead. I looked over the book, with its demonstrations of ways of exercising the fingers and hands, and said that whenever one has difficulties with certain muscles or the nerves that control these muscles, exercises can help to pull in other nerves or to strengthen the muscles. Robin said comfortably that she knew this and she liked the idea of doing this.

Robin then said that when she got angry or upset it always made her hand worse and she was worried about Eve going to the hospital and that was why she had trouble with her handwriting today. I suggested that we look at the diagram of the nervous system, with the cortex and the thalamus that we made last week. It seemed to me that something like this was happening: she had trouble with her hand, and this made her anxious. Ideas up there in the cortex then get connected with her hand. When she got anxious about something else—currently about Eve's operation—even though this was not going to hurt Robin or her hand in any way, anxiety about Eve got mixed up with the anxiety that was there all the time about her hand and made it worse. Robin was interested and added, "I guess there are some cobwebs up there that need to get brushed out too." I agreed and said that the cortex is where we can sort things out and get things straight. If she could sort things out so that she could understand that Eve's trouble with her knee had nothing to do with Robin or her hand, it might help her to keep things separate so that she would not get so nervous about her hand.

At one point I said, "You keep telling me about how nervous your hand gets, but it doesn't shake when you're here." Robin agreed, and we both agreed then that the anxiety is mostly in her head and comes out in her hand only when she has to do something with it in an anxious mood. I said this was another example of how we need to sort things out and how the anxiety could be less and her hand would get along better if she kept things straight.

Robin made a thoughtful comment: "I've never told anybody else this, but life has more meaning for me now. Really, in Grand Island it was rather empty, but somehow there seems more in it for me now." I said, "It sounds to me as if you feel more relaxed and related to the world," and she agreed. I added that I thought many things helped this, even including the interesting work about South America she had done in social studies—that maybe she felt she was living in a bigger world, and Robin agreed thoughtfully and warmly.

At one time during the hour, she referred to an amusing story her mother had told her, and I commented that she and her mother seemed to be communicating more; at another time she mentioned her father working with her when she did her homework—it all sounded as if the family was in a more settled phase now, despite the fact that Eve had to have an operation.

Also, I had picked up Robin's mosaic from the table where she had left it, and we talked about it. I told her how I thought it reflected her patience and care in being able to fit in all those tiny little bits and pieces, as well as the flexibility of trying different solutions until she could fit in different sizes and shapes, textures and colors. She then told me more about the pieces—how some of the pieces of glass came from church windows (that had been broken in the tornado), other pieces had been blown off the roof of their house (little bits of stone), other pieces came from a broken cup, and so on. I said, "Then, it has lots of meanings in it too, nourishment from the cup, protection from the roof, and the support of religion from the stained glass windows." Robin was interested in this and explained the sources of other pieces in response to each suggestion that I gave. Some of the pieces had actually been created to use in the mosaic—for example, little bits of "sagged glass"—to which I commented that there were different kinds of creativity in the whole piece. Robin then said she thought she might make another one, a mate to this, if she could find a suitable piece of wood.

✝   It was interesting that this creative work was integrated from residues of disasters, while it also integrated sources of strength and originality.

Recurrent Feelings of Being Left Out

In the middle of February Robin said that Eve's operation had been on Friday and that her mother had spent all of Saturday and all of Sunday with Eve in the hospital. Robin was awfully disappointed because she had counted on going with her mother to see *My Fair Lady*, but her mother wouldn't even take time enough away from the hospital to do that; Aunt Samantha had gone with Robin.

I asked how Eve was getting along, and Robin began to get weepy. "They won't tell me *anything* about it. I asked questions about how the operation was and what they did to her knee and how she's getting along, and they won't say a thing to me. Mother came back from the hospital, and I waited up to see her, but all she did was pick up her mail and go through that as if she wanted to say, 'Don't bother me.' Yesterday was the same thing. She spent the whole day at the hospital, and she and Daddy won't tell me anything about it. They won't let me go to the hospital."

It turned out that Ann and Jonathan had gone to the hospital and also several of Eve's friends, and Robin saw no logical reason why she shouldn't be allowed to go. She obviously felt left out and rejected, both in terms of talking it over with her parents and in terms of being allowed to go to the hospital. At one point, she said in regard to her mother, "I don't know what she looks like; I haven't seen her for two days."

I connected this with a discussion that we had had previously about the way in which "baby feelings" rush up at us, and I explained how when a baby's mother goes away for a couple of weeks or so, sometimes it doesn't recognize its mother—it really forgets what the mother looks like. Robin recited various illustrations of having been left when she was a baby and later when the family went to Disneyland with Ann and Eve and left Robin at home. I said when she was little she must have been very sad and angry at her mother for going away and leaving her. But now she was fourteen years old and probably her mother felt that during this stress of the operation Eve needed her most. Robin interpolated, "I know I'm jealous."

I agreed and said "and hurt and angry." I commented that a wise person that I knew had once made the remark that some people have to carry on a lawsuit against their parents their whole lives. Robin took this very hard and started to cry and said, "But I love my parents very, very much, and I want some attention once in a while." She said, "I woke up in the night and was thinking that maybe I'd break a leg or something like that so that they'd pay attention to *me* for one hour." I commented on how hard it was for her to stand her parents concentrating on Eve at a time when they thought Eve needed it very much and that probably she was angry not just about the operation now, but the fact that Eve had been keeping the center of the stage all fall, refusing to go to school and getting into so much trouble. Robin said, "I know Eve needs help, but she wouldn't take it."

I asked whether perhaps her mother and father felt that Robin was getting a great deal of help and attention here. Robin said, "And so they think that I don't need anything from my parents. But I do need my parents too." Robin added that her mother had helped her with her hair last night, and I commented that evidently she had wanted to give Robin what she could. I also explained that while I knew how angry and deprived Robin was feeling, it seemed to me that her mother was in a pretty difficult spot. When one stays in a hospital all day long, one can feel very tired and not have any margin of energy to give to anybody.

Robin seemed so very upset that I had a hunch that a physical factor was intensifying her difficulty. I asked about her period, and she said that she was "having her period right now." I reminded her of the times that we had talked about the way in which feelings get intensified before or during or after a menstrual period. Again I explained nerve connections of the autonomic nervous system. I showed her how these nerves go to the stomach and make cramps there and to other organs, and then I explained to her how, at the time of her period, the glands and hormones were sending different chemicals to the brain and into the blood stream and how this creates an increased sensitivity so that feelings we could ordinarily manage are ten times as acute, and I felt that this was what was happening now.

Robin said, "I'm glad I have a woman therapist because I wouldn't be able to talk about this to a man therapist this way." I said, "You feel that a woman therapist understands. You know that one reason why I understand these feelings is because I have had feelings like that so that I can recognize them." Robin agreed.

She quickly stopped crying, picked up her tape recorder, and said she wanted to show it to me. The rest of the time was then occupied with demonstrating to me how she was reciting the multiplication tables to the tape recorder so that she could then listen to them. She was going to ask her parents to turn it on after she had gone to bed at night so that she could hear the multiplication tables as she slept and then go over them in the morning first thing when she woke up.

I asked Robin if I could talk over with her social worker Robin's wish to visit Eve in the hospital and also to have her questions about Eve taken seriously. Robin agreed, and I said that I hoped she could work this out and talk things over with her parents.

✝   It is important to note here how overwhelmed Robin was during her menstrual period, and the openness with which she expressed her disturbed feelings and yet the very quick shift she was able to make when offered factual information about the relation of her menstrual tension and stress to the intensified feelings which had swamped her. She evidently felt the scientific information to be helpful and supportive, doubtless getting some satisfaction from a sense of being taken seriously. Also, the information functioned in essence both as a recognition of her potential ego strength and of her capacity to understand scientific information and as a bridge, as it were, away from the intense feelings. The organically determined abrupt shifts that Robin made under stress in the direction of disturbances could also be made in a positive direction when her intellectual interests were appealed to.

Most people have a typical range of variability within which they fluctuate, usually in accordance with variations in fatigue, health, stimulus, pressure, frustration, and so on. With Robin, these variations were striking and, while often predictable, sometimes they were unpredictable; the apparent unpredictability might be a result of the complexity of interaction of neurological and physiological factors with extreme variations in stress at home. There were also variations in level of work in therapy; times of working hard might be followed by hours of taking it easy in a chatty way.

In late February we saw another vivid example of this alternation: on the sixteenth she was casual; by contrast, on the twentieth the hour was very intense and complex, including a strange combination of giving and withholding or defensiveness; an intense assertion of a wish for autonomy repeated in different contexts paralleled recurrent examples of needs for attention. Feelings of being left or left out were reflected in various ways and also determinedly denied. Resentment and anger were reflected in occasional tense facial expressions and also denied. And a sense of being caught in a double bind of conflict with her conscience was part of all this.

Moreover there was something she wanted to tell me that she couldn't get out, and she felt the only way she would be able to tell me would be to have some sort of pill that would make it possible for her to talk about it. She repeatedly denied being angry at me in connection with recent discussions that might have evoked some anger. And at school she was having trouble concentrating because of the noise being made by the boys. Very intense and bottled up at the end of the hour, she volunteered that she was not letting me understand what it was all about.

Communication with the Team

Because of her great tension and her preoccupation with the idea that she needed some sort of pill in order to get at what was really bothering her, I felt it was important to alert relevant people.

I first called her social worker and asked what kind of discussion might have gone on at home to stir up this idea about the pill, and also asked whether Robin knew about the contaminated immunization shot that had made her so very ill when she was small. I wondered what else was going on at home. The social worker confirmed that Eve was crying all the time and did "take Robin down," and also everybody else. She also said that Robin was worried because she had "lied" to me, but there was no indication as to what the lie was about.

Since Robin had seemed upset about difficulties in studying during the hour with Jessie because one of the boys was very noisy, I called Jessie next. I explained that Robin had felt so happy about the progress she had made during the fall in reaching a more mature level of schoolwork, that this may have contributed to her frustration and anxiety at the feeling of not being able to accomplish much when she was constantly distracted by the noisiness. Jessie said she had been aware of and concerned about this. She had allowed Robin to work in the "tutoring room" to get away from the noise but, of course, she could not leave the boys to go to Robin and help her there. As she thought aloud about the problem, she said that she would try to see whether she could let the boys go to gym for half an hour so that she could have a sustained period of work with Robin alone.

She wondered whether Robin was being upset by the work on the nervous system. I told her that, on the contrary, my impression was that Robin had been very gratified by this; it was grown-up work. Also I was able to use it in the therapy hour to help Robin get some understanding of her neurological difficulties and to put these in perspective in relation to "nervous difficulties" that lots of other people have. Jessie was interested in this, and I added that it might be possible that Robin felt two ways about it, that while she was very satisfied, she might also have more anxiety than she was letting herself realize, and I would try to watch for this. I asked Jessie to let me know how things went.

Since Robin had been able to communicate quite well with Dr. Edmunds and Dr. Edmunds was very alert to Robin's moods, I called her next and reviewed the hour with her and my concern that people in contact with her be alerted to Robin's state right now and to her concerns. Dr. Edmunds said that she would be seeing Robin. She knew that Robin found it hard to admit any angry feelings toward me. I indicated that we had worked on this in therapy; also, Dr. Edmunds felt, as I had felt, that perhaps Robin resented my effort a week ago to help her understand her mother's situation after the long day in the hospital. Dr. Edmunds said that Robin felt that her family (and perhaps her therapist) had been expecting her to grow up too fast. She said also that she would be seeing Robin during the day.

Robin Faces Her Jealousy and Anger

The next therapy hour was again very intense and, during part of it, Robin cried. At first, she talked about how she wanted to do something desperate to get the attention of her parents. This was in the context of Robin's feeling that her parents had been so preoccupied with Eve that Robin did not receive a reasonable share of attention.

She again talked about the pill that would make it possible for her to say things truthfully that she otherwise could not say. She also spoke of how much she wanted to find out the "real reason" for her dreadful difficulties in spelling and math and how she wished she could pick the locks on the files at the residence and get at her records. Finally, she agreed when I suggested that she would like to know the results of her tests. Along with the intensity with which she communicated these things, there was much shifting of topics and defensive apologies.

Interestingly enough, at the very beginning of the next hour Robin offered me a piece of bread that she had made herself. She said that a friend of hers had remarked that "Making bread was good because when you knead the dough you can work out your hostilities and aggressions." I asked Robin if she knew what she was telling me and said, "Here you give me this lovely piece of bread that you've been kneading your aggressions into." We had been trying to deal with the problem of Robin's angry and aggressive feelings toward me, and she had been able to discuss this with Dr. Edmunds; still, she could not accept this remark and changed the subject. She went back to the almost chronic question of how much her sister was still preoccupying her mother and how Robin felt that nobody cared for her—they did things for her but she did not feel they really cared.

Robin reported that when her mother had gotten angry with her that morning over a card table that the mother had been looking for, not knowing it was in Robin's room, Robin had retorted to her mother's anger, "If you didn't want us why did you have us?" and added, "I've never felt as if I really belonged to the family; sometimes I think maybe I was adopted and that's why they couldn't care less." She went on to say that she was still thinking about doing something drastic to make them pay attention to her. She might break something like a leg.

She completely agreed with my comment on her competition with, and jealousy of, her sister but persisted in feeling that she had to do something, and she was extremely angry. She reverted to the idea of a pill and, when I asked her to tell me more about what she might be able to talk about with the help of a pill, she got more intense and said that she wanted to find out what was the real reason she could not spell and do her arithmetic.

Learning about Neurological Damage

I asked whether we really needed the pill to help us do this, and I began to explain something about the nature of neurological difficulties: "Many children break an arm or a leg. It is your nervous system that was damaged. When you were two or three years old you were extremely sick with a very high fever for several days, and we know that when this happens it can damage some of the nerves so that a person may have difficulties afterward." I explained that the different parts of the brain were important for different kinds of activities; one area of the brain has to do with coordination in motor activity, another has to do with vision, another with hearing. I said, "You can hear all right and you can see all right and you can get around all right." She interrupted to say that her coordination in games was not good, and I said, "Okay, but you *can* move around, and I don't see anything wrong about the way you walk," and she agreed. I added, "Probably those nerves were disturbed which are connected with the kind of abstract thinking that you have to do with math."

Now, dramatically, her mood shifted; she seemed relieved, and said she understood and she liked to know things like this. She continued that she would like to get at the records and had thought about picking the locks over in the residence and reading them. She didn't like the idea that the child-care workers and everybody over there knew a lot about her that she didn't know. I explained that the child-care workers did not have Ph.D.'s and M.D.'s and had not read all the records and that it was quite possible that they did not even know what I was telling her; she was surprised and interested and again became more relaxed—but then said that she would like to know what they said about her behind her back.

I replied that we were going to have a team meeting the next day and that I would want to know from everybody just how things were going at school and in the residence, what the difficulties were, and then we would talk about how everybody could help her to work on some of the difficulties. I commented that I knew that her teachers wanted to help Robin as much as possible. It would also be a good idea for Robin to talk over with Jessie her own ideas about a solution for the noise problem.

She had grown more relaxed during the hour but in view of her extreme curiosity about tests and records, I said, "Robin, I wonder whether one of the things you've been concerned about is that you want to know just what you did on the tests that you've had recently," and she agreed that she did. I said, "Well, I can tell you some of that too. When you first came here, your test records showed that you had a 'normal I.Q.,' and I was interested because I thought if a little girl who has this much trouble in reading and spelling and arithmetic can still come out that well on the tests, she must be a bright girl." Actually, Robin did not give me a chance to round out the picture and explain further about her range on the tests, from areas of marked difficulty to areas of good ability. Oddly enough, while beaming at my remark, she said, "When they first told me I was going to get you, I wondered who I would be stuck with if I didn't."

✛ It is hard to convey the enormous shift in level of feeling from one part of the hour to the other—from Robin's very angry feelings when she was griping about her family not caring about her and feelings of self-pity, to her alert, curious, and satisfied feelings after I had begun to give her information and also explained to her how we work together in team meetings. She seemed to accept the idea that I could not explain everything at once and also to trust that I really meant it when I said that I would explain the causes of her difficulties to her.

At one point, Robin also referred to her anger with me last Monday and said she knew that I really wouldn't laugh at her but she somehow felt that I was. I explained how we project our feelings onto other people. When we were angry at them and wanted to get rid of them, we imagined they wanted to get rid of us, and Robin agreed that that was just the way she felt.

Increased Anxiety about Her Sister

The next week home stress became more intense when Eve ran away on Thursday without leaving word about where she was going. The weekend had been a time of intense anxiety; for one whole day the family had not known where she was. Robin was also angry because Eve had taken the Siamese kitten and a record of Robin's along with her own records. Eve was staying at her grandmother's farm and turned out to be perfectly safe, but, in the meantime, Robin had had an anxious day at school, and her father had been irritable. Robin felt that she "fell apart" in school, crying as she practically never did there.

Realistically, I questioned her phrase "fell apart" and used this instance of cumulative stress to help her understand the relation between disturbed functioning and the stress she was under. I reviewed fall and winter crises

at home and at school and suggested that with so much stress many of us
would find it harder to work. Robin admitted that she had had a period
when she "couldn't care less" about school, and I suggested that she felt
drained by all the anxiety. Robin emphasized that her hand (chorea) got
very trembly at times of acute anxiety.

She went on to explore other possible factors in her vulnerability. She
asked whether she had ever told me about an accident that she had had
when she was about four years old when she had cut her forehead so that
it had bled badly and she had had to wear a bandage that "looked like an
Indian" for some time. She wondered if that could be connected with
anything. I said that if she had not been unconscious and had not had a
concussion, it was not likely that the accident would have contributed to
her difficulties.

I commented again that almost anybody would have some interference
with work with the amount of stress that she had been having. I added, "I
guess you're siding with a strong area in your family." Robin looked quite
sober and said, "I don't know," and then referred to times when she
didn't carry through well. I commented that she didn't stop trying for
very long—she always picked up again and kept on. Robin said, "Yes,
Ann stopped trying and so did Eve. I want to go to some kind of college if
I possibly can and get to be able to support myself, so I want to keep
trying." Then, she added that even when she felt like letting her homework go, there was something in her that made her do it. "It's my conscience that made me do it."

I said it was good that she could push herself to get the work done at
such times instead of giving up, and I repeated that she had a lot of
strength. She accepted this and then wondered whether she would be able
to take drivers' education. According to age rules, she would be eligible to
take drivers' education now, and then to drive when she was sixteen. I
said that driving a car was a big responsibility. Some of it would be easy
for her because she liked to stick to rules and there were definite rules
about driving that she would learn and master. But other things about
driving were not so easy to cope with. Robin then said that she did not
think her parents would let her start drivers' education until she was eighteen and then she would not be able to drive until she was twenty. I
suggested that this might be wise, that she had many things to learn. I
commented that she had conquered many difficulties she had had when
we first started to work together, and there were other things we needed
to work on.

She now wanted to know the results of the psychological tests she was
currently having. I asked how she felt about them—these tests were given
at a time of complex multiple stresses, despite our wish to avoid the test-

ing at a time of strain, because there had been no extended period since the beginning of the fall free from strain. Robin said that some days were bad, and she had not been able to do very well, but other days were better. It appeared that she had grown more comfortable with Dr. Grant through time and warmly commented, "She is very sweet."

I remarked that she had continued to progress through the fall and winter; for instance, one kind of progress was to bring in some of her angry feelings to the therapy hour, and I wondered why it had been so hard for her to do this; perhaps she was afraid that I would be hurt as easily as she gets hurt. I added that after all I had lived a long time and that I had survived a lot; I didn't think she needed to be so worried about whether some of her angry feelings would be damaging to me. Robin laughed and with a broad grin said, "You don't know me," as if to imply that she might be more dangerous than I suspected. However, when I said, "Perhaps I know you better than you do," she laughed again.

✝ Despite the anxiety of recent days, the hour had a warm, open, intimate quality of thinking together cooperatively, with moments when Robin appeared to be functioning well, reminiscent of the well integrated functioning shown in the fall after her good summer. Despite the worry about her sister the weekend had, perhaps, been easier for Robin without her.

With some exceptions, this quality of good integration continued through the next hour despite greater anxieties about dangerous activities on the part of her sister. Still, with Eve at a distance, and not incessantly beleaguering Robin, she was able to concentrate again on work. By this time the anxiety about Eve was mixed with criticism, but also it seemed that Robin had a clear determination not to let herself get caught in her sister's whirlpool.

She was feeling very good about school and said that she had had two As in social studies, and she was hoping to be able to work at a higher level in the summer. She wanted to enlist my help in persuading her teacher that she would be able to do so, but I emphasized the fact that the level of her own work would help her teacher to see what she would be capable of doing—especially if she could explore the library and get interesting books to read on her own. Robin then showed me parts of her work, especially a notebook in which she had provided illustrations of different tastes, smells, sounds, and so forth. Her illustrations of "repulsive smells" were a cat's box that had not been changed, cigarette smoke, and so forth. She also had a varied and interesting list of pleasant smells, such as bread baking.

✝   It was clear that Robin's commitment to progress helped her to recover resiliently from temporary losses of integration under severe stress. It was impressive to see that the neurological damage interfered with firm stability of control but not with the stability of this commitment and determination to reach her goal.

Team Meeting, February

This team meeting took place the day after Eve had run away, taking the kitten and the car. Eve had left a note saying that she wanted to get away to think for a few days and would come back. The mother had been extremely upset, crying, and had been unable to talk about it.

Robin had come to school and, crying, had told her teacher about this. However, her art teacher said that Robin had not mentioned it the second hour of the school day but was able to stick to her work and had a good time with one of the boys.

Their social worker said that Eve had been terribly upset, more so since getting well from her injury. (She was not allowed to participate in gymnastics or sports for a year, which upset her.) She had been sleeping all day, screaming and wailing in the evening. She had said she was going to move away and not have anything to do with her family. The day before, she had gotten up, written some letters, and listened to the radio.

In connection with this crisis, the parents had been trying to protect Robin from the constant battle and jealousy between Eve and Robin. Robin had been correcting Eve in reaction to Eve's picking on Robin. Eve would then blow up, swear, and storm. The previous weekend, the parents divided the house with Jim and Eve on one floor and Ann and Robin on the other. (Ann came home a good deal to do her laundry, and so forth.) Robin felt scared to be in the house with Eve alone so the parents had asked Ann to stay while they were away Sunday evening.

Robin told Jessie "everything"—that Jim told Robin that she could run away too. The group worker reported that Robin had tried to help Eve while she was sick but Eve would not accept it.

The social studies teacher reported that Robin told her that Jim was very difficult but veiled any anger toward Eve. In art class Robin attracted and enjoyed being with older boys. Robin did not talk about her family in home economics class. She could limit her anxiety but had not been accomplishing much recently.

When I asked about the quality of Robin's work in social studies, the teacher reported that they had been reading very difficult material in a

Weekly Reader. It dealt with a man-made river for the Los Angeles area. She also said that she had changed the approach in math; she was now going back to the old math book and the tape recorder for oral work on multiplication tables. She had observed that if Robin made an error, instead of correcting it, she continued the error through the rest of the table—evidently not remembering but simply adding. She also noted that Robin was responsive and curious. When she read something about the "Great Wall of China" in the *Weekly Reader* she asked, "What's that?" and wanted to write a report about it.

A visiting child psychiatrist asked whether Robin ought to be an inpatient in view of all the difficulties and pressures in the family. The social worker replied that the family does have strength, though at times it was hard for us to remember this. When Robin's interactions with the boys and enjoyment of Kelly were discussed, a teacher said that Robin was stimulated by some of the things the boys do. When she saw David working at the seventh-grade level, Robin looked at his book and said she thought she could do that. The teacher agreed but felt that she would have to work at it slowly. Her science teacher commented on Robin's ability to work independently, her interest in the nervous system.

Robin was now more able to accept changes. For instance, her schedule with art class had been changed so that she took art only three times a week, and speech class had been scheduled the other two days. Robin had been able to accept this without the anticipated difficulties.

I emphasized that it was hard to get a clear picture of the range of levels at which she worked—referring to the science teacher's comment that she had seen seventh- and eighth-grade pupils do less well on a project like the molds than Robin had done. Recently Robin's work had not been at such a high level. Dr. Moore felt that despite the constant crises, Robin's reaction had not interfered seriously with school. She did need support in the residence.

Dr. Moore reviewed Robin's difficulties in connection with the problem of flag raising. Robin had been disappointed because of the girls' resistance. I asked whether Robin was able to handle differences of attitude and opinion such as were involved there. The group worker commented that Robin did have difficulty in thinking about two points of view, particularly if it involved a commitment that Robin respected.

It was noted that she did seem secure with the older girls in the residence and in bringing her friends to parties. The tenor of the meeting seemed to be that, considering the extreme pressures and disturbances in the family, Robin had been doing pretty well.

✦ In contrast to Robin's integration in the fall, we saw the disintegrative effect of an overload of anxiety and frustration in the winter. Tension about the re-tests, competition with Eve stirring up old feelings of being deprived of her parents' attention, and anxiety about Eve, along with frustrations in Council and at school became unmanageable. Her thoughts about the fact that her damage had resulted in being left by her mother to the care of her nanny and aunt, while Eve's damage led to her mother's exclusive care of Eve, was probably the most unbearable stress.

13

Variabilities in Stress and Functioning

Overview of March

Robin's level of functioning in March was often in dramatic contrast to that in February; at times she had a special quality of serenity, relaxed responsiveness, cozy communication, and enormous charm—with spontaneous, subtle, sometimes humorous, often warm and pleasurable expressions. Her skin was rosy, in contrast to her pale and pasty look when under stress. In the hour of March 2, I was surprised at the steady, unbroken, comfortable tone and sustained integration. All this was so, despite continued anxieties in the family about Eve who was still acting up in potentially serious forms of teen-age rebelliousness.

A period of Eve's separation from the family and her safe pattern of life in Grand Island left Robin free from the immediate competitive, hostile, anxious pressures from her sister. She also had no further testing to bring her anxieties about her limitations into focus, and her mother had had time to share some activities with her. It was clear that when the pressures were reduced, Robin was able to maintain some distance from the family anxieties and to focus on her schoolwork.

During this phase of reduced stress Robin was more tolerant and at times empathic with her mother's difficulties. She again had a feeling of being left out when her mother was preoccupied with Eve at times, and her father spent his time with her brother. However, instead of getting enmeshed in tangled feelings, she was able to look at them more objectively—describing times when she was angry or even times when she did not sleep much, and summarizing with relatively modulated affect that things had been "bumpy." While she saw her sister as getting into deeper difficulties and being unwilling to use help, she felt that she herself could remain detached from her sister's problems. There were periods when she seemed discouraged and disappointed, and felt that her mother had been irritable with her, but she was willing to agree with my wondering whether her mother wasn't very tired from everything that had been going on with Eve.

In addition to her schoolwork as an anchor and support for keeping detached, Robin repeatedly brought in small treasures, souvenirs that Eve had brought her from Italy the previous summer—tiny crystal elephants, for instance. She also described little bone china Siamese cats in different postures. When I wondered what they meant to her, Robin remarked, "Well, they represent childhood," and she agreed with my comment that perhaps they represented some of the good things in childhood that she wanted to hold onto, perhaps play and imagination. Robin said she used to play with them when she was sick. By implication, childhood was in the past, and she now had a conscious identity as a teen-ager.

She was also exploring an identity as a helper. Robin talked about helping activities she wanted, like being a candy-stripe girl in the hospital, or an aide in a nursing home—she wanted to give. In other words, at this time, instead of reacting angrily to the actual situation of still being deprived by her mother's preoccupation with her sister, she mobilized her memories of, and symbols of, things she had been given, and also projected the giving through wanting to give to needy others. When I connected her wanting to give with her feeling of wanting more mothering, and also suggested that the childhood toys might have been brought to tell me that she would like to have more mothering before she was too grown-up, Robin looked at me solemnly and asked, "Have I ever had any?" She agreed acceptingly when I said it must be very hard at this stage, when she was wanting more mothering before she grew up, to have her mother so preoccupied with her sister that she did not have much margin to give Robin.

New Experiences with Boys: Teasing and Limits

It was in this context of the wish for mothering that Robin slowly described a recent episode at a party at the Children's Hospital. The gist of the story was that she had been sitting at a table with Steve across from her; she had accidentally upset her glass containing ice, and as she had reached out to pick up the ice, Steve had reached over and touched her hand. Another boy had seen this and had teased her again this morning in front of teachers. Robin had felt terribly embarrassed. I wondered whether he had used some obscene words that embarrassed her. Robin said, "Well, maybe," but when I finally got exactly what he had said, it turned out to be "Steve loves Robin."

During the slow process of this account and Robin's feelings about both the event and the teasing, her expression changed. At the beginning, she had seemed quite pale with a strained depressed look around her eyes, but as the story came out, her cheeks became rosy, then gradually her tonus improved and she regained the confidence that she had had the preceding hour.

In trying to explain why she had been upset Robin remarked, "I'm just beginning to look at those creatures across the room and try to find out what they're like. Even if I've grown up with boys all my life, I haven't known them this way." When I agreed that she was getting acquainted with boys in a new way but added that part of these new experiences would be to take the teasing of boys in stride and not take it too seriously, Robin conveyed that she was very sensitive and that words hurt her.

This led at first to a review of the many different circumstances in which she had been upset by teasing, by feelings of being ridiculed and rejected, and then to some discussion of ways of defending oneself and also of outgrowing the tendency to get hurt. "Another giant step would be to get to the point of not being so easily hurt by other people's words," I suggested.

Beyond this, I commented, "Maybe something has been going on—you were frightened by the idea of a little contact like that being interpreted as love, and you're not ready for love yet; it frightened you so much that it made you feel like going backward a little and playing with the safe childhood things again." She defended herself haughtily saying that she had brought the little elephants because I had been interested in them when she had mentioned them. I reinforced her ability to stand up to something that she evidently had felt was my misunderstanding her; I commented that part of being grown-up was the ability to talk back when she felt someone else was not seeing the whole picture.

In the next hour, Robin described more new encounters with Steve and, in addition, the fact that a psychiatrist and the head child-care worker were questioning their playful intimacies. When she wondered why, I suggested that in view of the overinvolvement of several other girls during the winter, they must be feeling they needed to help Robin to be cautious. I added, "It sounds as if Steve is very fond of you and you're enjoying it, but we have to think about keeping things within limits, not letting a boy fall in love so hard that he gets hurt." Robin agreed understandingly, "I know something like that happened in Grand Island; one boy insisted on liking me and I didn't like him at all." I also commented that it is possible to get acquainted with boys and still keep things within limits so that one does not get hurt oneself and also so that the boy does not get hurt. Quite seriously, Robin said, "I don't want to hurt anybody and I wouldn't want to hurt a boy."

This led to some discussion of what it means to be attractive and discover boys responding to you, and that it takes some time to find the kind of boy who is really right for you. Robin thought this over and suggested she would really like to find someone who was a combination of one of her uncles—"Strong like him, but not with too much money because I wouldn't want to give my children everything they wanted in a material way, it spoils them"—and a cousin who was a rancher.

After various detours, Robin shared her anxiety that she would never be able to have a child or, if she did have a child, it would not be normal. This was hard for her to talk about and she sobbed in despair. Again I came down to facts—there was no necessary connection between the neurological difficulties with her hand, or with math and spelling, and the problem of having a normal child. The neurological difficulties probably did not affect her uterus at all; her irregular menstruation in its first year was not at all unusual.

I arranged for a pelvic examination, which indeed confirmed the fact that her reproductive organs were completely normal. In the next therapy hour Robin's ability to accept my reassurance led to her reflection that she "Wouldn't want to have too many babies, not more than eight—or maybe four." I suggested that it might be a good idea to wait and see what her life was like, what her husband wanted, and how much energy she had. "Some mothers feel they have just about enough energy for two or three babies." Robin was thoughtful about this and agreed that it might be a good idea not to plan on having too many. She returned to thinking about the kind of boy or man she might like to marry.

✝   She seemed to be able to let the fantasy of raising a lot of children, along with a lot of animals on a ranch, drift off when thinking realistically.

Need for Father and Needing to Be Needed

The following hour, Robin commented first on altercations with others, then she told how she had wanted her father to go with her down to a certain area in the woods where there was a log. She had wandered off there after leaving a note on the door asking him to come down. But her father had not joined her in her retreat; instead he had sent Jim to get her. On the way back, Robin had fallen on some barbed wire and had scratched her knee, and she and her brother had bickered.

It looked as if her impulses were pushing her hard, and I said that it sounded as if she had not been able to control them very well over the weekend; Robin agreed rather blandly. She said she had just wanted to be alone with her father and not have anybody else around. When I suggested that since Eve had been having her mother all to herself so much of the time, Robin was wanting her father, she readily agreed and volunteered that she was jealous, in a bland way that seemed to fend off further discussion. She did comment later that she wanted to get her share of attention and "not have them babying Eve all the time."

In exploring her feelings about not wanting to spoil her children by giving them too much, while at the same time she said that she had not had the love and attention she needed, Robin said, "I do get love and they tell me I am wanted. But, I need to feel needed." I wondered whether she felt that I gave her a great deal of attention and care, but that I did not need her. She shook her head quietly after thinking for a moment, then said, "I need you."

✦   This expression of Robin's need to feel needed led to my exchanges with the social worker and the suggestion that the parents might give Robin more sense of being important or useful to the family; in particular, she had resented not being allowed to visit or help take care of her sister at the time of the accident.

It was interesting to see the alternation of the effort to get attention from her father (and one could carry this further) in the context of her many fantasies about marriage and having babies, and the fantasy about being one who helps and who cares for others. Actually, the wish to be a helper had recurred many times almost from the beginning of therapy and seemed to be so deeply rooted that it could only be constructive to give her opportunities to channel this drive.

Needing Help and a Volunteer Job to Give Help

In the next hour Robin spelled out in detail that she needed help from her mother on shopping and getting ready for a party for which she needed a new dress; she also wanted her mother to go with her to a concert this week instead of going with someone else to Kansas City. She said the only chance she ever had to visit with her was when they went somewhere together. When I wondered whether her intensified feeling of frustration at her mother's unavailability was connected with the fact that I would be away the following week, Robin agreed, saying that Dr. Edmunds would also be away and that she could not talk to her favorite child-care worker, "Because I'm supposed to be in my room doing my homework though I can't do it because my roommate chatters all the time."

She admitted that she was having premenstrual cramps for more days than usual before her period actually started. She felt she needed some medical attention for several things in addition to the menstrual problem; her brittle nails break very easily, and she bruises easily—she had bumped her back in gym, and she said the bruise would last for quite a while. She did not want to go to a new doctor. She had to have blood tests, and Dr. Edmunds had told her about a new nurse who did the tests and who was said to be very nice, but Robin was worried about this. I wondered whether she was also worried about the neurological examination which had been scheduled and reminded her that she was not seeing a new doctor— on the contrary, she had seen Dr. Thomas on her previous evaluation.

In this hour when so many of her own needs were stated, she again repeated that she wanted to feel needed. When I told her I had been thinking about some possibilities, and wondered about the Crippled Children's Center, Robin brightened, saying meaningfully, "Oh, I would very much like to work with children over there." I checked immediately and confirmed that they would be glad to have a volunteer. After her therapy hour Robin herself phoned for an appointment and set up a plan to work there in the late afternoons. She did so well that she was at times asked to give extra time in order to provide special help; for instance, when they were taking children on a trip.

Despite her comment that she needed to feel needed, she remarked in a slightly bitter tone that when her mother was away she was expected to do the cooking for the day. Certainly, there would be a realistic need at such a time, but Robin was evidently feeling that this was just one way of keeping her busy.

I Share Robin's Needs with Her Social Worker

I also shared a picture of what had been going on with Robin's social worker so she could help her mother plan more concretely for Robin at times when the mother had to be away. This memorandum was as follows:

To: Miss Miles   March 14
From: Lois Murphy

     As you know, Robin has been struggling with temptations to act out the way Eve does "to get attention." The overwhelming sense of need for attention and longing for her mother seems to be fed by a combination of sources:

     a. It's quite normal for many girls at puberty to have an intensified sense of need for mothering before they move into a more independent relation to parents and give up "the infantile mother." Robin is in the midst of this struggle. This is of course exaggerated by her realistic areas of difficulty of many kinds, and also the anxiety about how normal a life she will be able to lead, how much she will actually be able to manage by herself, and so forth.

     b. Also, the conflict about giving up the "infantile mother" is exaggerated by her angry, frustrated feelings about "never having had" the real acceptance from her mother the other children had.

     c. Being surrounded by threats and temptations from the impulsive actions of the rest of her family, and the girls in the hospital, has presented her with an almost unmanageable temptation to go and do likewise.

     d. Her own vivid responses to boys and their vivid responses to her are also intensifying temptations, and intensify her need to run back to her mother and to a dependent relationship, feeling that she isn't ready for all of the complexities that are coming with heterosexual maturing.

     e. Along with this is the constant reality that her neurological difficulties, especially at a cortical level, make the problems of control, management of complexity outside and inside, harder for her than they are for other less handicapped adolescents.

     She needs to be able to count on support outside in addition to what we try to do in therapy. It might help if her mother could anticipate with Robin what Robin's situation is when the mother is away for a day or two, and make a satisfying plan so that Robin could have the feeling that her mother was thinking about her. In general with her brain damage, enormous difficulty in adjusting to shifts, sudden changes in schedule, disappointments in plans, such thinking ahead is more than ordinarily important.

I have been trying to give Robin a sense that I have told her what I know about the causes of her neurological difficulties, including the fact that we don't have final answers. I have done this because Robin seems to gain strength from feeling (a) clear about what the score is; (b) having confidence that she knows the important things that people are thinking or saying about her, that we are all trying to understand and share and that I am sharing with her step by step the facts and understanding that may be useful.

For right now I am going to try to focus on a reality level confrontation: what are the things you really need your mother for? How can we deal with these when she has to be away?

Robin's Equilibrium Is Restored

In the following hour Robin was feeling better, her menstrual period having started shortly after the preceding hour with a consequent relaxation of the cramps. She was not only looking forward to going to Grand Island with her mother, but also expected to pick up an old friend. With these pleasant plans, the fact that I was to be away at a conference no longer mattered so much, but was an item for teasing laughter on Robin's part.

In contrast to the various shocked, indignant, rejecting feelings that Robin had had the year before about Grand Island girls who had gotten pregnant, she seemed more understanding about the fact that another teen-aged acquaintance had become pregnant—a girl whose mother had died and who was lonely. This led again to a review of Robin's feelings about boys; these were more casual now. But she was very interested in talking about the kind of man she might want to marry: "The man I marry—if I ever get married—will have to be stable."

In this hour she seemed to be letting go of the intensity of her longing for her mother, and I commented, "You know, it seems interesting that this weekend when you had a visit with your old friend (and also your grown-up friend, a former teacher) and you're looking forward to the coming weekend when your friend Libby will be here again and go to the party with you, you haven't been feeling such an overwhelming hunger for your mother as you did earlier." Robin was not defensive about this but looked interested and thoughtful. So I commented, "It seems to me that what you really long for is someone to be close to and companionable with; when there is a girl friend or someone else to talk to you, you don't really feel overwhelmed by the need to be close to your mother."

To this Robin nodded, and then wistfully and almost on the edge of a tear, said, "Yes, that's really one reason why I want a horse. Of course, a horse can't talk to me but. . . ." She left the sentence unfinished so I said, "He does respond to you," and she added, "And is a companion." We then spent some time talking about the possibility of making more effort to find girl friends in Topeka, but she seemed pessimistic about this.

Instead of pursuing this constructively, she spent some time sharing problems in her schoolwork—writing a paper on St. Patrick during which her hand had become too tired to write anymore so she had had to let it go and get up at six-thirty in the morning to finish it; difficulty that she had when trying to use a typewriter; trouble with long-division. I commented that she had actually done well to be able to stick to her schoolwork and make progress in working on her own problems during all the stresses of the past months. I told her, "Robin, you have more—and now I'm going to use a technical word—ego strength than you give yourself credit for; things have been swirling around you, but somehow you do keep going and you don't get stopped by it all."

Robin described rebellious episodes at home, where Eve had been yelling at her mother again and much conflict had ensued. Her way of describing her ability to keep detached was, "My watchdog takes care of me."

✝ It looked as if when Robin's functioning was not grossly disrupted by internal physical disturbances that aggravated the neurological difficulties, and when the strains of emotional assaults from her sister were not a constant threat, and when some of her needs for companionship were met, she was able to maintain her equilibrium. When the combination of external stress and internal disrupting factors piled up and interacted, the conflicts became nearly unmanageable. Robin's capacity to keep struggling in an outgoing way, demanding the support and intimacy that she wanted, seemed much less "neurotic" than withdrawal would have been. The effort to involve her mother in more planning for Robin had worked out well and had been helpful.

Robin's Conflict with Her Father

In the last hour of March, things dragged, and I had to work hard to get a clear picture of what was going on. What finally came out then was this: Robin was in acute conflict because she did not like to tell me how angry she felt at her father. On Sunday evening, they had been having supper at a restaurant. Robin had been trying to read the menu and decide what she wanted, and was just about to ask whether they had lobster tails, which they often had. Just as she was about to ask this, her father had "yelled at her" for being so slow. From her point of view, she had been trying to do the right thing and had been trying to ask in the proper way but then had been unreasonably criticized.

It sounded as if her father did not realize that she realistically needed time and support when she was trying to participate in a mature way. It was not only that she felt angry for being criticized when she was doing the best she could but that she had great conflict about saying anything critical about him. I said, "Well, you must have been angry at your father for not giving you the time that you needed."

Along with this, Robin had had a long dream that reflected her sense of deprivation. Then, in her neurological examination with a male doctor, she had been nervous when he had given her some simple arithmetic problems, and her tremor had been worse than usual when she had been asked to write.

She tried to avoid burdening her family but, according to the social worker, this effort was not successful. The cumulative and interacting experiences of frustration, anxiety, and anger were coloring her feeling about everything. Her own account of school included boredom with study of rocks in science class (with a male teacher) and extreme frustration in trying to master fractions.

While she was in the midst of current physical and neurological check-ups, which she dreaded, and was accenting the meaning of these for assessment of her handicaps, Libby, her best friend in Grand Island was now graduating from eighth grade while Robin was still working at different levels. She admitted to having times of feeling "fed up with it all"—she did not know whether she had the energy to keep on working so hard. Despite her discouragement (and in defense against it) she was able to fantasize about the possibility of helping to care for a new baby of a friend of her mother's.

Reflections on Robin's Need for Her Father and Factors in Variable Integration

✛   In this complex group of experiences we see how the different details interacted: Robin had been working hard at school and in the residence, not only academically but socially, to the limit of her energy; but she was acutely aware of her limitations in comparison with her friend Libby, and she desperately needed support from her parents. With her mother away and preoccupied with her sick sister, she wanted support from her father, and this intense need probably turned what could have been a minor incident—when a tired father tried to stimulate her to make her decision in the restaurant—into a mountain of anger and anxiety, augmented in turn by reproof (and an accompanying feeling of rejection) from her only remaining source of support, Ann. And the spilled-over anxiety intensified her fears of boys.

This cluster of episodes illustrated the importance of the role of the father at a time when a girl needs to outgrow dependence on her mother. If support from father is not available, the girl retreats to a mothering figure—first, her older sister; then, of course, her therapist. Parallel with the retreat from father, avoidance of boys and, later, of men in general became an added problem. In order to see why this episode became so important, it is necessary to recall Robin's reaction to the loss of medical care by her father (at the insistence of the Children's Hospital) who had always cared for her, his repudiation of her desire to play football with her brother and his friends, and the fear of dangerous boys aroused by the premarital pregnancies of several acquaintances.

It was as if the sense of rejection by her father who, she thought, ought to understand her realistic difficulties, was the final straw. Her relations with males were more difficult from this point on, and she began to tell of dreams which implied fear of sexual attack. Robin desperately needed a warm, supportive, safe father at a time of anxieties about dangerous boys.

Along with these anxieties, Robin was now confiding her fears of being left alone, being scared "when the wind howls." Being left alone was not just a matter, at that time, of being physically left by her mother—it was a matter of feeling emotionally abandoned.

But these feelings were complicated by Robin's concern for Eve, who had been acting up dangerously. Robin "would never forgive" her parents if they put Eve in the Children's Hospital against her will. It was as if Robin could tolerate the possibility of her sister's abandonment even less than her own abandonment: all the anger for herself she tried to bottle up flowed freely on behalf of her sister. But the Monday after Eve was brought to the Children's Hospital, Robin's expressions were fluid and kaleidoscopic—child-care workers reported that she was first immobile and mute, grumpy, irritable, then relaxed and warm. She was afraid she might get teased because of her sister; she did not like "having her in my territory," but she was "glad that she will get help."

Even while the multiple sources of increased anxiety, sense of deprivation in relation to her mother, and anger at her father continued, and

Robin's fear of dangerous boys, need for protection, and wish to escape from it all continued, she became more resilient and positive as she elaborated thoughts about helping other children.

It might have been Robin's satisfaction in her volunteer job of helping handicapped children, along with freedom from the stress of tests, which then shifted the balance so that she seemed to have more tolerance of the continued strains at home. Her sister's difficulties had climaxed. While Robin was anxious, she was not at all punitive, and she wished reasonably enough that Eve would do something drastic that "would make her realize that she couldn't handle her problems herself and that she needed help." While Robin continued to be a little annoyed that both her parents were so preoccupied, her attitude was stoical and her manner contained. She thought that she and her brother could manage by themselves. Again in a discussion of what it meant in a large family to be deprived of mothering when a mother was preoccupied with another child—for instance, a baby—Robin suggested that the older children "could help the mother." Thus, there was evidence that identification with a feminine helping role was becoming deeply consolidated as a way of coping with deprivation of mothering.

Team Meeting, End of March

Robin's marked variability when she felt threatened, fatigued, or unwell, and resulting variation in success in coping with stress made it hard for everyone to sort out and evaluate progress, lags in development, and transitory disturbances in development. The picture that emerged in a team meeting was sometimes in marked contrast with my impressions in therapy hours. For instance, early in therapy Robin tried consistently to convey her interests, needs, and positive efforts—at a time when child-care workers and teachers found her difficult, clinging, and whiny, and when the social worker's report emphasized angry outbursts and excessive complaining at home. Now, in the spring of her second year in therapy, teachers and other staff members were praising her progress while some therapy hours were full of angry, anxious reactions to home experiences.

Teachers now commented on her courage and growth: she was more relaxed and spontaneous in class, questioned the teachers' opinions, and was willing to argue. She had good ideas. In art class her products were good; she had a capacity to play around with material and see potentialities—she was more creative. Beyond this, she was more responsive to other children in her classes.

She still had difficulties in enunciation; her speech was sometimes mushy—reflecting a loss of control when anxious. Organic problems contributing to poor coordination led to feelings of inadequacy in gym and the reluctance of other children to choose her for their team in games. She also continued to reverse letters in spelling and to write tensely and laboriously in the effort to control her tremor. Organic problems continued to interfere with mastery in these areas.

Teachers agreed to try to help improve her enunciation by using a teletrainer kit, dictaphones, and tape recorders. Her home economics teacher emphasized how hard she worked, if slowly. She had received a C on a test of information in another class. She was free in her reactions to other girls' complaints—when two girls said they hated their parents, Robin protested, "You have to be thankful for what you have."

The group worker described her helpful and effective participation in Council and told of how she had brought two girls to a party, being hostess to both of them. Another time at a skating party, she had skated all evening.

✝ At the time I heard these largely positive reports from teachers, group workers, and child-care workers, Robin was bringing problems into therapy and not allowing disturbed feelings to spread through all of her experience. She did describe the party where she had brought friends, danced, talked with a boy, as the staff had mentioned. But Robin reported that right after this, when she went to Grand Island for a weekend, she avoided seeing other teen-agers because she was "too afraid of getting hurt," the boys would "mock" her, "would just think of her the way she used to be."

At the time Eve was brought into the Children's Hospital, Robin was momentarily in such an intense bind that she was mute in her therapy hour and had great difficulty in sorting out her bottled up feelings. While she was glad that Eve was getting help, Robin bitterly resented "having her in my territory." At the same time, she said intensely that she would never forgive her parents if they put Eve into the State Hospital because she would not get adequate help there. Robin had been afraid that she might get teased by other children in the Children's Hospital because of Eve, and this did actually occur.

At the same time, Robin seemed to be able to relax and turn her attention away from the immediate problems. She was thrilled upon reading a brief account of Helen Keller, feeling that "If she did it, I can." Her stoical and determined intentions were expressed at one time as, "God put these roadblocks in my way, and God gave me the strength to conquer my difficulties." She stated her determination to be independent and to master math.

Toward the end of April, Robin learned that Dr. Edmunds would be leaving in June, and she was able to talk about the difficulties she had when both Dr. Edmunds and I were away—how she needed someone to give her "a kick or a push." I commented on her capacity to make good relationships and the fact that she must have had good relationships when she was little. Robin described how Sadie and her grandmother had helped her by providing interesting activities—playing with pans in the kitchen with Sadie or painting with her grandmother. With these two, she felt she had had "real love," but it wasn't enough—she wanted it from her parents too. In a period of reminiscing, she also described mischievous activities of her childhood, such as running away from bean picking and avoiding pain from punishment by putting a book inside her blue jeans. She said that her brother got the "board of education" (paddle) more than she did. She remembered pleasant instances as well, such as being read to by her father.

Yet, she would end up discussions of the positive and negative aspects of growing up with the comment that it was hard to reach out to people because "I've been burned so often." Although she had originally presented Grand Island as much more friendly than Topeka, she was able by this time to admit that in Grand Island, as well, other children had mocked and teased her. She was "just an elephant who couldn't do anything." I tried to set these feelings, after ventilation, into a perspective in regard to the tendency of children to tease each other, ways in which other children are sensitive too—ways in which, as we grow up, we can conquer our sensitivities.

Robin Develops Perspective on Her Development

Robin sometimes talked rapidly, often with wit and gaiety, while at other times she was very serious and firm. She came to an hour early in May wearing a bright yellow jersey blouse with a very handsome handcrafted Indian necklace of turquoise and wampum. I commented on the clothes and then, as she beamed at me, asked what she wanted to talk about. She did not have any suggestions, so I told her that Dr. Edmunds had told me that she was going to San Francisco in June and that Robin knew this. At first, Robin responded humorously, "I disapprove, but there isn't anything that I can do about it; she'll be happier there." However, when I raised my eyebrows, indicating that she probably had some other feelings, she admitted that she had been very angry when Dr. Edmunds and I had both been gone at the same time in March and that it had been a difficult time for her. She enjoyed Dr. Edmunds's teasing as well as the fact that she had, in general, been "reliable" and available when Robin needed to talk with her. Robin said that, next to me, Dr. Edmunds was a person she could trust most. And she needed someone to reach out to her and sometimes to give her a kick or a push. She said there were times when she wanted to relate to somebody, but she could not get there all by herself; she needed to have the other person come halfway or more.

I commented that she had shown a capacity to develop good relationships and to communicate with various people, and that although Dr. Edmunds was leaving, there would be others, "because this is a place where good people come." She agreed but said that, still, she felt that Dr. Edmunds's departure would leave her without the reliable sense of someone she could depend on.

She wanted to talk about the section on Helen Keller in her reader—she had been so thrilled when she had finished it that she had shouted to her mother. Robin said, "You said a while ago that I didn't seem to get high, but I wanted you to know how high I was when I finished reading Helen Keller." She felt that Helen Keller had been stubborn and determined the way she was and had been able to accomplish what she had decided she would accomplish. We talked about the fact that Helen Keller had used all she had learned from mastering her difficulties to help others with difficulties.

I commented that evidently Eve's presence at the Children's Hospital was not bothering Robin too much. Robin responded with a very balanced remark: "She needs to get help here, but I don't like having her here." She also said that Eve's language was improving; as an illustration, Robin said that when somebody had asked Eve whether she had received a record someone had sent her, Eve had yelled back, "You bet your bottom I did." Robin laughed, "That's an improvement." Robin also added that Eve was doing better in her schoolwork and made one or two other positive comments in a big-sisterly fashion.

I had met Robin going toward the hospital at the time I was leaving a conference with Dr. Grant, and I told her that I had been talking with Dr. Grant and Dr. Roberts. The tests showed that things were at the same level—that is, the areas of difficulty were organic difficulties that she would have to continue to learn to manage. Robin wanted to know whether anybody said that things were better, and I said they thought she seemed more comfortable, less afraid, and able to manage better than she had before.

I explained how hard it had been for people to have a clear understanding of the complicated combination of organic difficulties and strengths that she had, and I thought the trouble in understanding this had made things hard at home when she was little. I said, "It must have been awfully hard when you were a little girl and you wanted to button your dresses and lace your shoes and ride a trike and do the things that other children did." Robin burst out, "I couldn't lace my shoes until I was in the second grade," and she went on to describe her difficulties in learning to ride a tricycle and then later a bicycle. I empathized that all these difficulties must have been terribly frustrating and must have made her very upset and angry at various times. I wondered whether other people besides Sadie understood this. Robin said she thought that Uncle Mark did and that in a way Aunt Samantha did, although really what her aunt did was "to shelter me"—that is, to protect Robin from difficulties and the consequences of them. She then said, "I wish you could meet Sadie," and I agreed that I would have liked to.

I commented that a long time ago when we first got acquainted, she had told me that she did not have real love, that she had been given material things but not the real love that she wanted. It seemed to me that she really had had a good deal of "real love" from understanding people and this had helped her to grow up. Robin said, "Yes, but I didn't get it from people I wanted it most from."

I said, "Well, you mean your mother and father, but I think they must have had a very hard time understanding what the difficulties were." I then told her that when I first came to the Menninger Foundation I did not know anything about children's neurological difficulties. When I found that, of the children who came here for testing because of emotional and behavior problems, 50 percent, or half, had neurological difficulties, I began to learn more about it. Actually no one had understood very well the subtle kind of problems that she had. Robin nodded understandingly and knowingly.

I asked whether she felt that her mother and father understood her better now, and she remarked again with her thoughtful tone "They're beginning to." I commented that if they were beginning, we could help them to understand better and that, as they did, I thought she would feel that she was receiving the "real love" from them that she wanted because this seemed to be so much a matter of understanding. Robin was thoughtful and didn't comment.

✝ She continued to look very charming through the hour, and I wondered whether her feeling of relief that Eve was getting some help was not a major factor in her good feeling—along with Eve's being kept within limits so that she did not impinge on Robin too much.

In the next hour there was more discussion of early experiences. I used her description of activities on the farm to discuss differences between things she could do and things that were too hard. In this context, she insisted wishfully that she could do anything she made up her mind to do. I commented that I knew there was great variability and that her hand had improved very much, but she had said that she had trouble with it during the examinations with Dr. Thomas and Dr. Grant. She agreed and added that she functioned badly when she felt that she might be rejected or felt that someone might not think much of her, "If somebody thinks I'm no good, I'm queer, or I'm not worth anything." She said, "If people accept me for what I am and if they give to me, then I can give to them. If they can see this in me, then I can give it to them." I said, "So we get back to what we were talking about earlier: the other person has to go more than halfway before you can respond at your best."

Robin said, "Yes, because I don't want to get burned, and I've been burned so often. If I'm not sure the other person really accepts me, I can't." Then, she went on to talk about how she had been hurt and how she couldn't stand teasing, except when it was friendly teasing like Dr. Edmunds's—"You can tell the difference between teasing when a person really accepts you and that's different from mocking or mean teasing." She gave examples of how Dr. Edmunds reduced her tension and pain during shots by joking or teasing comments.

I said it was very important for us to understand the conditions that helped her to be at her best and also how she could respond to other people to help bring this about. But Robin did not absorb this suggestion. Implicitly, she was caught in a conflict between her identification with Helen Keller—with her indomitableness, for example—and her own deep need for support, acceptance, and a friendly push from people she could trust.

She was, however, making a little progress—when meeting a doctor new to her but of whom she had heard, she handled the contact graciously, with less distrust than had been typical of contacts with new men. But in general, her suspicions of male doctors, her criticisms of them as cold and distant, continued.

✛ We have noted that Robin's progress was vulnerable to physiological variations. Even with the static condition of neurological damage her improvement in managing everyday problems was clearly seen. Evidences of her vulnerability during the stress of the winter and spring included a dissociative episode, abrupt and transitory, with accompanying flushing and change of affect and a breakthrough of primary process thought. It was as if there were a sudden burst of discharge or lesion in cortical-thalamic integration under pressure of exaggerated affect. This was apparently evoked in reaction to discussion of the fact that I could be in Topeka only half of each month the following year—an additional loss just at the time when Robin was struggling with a sense of inadequate protection from her parents and the need for protection from dangerous boys.

Reflections on Spring Development

Considerable ego integration evolved during the period we have just described; Robin coped with her feelings about deprivation of her parents while they were preoccupied with her sister by identifying with helpers and by reinforcement of her capacity to master her difficulties as Helen Keller had done. This whole experience put her image of herself into a different perspective—she saw her sister as needing more help than she did. She could forgive and support her sister probably because Robin recognized that the hostile, attacking, derogatory behavior was part of her sister's unhappiness. She could even tolerate her sister's taking the center of the stage at the next Children's Hospital party—dancing with a number of boys—while Robin watched. At the same time, Robin saw herself as established at Children's Hospital—"this is my territory." She was comfortable with many people, particularly teachers and child-care workers, and felt able to progress there.

It must have been this increased objectivity and use of strength which helped her to take the imminent departure of her favorite psychiatrist in stride. Empathizing with Dr. Edmunds's future plans—"She'll be happy there"—Robin could explain warmly how much Dr. Edmunds's availablility and friendly, outgoing teasing had meant to her. Similarly, she accepted the reports on her examinations—in essence, the neurological difficulties were as they had been, but she was managing them better.

She could also say that she found it hard when both Dr. Edmunds and I were away, and she had no one she found it easy to talk to. Despite the reorganization of her view of herself in relation to her sister and her sister's needs, she could not use the uncovering of early positive experiences to restructure her perception of her parents. Doubtless, the recent and current sense of deprivation reinforced the early perception of herself as left out by them when they took care of and shared activities with the other children.

Robin's increased tolerance, objectivity, and optimism was still vulnerable to physical disturbances which accentuated her sense of need for help. Toward the end of the period which had seen the progress reviewed just now, she came to her hour a little limp and glum. "I'm not feeling good; I was overdue" (with her menstrual period, which had recently started).

14

Coming to Terms with Sex and Losses

Coping with Inside and Outside Troubles

While family stress and tensions connected with Eve continued, and Robin's father was busier than ever, the last two months included more concern about Ann's departure, Robin's plans for summer, Dr. Edmunds's departure, my absence during the summer, and the fact that needs of my own family required a decrease of therapy hours the following year. Robin's physical reactions were more intense—having a very long menstruation, with cramps for some days before menstruation and during her period; medical help was arranged to alleviate some of this. Robin also had physical discomforts as a result of eating several foods to which she was allergic (pork, chocolate, and orange juice) and which produced a rash. It was as if when so much was being lost, she had to take in even things that were not good for her.

Robin's feelings of loss in regard to Dr. Edmunds or delayed anger about her departure led to exaggerated angry protests to a challenge by Dr. Edmunds. I interpreted the interaction of inside and outside troubles and their relationship, and the further depressed feelings that these interactions produced; and we discussed different ways of dealing with discouraged moods.

Robin talked about amusing compensatory activities such as playing with "silly putty" and aired her continued feelings of being left aside at home, jeered at by children, and defeated in her work efforts. Her teacher reported that Robin's work was now lagging in certain subjects, although she felt some progress was made in math. Coincidentally, when I suggested to Robin that she might enjoy Greek myths, she reported that the story of Pandora was the most interesting one!

Robin was able to explore the experience of contact with Kelly, who had held her hand on the way back from Council, which had given her tingling feelings that she enjoyed and feared. While she kept saying that she felt that she was not trusted, I commented that she did not want to be trusted too much; she really wanted protection so that she would not get into trouble as other girls did. All these feelings were intensified by Robin's recurrent experiences of Ann's baby. In this context a dream of being raped was interpreted as a combination of a wish for sexual experience and fear of being hurt, and Robin accepted the interpretation of the wish, saying, "Soft music makes me want it so much."

Some sublimation was reflected in Robin's bringing poems about the beauties of nature and finding comfort in a poem her Aunt Samantha gave her: "Taint what we have but what we give." A discussion with her mother about a boy's jealousy led to the mother's comment, "That's the way men and boys are," and also to her telling Robin that the reason for not having sexual relations was to avoid venereal disease.

I focused on the relation with Kelly and Robin's sensible efforts to protect herself, and feelings of fear that her impulses would overflow, especially around menstruation time. She also said that she felt secure in church, and I tried to encourage her attendance at church; but she could not go alone, and her parents were not able to go with her or help her find a companion.

During June, the departure of her sister Ann and of Dr. Edmunds, together with the departure for the summer of her two major teachers and myself and the change of staff at the Crippled Children's Center, all contributed to some deterioration of coordination and general functioning, as well as to hostility, protest, rebellion, aggressive gestures in the Children's Hospital, and an intensified need for warmth and support. It was as if the loss of so many supporting persons threatened to destroy the structure that helped to maintain her integration.

Robin's positive methods of coping included turning to her cat and trying to help Ann the last two weeks before departure. At the same time, there were diffuse protests: protesting against a male doctor giving her shots, protesting about her summer schedule—she did not want to have gym because other children ridiculed her there—criticisms of the new Crippled Children's Center staff. I interpreted her anger at Dr. Edmunds and at me and at the new teachers—intensified as so often by her instabilities during her menstrual period; and I interpreted her projections when she felt rotten, and the intensification of her need for her mother when so many others were leaving.

Positive supports included the arrival toward the end of the month of her cousin Wendy and a cousin of Wendy's, both of whom she enjoyed, and I commented that despite Robin's sadness about losing Ann and Dr. Edmunds, she had great resilience in being able to respond so happily to the arrival of her cousins. She also looked forward to the play that was to be given in July, and I helped her with this by providing a handsome robe for the "emperor" in the play. These developments constructed a new structure within which she could function well.

Robin began to think about possible future interests and activities and plans; these included wanting to work in a zoo, and she actually called the zoo director to find out if this would be possible, but he felt that she was too young to start now.

In therapy in June, there was further discussion of harmless and useful ways of dealing with anger versus the destructive projection that could make matters worse; the values of balancing sad memories with good memories as she had done recently in talking about childhood and balancing frustrations and losses with positive experiences.

Robin's despair and misery of the transition period did not interfere with her ability to utilize new opportunities of the summer, and the chance to take trips with her mother gratified her intense longing to have time with her.

While Robin continued to have recurrent difficulty, she was communicating with me independently and reliably. This helped her relationship with the child-care workers; I think this was a gain from therapy. Robin was sometimes inhibited by her consideration and concern lest she bother other people, but she generally showed a healthy perseverance. She liked one worker very much; she wanted his signature, and she used every device she could to try to get it. Again, she was not going to sit down and meekly take whatever life handed her. But she also needed to learn some tact. I saw her struggles with a multitude of feelings, and her achievements, in some of the therapy sessions of this period.

Robin Defends Her Rights as She Saw Them

This was a particularly vivid hour dealing with many of Robin's problems. The first ten minutes were occupied with satisfying matters—Robin showed me her new reader with fascinating excerpts from good literature, from Mark Twain to modern poets and writers. Much of it was taken from well-recognized adult books. Robin also described going to a play with her mother, a *Thurber Carnival*, and accurately described how they presented "The Last Flower."

Dr. Edmunds had told me about an episode in which Robin had gotten very angry at her but had said "I wouldn't give you the satisfaction of showing my anger." When Dr. Edmunds had prodded her that it was more grown-up to find ways of expressing one's feelings directly, Robin had left and cried in her room. The cause of the argument was that the child-care workers and Dr. Edmunds had been scolding Robin on the matter of repeating to her parents things Eve said that were upsetting to them; the general opinion was that Robin should not be carrying tales.

When I asked about what was going on here, Robin blurted out her feelings about the incident with Dr. Edmunds and her feeling that she had a right to talk to her sister and to talk to her parents. She felt defiant and perhaps slightly insulted by the feeling of "being pushed around and treated like a child." In the course of her complaints, she burst out again that people didn't trust her. I commented that this had come up before and that I thought we'd better get down to the bottom of it. After asking her just what she meant without getting any clear answer, I asked how she was getting along at the Crippled Children's Center and with her teachers at school. She said firmly that she enjoyed her work at the Crippled Children's Center and her teachers were all right. Then she said that she thought that this pushing came from her social worker "and right now I'd rather have Dr. Wilson for my social worker."

Interest and Concern about Sexual Feelings

About this time, she took out her name jacket and began to embroider "Kelly." Coming back from Council this week he had held her hand and jumped backward when he heard somebody coming. I commented that it sounded as if he felt a little guilty, and asked Robin about her feelings. She said it was a nice feeling. I asked whether she tingled all over and up her back, and she said she tingled but there was a sharp feeling in the place that's embarrassing to talk about. I said, "Well, that shows that you are growing up and you're even having feelings in your genital area." This seemed to free her to talk more about her concern about it. It was clear that she both enjoyed and was afraid of the sexual feeling, and I commented that it looked as if she had quite a conflict about it; on the one hand, it felt good and interesting and she wanted more of it, and on the other hand, she didn't trust herself, and she really wanted other people not to trust her but to protect her and set limits.

Through the rest of the hour, Robin agreed with every interpretation that I made relevant to this. Spontaneously, warmly, and sweetly, she described her feelings about Kelly, and I connected this with the experiences of girls in Grand Island saying, "You have seen what happens when girls get overwhelmed by wanting more of this feeling and are not protected." Robin agreed that she did not want to get into trouble, did not want to "hurt herself," and did not want to be in trouble with her conscience. She said, "It feels like wanting a piece of candy before suppertime." I agreed that sometimes it was very hard not to go ahead and take the candy before suppertime, and it must be hard for her when so many other girls did this.

Robin told me about Ann and said that her baby was due in the summer; the baby was very active and sometimes Ann let Robin touch her abdomen and feel the baby's activity. I said I knew it must be a lot of fun to feel the baby as a real live little person down there, and Robin then began calling it "junior" and said that maybe Ann's husband would have to leave for army duty. In that case, Ann would live either with her family or with Jonathan's family. I commented that I could imagine that Robin would like to have the baby living at their house, and she agreed warmly and tenderly. I added that sharing with Ann the pleasure of the baby and feeling it as very real and active must intensify her feelings about boys and particularly about Kelly when he holds her hand. She agreed.

She talked about a dream she had had, saying that it was like dreams she had had after she had been angry at somebody. Uncle Floyd and his son Kirk had been there in Grand Island, then somehow there had been a schoolroom and the teacher had been in her nightgown and all the students had been lounging around in their night clothes also. I asked Robin how the dream felt, and she said only that it seemed a little strange. We talked about Kelly again and night feelings, and Robin said that sometimes she wakes up in the night with a sharp feeling "in that place."

Then she said there was "something else in the dream that's embarrassing to say. There were some boys, one on each side, and one of them forced me to do it." She said, "I can't think of the word," and struggled for a word she couldn't remember; finally, after I tried to help her she said it was spelled something like *r-e-a-p*. I asked whether she meant "rape," and she nodded, again saying that it was embarrassing to talk about. I said it was natural for girls to have feelings and to want sex experience and more of these good feelings while at the same time they don't want to have such a dangerous experience, but sometimes they can have a dream about rape because they really wish it would happen without their being responsible.

Robin talked then about fear of being hurt—the boys had knives. I suggested that she felt it would be very dangerous and in a number of ways—emotionally and in terms of consequences. She added "and physically too." I said I thought she really wanted protection and that she wanted the grownups to set limits and to see to it that nothing dangerous would happen. It wasn't a matter of trusting or not trusting—but fourteen-year-old girls do need to have protection from grownups. Robin agreed.

I said, "The good thing about this is that you can be so honest about it and straightforward. You know what the good feelings are, you know what some of the dangers are from what happened to the other girls, you know it's possible to get overwhelmed and trapped. All this will help you to keep within limits yourself." Robin said, "When I hear very soft music, I have to run away from it because it makes me want it so much." I said, "Yes, it's that kind of music that's seductive," and Robin nodded.

I said, "Robin, another part of the problem is that you look more like sixteen instead of fourteen, and you can be a very attractive and seductive girl. Girls have to be careful and protect boys." Robin nodded and said, "Not get them too excited." I said, "Yes, because if the girl leads the boy on, it isn't fair to blame the boy if he goes too far too fast." Robin said, "If a boy tried to grab me, I could kick him." I said, "Yes, you told me that once, but it might not be necessary to do that. You could just tell him that you aren't ready for that much. You have to remember that you're only fourteen and that you want to wait for this until later." Robin nodded, and I said, "You know, something that people don't explain enough is that sex is much nicer later on when it's part of a real love experience and not just experimenting." Robin nodded. I said, "We'll have to talk about that some more." As we left, I said, "Robin, I know you have a lot of strength and you can handle this, and we can talk about it more on Monday."

✛ Robin's freedom to clarify emerging sexual feelings and dreams was impressive—and another important step in adolescent development. I was fascinated to see her capacity for cognitive and psychosexual growth while at the same time she was trapped in her need for restitution of parental care and in the stress of realizing the permanence of her deficits.

At the first hour after a party Friday night, preceding which Robin had talked about sexual feelings quite frankly, she took off her jacket and sat down in her vivid, stylish dress. She had brought a large armful of books and showed me two things that she had brought from Grand Island: one, a long poem by a ninth-grade boy on the theme of keeping one's eyes open to the beauties of nature; the other, an eight-line framed verse beginning "Tain't what we have but what we give that counts." Robin explained that Aunt Samantha had several of these mottoes on her walls and that Robin herself kept this on her own wall. I commented seriously, "That's what you really believe," and Robin nodded in her shy, quiet, serious way.

Then she told about a conversation with her mother in the car on the way home after therapy; she had told her mother that we had been talking about Robin's experience with Kelly and something of her feelings. She had also told her mother that Kelly was jealous of Robin's dancing with or spending time with any other boy. Her mother had said in effect, "That's the way men and boys are; they don't want to share the piece of candy with any others." Her mother had also said that one reason for not running around with boys (having intercourse) was the danger of "those diseases." Robin did not use the term "venereal disease," but she made it clear that it was embarrassing to talk to her mother about these things and that she didn't find it possible to tell her everything that we had talked about. I was impressed by her wish to share so much with her mother.

I asked about Robin's experience and feelings during the party. Robin said she had felt tempted when Kelly had said, "It's too bright in here"; also, "there are too many people around; it's too crowded." To these remarks, Robin said she had replied, "Oh, I don't think it's too bright at all"; or "I don't think it's so crowded." I commented that I thought she was protecting herself in a graceful and useful way; it was very sound not to run the risks that were involved when one moved into a dark corner or moved away from the group. Staying with the group was one good protection. I asked whether she had danced with Kelly, and she said it had been impossible to get him on the floor to dance, but she had danced with other boys.

We discussed the extent to which she felt she could handle her feelings and keep them under control. She said, "I know that sometimes my watch dog goes to sleep, and I do things that I shouldn't do." I asked for examples, and she gave the example of running away across the fields when she had been picking beans with the family. I commented that that was quite a while ago, when she was a little girl, and now at this age she might be able to keep things under control better. She agreed in a half-hearted way, and I said, "You're not really sure. We did talk about the way in which sometimes angry feelings can overflow, and sex feelings can overflow too sometimes." Robin agreed, and I added, "With you, these feelings seem likely to overflow at the time before menstruation or during your period." Robin agreed with this also and said, "I've been having cramps again." I expressed surprise, but she said, "I'm so irregular, it could happen again."

She then admitted that she had been tempted to get out of the group with Kelly, and I commented that she seemed to feel that she knew how to keep things under control, but at the same time, she was a tiny bit afraid that maybe she wouldn't be able to. Robin agreed. When I wondered what else might help her, she soon began talking about her Bible, which she read by herself in her room; sometimes she went down to a sort of retreat and read it by herself. I said that it would be important and helpful and satisfying to her if she could go to church, and she agreed, and said that in Grand Island she went with Aunt Samantha. She also said she might be able to go with Ann and Jonathan, although they did not go very often. When I asked about going with her family, she said that her mother sleeps late Sunday morning, and she felt that probably her mother needed the long sleep. She could go with her father, but Robin felt that he did not enjoy church. We talked more about what it meant to her, and Robin emphasized that she felt secure in church. I commented that church could be important in giving extra strength to our conscience, and Robin agreed firmly. I added that besides that, it was one place where she could be with a large group that was under control and quiet enough so that she couldn't be overstimulated or find it difficult, and she agreed with this.

✚   Robin was actively concerned with strengthening her control, in terms of her conscience and impulse control as well as mastery of the weaknesses in school and social performance.

An Educative Therapy Hour

In the next hour, Robin began by saying that Eve was going to stay in the Children's Hospital for several months. I asked how Eve was feeling about it. Robin said, "Partly she wants to and partly she doesn't want to." Then she went on to say that Eve had been particularly nice to her and recently called Robin "honey" or "sister." Robin felt quite warm and tender about Eve. We talked a little more about what it would mean to Eve to be in the hospital, and Robin said that she felt that Eve needed to have some of the things with her "that she loves—like her kitten and records." Then Robin said it would be a little hard to let the kitten come over here because it had been sleeping with her lately, and she would miss it. Their social worker had said that maybe Robin could get another kitten. I agreed that it was important for Eve to have things she loved with her and to be doing things that she enjoyed doing. As we talked about this, I felt Robin's real eagerness for Eve to have a good experience here.

It seemed inappropriate with this beginning to hark back to the problems about exchanges between Robin and Eve and the family—Robin seemed to want a quiet, companionable hour. She showed me a page of drawings of her one-celled animals; we talked about what they looked like under the microscope. Robin described their activity vividly, including a moment when her teacher was perhaps a little frightened by the jumpiness that one of them showed under the microscope, as if it seemed to be coming out at her, and Robin was vastly amused. She thought they were very interesting and was aware of many details. I commented that it was extremely important to make as much headway as she could now that things had quieted down and there was less stress.

She said she was expecting to work during the summer and, if she were allowed to, she would like to have her books and notebooks with her during August so that she could work ahead when she was in the mood. We agreed that it would be nice if she could sneak up on seventh-grade work in the fall. I explained that a younger level of schoolwork was unlikely to provide her with the information, vocabulary, and ideas that she would be able to acquire at the grade suited to her age level. She would have to fill in as much as she could by herself—listening to good radio programs, looking at television programs, reading the newspaper, *Reader's Digest*, and so on. She said she did like to listen to the news reports on the radio and to read the newspaper. She never resisted pushy remarks but gave examples of things she was doing in this direction and seemed to appreciate the "push." I had also been thinking about relationships with girls and other experiences outside the Children's Hospital. I suggested that after she once got acquainted in a church and felt at home in it, she might find that she could join a youth group. She agreed again that being affiliated with a church would be satisfying and important. However, she made a face and looked uncomfortable, then said that she felt uneasy and that she still was afraid that people would think her strange and that it was very hard to get into a new situation with new people. I said I knew exactly how she felt, that I had been terribly shy when I was her age too; it was important to remember that other people were shy as well—she was not the only one—and that if she could go half way she would find some other people going half way.

She talked about how much she had been ridiculed. I said I knew how hard that was, and I quoted my grandchildren's comebacks when they were teased or mocked. Then Robin illustrated comebacks in different situations; for instance, defending herself when she muffed the ball in tennis by saying, "The ball just doesn't seem to like my racket." I agreed that it was wonderful to be able to joke about it, and there were some things to say that would be appropriate to a specific situation and other things that might be just generally appropriate when she felt that she was being laughed at. She emphasized the point that it was hard for her to think fast enough when she was being teased to have a good comeback. I urged her to go ahead and try it and just have some things ready to say because it would get easier if she did.

Robin said she knew she really needed a kick and a push. I said I was giving her two right now; one kick was to get to church since that was what she wanted, and the other one was to make more effort to see girls outside the Children's Hospital. I asked whether she felt at ease with the two girls she had brought to parties several times. She did feel pretty comfortable with them. I said it seemed to me that there would be a variety of things that they would probably enjoy doing in the summer. Why couldn't she invite one of them to go swimming and have a picnic afterward? Why couldn't she invite one of them to go to a movie with her and her mother, and so forth? Robin said that when she went to a movie she liked to have her mother to herself. I agreed that it was fine to have her mother to herself on some occasions, but why not let her mother help her plan things that would bring other girls over? As Robin reflected, she thought that she might like to ask Carrie (a daughter of one of the doctors) to go to Grand Island with her. I agreed that most girls like to go visiting overnight or for a weekend.

Later, I told Robin that I had gone over her test scores in detail, and that I had noticed that, on the things that she did best, she was very high (actually in the top 16 percent), and then, laughing with her, said, "Of course in the low things like math, they're very, very low." Robin gave a half-humorous, half-embarrassed, half-appreciative subtle smile, and I went on to explain that one reason I was pushing her to listen to news reports, read newspapers, *Reader's Digest*, whatever interested her, watch good television, go to good movies and plays, and so on, was that she had a capacity for information and understanding which needed to be fed and that she herself had to take the responsibility for this if she was going to develop her best potentialities.

Very seriously she said that she really did want to, and that she would like to have her school reader with her and have it in her bed so she could read it late in the evening and in the morning when she woke up. I agreed with these devices of keeping at it.

I reminded her that since my husband was retiring from the Menninger Foundation and teaching in Washington, I would have to be there next year for about half the time, and wondered if it would be possible for her to write me or send me a tape at times when I had to be away. Robin was amused and pleased with this thought. I made the suggestion because there was to be for her this summer no stimulating, interesting trip that would be comparable to the trip last summer that contributed so much to her blossoming and integration. I felt that this was rather a critical period, and that every kind of support from her family, as well as from Children's Hospital, was needed to help her both to consolidate gains and to continue to make further gains.

I also mentioned that I had carefully gone over the tape of her discussion with Dr. Montrose, a psychologist, and I was impressed by the concise, clear, vivid way in which she answered a good many of the questions. Robin said she had noticed that some people ramble around too much in conversation and when they are answering questions. She felt that it was better to stick to the point (!), which was exactly what she did.

✝   This was an hour with a combination of stimulus for cognitive and social progress, along with coping and defense techniques.

During June, the departure of her sister Ann and of Dr. Edmunds, along with the departure for the summer of her two major teachers, changes on the staff at the Crippled Children's Center, and the awareness that I would be leaving at the end of the month for two months (and would be in Topeka for only two weeks each month from September on), all contributed to cumulative separation stress. This was reflected in poorer coordination, increased protest, rebellion, aggressive gestures in the residence, and an intensified need for warmth and support from her mother. Her anger was intensified, as it so often was, by her menstrual instability and tension.

Robin's coping efforts included trying to help Ann in the last two weeks before departure, greater preoccupation with her cat, more eating of sweets. She protested about her summer schedule—she did not want to have gym because other children ridiculed her there; she was critical of the new staff at the Crippled Children's Center.

Toward the end of the month her cousin Wendy and another cousin of Wendy's arrived, both of whom Robin enjoyed, and I commented on her resilient response to them. She also looked forward to the summer play, and I helped her with this by providing a handsome Chinese embroidered robe for the emperor (hoping this would provide a little restitutive sense of my caring). Her work in summer school improved as she got involved in the play.

In therapy we discussed harmless and useful ways of handling anger versus destructive projection that made matters worse. And we reviewed values of balancing sad memories with good ones, and balancing frustrations with satisfying experiences. Robin still felt unhappy at this time and momentarily wished she lived in the eighteenth century when all children did not have to go to school. But she was actually very busy with school activities in July, and in August with satisfying visits to relatives with her mother. Robin's flexibility and responsiveness were increasingly impressive despite continued frustrations.

Robin's Strengths as Seen by Dr. Edmunds

Before Dr. Edmunds left she wrote the following comments about Robin:

One of Robin's greatest strengths is her ability to form relationships. She has many difficulties still because of her sense of being defective, but she is a warm and responsive girl once it is clear that she is accepted and enjoyed for herself. In this kind of setting she has a keen wit, sometimes razor sharp, but never cutting, a spontaneous girlish appreciation of the whimsical, the funny, the sometimes merely ludicrous.

She is quickly responsive to any invitation to fun, for example, one day it was a cold day, and I felt like running. I asked her if she would run with me because that would give me an excuse to run, and about the only thing I didn't like about being grown-up was that I looked funny running. She was delighted both at the chance to help me and at the chance to take part in something with me, including the mild joke on myself.

Robin is always ready and willing and eager to help. She is endlessly patient with the little girls Becky and Barbara. She always speaks clearly to Missy. She is supportive with Lisa but avoids Prudence whenever possible. Her capacity for relationships contributes to the other qualities of character that are commendable and to her advantage. She has a zest for life, a zest for almost anything as long as she feels some sense of safety.

Because of her fluctuating physiological states, she is painfully and poignantly aware of her need for help. She is able to ask for help sometimes, calling attention to herself in this way in a fashion that can be misunderstood. She seems to feel safest and warmest when it is clear to her that people appreciate her difficulties, but "what does that have to do with how they feel about her?" It is as though then she is safe to expand and show her warmer, trusting side. I have the impression that basic trust is well established and that object relationships are alive, intact, and of great comfort to her.

I have been trying to think about why it is so difficult to talk about Robin without talking about her problems, and I think it can be looked at from at least five points of view. First of all, Robin has many problems with which she constantly struggles, often very ingeniously. She has learned that adults can help and will help, and therefore feels able to call on people for help, often putting it very clearly: "You know I need you to push me." Second, I have the impression that she may have felt most loved by her father when he was taking care of her as a patient and that this would then invest her sense of having problems with the value that these are a way of relating to, being cared for, being important to the other person. I would view this as a neurotic problem that perhaps she could outgrow with further help. Third, this is related to the problem of self-image. She hasn't as yet sufficient appreciation for her inner beauty and ability to love. I think that when she is able to separate the portion of herself that doesn't function too well and see it as a little more ego-alien (a process that is complicated by my second point), to separate this part of herself from her intact and healthy self, then this will be less of a problem and one will think of Robin less as having "problems." Fourth, in her family as in many families everybody has problems, and it's a kind of identification. A fifth point is that in the sibling rivalry in her family, he who yells loudest gets the most, and in the area of having physical problems this has been Robin's sort of excellence, through no fault of her own or of her parents. It is simply a fact of life related to her diffuse and spotty and confusingly disabling neurological difficulties.

Robin is very sensitive to many nuances and shades of feelings and relationships. . . . She is quickly responsive to appropriate praise and support. She is devotedly loyal to her family, and including Eve whom she loves very much no matter how obnoxious Eve has been to her on any given day. At the same time, she is quite clear that she doesn't like the way Eve treats her at times. She is protective of Eve in the residence, in part protecting herself to be sure, but I think truly protective of Eve. This was seen yesterday when there was a discussion of the fact that Eve's six-month-old kitten is in season and had run away. Robin was very worried about her. Becky and Prudence overheard the conversation and wondered in a frightened way who was lost, so we discussed it with them and said, "Please don't tell Eve." The other two girls understood and said that they would not. They responded quickly to Robin's wish to protect Eve. Robin's fear of Eve was also shown when she said, "If somebody has to tell her, let Miss Miles do it; I don't want to." From one point of view, it is for Robin a great gain that she is able to let somebody "do the dirty work" and not have to be embroiled in it at all times herself.

Robin has a keen and sensitive appreciation of the position of the underdog. She is kindly patient with the younger children in the group.

She is gay, vivacious, and flirtatious with the boy that she is attracted to. She has a tart, dry, perspective-restoring wit.

She can delay gratification as long as she is sure that she will get what is coming to her. She shows many intact ego functions. Her protectiveness and care for the other person was shown the other day. I walked by the sewing room and Robin was seated on the floor helping Cora (the woman who sews for the children) and Missy tie a quilt that Missy had made. Missy has the self-concept of being "stupid" and plays dumb constantly. I commented to Missy how nicely she was doing and also to Robin; she said with a quick glance at Missy that Missy sews three times as fast as she (Robin) does. How you interpret that depends on which side of the lens you use. From one side, you could say, "Well, Robin is saying 'Look, again I have problems,'" and another way of looking at it could be, and I think this was the more conscious one surely, "Let's let Missy feel good about this, can we? After all, it's Missy's quilt."

Robin's capacity for relationship and caring-for includes a nurturant kind of identification with her therapist, child-care workers, and so forth. I wish there were some place in society in which these qualities could be used to their utmost without demanding intellectual achievement. It gets harder and harder in our society to find such protected places for people who love. The only two situations I know of are in a Catholic convent caring for children and in the Salvation Army. Robin's religious beliefs don't push her in either of these directions, so I don't quite know where to go from there. She needs the structure, acceptance, and love that are present in both organizations which would then free her to do her work of loving, caring-for, attending, and nurturing.

Robin has a well-developed sense of right and wrong. She is particularly keen to the right way to treat people and what is the wrong way to treat people.

Robin is patient with other people's peculiarities. I have never heard her say an unkind or cross word to Lisa even during Lisa's longest, most boring, and most crude preoccupation with sex. Robin is fastidious and ladylike and somewhat offended by this but is tolerant of Lisa's concerns. She isn't just tolerant in a global undiscriminating kind of way. She is tolerant in a way that is tuned in to Lisa and who Lisa is. Robin is able to protect herself by withdrawal from Prudence, who is very sharp and cutting. She shows the same kind of sensitivity to all the other girls in the unit. She is also tolerant of Helen Alice's roughness and became amused by it as soon as she thought she could handle herself with Helen Alice.

15

Reflections on Robin's Second Year in Treatment

Introduction: Review of Progress

In the two years of treatment, Robin had progressed from her initial second-to-fourth-grade levels of work in school to sixth-to-eighth-grade levels, except for math. This impressive progress contributed to greater confidence, a more positive view of herself, reduced tension, and it even served as an anchor when she faced stress at home. But disturbed angry feelings and loss of integration occurred—chiefly when she was fatigued or plagued by physical discomforts, or burdened by unmanageable family crises, nagging criticism by Eve, or simultaneous losses. However, the angry or anxious feelings subsided more quickly and yielded to positive responses. She continued to emphasize her determination ("stubbornness") and areas of competence, such as skills with animals, children, and cookery. She responded with pride and even enthusiasm at some of her successes.

Her somatic integration also improved. She was speaking more clearly, showing less marked autonomic reactivity, and when not under severe stress, less menstrual distress. Allergy problems were under better control.

She was less fearful and, except when under the stress of tests and examinations which revealed her organic limitations, her reduced tension was reflected in better coordination, better cognitive functioning, and greater readiness for social participation and new activities. She had mastered fears of participating in peer groups in the hospital such as Assembly Committee and Council, making significant contributions to these group discussions. And she participated in plays and parties.

She reduced her dependence on her aunt. Except at times of severe stress, physical malaise, or fatigue, she was more tolerant of others in and out of her family; she was less critical, superior, and defensively disdainful; she considerably reduced the self-defeating defenses that interfered with the development of relationships with both peers and adults. In short, while her neurological state had not changed, secondary difficulties resulting from reactions to the frustrations it caused had decreased with an improved self-image and increased cognitive and social mastery.

During Robin's first year of therapy, developmental changes had been seen in her dramatic progress from childish behavior to experimenting with teen-age hairdos, clothes, and social participation. Feeling better about herself, she could let herself become a teen-ager. During the second year, increasing contact with boys stimulated new sexual feelings—interesting, exciting, frightening. Her honest and open discussion of these feelings helped her to understand why some teen-age girls in Grand Island and even in Topeka had become pregnant; her strong moral standards had earlier been reflected in harsh judgments of them. These standards, along with frank though shy facing of her own feelings, helped to protect her from too close involvement with boys who might have been overstimulating and overstimulated.

Conflicts Remaining to Be Worked On

Robin wanted to participate in social life with her peers, but her remaining fear of being hurt by ridicule or overwhelmed in new complex social situations still kept her from reaching out freely.

She said she "doesn't want to be different," but she did get secondary gains from being "special" which interfered with complete acceptance of herself as a person with a combination of strengths and weaknesses among other people who also had some weaknesses along with their strengths.

She wanted children but had anxieties about sex and boys.

She wanted to grow up, but her persistent longing for a satisfying mother-child relationship, which her burdened mother could not give her, slowed her relinquishment of dependence and the progressive individuation that would contribute to a more mature give-and-take with her mother. She was able to tolerate carefully planned absences of her therapist a little better but was still anxious about reducing therapy hours.

Although under optimal conditions Robin reached a vastly improved level of schoolwork, speech, emotional and impulse control, she was still an organically damaged young adolescent in the process of development. She still needed to develop better coping resources and useful defenses to handle frustration, teasing, and recurrence of feelings of deprivation and rejection; and she still needed to come to terms with inevitable losses and new opportunities in life.

Experiences Contributing to Progress

During the second year of therapy, Robin courageously came to an understanding of her neurological difficulties and was able to experience both appropriate discouragement and mourning. At the same time, in contrast to sleeping in school before she entered therapy, she was determined to make progress and even used the support of concentration on learning tasks to maintain her equilibrium through prolonged stress in the family. She was now able to express angry feelings and fears and to begin to understand how they aggravated social and physical problems and learning difficulties.

Medical help with menstrual discomfort probably contributed to improvement in somatic integration: Robin spoke clearly instead of with mushy speech, although this recurred under stress; there was less marked autonomic reactivity.

Both the child-care worker's and group worker's support helped her to participate effectively in the Council meetings; in summer school the opportunity to assemble props for the play was a useful stimulus. With the departure of her beloved resident psychiatrist, Dr. Edmunds, she welcomed the suggestion to correspond with her as a compensation for the loss of her companionship.

Robin had one friend in Grand Island and a cousin who visited during the summer; her relationship with both of them was quite intimate, but she continued to find it hard to toss off, or defend herself against, jibes and ridicule of peers who mocked her awkwardness and school retardation.

Robin's experiences in the residence and school were a major part of her treatment. Reports from child-care workers provided important data for therapy when I could connect her behavior toward them with her behavior toward me and work on alternative ways of dealing with situations.

The range of activities in the residence—parties, games, and Council, all provided opportunities for:

1. new steps in mastery of adaptational problems;
2. discussion of ways she could anticipate and prepare for varied experiences;
3. discovering her own initiative, the social values of her skills;
4. experiencing respect from her peers in the hospital;
5. discovering some potentiality for influence and leadership.

School provided experiences of using her strengths as in arts and crafts, science projects, reading about significant people (Pasteur, Helen Keller), and public events. Teachers facilitated progress in some of the difficult areas (oral spelling, special work in "speech," using the tape recorder for learning "times" tables). She valued concrete goals and appraisals, which helped to sustain motivation to continue the necessary drudgery.

The chief handicap in resources was the lack of variety in peers; she would have profited from being included in groups of normal girls, but she did not respond to suggestions about possible community groups.

Her large family and circle of acquaintances in Grand Island have had an almost unending series of emergencies and stressful experiences, as well as satisfactions, many of which provoked useful work in therapy on:

1. adolescent drives and problems (her response to pregnant girls in Grand Island);
2. the needs and stressful experiences of others;
3. the ways she and other members of the family cope with, and defensively deal with, stress;
4. her own need as she grows older to plan a life within limits she can manage realistically;
5. separation problems and disturbance over loss (of her grandmother or her Aunt Harriet);
6. significant new relationships

My absences were also used directly to deal with separation problems, dependence, and the relation of current problems to early experience and feelings about her place in the family.

Integration of Therapy with Casework

Because of Robin's pattern of reacting with inhibition, fatigue, or intensified emotionality to both stressful events and interactions at home, and also to various physiological conditions, it was very helpful to have the casework reports on the crises in the home, especially from October to her sister's entrance into the hospital the next April. When therapy required discussion of topics about which the parents might be expected to have negative feelings, as in the discussion of sex, I asked for their permission via the social worker.

As therapy illuminated specific problems in Robin's functioning related to her organic deficits or damage, the social worker was able to clarify these with the parents. Communications from the social worker helped to clarify Robin's expressions of intense longings for closeness and understanding from her parents and her self-defeating, aggressive ways of expressing these at times. There were problems in helping her parents to see Robin's strengths and potentialities while at the same time recognizing her realistic adaptational problems and needs for stimulating experiences.

I was not clear how much delight, fun, joy was shared in the family or how often the family setting evoked Robin's spontaneity, charm, understanding, and lively interest in the world, which she often showed in the therapy hours and to her teacher-friend, to Dr. Edmunds, and probably to her cousin Wendy.

Educative Aspects of Therapy

Some of the ways I tried to help Robin with coping techniques and useful defenses could have been used by others—her parents, other relatives, her big sister. But Aunt Samantha and Robin's family focused on propriety, control, and achievement without enough help in coping with overstimulation, stress, being ridiculed, and problems in orienting to new or complex situations. Consequently therapy had to include not only ventilating feelings, help in understanding the relationship of cumulative stress to the disintegrative overload, and the ways in which she projected distrust, and other negative feelings to other people; it had to include coping education.

There were other ways in which therapy went beyond dealing with emotional disturbances. Insofar as her anxiety was increased by confusion regarding the nature and causes of her difficulties, she needed facts she had never been given about these. Children who are deaf, aphasic, cerebral palsied, orthopedically handicapped, or have other obvious defects, do not struggle with so much uncertainty; it was very satisfying to Robin to learn about her neurological damage and about the results of tests showing her excellence in verbal areas along with her deficiency in math, spatial perception, coordination, and integrative processes.

Moreover, since she had not received sex education adequate to her needs, therapy had to deal with her emerging adolescent sexual feelings and the temptations that pleasurable contacts with boys brought; discussion of such problems fortified her coping with these feelings.

I also felt it was important to allow time for friendly sharing of Robin's interests, schoolwork, creativity, hopes, and pleasures. Her parents were too swamped with their own multiple sources of stress to respond to her interesting mosaic made during the winter, and to other normal interests. My interest in her creations and girlish activities helped her to develop a self-image as a growing girl with capacities, potentialities, and pleasures, as well as problems. Robin appreciated and responded to this normal sharing.

Robin's Increasing Understanding of the Organic Problem

In the first year, discussions of Robin's physical state began with obvious matters, such as her marked allergy problems and the need to get more help for this. As her mastery increased in the second year she became able to talk about her tremor and the difficulties it created in writing and spelling. She was intensely interested in what was in her files, what was said about her diagnostically, exactly why she had the difficulties in math, spelling, writing, and adjusting to changes and new or complex situations. I responded to this curiosity with simple schematic drawings of the nervous system and brain—the cortex, hypothalamus, and autonomic nervous system, and connections to different motor and vegetative areas. She felt a deep sense of relief in learning how the neurological damage affected her functioning and offered observations on ways in which her hand tremor got worse when she was anxious and similar worsening of her speech. She commented on her spelling difficulties: "I know what it should be but my hand mixes it up." This was consistent with our earlier observation that her oral spelling was two or three grade levels above her written spelling.

She also wanted to know how the damage had happened. With illustrations of consequences of severe illnesses and contaminated immunization shots, we spelled out possible factors, always with the emphasis that we did not yet know enough in medicine to be sure what caused it, but that it was not hereditary. Robin was satisfied after this review and did not have to return to the question in an obsessive way. Only later, long after therapy, she explained that knowing the facts relieved her from the sense of guilt that her difficulties resulted from being "bad."

In discussing her intelligence tests I explained that she had always had an average overall score, but this was the result of having some higher than average scores and some much lower than average. The high ones were related to her capacity to understand many things and the lower ones were related to her brain damage. She gradually became able to see that she was not only a slow learner but that she might never be able to go very far in the poorest areas. However she had capacities for grasping scientific, social science, and psychological ideas that might make it possible for her to take a special course in college if she kept on working toward it. She was able then to give up the idea of being a regular college student, but it took further work to help her see that medical training as a veterinarian might not be practicable.

Robin also became increasingly able to recognize factors in her fatigue, varied reactions to anxiety and increased difficulty (emotional and cognitive) during periods of physiological instability, such as menstrual periods or during a cold. Her tension tolerance, insight tolerance, and tolerance for transference involvement decreased at these times of decreased physical well-being. At such times she recuperated by "hibernating," or by extra sleep, after which she was refreshed and ready to go ahead.

Through constant attention to Robin's variable physical functioning we became aware of the variable heightening and lessening of her sensory acuity and her responsiveness to incoming stimuli. The neurological deficits interfered with maintenance of a stable level of input and of a stable capacity to integrate input, as well as creating problems in output. Under stress her control decreased more dramatically than happens with normal children, and this disturbed her neuromuscular skills.

Robin's organically determined variability included variability in pacing in different areas. She had been considered a slow learner, yet her sensory intake, both in vision and hearing, was rapid, and she made as much use of this as she could by eavesdropping and watching. Pacing of output, whether in action or speech, was generally slow; and the pace of integration of responses in complex situations was slowest of all. This imbalance of pace in different areas of functioning meant that all of those who worked with her—teachers, child-care workers, and other professional staff, including me—had to be sensitive to the pace allowed by her organic equipment in responding to a given demand.

Robin's Strength in Using School as an Anchor

At the end of the second year, looking back over the turmoil in the family and the frustrations, pressures, and conflicts Robin experienced at home, we had to marvel that she had been able to make so much progress at school in the midst of her anger, protests, demands, anxiety, feelings of being left out at home, and disturbed feelings and concerns about times when her parents were overwhelmed by the multiple problems with their children.

It was evidence of Robin's strength that she was able to use schoolwork to support her integration sufficiently to avoid destructive acting out. While her brain damage contributed to somatic and emotional instability as well as to coordination problems and difficulties in dealing with mathematics and abstractions, her values—deeply rooted in her identification with the strong members of her family—were unassailable. This included identification with their knowledgeability. In addition, her identification with the strong helping members of her family, and doubtless with her therapist, supported her capacity for constructive coping as well as taking on a helping role in the Children's Hospital and the Crippled Children's Center. The intensity of her commitment to the goal of being a helper was reflected in her ecstatic reaction to reading about Helen Keller as a strong handicapped woman who became a helping figure.

Patterns of Variability

Most people have a typical range of variability within which they fluctuate, usually in accordance with variations in fatigue, health, stimulus, pressure, frustration, and so on. With Robin, variations in affect and effort were more striking and, while often predictable, at times they were unpredictable. However, the apparent unpredictability was a result of the complexity of interaction of inner neurological and physiological factors with the extreme variations in level of stress at home and in the school and residence.

There were variations in mood reflected in periods of working hard in therapy followed by periods when she seemed to want to take it easy; at such times the hour had a rambling, chatty quality. There also were very intense hours.

Fluctuations in Physiological Functioning

The massiveness of Robin's reaction to fear of the Council early in the second year was reflected in her pallor, flushing, and in the edema that gave a different texture to her facial skin. But evidences of blood pressure changes and vascular shifts were also observed during the premenstrual, menstrual, and postmenstrual periods, as was hypersensitivity. They were sufficiently obvious that over and over again I recognized the onset of a menstrual period. I used this to try to help Robin understand relationships between her physical condition and disturbances in her perceptual functioning, as well as her extreme emotional reactions. Preoccupation with her body and her subjective experience, sense of inadequacy, and helplessness tended to emerge at these times.

The effects of changing hormone discharges exaggerated the adaptational problems inherent in her labile neurological condition. But Robin continued to find it hard to recognize and take into account this source of hyper-intense emotional reactions in order to forestall projecting blame onto others. We can speculate that referring blame to the outside helped to prevent her own suffering from becoming so overwhelming as to seriously undermine the ego strength she was in the process of consolidating. We can see that to admit to being overwhelmed would have felt like a surrender to helplessness. This was, then, a period of intensified conflict between a struggling ego and a periodically threatened, and threatening, loss of integration at the organic level, accompanying exacerbation of age-typical but dangerous sexual impulses intensified at menstruation.

At times of optimal organic functioning and freedom from stress, the neurological difficulties could be managed, and she could keep the integrative functions of the ego from being disorganized by variabilities due to neurological damage. But when combinations of physiological disorganization, pain, fatigue, and anxiety about family stress undermined her control, the higher functions could not be maintained and neurological vulnerabilities became dominant.

The constant danger of loss of ego control underlay, then, her own need to resist presssures and to avoid exposing herself to threats that could lead to disorganization. Largely for this reason she needed to feel that she could control her situation enough to maintain her equilibrium.

Reconstitution of Ego Control

A person with neurological damage has difficulty in coping with conflict and with intense negative feelings. Robin's recurrent dramatic reconstitution of ego control was an expression of a kind of functioning we see in some brain-damaged children. Imperfect subcortical-thalamic structuring contributes both to severe disorganization and to sudden recovery when stress is reduced. To combine support with action, involving other members of the treatment team, required constant vigilance on my part— vigilance oriented to determining instances where action was necessary to support or recover ego integration. With a fragile ego structure, consistent support for the ego was necessary for gains in ego strength.

Robin's strength lay in her positive goals, perceptiveness, energy, and identification with the best values in her extended family and others she knew. Her progress toward these goals was jeopardized by the organically determined external incoordination and internal shakiness of control and frequent threat of disorganization. A major requirement for the treatment team was to provide conditions that would avoid breakdowns of control and contribute to increased ego strength. There were, therefore, times when it was crucial to act as her surrogate. Of course, I faced certain risks in taking action in this way. Would the child-care worker, the residential psychiatrist, the supervisor of treatment disapprove or resent what I did? Would I be regarded as intrusive, as going outside my role? Would they reject my acting as a real person, going beyond my therapeutic role as interpreter of conflicts?

Since from time to time I was faced with the practical problem of how to cope with Robin's disorganized state, I had to take these risks. Fortunately, everyone involved understood the need for first aid to deal with the urgent necessity presented by Robin's disturbance before going on with a therapeutic discussion.

If we consider what ended the regressive disorganization, we can recognize the contribution of my combined action to gain time and to think with her as an expression of concern about Robin's state. This contributed a restitutive experience. I was then in the role of a caring mother-figure committed to help. With this sense of restitution the reorganization and restitution of ego control occurred quickly more than once.

Conditions for Maintaining Her Equilibrium

Robin's ability to maintain sufficient equilibrium and to cope with her handicaps depended upon freedom from too many simultaneous inner and outer sources of stress. In a complex new situation that involved several new people, too many choices, or lack of a comfortable directive, she became tense, awkward, and sometimes paralyzed. When multiple problems pressed simultaneously—as when she was disturbed by the pregnancies of two acquaintances, stealing by another, rejection and derogatory treatment by one sister, and departure of another—the anxiety aroused by each was augmented by the rest, and she was trapped in the circular interaction. At this point, she became confused, mixed up herself with her troublesome sister, and blamed the world at large, projecting her angry feelings onto the outside. She had to learn to select and limit stimulation to a level she could manage.

Self-Directing versus "Controlling" Behavior

Robin was sometimes considered "controlling" as well as demanding. All but the children who have given up hope of ever being independent find ways of expressing their initiative, their feelings, ideas, and impulses; and as they enter adolescence, their inner pressures for independence grow stronger. In a number of good boarding schools and day schools at the high school level, channels for independent activity, creativity, and problem solving dominate the program, and self-government takes over responsibility for most control of the group—within a few necessary ground-rules set by the adult authorities.

Handicapped children who are perceptive about their special areas of limitation and mastery, and the ways in which hospitalization circumscribes their initiative, sometimes have intensified needs to establish areas of autonomy where they can sense their own powers of decision. When such efforts conflict with staff assumptions about "appropriate" behavior, they are regarded as "inappropriately" controlling and therefore a problem, as with Robin.

The more obscure and complex the pattern of strengths and weaknesses in a child, the greater the appraisal gap between the patient and the staff. The child acts reasonably from his point of view but unreasonably in the staff's view. This appraisal gap cannot be bridged without serious efforts to increase mutual understanding, especially a sincere effort by the staff to understand the child's perception of the situation.

Robin's demandingness and stubborn resistance to pressures in new and complex situations were also seen as "oral" and "anal" fixations by certain psychiatrists in the evaluation and later. Yet it was precisely these characteristics that pushed her to receive needed help and to set realistic limits to what she could attempt. She fought for what she needed and fought against being forced into organically unmanageable situations. Respect for the fact that she realistically could not cope with everything at once helped her to progress gradually toward greater integration.

Shifting Emotional States

During the second year Robin's abrupt shifts from one emotional state to another were even more conspicuous at times than they had usually been previously. In addition, the spectrum of emotional reactions was much wider. During the first year we saw the shift from dejection, discouragement, distress, and sadness to hope, pleasure, and gratification. But this year, with increased evidence of progress in school and contacts with boys, along with disturbances at home, we saw shifts from intense anger or despair to an equilibrium, and a range that included excitement, intense eagerness, and joy accompanied by subtle expressions of tenderness. She was more open emotionally and less afraid of expressing negative feelings in therapy hours. But the surprising abruptness of some shifts reflected some inadequacies of control related to her brain damage. The strength of her wish for control was apparent in her effort to prevent being overwhelmed by sexual impulses. Lesser effort to modulate anger could be related to the pervasive patterns of expression of anger in the family, even by the grandfather.

Source of Difficulties with Peers

The discrepancy between Robin's poor performance in those areas most handicapped by neurological impairment and her high level of insight, creativity, and sensitive perceptiveness contributed to difficulties with peers. On the one hand she was not accepted on sports teams; on the other hand she functioned like an adult in helping younger children. This gap between rejection by peers and appreciation by adults created an acute self-image problem. Remarks like "I'm different," "I don't fit," "I'm a slow learner" expressed her attempt to formulate a realistic concept of herself. At the same time, her conscientious acceptance of adult pressures to get along with her peers, in line with identification with standards of correct behavior, supported anxious efforts to participate in group experiences. She was able to conquer her social anxiety in structured situations better than in unorganized ones.

Anxieties and Rewards with Examinations

Robin's resentment at never having been told the results of her many examinations and never having the source of her difficulties explained intensified her interest in and satisfaction in my sharing my knowledge and understanding. She trusted me and was deeply grateful to know the score. While I did not minimize or deny the difficulties, I emphasized her strengths and counted on Robin's strength to accept and integrate the knowledge about herself. This process of helping her to be "in the know" was, I felt, part of my effort to bring her into the world, to be among people who also had their different strengths to cope with their weaknesses. She did not have to be isolated.

The doctor's check on the state of her reproductive system which proved to be normal, laid groundwork for later heterosexual relations. Understanding all of herself helped her to be a more complete person.

It was extremely interesting to note that getting an answer to the question of Robin's neurological damage relieved her tension and freed her to turn her attention to other matters. It was impressive to see the effects of new understanding on recovery of integration and equilibrium. Cognitive mastery for Robin was important not only in relation to academic assignments but also in relation to her struggle to understand herself.

Robin's Anxieties about Sex

Robin's intense identification with Victorian aunts made her vulnerable to exposure to adolescent sex problems among acquaintances in Grand Island. The fact that several former schoolmates became pregnant within a few weeks of each other, and with resulting threats to the well-being of the coming babies, was utterly shocking to Robin, who reacted with intense righteous indignation. Beyond this, when a dear friend became pregnant the following year, she became angry. It was as if Robin were still living in the era of *The Scarlet Letter.*

With all the intensity of Robin's conflicts about expressions of sex in these contexts, it seemed important to introduce other ways of thinking about sex—namely, as a satisfying, joyous part of marriage, an expression of love and mutual responsiveness. It was significant that Robin did not have to reject this. She wanted support for control to defend herself against the pressure of sexual feelings especially around her period.

Problems in Communicating with Parents

Many adolescents long to communicate to parents how their treatment feels to the adolescent, what mistakes the teen-ager feels the parents made. It takes courage to talk to parents in this way, and many parents cannot take it—they may turn it off or react with protest or even punitively. The adolescent and the parents see the encounter very differently. And so it was with Robin and her parents. On Robin's side, it was a great effort to tell her parents how she felt about her growing up experience. Robin's neurological problems interfered with maintaining an equilibrium as she communicated her protest to her parents. She could not control her anger and the reverberating circuit led to rage. Her parents were understandably hurt. It is not until the young have matured to a level at which parents and offspring can talk to each other as equals that both sides can be at ease and keep a quiet perspective.

Robin's Mother-Hunger

Robin's persistent demand for closeness with her mother was considered inappropriate by some of the professional group. The fact was not recognized that she still felt deprived of intimacy with her mother and was therefore not ready for separation but needed a restitutive period that could compensate for her early deprivation. This year her mother was more than ever preoccupied with the problems of Robin's sister's hospitalization and extreme rebelliousness. Her mother's energy was realistically limited, and she could not respond to all of Robin's demands. Robin was not hostile, though she was often angry or jealous. Her loyalty and caring made it possible for me to try to help her to see her mother's situation, limits, and needs, and Robin rarely resented this effort even though she reiterated her need for her mother.

It was important to note that while Robin was so intensely upset about being left out when her mother was preoccupied with Eve, her anger and anxiety did not lead to regression in the spring of her second year of treatment. She protested, was jealous, cried, and expressed her anxiety; but she did not fall back into an accentuation of disintegrative functioning as sometimes occurred earlier when, as it were, the brain damage took over. Rather, she was looking at it as an existing reality that she wanted to understand and that presented certain challenges to her. As a matter of fact, she did not reject but was able to accept the interpretation that this experience of being left while her mother was taking care of siblings might be stirring up feelings she had had as a little child when she felt left aside while her mother was busy with the others.

Sibling Loyalty

During all the struggles with her sister, Robin's feelings were complex. While she could get very angry on occasion and disapproved vigorously of Eve's bad language and behavior, she never lost her loyalty to Eve or her awareness of Eve's needs for satisfaction or her own capacity to act constructively in the crisis precipitated by Eve's leaving home, when her mother was overwhelmed with anxiety. And she was ready to accept occasional warmth from Eve when it subsequently emerged, perhaps in awareness of Robin's loyalty. As we saw in her quick response to therapy in the first year, Robin was flexible and growing, while at the same time, she experienced endless upsurgings of old feelings.

Individuation and Separation from Parents

It was not always possible to sort out Robin's distortions from the realities of her parents' behavior and feelings. Her own deep need for their response to her longing for parental love and unconditional acceptance often exaggerated what she felt as their neglect of her when they were overwhelmed by the problems of their other children, their personal losses and stress, and their own middle-age developmental challenges. She was not able to proceed through a typical adolescent process of individuation and separation from her parents until she had had enough of childhood reliance on her parents and could also see them more objectively. Feeling my total acceptance, affection, and assistance in coping with her problems, her parents relied on this support for Robin. Gradually she understood, forgave, and loved them, as she began to realize their problems.

Dr. Edmunds supplied a "pal" relationship, which was an important part of the comprehensive treatment, and I was grateful that she could give Robin a degree of spontaneity and freedom of interplay which as therapist I could not give; we had no territorial competition. I was glad for all the support and help that was available. Robin deeply needed close relationships, and it could help to relax her own rivalry problems to experience our lack of rivalry. Fond as I was of Robin, I kept a commitment to our relationship as a therapeutic alliance. Moreover I was one element of continuity in helping Robin to adapt to change; others came and went, while I came and left for short periods and returned.

Differentiation with Loyalty

Robin's recurrent need to differentiate herself from the sick members of her family and to identify with the healthy strong ones, and also with the "strong pioneer woman," involved a conflict. She was very clear that she needed help, that her aunt would never accept help, and that her sister was resistant to help while Robin herself welcomed help and deeply wanted to cooperate. This clear perception helped Robin to maintain her own identity while also maintaining her loyalty to her family. In addition, Robin's family loyalty was colored by pride in her ancestry and her pioneer forebears. Whatever her own limitations, her good roots gave her a feeling of strength and potentialities.

Robin's reaction to her Aunt Harriet's death clarified for us Robin's own struggle between identifying herself with sick parts of the family and with the strong and healthy ones; and it also threw light on her repetitious emphasis on the strong pioneer woman, who contrasted with "pale, limp, weak" females. She herself was at times pale and limp with her multiple physical miseries, while at other times she was energetic and vigorous. She was always aware of being considered peculiar by children who ridiculed her, while she knew within herself that she understood far more than she could communicate and that she had healthy goals which she expected to reach, however slowly. It was indeed possible that she might have given up, as her defeated hangdog expression at the age of twelve seemed to imply. And the illness and death of her aunt, whom she thought she resembled, threw the weight on the sick side.

At that point my support of her strengths and my emphasis on the ways in which she was different from this aunt helped to prevent a consolidation of identification with the weak side of the family. I emphasized her strengths, her potentialities, the normal aspects of some of her problems as a growing girl, her achievements, and her qualities as a girl I enjoyed and cared for. I did this even to the point of bypassing some neurotic patterns that I felt she could give up as she gained confidence—because it seemed to me that a focus on illness would tend to support identification with the sick adults. My approach was an emphasis on mastery and coping within a realistic recognition of typical developmental problems, which in her case were exacerbated by neurological difficulties. With this orientation, interpretations within the transference of her projections, for example, were made with the attitude that this is one of the unrealistic or unfair things we all tend to do—not that she was deviant or sick.

Giving, Making, and Helping: Relatedness, Usefulness, and Self-Image

Much of the time, Robin had one or another project, usually a gift she was making for some member of her family or a friend. Some of these involved a considerable sustained effort and represented a true labor of love. She valued external symbols of relationship, and the gifts she made for others had this meaning. So did others' gifts to her, which she wore from time to time.

Along with these overt expressions of relatedness, we can see her wish to help—helping in the residence as at home seemed to give her a sense of belonging; and, beyond this, she repeatedly expressed the feeling that she was needed at home. She wanted to be needed, to be someone who had something to contribute, who was important to others.

Thus, we can see why Robin was so cooperative in Council and Assembly Committee, where the group worker repeatedly told me that Robin was forthright and open in expressing her opinions and often helpful in keeping the meetings on an even keel or progressing to solutions of problems presented. Here, undoubtedly, Robin could sense her usefulness as helping to maintain structure and to move the group in a sensible, socially minded direction. Her role was not unlike that of the "majority whip" in

Congress or assistant to the Speaker of the House. Her attention was focused on values and standards, proprieties to be recognized.

Along with bringing "props" for a play, she worked valiantly for its success. Here, she could give—even to the point of working on an acting role about which she had felt diffident. She could and did use opportunities to accept structured roles in situations like these, but she was dependent on these structures. She still avoided open, unstructured social situations or handled them awkwardly and with embarrassment.

As she became a giver, a helper, one who could take responsibilities, her view of herself changed from one with the inner hope to be useful to one who had actualized this hope.

Responsiveness, Understanding, and Progress

Robin's responsiveness to support in using new opportunities like the Council, parties, and learning tasks demonstrated how deeply normal she was in many ways. As with other children, success bred success. Functioning led to improved skill, and the emergence of the confidence that the effort was worthwhile. She developed a self-image of a girl who could cope with new challenges, and a reinforcement of her determination to make progress. She became an active participant in the treatment process through observing and sharing conditions that interfered or helped her participation in the residence and group activities, as well as in school. All in all, I was deeply impressed by her progress on so many fronts. I felt that we could not predict how far she could go, but I was confident that with her astonishing capacity for hard work and her range of understanding she would be able to finish high school, despite the fact that two psychologists said on the basis of tests that she would not be able to do so. The tests had helped me to understand her organic problems, but they did not do justice to her potentialities.

PART III

ROBIN'S THIRD YEAR IN TREATMENT

16

Struggles and Integration of a Whole Self

It was assumed that the third year of therapy should provide a period of consolidation; further mastery, including academic progress and clarification of Robin's potentialities; further work on management of feelings and also work on problems of management of realistic adaptive difficulties caused by her brain damage; further help to her family in understanding both her potentialities and her many problems and needs; and further help to Robin in her relations with her family.

This period of therapy began in September with acute problems at home and at the hospital and school. By fall, Eve had rebelled against further hospitalization. She had run away, and her whereabouts were unknown for about three days. Robin's mother was acutely upset, and Robin was more upset about her mother than about Eve. She handled this by phoning Aunt Samantha, whose calm response helped to soothe both the mother and Robin. When Eve refused to return to the hospital, the parents were afraid to act against her wishes and allowed her to stay home. In the course of one argument at home when Eve expressed her wish to stay home and Robin (perhaps trying to support the hospital) expressed the feeling that home was not so good, Eve kicked her so hard that Robin's thigh was bruised and had a 4-inch by 4-inch black and blue area for days. (All the children kick, slap, hit, and in other ways express anger physically. Both parents used corporal punishment and during the previous year had reacted explosively at a moment of acute tension.) All in all, it was a period of prolonged turmoil.

The social worker's notes repeatedly commented on the parents' anxiety and passivity in relation to Eve and, as the fall went on, their half-hearted participation in social work sessions. This led to a decrease of social work interviews to one per week; then, after Christmas, to one every two weeks.

The mother continued to support Robin's work at the Crippled Children's Center (where Robin felt a couple of girls were friends). Her father tried to get her interested in a judo group attended by Jim, but Robin felt that she could not cope with the coordination difficulties she would encounter. Her parents apparently never supported Robin's potential interest in church, expressed openly in previous years and still reflected in Thematic Apperception Test stories and discussed in terms of potential peer contacts.

Probably the effort to dissociate herself from Eve's status as an inpatient contributed to her resistance to participation in the four o'clock Friday unit (residence) meeting ("I'm not part of the unit"), but there was other evidence of effective individuation, explicitly discussed in therapy hours. At school, Robin became very frustrated with her program, which included only two academic hours in the fall; she felt the home economics course offered no new challenge and was unwilling to give much weight to suggestions that it could be useful to learn various ways of dealing with cooking, laundry, and other tasks.

In view of the fact that five out of eleven items on her last Wechsler Test, given in connection with a neuropsychological exam, received scores at an average to superior level, with "Comprehension" and the integrative processes involved in "Picture Arrangement" at a conspicuously high level, it seemed important to allow some academic work at her best level and not limit her to a focus on her deficits, which gave too little new information. Her "Information" score had gone down a little from the previous year, suggesting that she needed more content input; her deficit was conspicuous in geography. Examination of her Stanford Achievement test showed that, when allowed the time she needed, she was at about the ninetieth percentile for the level tested in several areas; this confirmed the desirability of offering more challenge.

So I had several discussions with the principal of the school, the teachers, the psychiatrist, and the social worker; these led to a plan (implemented after discussions with Robin) to enter an eighth-grade science course. By December, she had completed her sixth-grade reader and begun her seventh-grade reader; by spring, she was working at a junior high level in everything but math, which was fifth-grade level.

Peer relationships seemed decreased when her Grand Island friend, Libby, was unavailable during the summer because of the time she spent in Wichita helping her sister. However, during the year, Robin recaptured the relationship with Libby, who reported on the interest of a boy, Jerry, in Robin and tried to push her to go to dances, which Robin resisted. She never utilized my support and challenge to expand her peer relationships beyond her efforts within the unit.

The group worker consistently reported on Robin's useful participation and constructive suggestions in Assembly Committee; and Jessie commented on her helpfulness with younger children in the classroom. She continued her volunteer job at the Crippled Children's Center with enthusiasm; thus, several zones of helpfulness reflected her need to develop relationships in structured settings where she could feel that she had something to give.

Robin's picture of her relationships was somewhat different from the adults' negative picture of her social contacts. During the summer she found a relationship with Colleen, an eighteen-year-old cousin, as well as with her same-age cousin, Wendy, deeply satisfying. She also enjoyed a couple of group trips to drive-ins, and so forth, on her visit in Nashville, suggesting her need for structured protected settings for peer-group contacts. With repeated discussions in therapy of ways of coping with ridicule and teasing, she actively worked at becoming able to engage in mutual heckling with Lisa in the hospital, a big advance after her hypersensitive withdrawal from such interchanges. In addition, in response to discussions in therapy hours, she deliberately reached out to Paula, a new girl in the unit, and later responded positively to Paula's coaching in gin rummy, expressing a wish to know her better. She remained withdrawn from Eve's friends, whom others also thought inappropriate for Robin. While Robin lacked both a recreational peer group and a dependable available pal, she was not totally isolated from peers. In view of our feeling that more availability of compatible peer contacts was needed, the professional staff agreed in the winter that one course at public school summer session would be worth trying.

During the fall, Robin had prolonged and severe anxiety in regard to commitment to a plan for a group trip to Europe the following summer; impressed by her development, her former teacher, Joan, had invited her to go. Robin's parents seemed to accept this but did not support preparation for the trip or help her to think through the realistic difficulties she would confront. Robin was thus left to struggle between the inner pressure to go, as her sisters had gone, and her own overwhelming anxieties about it. This was discussed in many therapy hours; Robin was able to express many realistic fears about the demands of the trip but persisted in her determination to prove to herself that she could do it. A major unrealistic aspect of the plan was the fact that she was considerably younger than her sisters when they went on the trip and would be the youngest girl in the group. I commented on the difference between realistic thinking and wishful thinking about ways of dealing with multiple difficulties. Despite her refusal to give up, the usefulness of all the challenges in and out of therapy was suggested by the ease with which she gave up the plan after the aggressions of North Korea, which led her family to anticipate an international crisis and to decide the trip would involve too much risk.

Finally, a major stress for Robin in the fall was involved in getting adjusted to the changes in my schedule divided between Topeka and Washington, which meant half as many therapy hours. I saw her twice a week on the fortnights in Topeka which left her two weeks at a time without therapy; thus, she lacked this support during the periods of turmoil at some difficult points. At the same time, working through these separations in therapy probably contributed to the relative ease with which she coped with termination of therapy in the spring as well as to improved dealing with some other losses. At the time of the absences, she wrote me one or two informative letters, thus helping to maintain continuity in our relationship.

So from September to January, Robin responded to therapeutic efforts to step up the level of her academic work and to utilize contacts in the unit. She also made use of the support in the Children's Hospital for participation in a group responsibility (Assembly Committee) while at the same time individualizing herself both from her sister and from the inpatients in her unit; and for extended helpfulness as child-care aide and teacher's aide. This provided a needed sense of role and the opportunity to give. She dealt openly and actively with frustrations and stress resulting from my absences every month. She also worked through the interrelationships between somatic and affective reactions during menstrual distress at a time of special pressures; fantasies reflected identification with my work with motherless babies. Increasingly, as Eve's problems decreased, Robin and her mother became companions with restitutive satisfaction, probably on both sides.

By February, so much progress in integration and realism were reflected that the possibility of termination in May was broached and accepted. She had begun the new eighth-grade science course successfully; two front teeth had been inserted and her appearance improved; her family situation had quieted down and hostility from her sister decreased. It seemed clear that although therapy could not be expected to eliminate her brain damage—and the attendant susceptibility to stress, problems with over-stimulation, slow adaptation to shifts, changes, sudden events, loss of support, and so forth—it had reduced the inner anxiety to the point where potential for growth was released. Cognitive functioning was—though still hampered by brain damage—largely freed from emotional blocks; capacity for enjoyment of many experiences and people was extended, and a realistic view of her difficulties could be faced and dealt with. Somatic difficulties also declined: she no longer covered her trembling hand; there was no deterioration of speech; menstrual stress was somewhat less. And she felt clearer about how to deal with everyday stress such as distracting noises in the school situation. On her own, she applied for and obtained a promise for a job with a veterinarian in the summer.

The final period of therapy dealt with the stress of impending loss of therapy itself, along with multiple other losses of peers and child-care workers in the unit and several disappointments regarding summer trips, the most severe of which was collapse of her hope to visit Ann and her baby in Florida. Robin also raised some final teen-age questions about sex and pregnancy which she wanted to clarify and which were dealt with at a reality level, and reassuringly. Dealt with also were confusions about the plan for attendance at one public school summer session along with three hours at the Children's Hospital school. While displacing some final resistance to loss of therapy to the details of these school arrangements, she handled the termination with a combination of appropriate adolescent sadness, and appreciation and idealization of—as well as identification with—me and asked for continued communication. And at the same time, there were moments of denial as well as ones of regression in level of speech functioning in a few sessions before termination and intensified sadness at departures in the unit and the deaths of lifetime animal companions. Probably her recurring demandingness at home and in the unit was attempting to compensate for losses. It was not clear how much support she received at home—such as appreciation of the progress she had made, efforts to recognize and help solve her unavoidable problems related to her brain damage, physiological lability, and vulnerability or, at least, her sensitive reactivity to noise, adaptational problems in handling newness, changes, and so forth. However, from time to time, although altercations still occurred, Robin commented on her brother and sister being "nicer" to her.

As has been obvious, along with typical early adolescent problems, conflicts, anxieties, and somatic instabilities added to multiple congenital vulnerabilities as well as brain damage, the recurrent turmoil in life—the losses, changes, and home conflicts—had provided many stressful experiences for therapeutic work. But by midwinter of the third year, Robin's life had settled down, her progress in school was outstanding, her communication with her parents had improved, and it looked as if she could continue to make progress without therapy. Her parents had recently suggested termination.

17

Termination of Therapy

March through May

Reports from the current psychiatrist in the unit regarding Robin on the unit, from the group worker in regard to Robin's participation on the Assembly Committee, and from her teachers, almost uniformly described Robin's steady maintenance of good functioning during the last three months before termination of therapy. The psychiatrist commented that Robin was taking termination very well and that she showed appropriate sadness in connection with loss of her therapist and the departure of Lisa from the unit, as well as the departure of child-care workers.

At the same time, over the last three months, there were a couple of comments from the child-care workers about Robin becoming more cling-ing—which might be interpreted as, on the whole, a positive effort to turn to others in the face of the losses of this period. The group worker's reports also contained remarks each week about Robin's participation and help in solving problems; for example, when another child was bothered by the problem of writing a letter to Dr. Karl Menninger in appreciation of his assembly meeting, Robin actually took responsibility for writing this letter. Her eighth-grade science work received a B. Her papers were in-teresting and reflected real assimilation of what she had read; they were not just copying down statements from different sources. Comments on her art work included references to her humor and creativity, and her pleasure in the work in ceramics. Robin herself brought in examples of her work to the therapy hours with much pleasure. Her marks on other

subjects were As. She was ending the year at a junior high level in everything except math, having caught up four to six years since beginning
therapy.

Jessie commented personally to me that she was impressed by the fact
that Robin had continued to be able to make progress despite the fact that
she had been giving considerable time to helping younger children with
math, phonics, spelling, and so forth. Robin had been an asset, able to
stick with the helping tasks, patient, and resourceful in thinking up hints
that might help the children.

It was also noted repeatedly that she was helpful with the younger
children in the residence. Robin herself expressed the feeling of being
equal to the task of coping with Barbara, one of the children whom the
child-care workers found difficult to handle. It was also noted that Robin
watched the child-care workers, seemed to identify with them, and used
some of their techniques; She had been a sort of child-care aide and
teacher's aide. In addition, her volunteer work at the Crippled Children's
Center continued.

But, along with all these various positive comments, it was noted that
she did not participate in many of the available social activities and special events—for instance, she had turned down a weekend trip on the
grounds that her family would probably be going to Grand Island.

Reports from home during this period were less positive. While her
parents had expressed feelings earlier that Robin might well terminate
therapy, when faced with the reality, they expressed considerable concern
about the difficulties at home. The father was especially concerned about
difficulties in getting Robin to increase her responsibilities for work at
home—her share of chores, her dependence on her mother for shopping,
and so forth—and her lack of contacts with other teen-agers; and he was
also anxious about the years ahead in view of her realistic neurological
difficulties.

In therapy hours, this period contained much dealing with losses when
opportunities for displacement of her feelings about loss of therapy were
provided by the losses of child-care workers and peers in the unit, death
of an old horse she had known since childhood, and the death of an old
cow that had been, from Robin's point of view, part of the family since
her childhood. She seemed to feel the losses of favorite animals almost as
keenly as losses of people, if not more so, because the animals had been a
part of her life for a longer period.

The public school summer session did not offer the course Robin had
wanted, and there were other disappointments, such as the cancellation of
a family trip to Arizona.

Tears at moments, expressions of sadness and irritability, all appeared from time to time in understandable contexts. At the same time, these alternated with and, during the last week of therapy, were less apparent than her brave denial, accompanied by some slight somatic regression in the form of the tissue changes and fuzzy speech seen chiefly the first year of therapy. Robin was able to compensate with current and anticipated pleasures and a tendency to accent the positive (while avoiding the stresses of termination) with some realistic reviewing of what her therapist had meant to her, combined with warm adolescent idealization expressed in a couple of poems.

Major points in appreciation of therapy included her recognition of my help in "pointing the way" and, even more intensely, appreciation of my willingness to "tell me where I stand, what the trouble is, what I can do," and so forth. Her confidence and doubt both were reflected in her comment "I'll try" in response to a question about whether she felt able to manage now without therapy.

At the same time, child-care workers in the unit, the group worker, and others commented on Robin's attractiveness and even more significantly her willingness to accept an image of herself as attractive—not rejecting compliments about how pretty she looked. Various people in the unit commented that she no longer walked in an awkward, tiptoeing way, her carriage was better, and, in general, her typical appearance was that of an attractive teen-ager.

She did not seem to suffer as much from menstrual cramps; allergies were under better control, although house dust still bothered her; she was still hypersensitive to sudden noises—noises in school when the children moved chairs around, the noise of a vacuum cleaner, and, in general, other noises that might be mildly bothersome to other people but were sometimes intolerable to her. However, she was better able to manage this—in school by keeping her distance, finding a quiet area where she was less exposed to the noise, and at home by trying to convey her discomfort from the noise of the vacuum cleaner.

At the beginning of March, the unit report noted that Robin had expressed sadness about her favorite child-care worker's leaving. In the therapy hour, Robin talked about her pleasure in helping Barbara with her math and her problems in making contact with a new girl, Paula; Robin found it hard to find things to talk about with her, but Paula had taught Robin how to play gin rummy and was getting more friendly. Still, Robin said, "you have to work hard to get a smile out of her"—with which the unit workers agreed.

When I commented about the difficulties in making friends of her own age, Robin said that one of the boys at the Crippled Children's Center had asked her to go to one of their dances, but she had refused; it was difficult to get at the basic factors in her anxiety. When I asked whether it would be easier to get acquainted with people of her own age in a boarding school, Robin firmly said no, adding that her mother would not let any of them go until they were eighteen; but Robin agreed when I commented that she really did not want her mother to let them go. She stated that she wanted to get back home even when she was in places like Nashville where she felt happy, and we agreed that feeling close to home base was still very important to her.

We discussed the kinds of arrangements that could be worked out here in Topeka—the fact that there was no suitable school, except for the school in the Children's Hospital, and that it would be possible for her to continue here. I suggested that completing high school would be important in order to make it possible for her to take more responsibility than she otherwise could in work with children, for instance. Robin defensively said that if she did not complete high school, she could become somebody's cook, perhaps, because she liked to cook.

I called attention to her real talents in working with children and the need for people who work well with children and understand them. Robin was very intense in reaction to illustrations that I gave of people who do not understand children, but then she continued her defensiveness, saying that she did not see why it would be necessary to get so much training: "Don't you bring to children everything you've learned from your own life?" Robin gave the example of learning about children through a television documentary describing group care of children in Russia and the positive results of extra stimulation and exercise. In short, she seemed to want to be in a position to work with children but also seemed to be uncertain about the possibility of completing sufficient education or training to be able to do so.

At the same time, she brought in evidence of successful, satisfying, and interesting work in science, with drafts of papers on whales and on volcanoes, and so forth. She showed the most intense interest in discussions of volcanoes. She also brought in a little play she had written for Jessie—the topic was rather childish, about cats out on a fence under moonlight, but it was lively and amusing; she seemed confident in doing this, as well as in her description of what she was doing in art. In other words, her mood in regard to ongoing work was very positive. Her uncertainties came out primarily in relation to the future.

In the next session, she continued to talk about interesting work at school, particularly, a science experiment in which she had studied the effect of drugs on plants, making careful observations. She expressed pleasure about the time that her mother spent with her hunting for antiques and described in vivid detail specific things they had found. She seemed to be trying to show me that she was doing well and had things in hand on all fronts—in the mature way she described the immaturity of a couple of children who had tried to run away and also the difficulties of another girl in the unit with whom she had tried to make contact.

At the end of the month, in the school reports, Jessie commented that Robin continued to show improvement and, in addition, had adjusted very nicely to a new practice teacher. She also added that she had had many trying days, especially Mondays. In a meeting in the middle of the month between Dr. Moore, the social worker, the psychiatrist in the unit, and me, the reasons for termination were reviewed—namely, that for some time before the decision there had been practically no problems reported in the unit or at school or from home, and that Robin brought little to work on in therapy. The social worker said the family felt comfortable with the way things were and the mother was enjoying Robin, although the father questioned the amount of time the mother and Robin spent together, describing it as "not growing up." I commented again that Robin had been quite deprived in her relationship with her mother during her early years, and this period of having a good time together could be important restitution, satisfying to both of them, and could be a good foundation for steps toward independence later on.

Dr. Moore expressed concern that "Robin might be settling for less than she could be," that she might be setting her sights too low. I agreed with this, but I said that it was hard to move her in the direction of more effort toward teen-age contacts at this time; she did not seem to be ready to move on that now. Dr. Moore commented in response to the social worker's report that Robin retreated when Eve's friends came around, that Eve's friends "are a pretty tough group who would be hard for Robin to take" and added that she wished Robin had a friend something like herself with whom she could share her interests, with which we all agreed. The psychiatrist noted that Robin reached out to Paula and confirmed that they did play gin rummy a bit in the unit. Dr. Moore felt that it would be possible for Robin to go ahead in school at the Children's Hospital as long as she needed to, and the social worker said that an occasional conference with the family would make it possible for some continuing stimulation to be provided for the parents.

In discussion of what was ahead for Robin, I noted that Robin wanted to be self-supporting, and the psychiatrist asked whether she had in mind the possibility of an independent set-up. We agreed that a major obstacle to this would be her difficulty in handling money, but Dr. Moore commented that with so many relatives a plan probably could be worked out so that someone else could be responsible for the money; I added that it was not impossible that she would get married.

So far, Robin had not been able to communicate directly very much anxiety about termination; the psychiatrist felt that she was showing only appropriate sadness in response to the departure of her child-care worker. The group all agreed that she was practically functioning as a child-care aide, and we discussed the possibility of formalizing this a little more in the future.

At the beginning of April, much more affect began to come through than had been apparent in March—a tender birthday poem for me; irritability about the overlap of material in science and what she was reading in her health course. I interpreted her annoyance as connected with the amount of time she and I had spent on understanding the body and her wish to forget it now. Robin described a bad week; she was menstruating, which still bothered her, and had been to the dentist, where she had had four shots of Novocaine and a number of cavities filled at once. She admitted having been very irritable and in a bad mood all day the Saturday after that.

In discussing plans for the future Robin said she wanted to work with children and animals, and to take some psychology as preparation for this. She added that she learned a lot from animals that she could use with children.

In the next session, we were able to look at the actual summer school program, and Robin expressed her disappointment that what she wanted to take was not being offered. I commented that it was hard when she did not get exactly what she wanted, and Robin was able to recognize that she was not in a good mood that day and had been sick the day before. As we were talking about her nausea, she also commented that she had lost her horse—a very old horse she had ridden when she was a child. It seemed that her father had told her about the death of this horse the night before and this was intensely upsetting to her. She cried while talking about this, and we used it then for a more complete discussion of loss and the meanings of different losses. I interpreted that she was feeling very overwhelmed, not just about losing the horse but the many other changes and losses occurring now—missing the child-care worker whom she had known the longest time, other child-care workers and children in the unit who would be leaving, and also termination of therapy.

After summarizing the losses, I asked whether she felt she could manage by herself. She stopped crying and said, "I'll try." We stopped then to talk more about just how things would work out, and I explained that therapy would terminate in May and that school would end in May too. I would be back in June for a couple of weeks, and we could have a follow-up hour then. I also added that every summer when I'd been away for a long period of time, Robin had really had a very good time and had gotten along without the contact with me. She agreed, but a little resistantly, that she had been very busy (with visits from relatives, vacation activities, schools, and so forth).

She also expressed her deep disappointment that she was not going to be able to go to Florida to see her sister and the baby as she had hoped to be able to do. There had been some thought that she could go with a daughter of a friend, but the latter had given up the trip. Robin brought me the uncorrected copy of the poem that she had shown me earlier, and I thanked her, saying it was a beautiful poem. We then talked about poetry a little bit, including Emily Dickinson, whose poems I thought Robin might like. She expressed satisfaction about our plan to correspond and about her letters from Dr. Edmunds, which she received about once a month, as well as letters from her sister.

After this way of resolving her sadness and disappointment by reminders of compensations and substitutes, she discussed satisfying things that she was doing in school, especially her art work, including both the ceramics and an intriguing pin that she had made by melting a flash bulb into an odd shape. We talked a little about how things often turned out better than she expected, for example, the science course; she had not liked that idea at first but then found it extremely interesting. Robin ended the hour in a cheerful, relaxed mood.

The third hour in April was spent in unraveling some of the connections between her fearful and resistant feelings and her anger about terminating therapy and her difficulties in showing her anger to me. Robin blamed me in a huffy way, saying that "some people are so thick-skinned they can't catch on to any ideas." She was delighted at my protest that some people were so indirect and so evasive they did not make it easy for anyone to catch on to what their feelings were or what they were thinking. This kind of spirited exchange pleased her so that again she ended the hour very relaxed and in tune.

The last therapy hour in April was the Thursday before Easter. I came back to the poem that she had given me and the fact that she had given Jessie one that had been corrected and had brought the uncorrected one to me. I said that I wondered whether she wasn't telling me two things this way: that she knew how to do things well and also that she felt insecure at times. Robin agreed, but a little huffily, saying that probably most people felt that way a good deal of the time, and I agreed with this, but added that it was important for us to be clear about all the different feelings about ending therapy.

Robin had again brought in evidence of accomplishment—a bowl that she had made in art class with interesting colors that had been thoughtfully selected. We talked some about her experience in helping the younger children at school. She expressed the feeling that some of the child-care workers did not trust her with Barbara, and I mentioned to her that Dr. Moore had said that some of the child-care workers themselves did not feel sure whether they could manage Barbara and that it was not so much a matter of trusting Robin as not trusting Barbara. Robin explained in some detail that Barbara usually cooperated with her very well, and she felt that she could keep up with her if Barbara started to take off.

I commented that when we were close to ending therapy it was a good idea to think about where Robin was and what she had accomplished, and I said that I thought two things were very important: one, that she had been able to let me know when she was ready for something more, for a more challenging kind of activity or experience in school, and two, that I had been able to help her bring these about at times. Robin added, "But I got the vet job on my own," indicating that she felt able to take the initiative herself now.

I then commented that she had also been able to set limits and make it clear when she thought I was expecting too much of her. I wondered whether she could do this with other people. Robin said that, in connection with the question of being pushed too fast, when it happened at home she "gets grouchy" and that let her father know that she did not like the pace. I agreed that that let him know something but repeated that I thought it would be more helpful to tell him directly the way she could tell me.

Robin did not want to go on with this discussion and shifted the conversation to plans for Easter in Grand Island and news about her child-care worker's baby, with details about its weight, and so forth, and the fact that she would not be able to see it for a while yet.

She then began talking about movies, giving a rather vivid and sophisticated account of a series of movies she had seen over the winter, all of them good, top-level movies. She talked especially about *Doctor Zhivago*, urging me to see it. In the course of this discussion, she also said that she had not understood *Hamlet*, and I agreed that it was complicated and one needed to study it ahead of time.

In an hour in May, after ruminating on the white and blue dresses she had been wearing and her design on pottery, I commented at one point that I felt we both had been whitewashing the blues and that it was hard to end therapy. Robin reported crying about the loss of "Old Bossy," the cow she has known ever since she was a tiny child, and again we used this to talk about our feelings about the end of therapy, with Robin protesting a bit against linking all these things but able to absorb it. She said that she did not have a pet and wanted a new pet, a little one she could take care of.

I used this to move closer to termination feelings with her and said, "Well, you're not exactly my pet, but I'm going to miss you very, very much, and I guess I can't have a new one." Robin then tenderly said, "I'll miss you too . . . . you've been like a grandmother to me." I said, "I know what you mean because you've told me a great deal about your grandmothers and how much they meant to you and how your grandmother helped you when you got upset when you were very little." I wondered whether she was making the end of therapy even harder than it needed to be, thinking that I might die too, and she said, "Well, grandmothers do die." I agreed that there was no telling how long I would live but suggested that we just take one thing at a time—and what was happening now was terminating therapy.

Robin complained that she had had terrible cramps yesterday; I commented that they might have been worse because she had been shutting out feelings about ending therapy, and this was one reason why it was important to be able to talk about them and share them. We then spent a little time around some of the confusions about termination. Robin said she had wondered whether we were terminating because the family couldn't afford to pay for more therapy, but I explained that termination was possible because she understood her pattern of strengths and difficulties so much better now and had made so much progress in being able to work things out for herself. Just before the end of the hour, I commented that she had been laughing a good deal in spite of the fact that we both had been feeling pretty serious about termination earlier in the hour, and I asked whether she had ever heard the saying "I laugh that I may not cry." Robin understood this and accepted the fact that this was relevant to what she had been doing.

On Arbor Day I went over to the ceremony, meeting two of Robin's teachers there, Jessie and Dale. Jessie commented on Robin's ability to make good progress in school subjects, even though she was taking so much responsibility for helping a couple of the younger children. Dale said that Robin had "taken a jump" and that her current achievement test score in the science section of the examination was two or three grades ahead of where it had been before. It seems important to note that even during the stress of the termination period, Robin was able to maintain a consistently good level of work. The strain was shown in a slight jumpiness in her thinking in the therapy hour, a sensitive and depressed look around her eyes, and slightly fuzzy speech.

Also in commenting on therapy, Robin said at one point, "You're the only person who has ever told me straight where I stand—what I can do in different things. I've had so many tests and examinations, and they only gave me vague answers about what I had done. I really do need to know what I can do and can't do." I commented that she herself had helped me very much to understand her potentialities and to help her to stop "hiding her light under a bushel" and that she would need to go on being able to communicate to people when she was ready for more challenging work and activities. Robin said that she felt she could talk to Dr, Moore, and I agreed that Dr. Moore was concerned about her continuing progress and did not want her to sell herself short.

She had brought along another ceramic product from school, "a half cup," which we talked about just in terms of its artistic characteristics. Then I commented that Dale had told me recently that on a science achievement test she had "jumped a couple of grades."

In the next to the last hour Robin was quiet, but she then indicated that she was thinking of termination when she asked, "Is it all right to write?" I agreed that it was. Harking back to her comments about "Old Bossy" dying, I raised the question of whether it would be easier if I were gone completely, but Robin protested "that would mean that what we've been doing these years didn't mean anything at all." I said, "You're a little bit angry at me for even asking that question," and she nodded, saying, "I wouldn't have asked about writing if it didn't mean a lot to me to be able to." She seemed solemn and near tears.

Because of the intensity of the feeling at this point, I thought it would be appropriate at that moment to give her a little book of Chinese and Japanese poetry, which I had inscribed "To Robin, who loves many beautiful things in nature . . . after three good years of therapy." I opened the book to one of the poems and explained about the Japanese and Chinese style of writing very short poems and pointed to a haiku: "The mother horse watches her child while it takes a drink." Robin spoke very tenderly, saying, "That's sweet," and then she quickly began writing something of her own—she wrote quite steadily as if she had thought it all out ahead of time. It was called "The Rose and a Sunflower" and was about "one who will also point the way as a sun points out east and west. So wise that an owl might come to her looking for advice. This is my friend. . . ." After appreciating it warmly, I told Robin that she flattered me when she said that I was so wise that an owl might come looking for advice; and we were able to laugh together about that.

Then Robin's mood changed, and she said that she had to write something about children from three to six and couldn't find any material at home or in the library; did I have some? I pulled down the only thing in my office that was relevant, Gesell's *Infant and Child in the Culture of Today*. Opening it to the chapters on the three-year-old, the four-year-old, and the five-year-old, I showed her how the chapters consisted of general statements followed by sections with specific points and observations. Since she had been so responsive as we looked through it and checked points she might be interested in using, I told her she could take the book and bring it back later. Very intensely she said, "Thank you, thank you for everything."

Her speech was much clearer than it had been the previous week, and she seemed more integrated, although her little tribute had, as usual, a good many misspellings. But the writing was extremely clear and was done in a free and natural way, utterly different from the extremely labored, slow writing characteristic of the first year of her therapy.

Robin's last hour of therapy also began with an enormous pile of books which she brought in. She then showed me the Gesell paper which she had been working on. She said that she was not finished, and I agreed to let her keep the book and bring it back to me on June 6, which she wanted to do. Then I reminded her that I had been trying to find a little book of Emily Dickinson's poems for her; but since I could not find just what I wanted, I had selected some poems and had them typed out. I showed her the last poem, "Hope is the thing with feathers," which she enjoyed and said it reminded her of a poem her aunt had given her.

The conversation moved to home. Eve was sick, and Jim didn't even know that Robin was terminating. Robin had talked to her mother, but her mother had not talked to Jim. Robin did not know how her father felt about it. She then described some pleasant antique hunting she and her mother had done—this time finding a little antique desk that Robin described with enthusiasm and which I agreed would make a nice work and study place.

Going back to the question of kinds of work she could do at home, she said that she could do cooking and window washing without getting into allergy troubles but that house dust and grasses and things outside stirred up allergic reactions. We talked then about the kinds of stuff one used to clean windows, allergic and nonallergic. Talking about these home activities evidently reminded her of a very elaborate dinner that had been put on by some colleagues of her father's and Robin described it in great detail, as if she had seen it herself. I commented that her pleasure in so many things was a source of happiness and quoted a couple of verses, including Emily Dickinson's poem that ends "How much can come and much can go and yet abide the world," and emphasized that Robin would be discovering lots of new things.

Robin, in turn, stated, "What I care about most is people, people, people," and we agreed that one can keep on discovering new kinds of people all one's life, new things to enjoy in people, and people with new interests.

We were both rather quiet, and since it was coming close to the end of the hour, I tried to verbalize. "Robin, I think both of us have more feelings than we can put into words right now, but I do want you to know that you did it, it was your energy and your good work that made all the progress." Robin said, on the verge of tears, "I couldn't have done it without some kicks from you," smiling as she said this, and I laughed with her, saying, "Well, kicks, pushes maybe, but it couldn't have happened without all that you could put into it." Then as we walked out the door, I said, "Goodbye for now, and I'll see you June 6," and she looked back shyly.

Although the expressions came slowly, often indirectly, and in a muted form, I think Robin was able to convey and be aware of her major feelings about termination. While her great effort to tell me about all the interesting experiences and positive things that had been going on and that she looked forward to was, in the context of termination, being used defensively, it also seemed to be very healthy and valid. There was nothing unrealistic about her expressions of interest. Along with her warmly adolescent sentiments, she had her feet pretty well on the ground. Of special importance, I think, was her strong expression of appreciation for my telling her "like it is."

Robin certainly needed continued support in sorting out what she could comfortably do and could not do; how she could do her share without running headlong into her vulnerabilities; how she could make progress without overreaching her capacities. She would need help also in facing new situations, in clarifying them ahead of time, and in adjusting to unexpected changes or shifts.

Other writers on therapy with the brain-damaged, such as Sheldon Rapaport, have stated that, in the case of brain-damaged children, termination of a relationship should not be made in the same way it is made with neurotic children. Because of the difficulties families have in understanding all the subtle details and implications of brain damage, periodic help should be available in assisting the reality adjustments that are so difficult for the brain-damaged child. This is one reason for the provision for some sort of open door.

Robin's Afterthoughts

In the years after therapy Robin wrote to me from time to time; her letters included descriptions of her current activities and also thoughts about her treatment. I have excerpted these and organized them into one group on her thoughts about the needs of damaged children and another on her feelings about therapy. These few excerpts and my comments are given to emphasize the wide repertoire that Robin could use for growth.

On Needs of Damaged Children

ON TEACHING

A damaged child needs to be allowed to explore a wide range and find what feels satisfying.

✛ Only in this way can the child and helpers discover positive resources.

It is of the utmost importance for the strong areas to be noticed, in addition to the damaged or weak ones. While feeling good in the strong areas the child can more comfortably face the weaker ones that are so hurtful and scary. Thus the child has some good points to hold onto. If only bad areas are noticed, the child is so frustrated in some and so bored in others she thinks, "Why bother, I cannot do or reach anything of interest." The child needs to have a chance to work on the positive areas, not just concentrate on the weak ones.

✚   Recognition and use of the strong areas can motivate effort.

If the child is taught to compensate for the weak areas, make sure the feelings, the whys and hows are worked on, and the problem is not just covered up or pushed back into a corner.

✚   The child needs to understand and integrate the weak areas into the whole self so as to continue to accept and to cope with problems they create.

Usually compensation techniques are not new to a child with special defects or unseen handicaps. For example, when you can't spell a certain word, you use a word that means the same thing that you *can* spell, for example, "the next day" for "tomorrow."

✚   It is necessary to watch for the child's initiative in coping.

It's important for a teacher to drop a problem in a child's lap and let the child chew on it—not expect quick, immediate comprehension. Be ready for any question, tears or ruffled feelings. Let the child say, "I *can't* do it," and then allow time to take it step by step.

✚   Initial rejection reflects an anxiety that the child can overcome.

Funny sounding words are sometimes more of a challenge than dull, everyday words. For example, "egress" is more fun than "exit."

✚   This is how Robin feels, and how some other, not all, children might feel if they enjoy verbal skills.

I remember reading tutoring with Miss Mary, she was warm and not threatening.

✚   Damaged (and other handicapped) children are sensitive to failure and frustration and need support and warmth.

I remember how thrilled I was when I learned to tie my shoes. No one else was.

✝ The child needs recognition of progress whenever it occurs.

I enjoyed the library class with Jane. I felt she knew I could and would do things if they were just shown and explained. Books can be and have always been such good friends.

✝ This could apply to other activities with different children.

ON THE PROGRAM

The program could help with sensitivities, for instance, to noise; and skin sensitivities can be helped with warm salt baths, sponging, rubbing. It could help with respiration, making the body stronger, developing balance, seeing things more accurately. The program of patterning exercise was helpful to me; it helped me to see the difference between *b* and *d*.

✝ Exercises to strengthen muscles, to concentrate, to be aware of visual focus and of ways of handling the body can be helpful.

Pantomime might also be helpful to a child with special defects since expression at times is an easier tool than words, and is O.K. to use—it is not being a show-off, it can help others see and maybe feel good too.

✝ Nonverbal communication can contribute to relationships.

Maybe for this type of child a class in dance, yoga, or biofeedback would help them be aware of their *own* checkerboard.

✝ That is, to be aware of the range of strengths and weaknesses and possibility of developing control.

Music can make one feel good—maybe there could be a music class like an art class. Math can be taught with music, dance, yoga. Music helped me with the times tables.

✝ The rhythms of music and dance can be energizing and also provide pleasurable reinforcement.

Gymnastics might be included, as well as tumbling.

✝ But gymnastic exercises need to be selectively adapted to the capacities of the individual child.

Jumping rope depends on visual range scanning as well as being able to pick up the feet.

✚   Robin increasingly related her understanding to her previous difficulties.

ON PREVENTION

I think it would be great if the patterning program could be used with premies [premature infants] once they are stable [to begin stimulation early to help prevent neurological dysfunction]. It could help them to do a little catching up before they need to later on—maybe just five minutes patterning twice a day. Maybe the parents could help with the patterning if they feel up to it. Also their environment needs to be enriched to stimulate all their senses: a music box or tapes for listening; mobiles for vision; soft sheets of odors—so they don't have just stale hospital smells.

✚   Premature infants are too often cared for in isolettes in a ward where the light is on night and day; all nurses, bedding, walls are white, noise of constant activity of the ward is the only sound—a very depriving environment.

[To prevent severe emotional disturbances of children who have learning difficulties] It is important to tell the children [the cause of their difficulties] so they can understand. Then encourage them to be as much like other children as possible, and help them to understand they are O.K. and not "bad" because they can't do everything. With time and work and patience (of helpers) maybe a sport could be learned. I dislike tennis because the teacher yelled at me.

✚   This implies that Robin felt guilty about what she could not do.

I think it is important for other family members to be made aware of the child's difficulties, and that they are not getting so much of the parents' time because they are liked better.

✚   Family therapy in addition to the individual therapy could have helped to prevent Eve's acting-out reaction to Robin's treatment.

It is important for parents and others to let a child try things even if they look awkward or clumsy—not false, patronizing backing but deep, sincere backing. I learned to do front somersaults though I never could do a cartwheel. I'd still like to learn the parallel bars in gymnastics. I am still very uncomfortable doing any acting or "showing off" in front of others for I'm very concerned what others will say or think of what I do. This even comes up when I am doing a lesson for my Sunday School class. I enjoy watching those that can be spontaneous or open with others when teaching a class.

✝   Different kinds of performing in front of others can help to decrease this anxiety.

When I went to Dallas [to college] my whole world as I had known it since I was twelve was doing 180° change. I was to leave home for the first time and stay there. All Mom said was she could not understand why I wanted a "silly" scrapbook with a pink hippo on the front. Maybe it felt like a place to keep parts of my changing world. I still have the pink octopus you sent that February 14.

✝   Something familiar to hold onto in a new situation can help to reduce strangeness anxiety.

If someone gets mad at me and can talk about it to some degree, it does not seem so terrible.

✝   Unexplained anger can be frightening.

Parents might need help to realize that it was not their fault, so they would not be overprotective, and would let the child grow. Some parents don't realize why their kid may need special "T.L.C." and cannot just grow up.

✝   The damaged child who feels worthless needs extra emotional support as well as direct help in mastery.

It hurts when someone reads a piece I have written and sees only the spelling mistakes, and not the [ideas in the] piece itself. That can make "learning difficulty" children pull in and close their shells. [To prevent that, the ideas should be appreciated.] It's hard to be brave enough to show something you have written.

✝   A damaged child is all too aware of his inadequacies, and needs recognition of his positive contribution.

It's important to be yourself and grow and enrich yourself and not get in a rut. One has to learn how to look well put together, graceful, cheerful, even with "mud" up to their chins at times. Whether or not it stays up to their chin is their own decision. One must reach for the helping hands, grab a hold, and take off. Brush the dry mud off and you'll find you're not at the bottom of that mud hole.

✛ This is Robin's advice to other damaged children based on the development of her own mature commitment to let go of negative feelings ("mud," black moods of discouragement) and to evoke positive feelings through adaptive action.

It's important for children with defects to know that there are famous and not so famous people who had them [defects]. Hans Christian Andersen had to tell his tales to a scribe; Leonardo da Vinci did mirror writing; Einstein had learning problems too.

✛ This can add to the perspective given by sharing ordinary weaknesses we all have.

It's important to give the child books that show that with love, self-push, and encouragement things can work out—like *The Ugly Duckling, Tom Thumb*.

✛ Children need images and concepts of development and change.

It might help to use guided images; Dad used to tell me to think real hard about my cat show until I could see it, then tell him about it, when I got a splinter in my finger.

✛ This can help any child in a stressful situation.

Diet is important. If someone is sensitive to eggs and gets them, they will not do as well. A child who is tired because of lack of sleep, or underweight, will not do well. On one program I was down to 100 pounds and tired most of the time, to the point of sleeping in class again, and at times having a headache.

✛ Every aspect of physical functioning should be kept at an optimal level, so the neurological problems will not be exacerbated by unnecessary stress.

Pets can be very important to any child, especially a child with defects.

✦ Puppies and kittens are a source of fun in play, tactual pleasure, freedom from unmanageable demands, as well as being something to love that responds gratifyingly.

On Her Own Therapy

I know now that Mom and Dad loved me, though I didn't always *feel* loved by them. Even though I was a problem and a burden they kept me at home, they didn't institutionalize me.

✦ Robin sometimes expected they might.

You never threatened me. I never had the feeling that you expected me to be scared.

✦ I felt that Robin's disturbances were a reaction to her realistic frustrations and that she needed to be appreciated. Her comment about my not threatening her suggests that she felt in constant danger of being punished or at least scolded for her difficulties in conforming to adult demands and for her inability to control angry reactions to her endless frustrations.

One thing of many I have been thankful for, you allowed me to chew on new things, in other words, to drop an idea in my lap and let me chew on it, then proceed to try and tackle it. To have been allowed that freedom to back off at first, to see whatever it was, or hold it for a while, then in time to work on it. Something like the first time a small child sees a glass ball or a mirror—you may want to look at it, pick it up, and turn it over, but should you? Then later on, find out what a wonderful part of the world it opens up to you.

✦ I realized that Robin's organic difficulties would make it impossible for her to respond quickly to "new things"; and it would take her longer to assimilate new ideas.

I felt like a big, left-footed ox. I didn't know why I could do abstract things but not things with my body. I felt I couldn't do anything right.

✦ People rarely understand the discouragement experienced by a child with excellent to poor capacities. Her insight made her more than usually aware of her own variability in levels of functioning, even from day to day.

I felt worthless, no good, lost, unlovable. In therapy I felt loved. Feeling loved gives a foundation to grow on.

✝   Cognitive or interpretive therapy alone could not have provided the restitution Robin needed in order to mobilize her energy for work and growth. Feeling loved releases energy, melts defensiveness, mobilizes trust and confidence that it is worthwhile to make the effort to master problems, and supplies the motivation for doing so.

Being understood was indeed precious and gratifying for it was almost the first time for me, for someone finally to reach out and touch, like the sun or a new moon, or rain giving a thirsty plant a long needed drink. Being understood holds the string to many emotions.

✝   "Being understood" contributes nourishment and support for a sense of relatedness.

I am sure whether it is a new budding raspberry bush, or a child trying to take a first step, being understood makes them aware that they *are*.

✝   "Being understood" contributes to a sense of self.

If one becomes impatient with the child, he or she is just likely to shut the door in whoever's face and just plain not try. Why? Because they only get yelled at when they do. A sensitive child can be hurt when yelled at.

✝   I was asked how I could "be so patient" with Robin. I had a constant deep sense of how overwhelming her frustrations were; and how hard she tried to cooperate in therapy.

You also knew how important it was to let me give an angry refusal or even a pouty one at times.

✝   I thought that "angry refusals" were natural reactions of a damaged child to unmanageable stimulation.

I was always afraid of being pushed, of losing my balance, tears were always present.

✝ This conveys the constant strain and difficulty in motor and emotional control Robin experienced.

I couldn't stand it to be in a cubicle without a window. There was a closet with a window and a tree outside—it was *my* tree, it made me feel good, that there was my friend.

✝ Many people do not appreciate the deep satisfaction, even support, some of us find in nature.

The old feelings still come up when I run into the old problems. Starting ballet, I could not follow the class—all the old feelings were right there—the way I felt when I could not do something as a child—all the old feelings of you're no good, you can't do anything right, you look like a big ox. . . . I want to work with my body and learn about and with it. . . . One needs to realize the old feelings may show up now and then and that—O.K., just be ready to deal constructively with them and take time to see why they showed up.

✝ Robin's organic problems continue, but she can now recognize them, reflect on them, and cope with them.

I feel it is important for the person to realize maybe some patterns or feelings can be re-experienced and used as an adult; others must be seen, realized, and worked on so they don't crop up in an overwhelming way when the roads get rough or bumpy—or so you don't find yourself using them in the wrong place.

✝ This reflects the perspective and integration of her experience and feelings achieved by Robin, and her ability to distinguish between constructive patterns and patterns that could lead to blocks in growth.

When you gave me the book I felt warmth and deep intertwining understanding.

✝ This was a book of poetry, and giving it to her was a recognition of Robin's enjoyment of poems and an appreciation of the value of metaphor in sharing thoughts.

You were a grandmother to me. You treated me like a girl, not like some sick, queer person. You explained things to me—I had had tests and tests and tests and nobody told me what they found.

✝   More effort to explain the causes of learning and motor difficulties would help other children.

"Hope is the thing with feathers" [Emily Dickinson poem] helped many a time, since you dropped it in my lap one time when I was feeling worthless to anyone including myself.

✝   Images and anchoring ideas can mobilize positive feelings when negative ones threaten to be overwhelming.

You ask why I responded so fast to you and so differently from [my response to] the evaluation team. That is rather hard to pinpoint. Except your being was warm, soft, and open. Not cold, icy, almost cutting like theirs.

You let me show you me without being poky-nosed and pushy. You pushed, sure—but in a supportive way! You didn't demand things or make me feel inadequate, small, useless, and plain downright dumb. You were not afraid to touch me or let me touch you.

Later when I moved to the other office [with another therapist] I never felt as comfortable as at your old office. The next one was too bright, empty, cold, and with long halls! They seemed like the bowels of a large monster—not a nice one either.

I remember feeling like I was being made fun of or was seen as different. You never made me feel that being a little different was wrong or dirty.

You were like a photographer taking time-lapse pictures, letting me open so I would start showing different petals as I opened. You did not stick your hand in and try to pry the petals open. Later as we grew in and with each other, you could press, push, and pull without everything closing back up—usually opening some more.

✝   The achievement of competence is so rewarding that it becomes self-motivating. And insight gained through treatment opens awareness to new insights. Growth goes on.

Epilogue

J. COTTER HIRSCHBERG

In this chapter I will show how Robin has fared since her three years of intensive therapy combined with special education, group experiences, and medical and dental care. I can first briefly describe her present situation: she works as a nurse's aide in a hospital, has bought a house that she rents to a tenant, drives a car, and is an active member of a supportive church. She is living what, in many ways, is a normal life, functioning with considerable independence, and as is apparent from Robin's "afterthoughts," she has considerable insight into her own problems and into the needs of other children with neurological problems.

At this point some comments should be made about her dilemmas in traversing the distance from her adolescent life in the Menninger Children's Hospital to an active life in the "outside world." During the closing phase of her therapy, several issues were handled in ways that helped Robin achieve additional maturational steps that stood her in good stead. The first of these achievements was the recognition and clarification of Robin's awareness and acceptance of her increased mastery. The next was the recognition of her ambivalent feelings regarding this mastery, because it faced her with the responsibility of making her own choices regarding growth. In accepting the changes within herself, she had to ask herself, "What now?" and this brought new anxieties. She deeply missed the understanding of the hospital staff who knew her so well and the acceptance she had felt from her peer group there. She was also faced with considering possible courses of action without the constant, sustaining empathy and the perceptive psychodynamic interpretations of her feelings and conflicts as they were reflected back to her by Dr. Murphy.

Robin used the ending phase of the therapy to deal with her anxieties about losing her important relationship with Dr. Murphy. Robin was well aware of the need to choose constructively, which meant choosing the most appropriate of several realistic choices. As was expected, this mobilized doubts and anger. Sometimes she was angry toward Dr. Murphy because of the termination, while at other times she could realize that because of the gains she had made she would be able to make the constructive choices now available to her.

She successfully completed high school. However, her organic limitations in dealing with certain continuing realistic problems led her to explore various options. She wondered if she could handle her limitations in facing college work without becoming paralyzed by them? Could those limitations reduce her self-esteem and motivations for work?

An additional problem for Robin was whether she could deal with her anxiety about change. To alleviate her own anxiety, Robin continued to express herself and her struggles vividly and directly in letters to Dr. Murphy; even more important, this expression allowed her to use the anxiety to motivate action. In this struggle Robin gained considerable help because Dr. Murphy took a "growth stance," emphasizing her strengths without minimizing her limitations. Dr. Murphy continued to help Robin seek to work and to gain satisfactions at her optimal level. She expected Robin to face unpleasant tasks and conflicting attitudes of others as a part of life. It was clear that Robin brought some of her anxieties to test whether Dr. Murphy was herself secure about the gains made in therapy. The therapist did not participate in Robin's anxieties, but rather expected Robin to use the gains that she had achieved to search for solutions. Robin responded positively to this approach.

Robin even repeated certain of her earlier handicapping behavior as a way to ascertain that such behavior no longer had the same demoralizing effect now as it had before her therapy. It was almost as if she needed to experience some of her early behavior so that she could find out that anxiety was not disorganizing to her internal equilibrium. It was particularly important to Robin to learn that therapy was no longer necessary in order to succeed. Positive interaction between herself and her parents, herself and her siblings, and herself and her peers served to communicate to them that she now had assets and strengths she could use not merely to overcome new difficulties but also to conquer the anxieties rooted in her past. Robin used important adults as helpful resources and not as potentially critical figures, or people onto whom she needed to project her own anxieties and frustrations.

Robin accepted the fact that tasks could be accomplished with varying degrees of success, and that she did not need to achieve the same level of success in different tasks in order to feel secure. She was able to accept the fact that there would always be certain tasks that were more difficult. She realized that success or failure depended upon a constellation of factors within her and that by choosing to deal well with one of these, she could often bring about an improvement in dealing with the task at hand. She was able to manage the sense of unpredictability she sometimes felt due to her diffuse and persisting brain deficits and her autonomic nervous system variability. Her reactions were more predictable to herself; she was not utterly at the mercy of the fluctuating ego states that had been so typical earlier.

Robin's own development and adjustment, and the increased stability of her family interactions, were so impressive that therapy as such was considered to have served its purpose. It was clearly felt that what she needed was further special education. She was accepted at a coeducational college that had programs for working with students with learning disabilities. However, she found the program an extremely stressful situation. Without adequate understanding by the staff of her unique pattern of brain deficits, she was not able to cope with the pressures of her adolescent peers or with her realistic difficulties in learning. Robin still needed an extended time for adaptation to a new situation. She knew she had the capacity to cope if given a longer than usual time for orienting herself to new tasks.

In reviewing the work at college, it seemed clear that she resisted authoritative demands that conflicted with her view of her needs and capacities. She did, however, respond to a wide variety of positive challenges that she perceived as being within her capacity—with whatever effort this involved. Both her new school and she herself became aware that she responded most strongly to help with and support for undertakings she understood. She accepted criticisms and suggestions, if she perceived them as friendly. She also responded to warmth, appreciation of her strengths, and humor. In general, she was a hard worker, and as the gap between her areas of potentially good performance and those of limited capacity was no longer so wide, and as the many organic sources of variability in her level of function, control, and integration were better understood, she did not need to regress. Although she was still anxious about demands she could not meet, her determination was to get as much additional education as she could to be equipped for a mutually rewarding life in human services. She accepted suggestions and was able to increase her participation, feeling the potential support of others. As a way to reinforce her own comfort about relationships, she used her ability to give and to accept what others gave her. She found that a program of planned exercises was helpful to her perceptual and coordination problems. She became aware that she had realistic needs for help with certain motor tasks and did not need to feel guilty over "too much dependence".

Returning to Topeka, she continued to clarify her relationships with her family, and she came to realize that her own struggle toward healthy independence did not have to be felt as hostility toward her parents. She was able to involve herself with her parents in defining an adequate and realistic vocational choice. She entered nurse's aide training, which made it possible for her to be the helping person in the world that she had always wanted to be. As she takes care of babies in the nursery of a large hospital, she primarily impresses others as a happy and well functioning young woman. Even though a few adaptational problems are still present, she now copes with them consciously. She speaks of her "therapy experience" as an experience that continues to be relevant to the here and now, since it was always an exercise in living and not merely an intellectual process. She feels that her therapy, her family, and her faith as expressed through her church have allowed her to make use of important adults to derive "a security within which she can feel free." Robin now sees herself and other adults in practical terms, and she can appropriately reveal more of herself with important adults and give more of herself without threatening her own autonomy. As important relationships change, she allows herself to be aware of feelings of sadness and feelings of missing other persons. She does not have to struggle with feelings of abandonment and rejection; rather with appropriate affects she can now move ahead to new relationships and new settings.

From the beginning, Robin's treatment was planned as an integrated, pluralistic program that would support her strengths as well as favorably modify her problems. We wanted to avoid the limitations of a "reductionistic" approach. The problems associated with her neurological handicaps were clear, but so were her adaptive, compensatory, coping devices. She was sensitive about her motor awkwardness, but she sensitively used her social skills, her amazing verbal ability, and her favorable extended family to enable the comprehensive treatment process to bring about an increased capacity for relating to others and an increased knowledge about herself. There was a "good fit" between her free and secure therapist and her troubled, handicapped self. It made for appropriate timing of selective interventions.

Dr. Murphy was not only a transference figure, but was always a real person, available as a good identification figure. Dr. Murphy made consistent use of her work in supervision to achieve a dynamic understanding that made her interventions continually supportive to the furthering of the developmental process. Dr. Murphy in her own comprehensive approach never presented one single strand of truth as if it were the whole truth; instead she used each fact to increase Robin's understanding of the whole. Variations in constitutional and biological factors were considered in relation to variations in development and maturation. It was accepted that a child normally fluctuates from one level of adjustment to another in the transition between developmental stages or under particular stress. Sensitive use of interpretive work together with an awareness of the importance of cognitive and motor skill development led to acquisition of competence and mastery.

One cannot deal therapeutically with a child without also working with the parents and the family; occasionally a revision of treatment goals was necessary because of the parents' reactions and their acceptance of change within the child.

We hoped the treatment relationship could be used to clarify, confront, and interpret Robin's patterns of reaction and the family's interaction with the changes in her; we also sought to free her energies by the resolution of conflict and to become aware of her readiness to learn new methods of expression, to modify her own behavior, and to attempt new skills and acquire new knowledge. We considered our goal to be the modification of those ego and superego components that would allow for the appropriate gratification of instinctual needs in accordance with their various aims and the realities of life with which the patient had to contend.

We formulated our treatment plan to be a collaborative endeavor in which we included an optimum measure of communication between the therapist and the members of the treatment team, while maintaining the essential confidentiality of the girl's work. At the same time, we remained fully aware of the problem of unconscious or conscious competition in the team and within the family.

Through working with Robin we found that a more truly integrated approach to her treatment had to evolve, an approach in which the therapist was never working with Robin's feelings in isolation but was constantly aware of the actualities of her life in the residence, in school, in group experiences, and at home. Robin taught us that our comprehensive treatment plan for her had to be different from those we had heretofore been accustomed to, in which the therapy process consisted of enabling the child to build up those inner assets that would compensate for his or her liabilities in order to solve a neurotic conflict. Because of her various organically determined problems, Robin's treatment required continual availability and flexibility of contact between the therapist and the child-care workers, the teachers, the social worker, the group worker, and the physician. In this comprehensive approach, clarity of roles was maintained at the same time that the mutuality of helping individuals was stressed. Contacts between team members could be initiated by any one of the treatment team as the need arose.

Comprehensive treatment with Robin was directly and consistently oriented to ego integration, with a focus maintained on current realistic difficulties, feelings, and attitudes, and with transference problems related to the "here and now." Confronting interpretation of unconscious conflict was usually avoided at first. Instead, empathy assumed primary importance in the treatment process, and the willingness of any member of the treatment team to make himself available for identification became a central focus to the work of the treatment team. Each member of Robin's treatment team tried to help her allow feelings of anxiety to serve as useful guides, as signals, about her difficulties in dealing with current problems with other people. The treatment team tried to be able to *feel* itself into Robin's attitudes without losing its own identity. Also, the team tried to evaluate not only what help Robin needed but also what would allow Robin and her family to use the help. The team tried to help Robin look at herself realistically and honestly by sustaining her through warm understanding in the difficult task of giving up defenses that she had developed to handle her troubled feelings about the way in which the neurological impairment had disturbed her life.

The team tried to remain continually aware that Robin's brain dysfunction had led to her feeling helpless and vulnerable and that her emotional or behavioral disability may have resulted from her attempt to reduce her anxiety about the maturational lags and the developmental tasks. Thus, comprehensive treatment saw not only the unevenness in different aspects of development, but also saw that continued maturation and continued mastery of developmental tasks were fostered by Robin's achieving from each phase of personality development the appropriate and realistic satisfactions that would enable her to proceed to the next developmental stage.

The treatment team was not merely interested in her diagnostic label, but rather sought to achieve an integrated understanding of her physical, emotional, familial, and social difficulties, including the relationship of these to each other and the ways she handled these difficulties as well as the ways she used her biologically given resources. In comprehensive treatment, the team members knew how crucial these diverse factors were to the neurologically damaged child's concept of herself and to her concept of other human beings and of the world itself.

As Robin went through her growing up, the team had to have the ability to adjust to change and be able to modify their views and expectations of her responses to the developmental changes. Achieving this was as much an empathic process, requiring a limited identification with Robin, as it was an intellectual process involving observation, interpretation, and application of multidisciplinary scientific thinking. Organic brain damage not only posed handicaps to which Robin and her parents needed to adjust, but it also altered her adjustive process. The task of the comprehensive treatment process was to remain aware of the meaning of the symptoms, of the behavior, and of the feelings of the girl as *adaptive* within her limits. With this neurologically handicapped child, behavior had often been transformed by people into fixed images.

It was the task of the comprehensive treatment team to avoid rigid generalizations and arbitrary concepts. This required a recognition of the variable and changing neurological "baseline of behavior." Such an attitude meant evaluating the patient's conscious and unconscious efforts to compensate for her neurological deficits as well as her effort to adapt more adequately to her achievements and her aspirations, with a commitment to continued growth.

References

Hirschberg, J. Cotter. 1953. "The Role of Education in the Treatment of Emotionally Disturbed Children through Planned Ego Development," *American Journal of Orthopsychiatry* 23:684–90.

McFate, M. Q.; and Orr, F. G. 1949. "Through Adolescence with the Rorschach." *Rorschach Research Exchange and Journal of Projective Techniques* 13:302–19.

Moriarty, A. 1961. "Coping Patterns of Preschool Children in Response to Intelligence Test Demands." *Genetic Psychology Monographs* 64:3–127.

Murphy, L. B. 1962. *Widening World of Childhood: Paths to Mastery.* New York: Basic Books.

Murphy, L. B.; and Moriarty, A. 1976. *Vulnerability, Coping and Growth: From Infancy to Adolescence.* New Haven: Yale University Press.

Redl, F. 1943. "Preadolescents, What Makes Them Tick?" In F. Redl and D. Wineman, *When We Deal With Children.* New York: Free Press, 1966.

Sechehaye, M. 1951. *Autobiography of a Schizophrenic Girl.* New York: Grune & Stratton.

Sheldon, W. J. 1940. *The Varieties of Human Physique.* New York: Harper.

Stolz, H. R.; and Stolz, L. M. 1971. "Somatic Development of Adolescent Boys." In M. C. Jones et al. (eds.), *The Course of Human Development.* Waltham, Mass.: Xerox College Publishing.

Williams, R. J. 1956. *Biochemical Individuality.* New York: John R. Wiley.

INDEX

(An alphabetical list of subheads follows the main index, on page 360.)